Brest-Litovsk - Volume II
Encyclopedia of the Jewish Diaspora (Belarus)

Translation of:
Brisk de-Lita: Encycolpedia Shel Galuyot

Original Yiddish Volume
Edited by Elieser Steinman
Published in Jerusalem, 1958

Published by JewishGen

An Affiliate of the Museum of Jewish Heritage - A Living Memorial to the Holocaust
New York

Brest-Litovsk - Encyclopedia of the Jewish Diaspora (Belarus) - Volume II
Translation of *Brisk de-Lita: Encycolpedia Shel Galuyot*

Copyright © 2014 by JewishGen, Inc.
All rights reserved.
First Printing: May 2014, Iyar 5774
Second Printing: October 2019, Tishrei 5780

Layout: Howard Morris
Cover Design: Jan R. Fine
Publicity: Sandra Hirschhorn
Translation Project Coordinator: Jenni Buch
Yiddish and Hebrew Consultant: Josef Rosin
Indexing: Jonathan Wind

Published by JewishGen, Inc.
An Affiliate of the Museum of Jewish Heritage
A Living Memorial to the Holocaust
36 Battery Place, New York, NY 10280

Printed in the United States of America by Lightning Source, Inc.

Library of Congress Control Number (LCCN): 2014902440
ISBN: 978-1-939561-17-6 (hard cover: 510 pages, alk. paper)

Front cover: Photograph by Eli Rabinowitz
Back cover: Brest Synagogue, now a movie theatre

JewishGen and the Yizkor-Books-in-Print Project

This book has been published by the **Yizkor-Books-in-Print Project,** as part of the **Yizkor Book Project** of **JewishGen, Inc**.

JewishGen, Inc. is a non-profit organization founded in 1987 as a resource for Jewish genealogy. Its website [www.jewishgen.org] serves as an international clearinghouse and resource center to assist individuals who are researching the history of their Jewish families and the places where they lived. JewishGen provides databases, facilitates discussion groups, and coordinates projects relating to Jewish genealogy and the history of the Jewish people. In 2003, JewishGen became an affiliate of the **Museum of Jewish Heritage - A Living Memorial to the Holocaust** in New York.

The **JewishGen Yizkor Book Project** was organized to make more widely known the existence of Yizkor (Memorial) Books written by survivors and former residents of various Jewish communities throughout the world. Later, volunteers connected to the different destroyed communities began cooperating to have these books translated from the original language—usually Hebrew or Yiddish—into English, thus enabling a wider audience to have access to the valuable information contained within them. As each chapter of these books was translated, it was posted on the JewishGen website and made available to the general public.

The **Yizkor-Books-in-Print Project** began in 2011 as an initiative to print and publish Yizkor Books that had been fully translated, so that hard copies would be available for purchase by the descendants of these communities and also by scholars, universities, synagogues, libraries, and museums.

These Yizkor books have been produced almost entirely through the volunteer effort of researchers from around the world, assisted by donations from private individuals. The books are printed and sold at near cost, so as to make them as affordable as possible. Our goal is to make this important genre of Jewish literature and history available in English in book form, so that people can have the personal histories of their ancestral towns on their bookshelves for themselves and for their children and grandchildren.

A list of all published translated Yizkor Books can be found at:
http://www.jewishgen.org/Yizkor/ybip.html

Lance Ackerfeld, Yizkor Book Project Manager

Joel Alpert, Yizkor-Book-in-Print Project Coordinator

This book is presented by the
Yizkor Books in Print Project
Project Coordinator: Joel Alpert

Part of the
Yizkor Books Project of JewishGen, Inc.
Project Manager: Lance Ackerfeld

These books have been produced solely through volunteer effort
of individuals from around the world. The books are printed and
sold at near cost, so as to make them as affordable as possible.

Our goal is to make this history and important genre of Jewish
literature available in English in book form so that people can have
the near-personal histories of their ancestral towns on their bookshelves for themselves and for their children and grandchildren.

Any donations to the Yizkor Books Project are appreciated.

Please send donations to:
Yizkor Book Project
JewishGen
36 Battery Place
New York, NY 10280

JewishGen, Inc. is an affiliate of the
Museum of Jewish Heritage
A Living Memorial to the Holocaust

Title Page of Original Yiddish Yizkor Book

אנציקלופדיה של גלויות

ספרי־זכרון לארצות הגולה ועדותיה

ענציקלאפעדיע
פון די גלות־לענדער

גערענק־ביכער פון לענדער און שטעט פון יידישן גלות

דירעקטאר פון „אנציקלופעדיה של גלויות"

ח · ב ר ל ס

הוצאת חברת „אנציקלופדיה של גלויות", בע"מ

ירושלים — תל־אביב

אנציקלופדיה של גלויות

ענציקלאפעדיע
פון די גלות־לענדער

בריסק־דליטא

אויפלאג אין יידיש
דערשינען אין העברעאיש אונטער דער רעדאקציע פון
אליעזר שטיינמאן
„אנציקלופדיה של גלויות" ברך ב', 1955

פערלאג פון „אנציקלופדיה של גלויות", בע"מ

ירושלים — תל־אביב

Translation of the Title Page of Original Yiddish Book

ENCYCLOPAEDIA OF THE JEWISH DIASPORA
A Memorial Library of Countries and Communities

BREST-LIT. VOLUME

אויסלאנד אין יידיש

Hebrew Edition
by
ELIESER STEINMAN

(Volume II of the Encyclopaedia of the Jewish Diaspora)

Published by
THE ENCYCLOPAEDIA OF THE JEWISH DIASPORA CO., LTD.
Jerusalem — Tel-Aviv

Dedication to the Publication of the Translation

This book is dedicated to Dr Samuel Chani, a true *Brisker* son, 1921-2011.

And in Memory of the Jewish Community of Brisk D'Lita that was totally destroyed in the Holocaust.

Acknowledgements for the Publication of the Translation

This book would not exist in English if it were not for the dedication and hard work of Jenni Buch and the late Dr. Samuel Chani, a native of Brest. They translated the whole book themselves. We are very grateful for the additional cooperation of Jenni Buch in the publication of this book. This was a tremendous undertaking and we hope all the readers of this book appreciate their dedication.

Joel Alpert, Coordinator of the Yizkor-Books-In Print Project

April 2014

Brest-Litovsk in Belarus

Geopolitical Information:

Brest, Belarus is located at 52°06' North Latitude and 23°42' East Longitude
203 mi SW of Minsk

Alternate names for the town are:
Brest [Belarussian], Brest Litovsk [Russian], Brześć Litewski [Polish], Brześć
nad Bugiem [Polish, 1918-39], Brisk [Yiddish], Brasta [Lithuanian], Brest
Litowsk, Brisk Dlita, Brisk de-Lita, Brześć-Litewsk, Brist nad Bugie, Bzheshch
nad Bugyem, Bieraście

	Town	**District**	**Province**	**Country**
Before WWI (c. 1900):	Brest	Brest	Grodno	Russian Empire
Between the wars (c. 1930):	Brześć nad Bugiem	Brześć nad Bugiem	Polesie	Poland
After WWII (c. 1950):	Brest			Soviet Union
Today (c. 2000):	Brest			Belarus

Jewish Population: 30,608 in 1897; 21,796 in 1929

Nearby Jewish Communities:

Terespol, Poland 6 miles WSW
Chernavchitsy 8 miles N
Kodeń, Poland 14 miles SSW
Zhabinka 15 miles ENE
Piszczac, Poland 16 miles SW
Volchin 21 miles NW
Zamosty 21 miles NNE
Kamyanyets 21 miles NNE
Janów Podlaski, Poland 22 miles WNW
Charniany 23 miles ESE
Vysokaye 23 miles NW
Biała Podlaska, Poland 24 miles W

Abramovo 25 miles N
Domachëvo 25 miles S
Sławatycze, Poland 25 miles SSW
Łomazy, Poland 27 miles WSW
Niemirów, Poland 27 miles WNW
Malaryta 27 miles SE
Konstantynów, Poland 27 miles WNW
Wisznice, Poland 29 miles SW
Kobryn 29 miles ENE
Rossosz, Poland 30 miles SW

The History of This Book

by N. Chinich

Translated by Dr. Samuel Chani and Jenni Buch

At a general assembly of the Organization of Brest Immigrants in Israel that took place in Tel Aviv in 1944, it was decided to publish a memorial book about this famous and historic community.

I undertook to manage this difficult task and issued a plea for support in the press, both in Israel and abroad. I requested that all the Briskers in the world send in their memoirs, recollections, photos, memorabilia, political and institutional records. This request was printed in the U.S., Australia, South Africa, Argentina, Europe, Mexico and Brazil. I also sent more than 300 personal letters, both in Israel and overseas.

Over the following eight years we collected enough material for a book.

A huge amount of material was collected; everything remained as a collection of works as we were unable to edit the work for publication. Our comrades also lost hope that it would ever appear in book form but then we found a saviour in Chaim Barlas. A native of Brest, Chaim Barlas was the editor of the Encyclopedia of the Diaspora and he made our goal a reality. Praise should be given to the book committee of the Organization of Brest Immigrants in Israel:

B. Kastrinski, A. Shtrickman, S. Orchov, M. Neumark who gave their hearts and souls to this project, also A. Zamir, blessed be his memory, who helped a great deal with the collection of material. The many people who helped collect and edit the information – M. Zinovitch who gave us valuable information about the rabbis of Brisk D'Lita.

Special thanks should be given to the Brest Relief in New York and the members of its book committee: H.H. Gonsher, Y. Finkelstein, B. Wolsky, Frieluk and others who assisted greatly to make this matter a reality and get this book published.

The Memorial book for our great and famous hometown of Brest, its people, their sufferings and torments, and the tragic demise of the ancient city of Brisk D' Lita.

From The Brisker Relief in the U.S.A

In 1947 the idea was formed by the Brest committee in Israel to perpetuate the memory of the murdered 30,000 Jews of Brest by the publication of a Yizkor (memorial) book. P. Chinich wrote us that he was collecting material for a Brest Yizkor Book, and that the Brest committee in Israel would prepare it for publication.

J. Finkelstein replied that the decision of the Brest Relief was to publish a book by themselves. However, the problem arose of publishing the book with the cooperation of several countries: the U.S., Israel, France and Argentina. This plan was discussed at great length and with much correspondence between the various countries. In 1952, Chaim Barlas came to the U.S. as representative for the Encyclopedia of the Jewish Diaspora, which wanted to commemorate Jewish cities and communities, amongst them Brisk D'lita.

The Brest committee in Israel proposed to publish the book within this format, but at the same time established a book committee to prepare the book for publication. The members of this committee were: Gashner, Rosinsky, Tepper, Ravin, Hari and Wolski. The issue was much discussed and debated at great length at Relief meetings until a compromise was reached and it was decided to form a United Brest Yizkor Book committee that would collect and supply it's material for this book.

Note: Although this article was not part of the original Yizkor Book, it is included here because it was felt it was very significant.   [J. A.]

A Town with four names:

Recollections of life in Poland prior to World War II

by Dr. Samuel H. Chani

Brest (as the Russians call it) is a city with about 200,000 inhabitants, in the USSR on the Polish border. It is situated on the River Muchawiec as it runs into the River Bug and is on multiple railway crossings. It is located on the road between Moscow and Warsaw, and, as tourists often stop there before returning from Russia to Poland and Western Europe, it has in recent years been turned by the Russians into a show place, with large squares and imposing monuments to the heroes who fought the Germans in the nearby fortress one kilometre to the west, when the Germans invaded Russia in 1941. The commandant of the fortress happened to be a Jewish officer, who died valiantly in its defense after the German army advanced deep into Russian territory. These changes in the city's appearance must have taken place in the last twenty years, however, because when I visited London in 1965 I was repeatedly refused a visa of entry into Brest by the Russian Embassy on the grounds that Brest "was of no interest to tourists and had no accommodation for tourists."

Nevertheless, in September 1965, I did cross the Polish border in my little Fiat, carrying a permit to visit Minsk, and persuaded the officers at the border to allow me to spend the day there, on the grounds that I had been born and raised in Brest. Contrary to the information given me by the Russian Embassy in London, who told me that there was nothing to see there, since the old city had been "wiped out" by the shelling and bombing of World War II, I found the city almost intact; but it was a pathetic sight. The buildings were in a state of neglect; the shops were used for housing; and the once beautiful synagogue in the centre of the town was now shabby and used as a cinema. Trees lining many of the streets were over-grown and untrimmed, and hid the neglected little houses.

After photographing my old school, the synagogue (or rather cinema), and the old weatherboard house where I had spent my childhood and adolescence, 1 located a small, insignificant monument which had been erected by the Red troops after they reached Brest in 1944, to mark the spot where, two years before, nearly the entire remaining Jewish population of about 30,000 had been shot and buried. Earlier, between 5000 and 8000 able-bodied men had already been taken outside the city, on the pretext of going to a work project, and murdered there. My family and I, through a set of peculiar circumstances, had emigrated just before the German invasion. If we had stayed, we would surely have joined all our friends in death.

Geographically, and historically, my birthplace is known as Brest-Litovsk, the name being indicative of its link with Lithuania. Although founded by the Slavs in 1017 and invaded by the Mongols in 1241, it became part of Lithuania in 1319. In 1569 it became the capital of a unified Polish-Lithuanian state.

Former synagogue - now cinema

The treaty between the Germans and the Russians towards the end of World War I was signed in 1918, and is recorded in history books and encyclopaedias as the "Treaty of Brest-Litovsk." This took place in the nearby fortress, which is surrounded by a mediaeval wall and moat. In 1936, I had an opportunity to visit the fortress with my school. It was pointed out to me that the Russian graffiti on the wall of the conference room stating "No Peace and No War," was attributed to Trotsky; it must have been scribbled during a moment of frustration, which peace negotiations can invoke. The city acquired its Polish name of Brzesc Nad Bugiem (the last two words, sometimes abbreviated N/B, mean "the River Bug") in the year I was born - that is, in 1921-and continued to be known by that name until 1939 and the outbreak of World War II.

Yet there is a fourth name by which the town is known - that of Brisk, a name dear to me and of great sentiment to the Jews who lived there for about six centuries. The origin of this Yiddish name is obscure to me, but I have always referred to the city as "Brisk" and have taken pride in being a "Brisker." The Jewish Brisk had had a great history, producing such famous rabbis as Solomon Luria and Joel Sirkes in earlier periods, three generations of the Soloveitchik family in more recent times (right up to the last war), Jacob Epstein the great Talmudist at the Hebrew University, Menachem Begin, and many other major religious, literary and political leaders.

The Landsmanshaften (immigrant clubs) in the Americas, Australia and Israel are called the Brisker Landsmanshaften, and an obscure little street in Tel Aviv, Rehov Brisk, has been named after it - a small tribute to an old Jewish community which provided so many personalities, Rabbis and Gaonim, and which is now extinct. It lives now only in memories. It was a cool September night in 1938. The sounds of the horse's hooves and the carriage's wheels echoed in the empty streets as our family left for the station with our meagre belongings. My heart was heavy. For the moment, the excitement and anticipation of going to a new exotic land which would offer me freedom and opportunity was forgotten. I was silently saying goodbye to every building, to every cobblestone in the street, and to my friends, who would be asleep by now, nearly midnight. I did not get the chance to say goodbye to most of my friends as, a week earlier, after a farewell party by the committee and members of "Masada," of which I had been secretary for nearly two years, I developed quinsy [tonsillitis] which subsided only on the eve of our departure. A few close friends had come earlier in the evening to say goodbye. The others were not aware of my illness, nor the exact day of our departure.

As, one after the other, the buildings and streets receded from view, I strained to have a last lingering look at the so familiar surroundings into which I was born and where I had spent the most formative and influential seventeen years of my life. When would I be able to visit my friends and see "my" Brisk again? Brisk was a town that I loved so dearly, regardless of its poverty and the bleak, uncertain future it offered me. Because of that uncertainty, my contemporaries and I were dedicated to finding a way to create a better future for ourselves and, in our young minds, we thought ourselves to be idealists. But, just as there is no pure altruism in this world, I believe there is no unmotivated idealism. Most of the youth in Brisk unwittingly became "idealists" because of that uncertainty about our future. To establish a future that held out something better than second-class citizenship and the increasing misery, nearly everyone belonged to some organisation, whether it was "Gordonia," "Betar," "Poale Zion," "Bund," "Mizrachi," "Masada," etc. The Communist sympathisers, and there were many of them, did not declare themselves openly. For that, they could easily end up in the nearby concentration camp: Bereza Kartusk.

In our quest for a better world of justice, freedom and tolerance, we thirsted for knowledge and education. I had formed strong bonds with many both from my own age group and among older folk, but on this particular September night I did not imagine that those bonds were about to be broken forever.

Брестъ-Лит.
Brest-Lit

Вокзалъ
La gare

Brest Railway Station

The station of Brzesc N/B was brightly lit and as busy as usual, serving as an intersection for three different railway lines. Shortly after midnight we boarded the train for Warsaw. It was half empty, which was so different from only a short two months ago, in the summer of 1938, when the trains had been full. I had criss-crossed Poland that summer with the few zlotys I'd saved up from my earnings as a tutor in Latin. Most of my earnings went towards the cost of books and school fees, these being nominal as my school was a government school.

Soon after boarding the train, I left my parents and sister in their compartment and found myself a completely empty one, where I could stretch out and go to sleep. I wanted to arrive in Warsaw refreshed and thus to be able to revisit some of my favourite spots there the next day. The rhythm of the train sounds, the lateness of the hour, the tiredness and weakness following my recent fever, all these should have sent me off to sleep fairly quickly. But I couldn't sleep, and kept on dwelling upon the great new change in my life. The past few weeks had been hectic, although events had been set in motion nearly a year before, when I manipulated my mother (my father would not hear of it) to lodge an application with the Hebrew Immigrant Aid Society (H.I.A.S.) for a visa to Australia - a land familiar to me only through geography lessons and from a book by Jules Verne I'd read as a child. Now it all seemed like one of Jules Verne's adventures. I was trying hard to get to sleep, but even the rhythm of the steam train did not help. Past events passed through my mind like snippets from a movie, and our present long journey suddenly seemed unreal.

My paternal grandfather had migrated to the USA early this century, intending to save enough money there to be able to bring his wife and three children over. The Jewish population in Czarist Russia (as now in 'Free Poland') was poor, and he could not afford tickets for the whole family. By the time he had settled in and gained enough money, World War I had broken out.

My father was conscripted into the Russian Army and eventually ended up in Kiev and other cities on the Dnieper. My mother, his girlfriend at the time, followed him there and they eventually married in Yekatherinislav (or "Dniepropetrovsk," as it is now called), just after the Revolution, in 1917 or 1918.

In 1923, my grandmother and two aunts went to the USA to join grandfather; however, my father stayed on in Brzesc N/B In spite of the difficulties in making a living as a watchmaker (and a good watchmaker he was): in a town with a population of 60,000, there were about 20 watchmakers and few watches about. Yet he stayed on. We had the papers to migrate to the USA but, as time passed, their validity expired and with the onset of the Great Depression, entry to the USA became difficult. In our case, my father was determined to stay in Brisk, not because of the great love he had for Poland, but because of his involvement in numerous communal activities He was secretary of several organisations, such as the Handverker Ferein, a Jewish trade union, and secretary of Z.T.S., a local Jewish sports club. He was active in the leftist Poale Zion movement, Ort (a. Jewish trade school), and so on. He enjoyed the prestige of his positions. He loved his activities in the Yiddish cultural circles of our town. Sadly, the family came last in his thoughts and plans. He certainly took very little interest in me. My mother had to work hard to supplement our meagre income (mostly consisting of gifts from the USA) with dressmaking, her customers being peasant girls from nearby villages, and with cooking meals for subtenants. She, too, had little time for me. Thus I learned early in life to be independent.

Poverty and "scraping for a living" were part of Jewish life in the smaller towns where no industries existed. But this got worse with the creation of the new Polish state, formed after a century and a half of foreign occupation. The new state was supposed to be democratic; but the rulers of Poland, like those of the other newly created states after World War I, had no conception of what democracy was, and they certainly had no intention of enforcing its principles as proposed by the Versailles Treaty and Woodrow Wilson. Jews were excluded completely from the entire civil service, and from transport and state-owned manufacturing monopolies. Already, in the early 1920s, the government resorted to etatism - a kind of state capitalism which nationalised the tobacco, liquor, salt, timber, matches and other industries. These were industries which Jews had created and in which they had long been prominent. As the government took these over, the Jewish employees were dismissed.

In a town like Brest where there was practically no industry. The Jews, who made up 60% of its population of 60,000, had to rely on small trade and commerce. The local shops and tradesmen - tailors, bakers, butchers, shoemakers, photographers, etc. - supplied the peasants from nearby villages and the army and air force, which were heavily concentrated about Brest. Brest was also the capital of the administrative district of Polesie, although located at its border. Consequently there were many Polish Catholic civil servants here, and a few of the Jewish shopkeepers and tradesmen were able to make a reasonable living.

Some Jews had small, back-yard factories, producing things like soap, cosmetics, sweets, and so on. The few professionals such as doctors and lawyers lived fairly well. They had running water, indoor toilets, radios and even telephones - all unattainable luxuries for more than 90% of the Jewish population before World War II.

There were, on the other hand, smaller shopkeepers and tradesmen who struggled to make ends meet. There were also many, many beggars existing on handouts. Things got worse when the global economic crisis set in, and those who relied on dollars sent by relatives in the USA suffered most. None of this, however, led to our journey. My father, like most others, accepted the status quo.

As far as I am concerned, the real process leading to our journey probably started years before, in my own hungers and longings. As a curious youngster and avid reader, I developed a thirst for knowledge and, subsequently, a desire to become a doctor. At the time, I did not realise that the motivation for this desire had deeper psychological roots. It appeared to be an unrealistic dream at the time, not only because I came from a poor home (that, perhaps, could be overcome), but because of the existing *numerus clausus* (Jewish quotas) at the government high schools and universities. There were three private high schools in our town, but they were beyond my means. The government high school was supposedly free, save for a nominal half-yearly fee. This school accepted about two Jewish youngsters per class (of 40) - this was in a city with a 60% Jewish population! The situation was even more paradoxical, because only a wealthy Jewish child whose parents could bribe the teachers had some chance of getting into this "free" government school.

Sheer persistence won out. Knowing that I could not afford a private school, I sat three times for the entrance exams for the government high school and was failed twice. By the third time, they had become exasperated with my perseverence and allowed me to enter. I learned this later from my Latin teacher. Somehow I had become expert in Latin, and I was her favourite. One day, she said: "My, how the years have flown! Here you are going for your matric already. It was only a few years ago when the priest (Catholic religion teacher), during the pedagogic conference selecting entrants to the school, insisted that: 'If we don't let this little Jew enter, he will return for the fourth and fifth time for his entrance exams.

There were two Jewish boys in our class. I was accepted by my classmates and experienced no anti-Semitism. Coming from an atheistic background, I adjusted easily to the Gentile environment. Neither of my parents were religious Jews. They were Bund sympathisers, although my father was active in the leftist Poale Zion. I had read a lot of Yiddish literature in my childhood, but I knew no Hebrew and little of the Jewish religious laws. My upbringing had been in Yiddish, but had excluded the Jewish traditions. Most of my teenage years, from the age of 12 to 17, were spent amongst Polish Gentiles. My language at home slowly changed from Yiddish to Polish, but I never drifted towards assimilation. I have always been proud, and shall remain proud, of my Jewish heritage. This pride I owe largely to my city, Brisk. It was an entirely Jewish city, the Gentiles living in the suburbs, particularly in the newly built suburb called "Clerical." The school provided time for Jewish history lessons once a week, where all the Jewish boys from our school, and later also the girls when our school became co-educational, turned up voluntarily. It aroused my curiosity about my religion, which was not practised at my home.

At the age of 15, using my own earnings as a tutor in Latin, I hired a melamed (Hebrew teacher), who taught me how to lay tefillim and who introduced me to the Hebrew prayer books. When, after some months, I could no longer afford the private religious lessons, this melamed, who lived in extreme poverty with many children to support, offered to give me free lessons. I declined, because at the time I had thrown myself into other activities. But I never forgot this gentle, saintly melamed's gesture. Somehow I recalled him on the memorable September night of 1938 when I left Brisk. I hoped that one day I would be able to return to visit Brisk as a man of means and could reward this man and others who had been kind to me. There were many "beautiful" people in my town, people dedicated to their faith, honourable people, notwithstanding heir miserable circumstances. Thus, at the age of 15, I had mixed emotions about my national Jewish background and the land in which I had grown up, a land I had learned to love through the influence of the Polish school and the national romantic Polish literature. By this stage of my young life, I had absorbed nearly all the fervently nationalistic writing of nineteenth and twentieth century Poland.

The 1930s were in particular a time when there was a tendency for writers in the newly created eastern European states to glorify their histories and to romanticise their national heritage and their countryside. This spurred me into travelling and exploring as much of Poland as I could during school holidays, despite my limited financial resources. Drawn though I was to Polish nationalism, like the few other Jewish boys in my school I felt that to deny my Jewish origins would have meant to be a renegade.

During the next couple of years, several things took place that changed my outlook. The death of Marshall Pilsudski in May 1935, a man who had been a benevolent dictator and who was opposed to official anti-Semitic policies, was a turning point for Polish Jewry, and for me specifically. In actuality, Pilsudski did not particularly care for Jews, but he recognised their potential contribution to Poland, and therefore, did not adopt an official anti-Semitic platform. Like many other Jews, I admired the "Grand-dad" as he was affectionately known. I thought of him as an upright tower of strength in a government which otherwise tended to be corrupt. Jews genuinely mourned his death. When, towards the end of 1936, Rydz-Smigly took over, the stability of the Polish government had already weakened and corruption had increased. Economic conditions worsened. Anti-Semitic legislation was being passed through the Sejm (Parliament). The Jews, who had already been legislated out of certain industries, were now legislated out of the professions. Numerus clausus became numerus nullus. It became obvious that medicine would be closed to me. Anti-Semitic slogans and anti-Semitic articles crept into the press; boycotting of Jewish merchants and tradesmen was repeatedly called for; some of my Polish school friends became members of the party, Mloda Polska (Young Poland), a similar body to that of the Hitler Youth. We became estranged.

It was early in 1937 that I went to a meeting of a Jewish students' organisation called "Masada." A fellow from a different school, whom I was tutoring in Latin, talked me into attending this meeting. There were about a dozen members present. The meeting was addressed by a lawyer from Warsaw, who had come to visit his parents in Brisk, and who, I later learned, had graduated from the same Polish high school that I had attended some seven or eight years earlier. He was known to be second only to Jabotinsky in his powers of oratory. I was curious to see if he would live up to his reputation.

I was not disappointed. Menahem Begin was indeed an excellent orator and, though the auditorium was small, he spoke with pathos and enthusiasm. The subject was not new: the hopelessness of our future in Poland, and the urgent need of our own State in Palestine. He spoke in Polish, but would use some clichés in Yiddish or German. I became interested and joined the "Masada," a student wing of the Revisionist Party. I was asked to contribute to its magazine, also called "Masada." I wrote about my dilemma, that of a Jewish boy in a Polish environment trying to find his identity. My article, simple but genuine, impressed the leader of the group and I was asked to become its secretary. I was flattered and I needed this. I threw myself into the party's activities with great enthusiasm. I read all I could about Zionism, and was particularly impressed with Jabotinsky's report to the Peel Royal Commission. There was a man with practical answers to our problems, not just theories and weak aspirations. I worked hard for the organisation. As a result, my school marks suffered, but I found myself fulfilled. By mid-1938, the membership of Masada had increased ten-fold to about 200.

As I became imbued with Zionism and Jewish nationalism, and disenchanted with my "fatherland," Poland, I developed the desire to migrate and settle in Palestine. There were, however, two problems: first, certificates of entry into Palestine were almost impossible to obtain at the time, and second, there was no medical school there, as far as I knew, and I still felt that I was destined for the medical profession.

On the 13th May, 1937 - by some weird coincidence, it was the second anniversary of Pilsudski's death - something else happened to affect my outlook.

One of the anti-Semitic laws introduced in the past year or so was a restriction on the number of cattle which the Jews could kill ritually - a sort of numerus clausus on cows. The number was not sufficient to cater for the needs of the Jewish community, which was more than 80% orthodox. As a result, much illegal killing of animals was carried out by the local butchers. Naturally, the police had to be bribed. On that particular May morning, a government officer assisted by a constable carried out an inspection of the meat market. In one butcher shop, a quantity of meat above the allotted quota was found and was confiscated by the officer. When the middleaged butcher protested that he had paid off this particular constable, the constable feigned indignation in front of the government inspector, lashed out "You lying, bloody Jew," and pushed the butcher, who stumbled and fell. The butcher's hot-headed son, seeing his father injured, stabbed the policeman, who subsequently died. A pogrom spread immediately throughout Brisk, and raged right on through the night. It was not a spontaneous riot. It was too well organised to be so. At the time, there were agitators from the north of Poland (from the Poznan district) who had been planning for just such an opportunity. Until then, their propaganda calling for a boycott of Jewish tradesmen and shopkeepers had not been very effective. But on this day in May, 1937, they had collected an army of nearby peasants and hooligans, who looted every Jewish shop in town, while the police stood by to protect them. Any resistance offered by Jews was frustrated and stopped by the police with drawn guns. The pogrom only ended the next morning, when auxiliary police arrived from Warsaw. Witnessing all this was a traumatic experience and it remained vividly in my mind. Until then, 'boycott' and 'pogrom' had just been words to me.

The general idea of the pogrom was that, with their shops empty, the Jews would not be able to replace their stock quickly and therefore would not be able to carry on with their trade. This would provide an opportunity for the few existing Polish shopkeepers, merchants and tradesmen to take over. The plan failed. All Polish Jewry rallied and helped replenish the shops within a few days, and trade went on as usual. The solidarity of the Jews from other cities was just magnificent.

At about the same time in 1937, there were several other pogroms in Poland, but not on such a large scale as that in Brisk. The clouds over the Polish Jewish community were getting thicker, and the gloom deepened in the following year.

The impact of the pogrom was reflected in the numerous applications that the local H.I.A.S. office received from Jews wanting to emigrate. The only country which had its gates open at the time - the world was starting to recover from the Great Depression, and no-one was keen on receiving immigrants - was Australia. Even this was mainly for German refugees from Nazism; but Australia, which had been very hard hit by the Great Depression, must have had a quota of the numbers she could receive. Although hundreds of Jews applied, only about twenty families from Brisk were given visas. We were fortunate to be amongst them. There was one catch though. Immigrants had to have 200 Pounds Sterling, to show that they could support themselves for a while on arrival in Australia. 200 Pounds Sterling was a fortune in 1938, and our family did not even have a small fraction of that sum in cash. Our immigration permit arrived on the first of August, 1938, my seventeenth birthday. It was a hot summer day and I was jubilant. I knew that, in Australia, I would be able to study medicine and, later after graduation, immigrate to Palestine. But my father would not have a bar of it, and besides, we did not have the two hundred pounds nor the fare. No matter how hard we try to guide our lives or "forge our futures ," no matter how determined we may be, we can fail. It is said, "where there's a will, there's a way"; perhaps yes, but not always.

I have seen some strange coincidences in my life. The one that occurred in September 1938 was one of them. It was not possible for me to go to Australia on my own, but then the following happened: in the beginning of September 1938 Hitler marched into the occupied Sudeten, the western part of Czechoslovakia. This was a signal for Poland to demand the Cieszyn area, a part of Czechoslovakia which was ethnically Polish. The Czechs refused, however. The Polish government responded by declaring a general mobilisation and threatening to take the disputed area by force. There were massive rallies all over Poland, with slogans - Na Prage ("On to Prague") - calling for a full invasion of Czechoslovakia.

My father had never been a great hero and certainly not a Polish patriot. In his forties, he was still of military age. And we did have papers to go to Australia.

Things happened very swiftly. It took less than one week to sell our house, which we owned, and this provided us with the money for our fares and our deposit for entry into Australia. A few days later, Czechoslovakia capitulated and, for the sake of peace, handed over the small disputed area of land to Poland. But by this time, our house was sold and the ship tickets paid for. There was no backing away for my family. Now this long journey to the other side of the world was ahead of us. I nodded off to sleep eventually, and awakened when the train pulled up in Warsaw in the morning.

Brest - the Shoah and Today

There were perhaps 200 to 300 Brest survivors of the massacres in the Shoah; most of then survived because they were deported to Siberia by the Soviets during 1939 to 1941. A handful survived by hiding in Brest and surrounding villages. After the war in 1946, there were about 30 Jews living in Brest - not all of them native "Briskers," so it is fair to say that almost the entire Jewish population of Brest were murdered during 1941 to 1944.

The main massacre was at Bronnaya Gora on the 15th to 17th of October 1942 when the Germans shot over 50,000 Jews from Brest and the district into eleven pits. Brest was the first city to fall on June 22, 1941 when the Germans invaded the Soviet Union.

Brest was right on the border and it fell to General Guderian's tanks in a matter of hours.

The Brest survivors in the Soviet Union returned to Poland in 1946 - they assembled in a Displaced Persons camp in Stettin and most eventually emigrated to the United States, Austria, Argentina, Israel, France, etc.

Today, there is an active Jewish community of about 40 families , mostly reform Jews, but including a smaller orthodox group led by the Chabad Rabbi of Brest.

These Belorussian Jews have settled in Brest since 1945, none of them are descendants of the original 'Briskers'.

Jenni Buch

April 9, 2014

Notes to the Reader:

Within the text the reader will note "*[Page 489]*" standing ahead of a paragraph. This indicates that the material translated below was on page 489 of the original book. However, when a paragraph was split between two pages in the original book, the marker is placed in this book after the end of the paragraph for ease of reading.

Also please note that all references within the text of the book to page numbers, refer to the page numbers of the original Yizkor Book.

Family Notes

TABLE OF CONTENTS

THE OLD TOWN OF BREST-LITOVSK

The story of the Jews in Brisk D'Lita

S. Edelberg
Translated by Dr. Samuel Chani

1) Brest-Litovsk was a famous city since the times of the Polish Kingdom and the Lithuanian Duchy This town had a special important significance because of its geographic location, thanks to which it served the West as a window to the East. Brest – Litovsk linked Warsaw to Moscow, and it also linked Poland to Wolyn.

Two rivers, the Bug and the Mukhavets, formed the natural boundaries of the town.

The river Mukhavets formed a link to the forests and the marshlands. The river Bug connected the land with the west – the shipping links went through the Vistula to Gdansk and the Baltic Sea, and the Dnieper to the Black sea. In the old Polish kingdom Brest was the provincial capitol. In the times of the Lithuanian Duchy it was an important center of the province. Brest – Litovsk was the first city to receive rights under the Magdeburg Charter as an autonomous city. In the middle Ages it was the eastern frontier of the Polish State. It was surrounded by a lot of old forests and marshes, it's inhabitants were not very civilized – the central power of the Church had difficulty in reaching them – the new colonizers were not in a hurry to settle there.

Trade and commerce were not developed and the government did not place much military importance to it, the Catholic and Orthodox churches were seeking to establish their influence over this poor region.

We don't know exactly when Brest was established, but there is hearsay that Brest already existed in the 9th century because of its' importance to the western lands.

Granduke Vitold was looking for a means to interest Jews in all the aspects of Lithuanian development - Lithuania distanced itself from Poland in all aspects.

The Jews at that time were more experienced in business, trade and cultural matters – this was his main reason in enticing the Jews to come from the Polish Recz Pospolita (Commonwealth).

When did the Jews come to Lithuania?

According to the official documents of the Grand-duke Vitold in 1388, the Jews were given inhabitant rights. These decrees indicate that he knew years earlier of the benefits in having Jewish communities. Everything showed that the Jews of his Duchy excelled themselves with their ability and diligence – the duke saw in the Jews a serious force in the development of trade and commerce.

There is evidence that the Jewish community was settled there by the first half of the 14ᵗʰ century. There are no specific details of the Jewish community – because of all the wars and subsequent fires; all the documentation has been lost.

It's very hard to determine where the Jews of Brest-Litovsk came from; the majority came from Poland where they had come to after being expelled from Germany.

Their various customs and the spoken Yiddish proved this.

It is also possible that some of the Brest Jews came from Russia, because it was found that some of the Jews were involved in agriculture. This proving a more eastern origin, as trade and money matters were more representative of the western Jews.

The first official mention of the Brest-Litovsk Jewish community is found in the Right to Inhabit Decree of the Grand-duke Vitold in 1388. The Grand-duke knew of the Privileges granted by the Polish king Wladislaw to the Polish Jews in 1264, the contents were very similar to those granted by Vitold., it was highly probable that the Brest- Litovsk Jews knew of the privileges granted by the Polish king to their Polish brethren, and gave this example as a precedent when negotiating with Vitold.

In the decree, Vitold granted the Jews of Brest, and all the Jews of Lithuania, equal standing in rank and jurisdiction. For example: ordinary disputes between Jews could be determined by a Jewish judge – more serious cases involving the death penalty must be heard by a government judge.

A Christian who disturbed a Jewish grave would be strongly punished and his assets confiscated. It is forbidden to accuse the Jews of ritual murder, the king would determine the penalty for such a crime.

Jews were exempt from military service to the government.

A Christian who murdered a Jew would be executed and his belongings confiscated.

A Christian who beat a Jew would be punished the same as for beating a non-Jew.

It is forbidden to persecute a Jew, who goes from one place to another, for the importing of goods, he should pay the same tax as the rest of the population.

If a Christian attacks a Jew at night, the Christian neighbours are obliged to come to his aid, if they don't, they will also be punished.

This decree strengthened the community and re-enforced the leaders in their powers.

The Duke decreed that special attention be given to the Jews to enforce the verdicts given by the Jewish judges. The Duke allowed Jews to buy land and to cultivate the soil and plant seeds. From that time it proves that the Jews of Brest were involved in agriculture.

'The Right to Inhabit' decree had several important statutes which were granted to the Jews of Brest, these were much later granted to the other

Lithuanians communities under the Kings Zygmund the First (1507) and Zygmund the Third (1570).

The Brest community had striven to obtain these privileges so that they could conduct honest livelihoods according to the laws of the land – actually this was the aim of all the Diaspora Jews.

We have no documents about the spiritual lives of the Jews of Brest in the 16th century; it is not known who their leaders were. There is superficial evidence of the first Brest Rav, HaGaon Yechiel Luria, the grandfather of Rabbi Luria who came from Alsace Lorraine and became Marah D'Altra (Chief Rabbi) of Brest in 1470.

According to different documents, there were in Brest Jews who were landowners, some of whom owned villages that ruled the local peasants, merchants who traded their goods well beyond the borders of Lithuania.

At the time of Kasimir Jagiello (Kasimir 4th) 1447-92, the laws pertaining to Jews were observed and the king, as had the previous king, benefitted from the town and Lithuania generally. During the 100-year period between Vitold and the death of Kasimir the Forth – the Jews of Brest lived in peace. They established important bases for the gold trade and finance.

2.) After the death of Kasimir Jagiello in 1492, the fortunes of the Brest Jews were to be shaken. The king had 2 sons, the first, Jan Ulbrecht, was crowned king of Poland, the second, Alexander, was crowned Grandduke of Lithuania.

The news of the expulsion of the German Jews, the expulsions of Jews from Spain, Portugal and Provence, and the confiscation of the Jew's assets, came to Lithuania.

The aristocracy and the Lithuanian Boyars under the Duke Alexander wanted to confiscate the Jewish assets – they coveted the wealth of the Brest Jews.

The duke issued a proclamation stating that whoever would not convert to Catholicism by April 1495, would have to leave Lithuania. Despite the economic strength of the Brest Jews, they were forced to migrate from Lithuania for Poland. There was instability between the church and the Lithuanian ruling class, the rulers of Brest took the houses, estates and villages of the Jews and apportioned them amongst themselves.

There was a Brest Jew, a rich landowner who left his brethren and converted. This was Avraham Josefovitch, the brother of the famous Michael Josefovitch. Avraham Josefovitch reached the rank of Adelikan, in spite of the fact he had many enemies, he became the finance minister of Poland and his family assimilated into the Polish aristocracy.

In the year 1501, King Jan Ulbrecht died. His brother, Alexander inherited the throne of Poland and Lithuania. Within a short time it became clear to Alexander that the expulsion of the Jews had badly affected the Lithuania's finances. The economy of Lithuania had sunk to a very low level and the country was also suffering greatly from the Tartars attacks, which had razed

Brest to the ground. In 1503 Alexander allowed the Jews to return to Lithuania, he ordered his ministers to return their fortunes to them. Alexander decreed in 1505, that all the rights of the Jews be reinstated, all their assets and goods be returned to them, and he also decreed that a hospital and public baths be built in Brest.

Many Jews petitioned the king, reporting those gentiles who refused to return their goods and property. Then king then ordered that their assets be returned, plus interest accrued during the period they were confiscated. The situation of the Jews of Brest was unchanged until 1507, when Alexander died. After Alexander, two brothers came to the throne.

The first, Zygmund 1, was an enlightened man with good intentions towards the Jews, he appreciated their value. In both 1507 and later in 1511, he reissued Vitold's edict of 1388. Under Zygmund 1, and the Jews of Brest lived peacefully.

They were engaged in business, trade and agriculture, they were also artisans, tavern -keepers, and plowed the fields. They also were suppliers to the Polish Army of munitions, clothing and goods that King Zygmund needed in large quantities due to the ongoing wars with his enemies both to the east and the west.

In 1514 the king cancelled an extraordinary tax that his brother Alexander had levied in times of war - 1000 army cavalrymen.

In those days, commerce and business flourished and Brest became a town of merchants. The Talmudic scholars studied day and night in the Yeshiva of Brest which had become world famous – it's students went all over the world.

King Zygmund 1 believed that for his own aims, the cultural life of the Jews was important to the Jewish community. The first step in interfering in the internal affairs of the Jewish community of Brest was a prohibition that Zygmund issued forbidding the marriage of the daughter of Rabbi Moshe Rascovitch, who was known as the second Brest Rav, to the son of the Rabbi of Cracow, who had been expelled from Poland for a political transgression.

The second step was to establish a leader from amongst the Jews to collect the taxes and supervise all organization for the Kehilla (community). According to the king's wishes, Michael Josefovitch was elected as head of the Jews of Brest and all of Lithuania. In a letter he decreed that Michael Josefovitch had served him honestly and faithfully, and ordered that he be the intermediary between himself and the Jews. All taxes that were levied on the Lithuanian Jews were to be brought to Michael Josefovitch to transfer to the State Treasury. Thanks to his diligent efforts he was established as the king's representative. Michael Josefovitch was not a great Talmudic scholar but he was a religious man. He used the powers granted by the king and became autocratic and arrogant. At the time there was a revolt against Zygmund by the Duke Galinski.

Michael Josefovitch openly dealt with two Jews who sided with Galinski and confiscated their fortunes.

Some Jews complained to the king, Zygmund heard both sides, both of whom quoted Torah, but he upheld Josefovitch. To enforce his power, Michael Josefovitch requested that the king establish as Rabbi of Brest and of all Lithuania, Rabbi Mendel Frank, a famous Talmudic scholar, formerly Chief Rabbi of Posen, known as the Gaon of Lublin.

The Jews of Brest, who were fighting for their rights, did not want a Rabbi established by the power of the king, but an independent who was chosen by their own community. Mendel Frank complained to the king that the Jews were not obedient to him; they took their disputes to the civil authorities at the Town Council. The king threatened them with punishment, but then relented – Mendel Frank left Brest and for a long time after the Rabbis of Brest had the title 'Rav Kollel'.

Michael Josefovitch and his brother Yitzhak served without interruption as chief ministers and advisors to the king. They managed his finances, they supplied him with munitions and it is worthwhile to note the activities of the brothers Josefovitch.

An example – a Jew called Aaron the Blind was suspected of having poked out the eyes of a gentile in Brest, and then rubbed salt on the wound. The Jewish court demanded that Michael Josefovitch guarantee that he would put the accused in his own custody, and free him eventually. It came to light that he was a criminal and Josefovitch refused to give this guarantee and claimed that a Jewish community court had no power over the accused.

The Town Council (gentiles) tried him according to the Magdeburg law and ordered that his hands be cut off. After that, Michael Josefovitch realised that he had made a mistake in handing over a Jew to the gentile court, the case was judged on suspicions, not circumstantial evidence, and the verdict was carried out.

Michael Josefovitch was involved in many large business ventures; nevertheless, he did not stop furthering the cause of the Jews of Brest.

In March 1527, King Zygmund decreed that there be a travel tax on all coaches going through Brest. The Christians who collected the tax did not want to give the Jews their share. After the Jews of Brest through Josefovitch, petitioned the king, requesting that the powers of the Brest rulers be used, and that the Jews be given their share.

The king wrote that the Jews paid taxes like everybody else, so they should also be able to receive income from the State.

King Zygmund generously rewarded Josefovitch for his loyalty. He gave him the title of Adelikin - the ceremony was in the marketplace of Cracow in 1525. This is the only example of a Jew receiving a title despite not having renounced his religion and adhering to his religious beliefs. After the death of Josefovitch, the rank and privileges of the father went to his children. Josefovitch himself did not accomplish any special historical deeds to distinguish himself in the history of the Lithuanian Jews.

3.) In the first half of the 16th century, after the death of Zygmund 1, we find the Jews of Brest in good economic and social conditions. They were protected by the king against the church and the aristocracy, who wanted to take away from the Jews their economic privileges.

The Jews received a proportion of the city taxes and together with the other inhabitants of Brest carried out their share of city maintenance and such work as maintaining the bridges over the rivers and the city fortifications.

In 1548 Zygmund Augustus became king of Poland. He strove to bring the West and East closer together. During his reign many Jews came from the west to Poland.

There have been many documents showing the good relations the Jews had with the gentiles during the time of Zygmund Augustus. Their rights were confirmed and furthermore, the management and collction of taxes was placed in Jewish hands.

One time, it was brought to Zygmund Augustus' attention - a dispute between the gentiles in Pinsk and the Jewish tax collectors of Brest. The Jewish Finance Minister confiscated salt belonging to the gentiles, because the gentiles were stealing the salt taxes. The king supported the Jew's actions in this case. However, Zygmund Augustus burdened the Jews of Poland and Lithuania with heavy taxes.

In 1566 there were 106 Jewish house owners in Brest as against 746 gentiles in Brest.

The houses were timber, and there were about 14 inhabitants in each house. However, the economic situation of the Brest Jews was considered good.

In those days, the study of Torah flourished in Poland, which had replaced Germany as the European centre of Torah learning. The Union of Poland and Lithuania (Lublin 1569) had brought the two communities closer together.

Brest became the central community in Lithuania and became known all over the world. Even a Jewish printing press was established there, and dynasties of Rabbis were founded there. In the first half of the 16th century, Rabbi Klonimus was seated on the rabbinical chair; he was the son-in-law of the Gaon Rabbi Shlomo Luria (known as the Rashal)

His pupil, Rabbi Jakob Kitzingen, wrote in his book "Hag HaPesach" page 21, "and this happened - whilst I was studing Torah with my great teacher, the Rashal, of blessed memory,who was then Rosh Yeshivah of the holy Kehilla of Brest, in the house of the generous Reb David Drucker that mice ate up the Afikoman."

This Rabbinate of Brest was recognised as the most prestigious and important in Lithuania, and the Brest congregation was mentioned amonst the most important in Poland at that time, the others being Lublin, Posen and Cracow. This we also learn from the words of the

Gaon Rabbi Meir of Lublin (known as the Maharam), who wrote in his Questions and Answers page 88: "All the elders and great teachers, and the great Gaonim(Sages) of all Poland, Lithuania and Russia, are therefore, the great Gaon Rabbi Mordechai Joffe, head of the Holy congregation of Posen, and the Gaon, the Wonder, Rabbi Moshe, Rosh Bet Din of the Holy congregation of Cracow, and the Wonder in Torah and in Chassidut, Rabbi Leib, Rosh Bet Din of the Holy congregation of Brest".

Thus wrote Rabbi Moshe Isserlich (known as the Ramo) of the Sages of Brest in his Questions and Answers, note 1: "Together, our Rabbis from Brest, that everyone is blessed and uplifted by their position, Shalom." From this source we learn that the rabbis would swap their positions in the Kehilla (community council) .

In the beginning of the 17th century, in the year 1618 the Rabbi of Brest was the Gaon Rabbi Joel Sirkis, who was known as the 'Bach', after his book, Bayit Chadash (New House), an explanation of the 4 parts of the 'Turim'. In the year 1618, Rabbi Joel Sirkis, the 'Bach', went to Cracow. According to legend, the Bach left the Rabbinate of Brest, because members of the congregation accused him, that one night the light in his house did not burn after midnight, a sign that he did not sit and study until late.

(A similar accusation was written many years later by the Gabbais of the Vilna Congregation, against their Rabbi, the Gaon Rabbi Shmuel, that sometimes he did not stay up late and studies, as there was no light in his house past midnight).

In the year 1618, Rabbi Joel Sirkis, the Bach, signed an excommunication order, which was brought about by the great rabbis of Poland and Lithuania, against a doctor from Amsterdam (Holland). This doctor was also spokesperson of the Dutch Jewish community.

The excommunication order was taken out against him because he made a mockery of the words of our Sages and only believed in the wisdom of Philosophy. The Bach formulated the words as follows: " there is no doubt that this man deserves the death penalty,isolation, and to be thrown out of town, because even if this had happened in the time of our Sages, he would have been isolated, as it is quoted in the Talmud and 'Masechet Velo Megalchin'.

Even more so when it is a matter of making a mockery of Sages and speaks negatively about the wisdom of the Kabbalah, which is the source of the Torah and it's principal text- as a whole it is full of fear of heaven, and he deserves ex-communication, and in addition, he follows the philosphy of the free-thinker (Apicorus).

"There is no doubt that a person, whether he be a learned person, who laughs off the words of the Sages and the wisdom of the Kabbala, deserves to be killed and ex-communicated,

because this is the free- thinker in all his power."

4.) In the year 1568, there was a great fire in Brest and the entire Jewish neighbourhood burnt down. King Zygmund Augustus relieved the Jewish community of one third of their taxes in the New Year, on the condition that they would rebuild their houses in stone or brick.

This helped the Jews build a new district; they also built a new Beth Hamidrach, according to the designs of the builder Patronka of Posen. Near the Beth Hamidrach was the Great Yeshiva; the Beth Hamidrach remained until 1842.

During the reign of Zygmund Augustus, the native inhabitants were inventing various blood libels accusations designed at expelling the Jews from the commercial life of Brest.

In 1564 there was a blood libel against a Jew from a neighbouring town – he was accused of knifing a Christian girl to use her blood to make matzot. The king released him and decreed on the 10th May 1566, that only under the conditions of 3 Jewish and 3 Gentile witnesses could such an accusation be levelled, and only the king could judge such a case of ritual murder.

The same decree was confirmed by his successor, Stephan Batory on the 9th August 1576.

According to historical information we have concerning the Brest Jews in those days, they were involved in importing fabrics and raw-materials from Germany and other lands.

They would manufacture clothing and other goods and send them to Russia.

Then Ivan the Terrible, who was known as an enemy of Israel, forbade the importing of these goods into Russia.

At the same time, the Great Yeshiva in Brest was established, and talented students from all over Europe streamed towards it.

5.) In the year 1572, in the transition period before the election of Stephan Batory in 1576, Ivan the Terrible attempted to take the kingdom by force, but the Poles repelled him.

Then Batori was elected as king in 1576. The Jews rejoiced at the defeat of the Enemy of Israel – the youth of Brest arranged a Purim play in 1577 in which Haman was depicted as 'Ivan of Moscow'.

In the second half of the 16th century amongst the young students who came to study at the Brest Yeshiva, there was a Saul Wahl from Padua in Italy. There in Padua his father was the Gaon Shmuel Yehuda Katzenellenbogen -Minc, the son of the famous Maharam of Padua, famed as a Posek (Rabbinic judge and authority). In Brest Saul Wahl married Devorah, the daughter of a rich merchant Reb Yehuda Krocker. Reb Krocker was the Parnas (community leader) of the Brest Kehilla.

Thanks to his great knowledge of the Torah and wisdom, Saul Wahl became very important amonst the inhabitants of Brest. He also found favor with the king Stephan Batory who made him one of the greatest Arendars in Lithuania- Poland.

According to legend, after the death of Stephan Batory in 1586, there was a meeting of the Council of Ministers in Warsaw to elect a new king, however, they could not reach agreement and followed a suggestion by Prince Radzivilll that Saul Wahl be made king for one night, until they could reach agreement. The next day they elected Zygmund the Third.

Naturally this is a legend, but the Wahl family folklore claimed that during that one night, Saul Wahl affirmed all the decrees pertaining to the welfare of Jews.

In 1578, Saul Wahl was in charge of all the salt manufacture, and was Controller of all the king's finances in Brest and vicinity. Notwithstanding his heavy business responsibilities for all of Poland, we find his name mentioned in many documents that confirm his status and endeavors for the Brest community. Saul was special envoy to the king, because of his relationship to the monarchy he was able to ceaselessly campaign for the Jew's rights.

In 1582 Saul Wahl requested one quarter of the town's taxes for the Brest Jews, and King Zygmund the Third ratified this.

In 1593, Saul Wahl brought forth an accusation against the city elders in front of the king. The elders of Brest were interfering in Jewish affairs and were oppressing and beleaguering the Jews with their demands for heavy taxes. Zgymund the Third sent a letter to the Town Council of Brest forbidding them to interfere in Jewish affairs. Also in the Christian population, Saul Wahl was respected and esteemed as the king's' representative.

In 1595, all the inhabitants of Brest approached Saul Wahl and requested that he intervene with the king on their behalf, to lower their taxes. There are no further references to Saul Wahl in that year. We don't know the date of Saul Wahl's death, but before his death he allocated part of his fortune to the poor and the Yeshivot.

Wahl's family lineage was far -reaching. His son the Gaon Rav Avrashka Wahl, became Head of the Brest Yeshiva, he was the son-in-law of the 'Tosfot Yom Tov', Rabbi Lipman Heller. In Avrashka Wahl's time there was in the Brest Yeshiva a great scholar named Rav Josef Isserlich, the brother of the Ramo, Rabbi Meir Isserlich.

In his elder years, Rav Avrashka was the Rabbi of Lwow, and until Rabbi Jacob Padua, who was a great-grandson of Saul Wahl's, who died in Brest in 1855, all the Brest rabbis were related to the Wahl dynasty.

Towards the end of the 16th century the importance of Brest to the central government and the Sjem (Polish parliament) had increased. The Sjem assembled there in 1594-96.

Brest was also a meeting place of the bishops. Brest was the most respected community in Lithuania and actively involved in the meetings of the Council of Four Lands. In a meeting of the Four Land's Council in 1607, there was a Rabbi from Brest, Rabbi Yehuda Eilenberg, representing the Jewish communities (Kehillot) of Lithuania, which belonged to Poland.

In 1623, there was a split between Lithuania and Poland because of their many differences and different systems of government. There were many reasons for the formation of the Council of Lithuania

. In 1644, the Jews of Brest complained to the Lithuanian government that students from the Theological Seminary had attacked and molested them in the streets. In the same year, there was a counter-complaint from the

Seminary students that Jews had attacked and beaten them. The atmosphere of anti-Jewish sentiment and the ill will of the Church was increasingly felt, and the Jews were seeking to counteract these troubles.

6.)In the years 1648 and 1649, great suffering came – with the Cossack uprising under the leadership of Bogdan Chmelnitski. In this revolt against the Polish king, Wladislaw the Fourth, much Jewish blood was split, mainly in eastern Poland. According to sources, the Jews suffered greatly, hundreds were murdered, and these hundreds were the Jews that had not fled from Brest. The Jew's homes were looted and destroyed, and their belongings stolen. From a book by Nathan Hanover " in the other large communities of Lithuania there were thousaands and tens of thousands of Jews murdered." From the communities of Slutsk, Minsk and Brest, many fled into Greater Poland, by using the Vistula River, many even reached Gdansk. The poor people who remained were slaughtered. In another chapter " how many souls of the remaining poor, the holy people who were the remnants of the Brest Kehilla, were murdered in the glory of God in that year (1648)".

A priest called Gregory Kanakov has left a list of Brest murders from the time of the massacres. He describes how the city was ransacked, the Jew's worldly goods looted and destroyed, and most of the Jews killed. The Polish soldiers who arrived and chased the Cossacks away, killed the small number of Jews that had survived, whilst searching for their hidden treasures.

From the books of that time is a book called 'Helkat Machkok' by Rabbi Moshe Lima, son of Rabbi Yehuda Lima, who had left the Rabbinate in Lithuania and was in that year was the Rabbi of Brest. In this book we read of the Cossack atrocities. A woman eyewitness to the atrocities of the Cossacks reported that the Cossack murderers killed their victims by swinging their axes and cutting off their victim's heads. Then they wiped their axes on the victim's clothes. Another description:' Our own eyes have seen many people slaughtered and taken prisoner.' The Gaon Rabbi Moshe was the pupil of the author of the book 'Pnei Yoshua' and many rabbis corresponded with him, he died in Brest.

The decrees of the years 1648 –1649 were reflected in the decisions of the Lithuanian Jewish Council that was assembled in 1649. " Until our own eyes saw, because of our many sins, how many Jews were abducted and assimilated with the gentiles, and so forth...."

"Because of that we are now writing to all places and congregations where there are at least 10 people (a minyan), that they have the right to pay ransom for every soul under the age of 17, without hesitation, or having to ask permission."

" And also in regards to the poor dispossessed people, who have became like nomads in our land and wander around"." This ruling, which was to be strictly enforced on the movement of these homeless masses, we should now, after the tragedy, hasten with saving as many Jewish lives as possible."

7.) The revolt of the Cossacks and the wars that Poland waged against Moscow and the Swedes, as well as the Turkish attacks, all contributed to the deteriorating position of the Jews in Lithuania and Poland. As in other towns, the Jews of Brest became impoverished, those who were once affluent became homeless, and Jewish fortunes were lost.

In 1661 King Jan Kazimir freed the Jewish citizens of Brest from the compulsory billeting of Polish soldiers, and relief from various taxes. This is because they were impoverished and unable to pay. The king, Jan Kazimir, genuinely wanted to improve the conditions of the Brest Jews and to influence them to return to normal life. Therefore, he issued a special manifest on the 13th June 1665, in which he exhorted his ministers to protect the Jews and to look after their interests. However, the attacks on the Jews increased, especially from the nobility.

The king, who was courageous enough on the 13th May 1665, to sentence an nobleman to death. This nobleman had ridden his horse into the Bet Hamidrach in Brest, brandishing his sword, and killed the caretaker of the synagogue. The family of this nobleman was also forced to pay compensation to the family of the murdered man.

However, the overall situation of the Jews in Brest was grim. Commerce dwindled, and the Christian population in Brest became saturated with the hatred of Israel. The Church incited against the Jews, and the nobility found revenue through robbery and corruption.

In 1679 in Brest, there was the trial of a long drawn -out dispute over land ownership.

The head of the church in Brest claimed large areas of land on which Jewish houses had been built, claiming that this belonged to the Church. On the other hand, the Jews had the official documentation proving that the land indeed belonged to them before they had erected their homes. This dispute had dragged on for years, and led to violence and blows, but the Jews won their case in the end.

In 1669, Michal Wiszniewski, who was the king's representative, affirmed the rights of the Jews in Brest. He allowed the Jews to build gates that were locked on the Sabbath and Holy days, so that their Gentile neighbors could not molest them.

This statute did not appeal to the anti-Semitic nobility and at a meeting of the Brest Assembly in 1669, the nobility requested that heavy penalties be imposed on Jews who employed Christian workers and servants.

The rights of the Jews werer affirmed by the king, Jan Sobieski in 1676, who was known as a friend of the Jews. He strengthened their rights. Because of this, a charge of conspiracy was levelled against the Jews in Brest. It was alleged that the Jews had murdered a Jewess that had converted to Catholicism and then disappeared. Several members of her family were sentenced to death.

The grave situation of the Jews was illustrated by the following events:

In 1682 elected representatives of the Jewish Community (kehilla) appeared before the governor of Brest with the following petition. Many Jews had borrowed large sums of money from the nobility without consultation. The kehilla was held responsible for these large debts. The kehilla requested that it be made compulsory to first ask permission of the kehilla before borrowing money.

In 1670 the plight of the Jewish borrowers was illustrated by the reform amendment (Takanon): "those who give their wives and children as sureties will suffer in both worlds."

Amongst the signatories of this amendment was the Gaon Benjamin Ginsburg, the Rabbi of Brest.

In 1676, the king Jan Sobieski agreed to heavily punish those that did not honour their debts, and gave permission to the kehilla to treat this as a criminal act and punish them.

In 1684 the government closed the Brest Beth Hamidrash (prayer house) for not paying a debt owed by a Jew to the Brest Government. Only after that debt was repaid was the Beth Hamidrach reopened. During this period, some of the assets of the Jewish community were sold to the Church as repayment of debts.

After Jan Sobieski's death in 1696, war broke out in Poland. Civil war erupted like flames between the followers of Stanislaw and the followers of Augustus 11, who was eventually elected as king. Augustus 11 reigned between 1697 and 1733. The Jews of Lithuania felt the impact of these conflicts more than the other citizens, they were oppressed from all sides, and not helped by the affirmation of their rights by the king.

The importance of Brest was diminished by the central powers. Many new towns were established in the area and grew in importance. Amongst the Jewish communities of Lithuania, Vilna became more important. The significance of Brest began to waver. An example of this diminished power was illustrated by the kehilla of Slutsk declaring that they wanted to be independent of the Brest kehilla. A member of the Four Lands Council requested that he be appointed the leader 'of the famous and beautiful Slutsk community'.

As Brest did not respond to this request in time, the Slutsk kehilla decided to grant this request by themselves.

Brest, which had served as an example to other Jewish communities by their punctuality in collecting and paying taxes, protested against soldiers accompanying the tax collectors.

The war minister requested that the Jews of Brest attend a military tribunal for attacking soldiers. When King Augustus the Third came to the throne in 1733, he promised to uphold the rights of the Jews and their protection. However, the Adelikan strengthened their persecution by reinforcing the locals who wanted to expel the Jews from the business and commercial life of Brest.

In 1759, there was a meeting of the Polish parliament in Brest, several members of this Parliament attacked the Jews in the Great Synagogue, and demanded money. The criminals were brought to justice, but their leader was lightly sentenced and the rest were exonerated.

8.) Notwithstanding its economic decline, the town of Brest retained its greatness. It was a large community, full of Talmudic sages and clever Talmudic businessmen who respected the Torah, and the names of the Brest rabbis shone in the list of Sages (Gaons) of the Polish and Lithuanian rabbis.

Amongst some of the Sages and rabbis who were recorded in the list of Brest rabbis after the decrees of 1648 -49 were:

The Gaon Yakov, son of the Gaon Ephriam Zalman Shor, the son-in-law of Rabbi Yeshayahu, the son of the Nagid, Reb Moshe Lisras.Reb Moshe Lisras left a lot of money in his will to the Council of Lithuania. These monies were supposed to help the communities, specifically to build Beth Midrashim (prayer houses and schools). After him, there was a rabbi of Brest in the year 1655, Reb Moshe Lima, who wrote 'Helkat Mechokek'.

And after Rabbi Lima, the Gaon Rabbi Aharon Shmuel Kwidenaver, author of the books "Birkat Hazevach" and "Birkat Shmuel". Then the Gaon Rabbi Tzvi Hirsh in the year 1664.

Until the Gaon Mordechai Ginsburg was the rabbi of Brest D'Lita, the custom was not to retain the rabbinical seat for more than 3 years. With Rabbi Ginsburg, this custom changed.

Rabbi Mordechai Ginsburg was succeeded by the Gaon Rabbi Mordechai Zyzkind Rottenberg, the author of the book "Questions and Answers of Rabbi Mordechai Zyskind" In 1691,the rabbi of Brest was the Gaon Rabbi Saul, the son of Rabbi Heshel. Rabbi Saul, was later the Rabbi of Krakow.

In 1713 there was in Brest a rabbi, Aryeh Yehuda Leib, the grandson of the author of the "Shaagat Aryeh"

In 1718, the rabbi was Nachman Sirkin, who was praised by Rabbi Yaakov Emden in his books, " Torat HaKanaut" and "Ezrat Yaakov".

At the time that Stanislaw Poniatowski became king of Poland in 1764, conditions were very difficult for the Jews because he followed the laws of the Russian Empress, Catherine the Great. At that time there was a Russian law that each community was responsible for collecting their own revenue and taxes. The Polish king followed the Russian laws in relation to the Jewish communities and ordered that the Council of Lithuania be continued.

In 1768, the Polish parliament issued an edict forbidding Jews who held no special concessions, from owning taverns. Not all the tavern owners could produce such concessions, and therefore many Jews lost their livelihoods. As many Jews were innkeepers in Lithuania and Wolyn, this main source of income was lost.

In 1761, the Council of the Lithuanian State held it's last meeting in Slutsk. The first signatory on this final proclamation was the Gaon Rabbi Abram Katzenellebogen, who was previously the Rabbi of Slutsk. From 1760, Rabbi Katzenellenbogen was famed as a Gaon, and as an opponent of the Chassidim.

During the time of Rabbi Yacob Meir Padua's term as rabbi of Brest in 1847, there was a great fire in Brest and the Great Synagogue burnt down. On the main street of Brest in the central Jewish business area, all the shops burnt down, and 12 men died, incinerated in the fire. With much difficulty, Rabbi Yakov Meir made great efforts on behalf of their widows that they should not remain as Agunot (deserted wives, unable to remarry), according to the law in Tshuvot.

The Great Synagogue that was destroyed had been built in 1759,and improved by Saul Wahl. The erection of the new synagogue lasted 10 years, 1851-1861, due to many shortages. The designs for the new synagogue were according to the sketches of the Rabbi, Yakob Meir Padua, who was the Rabbi of Brest 1840-1855.

After the death of Rabbi Yakov Meir, Rabbi Tzvi Hirsh Orenstein occupied the rabbinical seat in 1865. Rabbi Orenstein was a Gaon of Torah and also a very efficient organizer. Under his leadership, the communal hospital and old people's home were built. In those days there was a law that every Jewish community had to provide a certain number of recruits for the Russian army, or buy their exemption with money. Rabbi Orenstein was always seeking means to ransom these recruits and to provide money for their release.

Rabbi Tzvi Hirsh did many good deeds for his community until the Russian authorities exiled him in 1874, on the pretext that he was from Galicia, and therefore, a foreigner. In his last years, he was the Rabbi of Lwow, his book "Brachot Tzvi Hirsh", was published after his death in 1888.

To the rabbinical seat came another Gaon, Rabbi Yehoshua Leib Diskin, who previously had been the rabbi of Lomza, Kovno, and Shklov. Rabbi Diskin was a Gaon who was extremely orthodox and uncompromising – in Brest he had many conflicts with the Russian authorities.

In 1877, Rabbi Diskin issued a rabbinical ruling that was in opposition to the law of the Russian government. Due to this, he was forced to leave Brest after 3 years of being the rabbi. He went to Jerusalem and whilst there was a vehement and passionate opponent of the Zionists and the enlightened (secular) Jews. He forbade the "Heter Shmita", which was a law passed in 1889, by the sages and rabbis, amongst them the rabbi of Kovno, Yitzchak Elchanan Spektor.

In Jerusalem, Rabbi Diskin established a large orphanage, and the Yeshiva "Ohel Moshe". He died in Jerusalem in 1898, his book "Question and Answers of Rabbi Y.L. Diskin", was published after his death.

By the end of the 19th century the Jewish population of Brest had greatly increased.

The military Garrison at the Fortress, one of the symbols of the Russian Empire, brought much business to the tradesmen and artisans of Brest. From the surrounding shtetls (villages), Jews came to settle in Brest. In the 1880's Jews were 50% of the town's population.

They were engaged in trade, craftsmen, light industries and building enterprises.

In the year 1878, the Sage and Righteous, Rabbi Joseph Dov Ber Soleveitchik, (Rabbi Yoshe Ber) was elected to be Rabbi of Brest. From 1878, up to the great disaster of 1939, the rabbinical seat of Brest was occupied by Rabbi Yoshe Ber, his son Chaim and his grandson, Ze'ev Wolf Soleveitchik, until the destruction of the town. Rabbi Joseph Ber was born in Niesvitz in 1820 and studied in Volozhin. For many years he wandered through various yeshivas, he was the Rabbi of Brest until he died in 1892. He was much loved by all. Yoshe Ber was a sympathizer of the ideas of "Yishuv Israel", which was founded in 1860 in Brest. He was the author of the book, 'Beth Halevi', which was four parts of questions and answers, and sermons.

In 1891 there were 30,000 Jews in Brest out of a population of 46,000. In that time, emigration from Brest and all of Russia greatly increased. Many left for America, Argentina, etc. Amongst the Zionists (Chovevei Zion) that made Aliyah to Israel in 1884, were some from Brest. The Russian authorities were very distrustful of the Jews of Brest, because of the town's strategic position; the Russian rulers doubted the Jew's loyalty in case of war.

In 1892, the rabbinical seat passed on to Rabbi Chaim Soleveitchik, Rabbi Chaim played a very large role not only as Rabbi of Brest, but also as Chief Rabbi of the general Jewish community of Russia. The Brest community was very proud of Chaim, he was known as Chaim Brisker. He was recognized by every scholar and learned Jew.

He wrote the following books: 'The Renewal of Rabbi Chaim Halevy'. 'Explanations of the book of the Ram Bam'. 'New explanations of Questions that have arisen in the Talmud'. With the death of Rabbi Chaim in 1918, the Jewish community of Brest became orphaned.

It's a wonderful thing in the history of the Jewish people that the city of Brest D'Lita, over a period of many generations, developed into the chief Jewish community of Poland and Lithuania. The Brest Rabbis and Sages extended their influence over the whole of European Jewry, and retained and continued their influence until the great tragedy and demise of this community.

A 17th Century Purification Cup

[Page 45]

Map of Council of 4 Lands 1667-1764

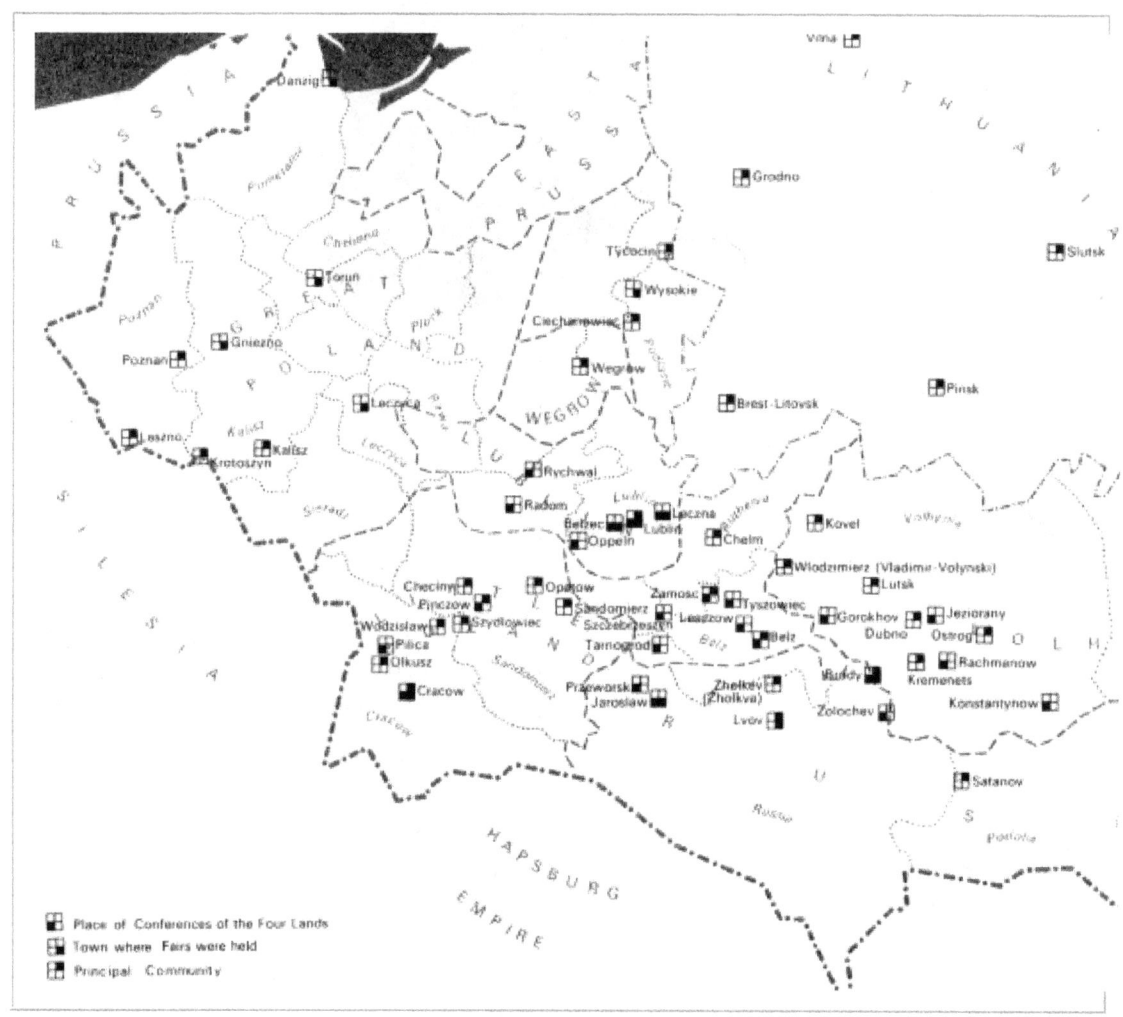

Map of Council of 4 Lands 1667-1764

Main Jewish Communities in Poland and Lithuania under the jurasdiction of the autonomous Jewish organization of the Council of Four Lands and the Council of Lithuania. After I. Halperin, *Pinkas Va'ad Arba Arazot* (1945).

[Page 47]

Brisk D'Lita in the Council of Four Lands

By C. Barlas
Translated by Dr. Samuel Chani

A. During the entire period of the Jewish Diaspora the Jewish people strove to organize and attain for themselves in different countries, some sort of autonomy - an autonomy that would help them defend themselves. As it says " A nation that dwells alone will not be considered a nation". In the lands that had concentrated settlements of Jews, sometimes they were able to establish their own special institutions and regulations through laws and statutes. Those Jews voluntarily undertook to oversee their communities. Cells of Jewish autonomy already existed in the period of the Babylonian Diaspora." The Heads of the Community and the Sages".

When the spiritual center transferred to the Jewish communities of Europe, the form of self-rule crystallized through the rabbinical customs and administrators, first in Spain, then in France and Germany. Thanks to the statutes that were enacted by the heads of the community as "laws that were not to be broken" the Jews achieved a greater degree of independence in Central Europe. In the 15th century there was established the "Council of Lands" in Poland and later a "Council of the Nation" in Lithuania.

The political upheavals and rebellions that took place under the Polish monarchy forced the kings to enforce heavy duties and taxes on their countrymen and to seek methods to centralize their power, frequently with a strong hand.

The privileges that the Polish kings had granted thanks to the emissaries of the heads of the communities served as a basis by which the community leaders could administer and carry out their duties. Whilst the Jews were differentiated from the local inhabitants by their different customs, they became enclosed in their own communities, having received permission to organize their affairs amongst themselves. The state benefited economically as the Jews had talents and commercial expertise and the Jewish communities with their practical abilities and skills set an example of communal life.

The 'Council of Lands" was established due to the tendency of the ruling powers to oversee the collection of taxes through the Jewish leaders and officials that worked within their own communities. These leaders and community officials thereby found a means to broaden their powers and extend it to the establishment of administrative cells that had full autonomy. These functioned in all areas of Jewish life within the borders of that country. The 'fairs' in all the main cities that the Jews came to en masse for trade and commerce were an opportunity for all the community leaders to gather together. This was very useful for deliberation and decision-making about economic affairs, the collection of taxes that the king and the central power imposed on the cities. Therefore, this autonomous situation ultimately concentrated economic decision- making in the hands of the administrators of the communities. This was the Council of Four Lands, in which the rabbis and leaders of the important and influential communities met and decided on essential matter in their meetings. They dealt with edicts and customs that became strictly enforced laws in the Jewish settlements.

Circumstances of the central and local bodies,(The king and the Parliament)

Organization of the living conditions of the community, e.g. election of leaders, judges, tax collectors, synagogue officials by secret ballot.

Tax collection for the Government and the local community, and the distribution of these taxes according to priorities and categories.

The administration of religious education and affairs. (Yeshivas and synagogues).

Trade and business affairs. Arendars (leaseholders) of estates and tax collectors. Taverns in the villages, Rights of ownership and preserving their property borders.

From the above came the rules and customs, spiritual and ethical codes, which were etched on the character of the Eastern European Jews for generations. Prior to the establishment of the Council of Four Lands there were a series of gathering and meetings by rabbis and heads of communities at different times. In 1580-81 there was a meeting and there remained the first documents about its existence. The structure of the Council of Lands varied in different periods. At first there was the Council of Three Lands – Little Poland, Greater Poland, and Russia. After that Lublin merged with the community of Wolyn and joined thus becoming the Council of Four Lands. In the constitution of 1588, five countries are mentioned - Greater Poland, Little Poland, Russia, Lithuania, and Wolyn. The assemblies took place twice a year at the times of the fairs in Gramnitz, Lublin or Yaroslav. The first communities who participated in the first council were Posen, Krakow, Lemberg (Lvov) and Brisk D'Lita.

The organizational body in the lives of the Jews of Lithuania and Poland was the "Kehilla". Some of the communities set up centers for their provinces. In the confederation of the Council of Four Lands, Lithuania was represented by the taxation system in Brest, the chief Jewish community of Lithuania. In the meetings of the council the distribution of the taxes to each country was decided, the elections of rabbis, scribes, shammes (beadles). The meetings usually took place every two years, and in the period between the meetings, the communities were represented in the central government in Warsaw by lobbyists (those who had the authority to stand in front of the King and his ministers). They represented their interests (the Jewish communities) to the central government and bureaucracy and tried to protect against adverse edicts with righteousness and prayer.

B. The Kehillot of Lithuania participated in the Council of Four Lands for over fifty years, until the Assembly of the Heads of the Communities in 1623 in Brisk D'lita when they founded their own Council of the Communities of Lithuania. From this assembly a wonderful regulation was adopted. It spread over 100 points that covered everything - all that concerned the social, economic, religious and ethical issues of the communities and their members

The foundation meeting of the Council of Lithuanian Communities was a turning point for Lithuanian Jewry, which apparently could not live under the same roof with the Council of Four Lands. After the communities developed and became economic and spiritual centers, specific customs and methods crystallized as community standards.

Early on in the Council of the Lithuanian State the delegates were representatives from Brest, Horodna, and Pinsk. Later on Vilna and Slutsk were added. The Vilna community was co-opted at the session of the Council in 1652, with the decision being made to present the proposal to the Head of the Vilna community residents Only 35 years later in 1687, did Vilna get equal status in the Kehilla of leaders through the representation of three leaders, a scribe and a Shammes.

The Slutsk community was co-opted under the supervision of Brest until 1691, when it received full status in the council whose activity already governed five provinces with all their communities.

Two or three leaders of each main community, together with the chief rabbis and the number of participants reached 15 attended the Council assemblies. Once every two or three years, the Council assembled in one of the cities of the communities and the meetings lasted from three up to six weeks. The leader of the community of the Host city was the chairman of the meetings. The expenses were covered by a levy of all the communities. As planned, the meetings first dealt with the summation of accounts and expenses (budget), and then with laws and statutes, lastly, education and charity.

The competence of the main kehillot was defined in the foundation statutes of the Council of 1623 that was composed of Brest, Horodna and Pinsk. Brest had 30 communities, Horodna 7, Pinsk 8.

The community of Brest was composed of the following: Mezrich, Warin, Yanov, Rashes (Rashi), Lamaz, Bila, Beshatz, Wlodawka, Slovatitz, Kadna, Wysokie, Amystivaya, Kobryn, Horodetz, Pruzhany, Maltesh, Seltz, Chernowitz, Kamenetz, Sherchavi, Rushanik, Slonim, Dvoretz, Novordok, Nezvitch, Slutsk, Minsk, Malavny, Orhsa and the inhabitants of Rus.

To Horodna belonged: Ambur, Mustetzki, Kuznitza, Nowy Dor, Ostrin, Rashin, and Litza.

The community around Pinsk encompassed: Kletsk, Lachovitz, Hamsak, Brahin, Dovrovitch, Wissotsk, and Torava

Apparently in those days Brest had so much importance that it ruled over distant cities in Russia – Minsk, Mogilev, even until Orsha. Brest was the leading community because of its geographic position to all the neighboring communities, as well as it's economic importance and being the center of Torah learning.

At the first meeting of the Lithuanian Council the following was decided: During the life of our leader the illustrious Rabbi Meir who is old in his days and will not be able to leave the city anymore, every time there is to be an assembly of the Heads of Communities, it is to be held here in Brest, in honor of Rabbi Meir (son of Saul Wahl who was the King of Poland for one hour)). It was agreed that Brest would be the venue for the Council because "the eyes of the nation were focused on Rabbi Meir" who would ratify the documents of the Council. Rabbi Meir the chairman, who is ailing, gave full legal empowerment to the scribe to sign in his place.

After his death it was decided that the seat of the council be in Pruzhany. Then it returned to Brisk. At times it was held in Shiltz (1632-47). The council alternated from place to place. The assemblies were not precisely decided according to the town; rather the circumstances of the times dictated the venue.

The sessions of the Council of Lithuania that were held in Brest were:

Elul 1623, Adar 1626, Elul 1627, Adar 1631.

———

[Page 71]

List of Rabbis of Brisk D'Lita

Segment from original list

	Name of Rabbi	Year	Title	Notes
1	Issachar Aron Luria	About 1470		
2	Michael Josefovitch	1475		
3	Mendel Frank	1529	Head of the Beth Din	
4	Joseph ben Moshe	1559/60	Head of the Beth Din	
5	Naphtali Herz	1568/69	Head of the Beth Din	
6	Klominus Schor	1573	Head of the Beth Din	
7	Mordechai Reis	1573	Head of Yeshiva	
8	Shimon		Head of Yeshiva	
9	Yehuda Livo ben Ovadia Ellenburg	1589		
10	Moshe Livshitz	1609		
11	Hirsh Schor	1612		
12	Joel Sirkis	1614-18		The "Bach"- Author of Bayit Chadash.
13	Beinish Livshitz	1619-20		Son in law of Saul Wahl
14	Meyer Wahl	1622-25		Son of the Minister Saul Wahl.
15	Avrashka Wahl		Head of Yeshiva	Son of the Minister Saul Wahl.
16	Joseph Kazak			
17	Zeev Wolf			
18	Ephraim Zalman			
19	Yakov ben Ephraim Naphtali	1631		
20	Avraham Epstein	1635		

21	Avraham ben Benjamin Aron Solnik	1639		'Baal- Tov'
22	Joshua			Baal M.S.'
23	Shlomo Zalman ben Yermiahu Yakov	1646		
24	Yahov Kahana		Head of Yeshiva	
25	Yakov Schor	1651		
26	Moshe ben Joshua Lima	before 1657		
27	Shaul Ben Rabbi Moshe			
28	Tzvi Hirsh ben Moshe Yakov	1663	Head of the Beth Din	
29	Yehuda of Troppa	1664		
30	Shmuel Kaidanover	1657-60	Head of the Beth Din	
31	Moshe Pesach ben Rabbi Tanchum	1673		
32	Mordechai Pinchus	1683		
33	Mordechai Ginzburg	1685		
34	Mordechai Zyskind Rottenberg	1691		The Ramaz
35	Heshel Ben Yakov	1691-95		
36	Shaul ben Heshel			The Rasha
37	Moshe ben Mordechai Zyskind			
38	Menachem Mendel ben Benjamin Katz			
39	David Oppenheimer	1698		
40	Arye Leib ben Shaul Heshel			

41	Avraham ben Rabbi Shloime	1711		
42	Shmuel Tzvi Hirsh	1714		
43	Nachman ben Shmuel Tzvi Hirsh			
44	Israel Isser ben Rabbi Moshe	1757-60		
45	Avraham Katzenellenbogen	1760-1804		
46	Nachman Halperin			
47	Joseph Katzenellenbogen	1804		son of Avraham Katzenellenbogen
48	Arye Leib Katzenellenbogen	1798-1837		son of Joseph Katzenellenbogen
49	Yakov Meir Padua	1840-55		
50	Tzvi Hirsh Orenstein	1865-74		expelled by the Russians as a foreign agent, died in Lwow 1888
51	Yehoshua Leib Diskin	1874-77		expelled by the Russians, died in Jerusalem.
52	Joseph Ber Soloveitchik	1878-92		
53	Chaim Soloveitchik	1892-1918		
54	Yitzchak Zeev Soloveitchik	1919 -40		The Last Rabbi of Brest, died in Israel 1959.

[Page 73]

The Jews of Brest in the 16th and 17th Centuries

By K. Lichtenstein
Translated by Dr. Samuel Chani and Jenni Buch

1). Brest has a premier position in the archives of literature about the Lithuanian Dukedom. In the publication of the "Vilna Archival Commission" 1865-1915, which was edited by the Russian Government, there are 5 volumes containing documents about Brest 3 volumes are chronicles of the town's courts, and 1 volume is of the Brest district's court. I more volume chronicles the city's administration.

The same is to be found regarding other publications and collection of documents from the archival sources of the Old Lithuanian Duchy and the Lithuanian Metrical Books. The number of documents of the Brest Courts and Government organizations to be found is far more than the documentation of any other Lithuanian town, including, Vilna, Grodno and Pinsk.

This is not just a coincidence, those who brought the material into order and into print, favoured the significant 'Altertumlichkeit' (precedence or antiquity) of Brest over the other Lithuanian towns.

The reason is the special significance Brest had compared to Vilna, in the story of the Lithuanian Duchy of the 15th and 16th centuries. Also in later times, at the end of the 16th, and 17th centuries when Vilna became the capital of the Lithuanian state and was in full bloom, Brest was still recognised as one of the most ancient and important provinces of Lithuania.

The volumes of the 'Vilna Archival Commission', 'Documents from West Russia', as revealed in the St. Petersburg Archive Commission 1846 –1853, '14 archival collection' about the History of 'North-West Russia', published in 1867 by the Bureau of Public Education of the Vilna district. The documents of Bershavski (3 volumes of Jewish Russian Archives). The volumes registered in 'Registi I Nadpisi". The material contained in the 'Society of Spreading Education Amongst Russian Jewry' and other contents, besides the clear historical material about the Jews, contained a treasure of over 100 documents pertaining to the Jews of Brest and district.

It is therefore very important to concentrate and work through methodically and scientifically the very descriptive material which is vital to the history of the Jews of Lithuania and White Russia and kehillat Brest specifically. Amongst the documents published till now about the Jews of the Lithuanian Dukedom, there is special significance in volumes 28 + 29 of the 'Vilna Archival Commission', that are almost entirely dedicated to the topics of Jewish life.

The editors, who were appointed by the Russian authorities, in reality, endeavored to uphold the Russian official position towards the Jews, with a specific method of selecting documents and publications. The documents selected were ones that depicted Jews in a negative manner. Notwithstanding this, the significance of every document is that they throw light on the domestic, internal and external lives of Jews of Lithuania in the 16th and 17th centuries.

The first of the 2 volumes, number 28, appeared in 1901 and holds 332 documents, which cover 1560 –1667, over 100 years of turbulent and stormy Jewish life afflicted with troubles. The day to day worries which punctuate the chronicles and reports of the city courts of Brest, Kovno, Minsk, Grodno, Pinsk, Slonim, Vilna, and Troki, in addition to the Lithuanian Supreme Tribunal. In those 100 years, the Brest community continued as the foremost community of Lithuanian Jewry.

In this period, there were statutes and laws formulated that crystallised the establishment of Jewish autonomy, their protection enabling those leaders who created the administrative separation of the Jewish Lithuanian bloc, and the establishment of the Council of the Land Authority of the Govt. of Lithuania, which included the community of Brisk. The Brest Community heads were considered leaders and responsible for the fate of the Lithuanian Jews

2). In order to further our knowledge of the Brest community and Jewish life in general in that period during which occurred the time of greatest historical responsibility, it is necessary to delve deeply into many documents in Volume 28. In this volume we come across 42 documents in this collection relating to Brisk, revealing protocols and chronicles of the town's court, divided into 5 groups which include:

1. One document taken from book 7012, which cover the years 1577-1586
2. Fourteen documents taken from book 7075, which cover the years 1589 1596
3. Seven documents taken from book 7078, which cover the years 1589 – 1596.
4. Fourteen documents taken from the book 7079, which cover the year 1644.
5. Six documents taken from the book 7083, which cover the year 1663.

The description contained in document no.30 (15th March 1580) from which we learn about the dwellers of the Jewish quarter of Brisk towards the second half of the 16th century. It shows that an earthen wall had been built previously (in the 14th century) to protect the town, which had become a fortress. That wall encircled the whole settlement from the river Mukhavets to the river Bug. The entry into the town was through 2 gates that were cut into the wall. One of the watchtowers was on the road to Vilna (to the north) Zagrinski St., and the second was on Piesaki St. The Jewish dwellings were close to the wall, the gate went to Zagrinski St and the road stretched to the Bug River.

From these documents it is shown that the Jewish settlement had separated itself from the safety of the walls and spread to the other side of the walls, in those parts of the wall that reached the Jewish houses, the wall had been broken and destroyed because of the Jewish expansion.

It shows that due to the growth of that century (16th), the Jews wanted to settle in the open fields on the outside of the wall rather than live in the congested town, squeezed together by the wall, in close contact with their fellow townsmen, who were not noted for their friendliness to Jews.

The second group of documents are very important pertaining to the Jewish economic situation and their difficulties with the Polish – Lithuanian society and it's conflicts, the opposing interests of the ruling feudal landowners and the influential bishops, and the Meschanes (townsmen) who fought with great tenacity for their existence, and the tavern owners who were accustomed to suffering and persecution.

Doc. 34, 1st May 1589, describes the drunkenness of the innkeepers. There was also the head of the Brest community, Shaul ben Yehudah, Joseph and others who complained about the damage caused to them by the Bishop of Lutsk, who had exempted taxes on liquor. This innkeeper, Shaul ben Yehudah was the treasurer of the Jewish community, and head of the Council of Jewish communities, and is mentioned in Pinsk. In the document we find that 34 years before the establishment of the Council of the Lithuanian State, which was the jewel in the crown of the community existence.

In Chronicle no.3, 30th March 1589, we find the activities of a Brest merchant, Yakov ben Eliezer who transported merchandise from Slutsk to Brisk and had entered into disputes with his driver.

Relating to the protection of Jews who hid in the shadows of the 'Paritz' (the nobility), and were involved in the conflicts between one aristocrat and the other, we found the chapter of Biala in the district of Brest. In that neighbourhood lived Prince Nicholas Radzivill and the aristocrat Kishkin of the Kadkevitch family (docs 35,36,41,42,.17th May, 14th August 1589). It eventuated that in 1589 that there was a tense relationship between these well-known noble families, to the extent that the guards of Kishkin Kadkevitch allowed themselves to attack the Arendar (leaseholder) of the Radzivills' estate, Israel ben Eliezer, who was severely beaten, tied in chains and threatened to be burnt alive.

The same fate was also threatened to his associate Marek Yaskevitch (Mordechai ben Yitzhak), Eliezer ben Yehoshua and Freide the wife of Joseph, who were all underlings of Radzivill. However, luck intervened and the guards of Radzivill saved them at the last moment. As it turned out, Radzivill had the upper hand and the opposing side had to capitulate to his demands and paid 1000 groschen surety that they would not harm the Jews that worked for Radzivill, and would enter the areas under his noble jurisdiction.

Then the noblewoman of the Katkevitch dynasty demanded from the Jews in Radzivill's service that they take an oath in the Brest synagogue as to their innocence, in the presence of the very men that had attacked and beaten them, these were the actual thugs themselves, the beaten victims came to take the oath but waited in vain as the guilty hooligans did not appear, thus showing their guilt.

The 'Mitnik' (Tax Arendar) from the shtetl Divin near Brest, Mordechai ben Nachman complained that he had been severely beaten by the tax collectors without any cause – was documented on the 30th May 1589.

The arendars of customs and of the many taxes in Brest and Brest district, because of the nature of their profession – the collection of taxes on alcohol, roads and river usage, etc., were depicted as having to endure all kinds of tribulations and incidents more so than people of all other classes. The Brest tax-collector representing the Prince Micholai Sapieha, Moshe ben Tuvia, complained about the estate owner Zhitavieski, claiming that he broke into the tax office on Pisatski St. in Brest, whilst the complainant was busy cashing the in the money collected from the Jewish merchants of Pinsk and district, and hit him without cause... December 17th, 1589.

The arendar of the estate Tiachinitz, who was born in Brest, with the name of Aaron ben Pesach (who was also customs collector), his servant Moshe Patzalnik, and his guest Betzalel ben Moshe, told how they had been beaten up by the Pravoslavnim (the Russian orthodox priests) in the village, because they had requested distribution of the tax. (Doc. 45, 4th October 1589).

On the other hand, Moshe ben Yoske, a Brest inhabitant, does not detail why he was attacked by the district official in his town of Skivitch and beaten and robbed of certain articles, amongst which was a hat of fox fur. (Doc 43, August 1589).

Yes, not all Brest Jews were involved in collecting tariffs and taxes, which gave a good income, but was linked to many troubles. Others had studied law and the science of healing the sick. Doc.no.24, 24thMarch 1589, does not tell whether a Brest Jew, Yoske, was a doctor who studied medicine, or someone who healed the sick by special means, as was the custom in those days. However, this did not provide him with a secure livelihood. Yoske the doctor had to flee from Brest to unknown whereabouts because of the promise he had made to cure the sister of a peasant, Martin Kalitztich.

Better was the episode of the holy vessels. A shochet (ritual slaughterer), Pesach ben Shlomo, began to build a house on a plot which he had leased from a gentile in the Judenstrasse, and ended up by buying the plot for it's full price.(Docs.nos.39, 40, 20th July 1589). From these documents we learn, by the way, that a gentile could not withstand (hold out) in the Judengasse. A plot that the gentile bought in 1571 was bought by a Jew, Peretz ben Hillel and his wife Hannah, which was surrounded on both sides by Jewish homes, the gentile held on for 18 years, in the end he sold it back to a Jew.

The year 1629 was a year of grievous slander against the Brest Jews - 6 years after the demise of the Council of the Lithuanian State, which had been situated in that community, every filthy accusation and slander was levelled against the Brest Jews, this was likely to spread to every other Jewish community. The heads of the kehillot warned of the spreading of local blood-libels into widespread hatreds.

In the docs.101-4, 106, (4th March, 17th-18th April, 19th June, 1629) there arose a terrible slander against the heads of the kehilla, Eliezer ben Eliezer and Zalman ben Shmuel, and the whole community of 'unbelievers' (the Jews) of Brest and the other cities. In this episode are all the signs of the familiar blood-libels. A web of drunks, false witnesses, claiming that Jews poisoned a Christian, that they beleaguered the courts and the Christians, and tried to introduce rabbinical law. The same blood-libel charge which arose in the Middle-ages in all it's details. Like all blood libels this turned out to be false and the truth triumphed. But how much pain and fear was endured by the head of the kehilla until he proved his innocence and justice was done? In their defence, the Jews protested against the blood libel "with pain and deep distress in the name of the whole of the Brest community, and in the name of all the Jews who live in the land of his Illustrious Majesty," the blood libel cannot be washed clean entirely until the accused swear an oath in the Brest synagogue in the presence of the State authorities that he is clear of any guilt.

In doc. no.25, 18th April 1629, we come across traces of the edicts that were made by the Council of the Lithuanian State. Concentration of the tax collection through the head of the community:

Zalman, in the name of the Brest community.

Israel ben Yosef in the name of the Kobryn community.

Yitzhak in the name of the Sherechev community.

Nissim ben Yakov in the name of the Pruzhany community.

Yechia in the name of the Yania community.

Yitzhak ben Mendel in the name of the Biale community.

Eliezer in the name of the Chernovitz community.

Each of them paid sums for the road taxes that were levelled on the community according to the number of families. The image of the Jewish trader of merchandise, who sold on credit to the nobility and risked his money, this image was familiar to us all in the towns and villages of Lithuania until 1939.

This example we see in doc.no.107, 12th August 1629. Josef ben Yakov, a merchant from Brest, was honoured by the visit of an exalted visitor, the aristocratic Barbara Shaliska, from the house of Lipnitski, owner of the Matrikel estate near Brest. From the list of clothing we can see what sort of silks they bought in 17th century Brest. After she chose linen according to her taste, and sent them with her servant to her estate. She said that this time she would take it on credit to her father's account, not her husbands'. When the merchant presented the account to her father, he refused to pay. The merchant, Yitzhak ben Yakov, exhausted his legs between the estates of the Lipnitskis - the matter eventually went to court – the document does not record whether the creditor was eventually paid his due, and by whom.

Just as 1629 was a year of blood-libels for the Jews of Brest, the years 1643-44 were filled with pogroms. Despite the terrible events of 1648 (4 years later), we should not see in them the beginning of these later massacres. The pogroms of 1643-44 were carried out by Poles alone and had no connection with the tensions between the peasants and the Cossacks against the Polish aristocracy and the Ukrainians. These started with wild attacks from gangs of Jesuit students on the streets of Brest – we have no exact information as to the establishment dates of the Jesuit colleges in the city of Brest. In 1643 there were already a number of hooligan groups in Brest, namely students, spoiled brats of the aristocracy, who went over to the Jesuit upbringing. All this started in essence in 1644, when the students made a blood-libel charge against the townsfolk, to embitter and create trouble in the lives of Jews, inciting hatred. The Jews were not afraid and responded to the young Jesuits, as they should. This Jewish 'chutzpah' brought out the wrath of the Jesuit leaders. They had not expected such a strong response from the Jewish community. Therefore, they expressed their anger not only against the Jews who had defended themselves from the hooligans, but wanted revenge on the Jewish community of Brest in general. There is a fragment of the accusation found in the town's court (doc.no.143, March 1644), wherein the accusation is brought by the priests Jan Rachowski and Kristof Jankowski: "we accuse the heads of the community of 'unbelievers' as well as the all the Jews of the Town of Brest, of being great enemies of Christian blood, not only of having attacked those students under our supervision, and insulted and beaten them, they also attacked the sons of the nobility with sticks and endangered their lives. One of these sticks is at present in the Jesuit seminary as evidence of the Jewish chutzpah". It was obvious at first glance that this wild incitement the Jews experienced as the Jesuit fathers and their young hooligans were preparing for more serious "Tumult" – in the Polish judicial terms of those days. By the way, a new agent for the Jews brought the community an accurate and detailed intentions of the opposing side, with all the details of the intended pogroms (doc.no.146, 1644). The pogrom was planned to break out on the 16th May 1644, with all the participants of the town, the low-lives and rabble being incited to rob and plunder the Jews. this time they did not rely on their own forces , but applied for help from the Town Council and to the mayor and his advisors.

Behind the scenes, the Brest Town Council, were planning a pogrom against the Jews, in the doc.no.145, 1644, the mayor incited the military representatives against the Jews who would not deliver wagons to them, a duty that belonged to the town's magistrate, and from here it must be stressed that from this document we discover the inner workings of the kehilla administration which each month issued new edicts from the head of the kehilla.

The magistrate could not officially ignore the main plea of the Jews, and he had to come to an agreement. With no alternative, he devised a method whereby each side of the abovementioned parties (the magistrate and the Jewish kehilla) would be obligated to come to the help of each other in the case of wars and attacks on the city, and in reality on the 7th May, 1644, the kehilla turned to the town's magistrate to uphold the terms of their agreement when the news of the impending attacks by the hooligans arrived.

The pogroms subsequently took place according to previously detailed plans by the Jesuit provocateurs in the Town Council. The help from the magistrate, understandably, did not eventuate.

From the accusations of the head of the Jewish kehilla and in the name of all the Jews of Brest and all those who were persecuted, the double treachery of the mayor, Jan Kutanovitch became clear. After he received the plea for help, he ordered the town's militia and the members of the town's guilds to assemble and be ready. On the other hand, in his house he assembled the leaders of the Meschanes (the town's residents), the leading organisers of the pogrom, and immediately after that he assembled students and the common rabble that were prepared to do their tasks. Then the mayor ordered the police to go to their homes, and the 'progromchiks' were given a free hand.

In order to frighten the Jewish self-defence, and not to interfere with the 'progromchiks' work of breaking down the windows and doors of the Jewish stores, as it turned out, the Meschanes and the town's police overran the streets to frighten the defenders and to increase the confusion and uproar. In doc.no.49, 16th June 1644, the empty defence of the mayor was that he did not deceive the Jews, he tried to assume the guise of an idiot (Tam). His arguments were full of loopholes, until he tied himself in knots, and in the end, had to confess that he had ordered the police to go home, and then he added that the Jews were themselves responsible and guilty of the atrocities committed against them.

The attitude of the Jesuit clergy towards to the Jews is shown by the hostility expressed in the documents. In the meantime, also the Russian Orthodox clergy, followed the same path.

Docs 151-3, 29th –30th July, 1644 describe a dispute and blows between the Jewish hat-maker Shimon and the Russian priest Ivan Trasevich, a dispute which spread from the confines of a private argument and grew into abuse against the whole Jewish community, and united against the Jews all those Christians - Catholics, and Russian Orthodox.

The chronicle no. 154 of Sept. 1644, is again evidence that a Russian priest had made accusations against an Yitzchak ben Israel, a Brest Jew who travelled from village to village buying cattle, claiming that he had caused the outbreak of a plague from the fields of the villages and that he had bought diseased cattle and placed them in the villages.

There are 3 other documents in 1644 dealing with attacks on Jews. The nobleman Chitavetsky beat Hersh ben Faivel of Brest, his arendar. In the kehilla of Wysokie, district of Brest, and hooligans disturbed the celebrations of Succoth. In the middle of prayers, hooligans broke into the synagogue and attacked the praying Jews, five of whom were severely wounded, stole the silver etrog and the women's jewellery – they promised to return and kill all the Jews of Wysokie. Interestingly, the prosecution's documents had details and names of all the people who were inside the synagogue at the time of the attack.

In doc.no.148 (May 1645), the issue at that time was pertaining to the competence of the synagogue's Shammes (beadle) and other learned members of the community, and throws some light on the organization of the synagogue. A bundle of documents from 1637 end this documentation of Brest – a plague, wrongful accusations and even blood-libel.

In 1662 there broke out in Brest and district a plague that caused a diminishing of the town's population. But the arendars (leaseholders and agents) who collected the town's taxes had to fulfil their tax obligations to the government. In relation to this, a document tells of those days. Yakov ben Shmuel, an tax collector of the 'Tchapavi' and 'Shasavi' taxes for the estates Rasne, Wysokie, Zubatch, and others that belonged to the great Hetman (chieftain) Pavel Sapieha, was forced to confess that his people were not able to collect a cent from the populace because of the taxes of 1663. (Document 313, 9th January 1663).

An aftermath of the Brest pogroms of 1644 eventuated 19 years later - the action was carried out by a military commander and his men on a pretext that the head of the kehilla, shielding behind the privileges granted to the kehilla by the Polish king, had refused to obey an order to provide food and drink by one of his officers, Hiranim Dubiner. Dubiner was enraged and attacked the Jewish shops and the synagogue. Thereupon a huge panic broke out; there were much beatings and violence, followed by looting. The town square next to the synagogue was left in a terrible condition, destroyed houses and shops, salt and food littered the streets, groaning wounded, the result of this bloody day was about 20 wounded, and dozens of destroyed houses and shops.

The shtetl of Wysokie, Brest district, was a place ready for incitement, even from earlier times. In the book that recorded it, the catholic priest Ange Zhivnitski, harassed the arendar Laizer from the estate Gubatch, the arendar Yitzhak ben Aharon Batiak from Wysokie, Pesach Ruchotski, and others. He accused them of inciting hatred and attacking people of the local Catholic Church. This conflict occurred because the Jews had rescued a thief from the power of the church. (317-321, 30th June, 20th Sept. 1663).

The most interesting part of these documents deals with the Meschanes (townspeople) of Wysokie that did not participate in the priest's accusations and the ensuing trial. The Mayor (Voijt) and his council of townsmen, were as it happened, guests of the arendar in his house. According to these documents, at the head of the Jewish side stood a woman of valour, the wife of the arendar Yitzhak, in her honor and by herself.

A proven method by the healers of Brest in case of failure was to flee from the city. We have already seen in 1589 the fate of the healer/doctor Yoske, who ran away from Brest because of the accusations of the peasant Kaladich. Also in 1663 the healers of Brest did not know how to defend their honour or lives. Aharon ben Yakov, one of the heads of the Brest kehilla, complained about the healer Shmuel Shreiyer, that his son, Dovid ben Aharon, a goldsmith, had died because of improper treatment. (Not according to the doctor in his wisdom) "Not an erroneous treatment, and not according to the doctor's knowledge". The doctor, who had received a proper fee for his treatment, ran away to unknown whereabouts at the time of his patient's death. (Chronicle 320, August 20th 1663).

A story of a blood-libel ends this series of docs. The libel was proved to be false, but in this case all the familiar signs of blood-libel, which tragically prevailed over hundreds of years. It began with a dead child being discovered with stab wounds to its corpse, a sign that the Jews had drained it of its blood. These wild accusations were admitted in the time of the torture during the interrogations – the accused have confessed to this crime. (doc.318, 1st July 1663).

A deed will be recorded as it was: In the shtetl of Vanya, Brest district, a Christian child drowned. When he was pulled out of the water, there were no signs of torture or wounds, besides the signs of drowning. The townsfolk, who wanted to get rid of their Jews, grasped this opportunity and exploited it, so that whilst the mother went and reported the tragedy to the authorities, they stabbed and mutilated the body to give it the appearance of murder and torture. When the mother, who was alone without a man or family, returned, she was astounded at the fresh wounds on her child's corpse. The neighbours then attacked her with the accusation that she herself had wounded and killed the child. Their intention was to frighten the unfortunate mother, and through her to obtain the grounds of a blood-libel. The town's authorities were linked to this gang, who intimidated this woman, keeping her imprisoned. At night, they let in their emissaries to convince her 'have no fear, we won't harm you'; on the condition that you claim that 'the Jews murdered your child'. 'We Christians' lives are blighted as long as the Jews live in Vanya – this town is theirs not ours. Do as we ask, madam, and nothing will happen to you'. To their great astonishment, the soul of this simple peasant woman shone with honesty and truth, and she categorically refused all their persuasions. Threats did not move her; she declared she would not denounce innocent people.

When the story became known to the Jews of Vanya, they demanded of the court that it investigate the holding of the woman in jail, in the presence of the court's representatives, the woman absolutely swore in front of witnesses that the Jews had no part in the death of her child, and that she had retrieved the body from the river without a single wound.

The initiators of the blood-libel did not desist and received an authority from the court to submit the woman to torture; the townsfolk urged the court to torture her without pity until she accused the Jews. This document does not mention the instrument of torture, but it mentions that the woman was burnt on her fingers and feet, such tortures were made at intervals, and the woman asked if she confessed to the Jews crime. However, she obstinately stuck to her story. 'Only the Jews could have sent her a magical potion to prison' the heroes of the blood-libel claimed, and they requested to apply even more tortures, with renewed energy. With her last strengths the peasant woman screamed to her torturers 'I am going to die of all this pain and torture, and with my last breath I will not denounce innocent people'. She died in prison on the 1st July 1663. The blood-libel was cancelled due to lack of evidence, and failed to ignite a fire against the Jews. The cesspit of accusations, blood-libels, floated in a sea of hatred before our eyes when we recall those sorrowful times of the Brest Jews. It is obvious that the deepest nature of humanity to sacrifice the body for truth, and that, with her sacrifice, humanity was saved through this woman - her name was Mariana Ivanova Litvianka.

[Page 89]

The Destroyed City

By Arieh Leib Feinstein
Translated by Dr. Samuel Chani

The year 1831 (fear and panic in the city) saw great changes in the situation of our city, Brest. This was due to a great tragedy, which was unleashed in the country of Poland – war and insurrection broke out. The Poles rebelled against the Russian Tsar, who had increasingly spread his domination over them since the partition of Poland decided at the Congress of Vienna in 1815. The city of Brest, located at the gates of Poland, was besieged and the inhabitants began building fortresses and barracks, which were surrounded by high earthworks with deep canals so that they could defend themselves against the Poles who had mobilized their last forces to try and take the town.

Arieh Leib Feinstein

A year later, when the fighting had subsided, an edict was issued by Tsar Nicholas ordering that the town, which sat between wide rivers and lakes, be rebuilt and strengthened. A large fortress was built with large buildings housing munition stores and factories, and barracks for housing the garrisons. In order to make space for this fortress an order was issued to demolish and raze the houses that had stood there previously, so that in their place, a high wall with a gate in the middle of the town stood there, and high earthworks were built up around the town. When the builders began their work a proportion of the inhabitants left their houses

and moved to the new houses which were being built inside the city. These places were called suburbs, which the government had bought in order to resettle the population. One of these areas was a large suburb to the west, which was called Kobryner Forshtadt or the New City, and to the south a smaller area that was called, Volyner Forshtadt. The whole town was called Brest D'Lita or Brest – Litevski.

The year 1835 was the year of the great fire, in which God's wrath was poured over the old town, which was consumed by fire, on the holy Sabbath, the fire became a blaze which consumed several streets in the centre of the city. About 500 houses were destroyed and the frightened residents rushed to find shelter and build new houses in the grounds of the new city. In order to provide shelter and protection, they rushed the building works with all their strengths, and within two years, in 1837, it was completed. The new town stood in all its' beauty, and tens of thousands of people filled it's streets – large good quality stops were created, and the commerce and trade returned to normal and Brest once again became a joyous city. In the old town were the ruins of the burnt houses, which were demolished one by one, no memory of them was left. At the same time as the new buildings were growing in the new town, the town's rates and taxes increased five-fold. Also at this same time the government built storehouses for military equipment and uniforms. They also built barracks and residences for their employees. They built a beautiful and magnificent railway station. The houses that were built for the town's inhabitants were built on town land, so that the town spread to a village called Trishin, creating a new suburb called Horodek (small town in Russian).

As was the fate of all the residents houses, so followed the fate of the synagogues, which had been partially burnt down, partially vandalised, and then destroyed. These were rebuilt in the new city, and given the same names as the old ones, according to the size of their congregations, which multiplied and grew in the new city. This large city attracted masses that streamed to it from all the corners of the land to settle there. But the great synagogue was left in it's place until the year 1842 when the bitter cup overspilled itself and it was destroyed to it's foundations. 8000 roubles were given as compensation by the government for the damages. During the demolition of this synagogue, they found a damaged stone tablet that was built into the walls of the synagogue inscribed with the following:

'The officer Saul, son of the Gaon (genius) and Rabbi Shmuel Yehuda from Padua, built this synagogue for women and Torah and in memory of his wife Deborah, who was pious and righteous and the daughter of......' These words had been partially erased by antiquity. Deborah was the daughter of David Drucker, one of the leaders in Brest, in the list of Brest luminaries.

———

[Page 93]

The Jews of Brest in the 19th Century

By M. Kaplan
Translated by Dr. Samuel Chani and Jenni Buch

Great Synagogue

In the year of 1793, after the partition of Poland, Brest fell into the hands of the Russians. Then Brest- Litovsk came into a new and difficult period. The ruling powers decided to build a fortress in the city.

The orders to build this fortress and to move the town to a new suburb, Kobryner Forshtadt, were issued in 1837. Under these edicts, the government was to pay the full value of the property assets that were in private ownership, so an assessors' office was established.

The order of moving the houses in order to build the fortress was established according to the street plan. It was also forbidden to bury the dead in the old town's cemetery.

The committee set aside an area for burials in the new town, which later became Spitalna St., the intention being that the new town would be established away from this area.

After a competent authority finished the plans for the new town, it became obvious that the area allocated for the new cemetery (people were already buried there) had become developed with small factories, so they were forced to move the cemetery to another area.

The Jewish community received a certain sum as compensation for the old synagogue and decided to build a new synagogue. The plans were presented to the military authorities at the fortress and from there it was sent to the 'Supreme Power'. After personally inspecting the plans and not liking them, the Tsar wrote the following remarks with a pencil, saying: 'not beautiful, the synagogue should be built according to the Viennese design'.

The Tsar's wishes were presented to the head of the kehilla, and the Jewish community sent a man to Vienna to design a synagogue based on the Great Synagogue of Vienna. The Viennese architect prepared plans that were adorned with artistic drawings of men and women in the grounds of the synagogue. The men wore shtreimls (fur hats) and the women wore wigs in the style of the orthodox Viennese Jews. The drawings were delivered to the office at the fortress and endorsed as being in accordance with the wishes of the Tsar. The community leader and historian A.L. Feinstein discovered these drawings in 1885. This is the story of the Brest –Litovsk synagogue being built in the "style of the Great Synagogue of Vienna".

The historic synagogue in the old city was built in the time of Saul Wahl, on the wall of its lobby was a white marble plaque about one metre in length, which read: In memory of the Sage and Genius Saul Wahl, under whose patronage and generosity this synagogue was built in the year .... During the transfer of the holy vessels from the old synagogue to the new one, they tore this plaque off the wall and rebuilt it in the lobby of the new synagogue, also in the rebuilding of the plaques, words such as the year were missing, so they just inserted dots.

Opposite the white marble plaque there was a black marble tablet with the inscription:

This Synagogue was built according to the plans and under the supervision of Tsar Nicholai 1.

The terrible fire, which broke out in the town on the 4th May 1895, destroyed half the city – 45 souls perished by fire or suffocation. But the fire did not spare the beautiful Great Synagogue of which only four walls remained; also the historic plaque of Saul Wahl was destroyed. The synagogue was rebuilt in 1896, but it was not as beautiful as before. During the German occupation of 1915-1918, the synagogue was also badly damaged, but thanks to the dedication of the Gabbehs, the synagogue was restored and surpassed the earlier building.

Rebuilding of the New City with Its Institutions

The Jews of Brest were very diligent in commerce, and in this sphere they showed a wondrous talent, after all the fires and wars and pogroms and plagues that the town endured, after all that, the Jews managed to rebuild their town with great energy. The city was built anew after several years and became much larger and more beautiful than before. An important factor in the development of the Brest was the digging of a canal connecting the Dnieper with the Bug in 1841. This canal connected the Pina with the Mukhavets, thereby allowing the movement of ships between the Dneiper and the Vistula. In the year 1899, 11 steam ships, 279 cargo ships, and a great many smaller fishing vessels used it. The export of timber and wheat also developed. - almost all the trades and manufacturing were entirely in Jewish hands. Industry could not be developed more because of the law prohibiting the building of tall buildings, higher than the fortress. Yet there were factories of soap, leather, luggage, uniforms and others. Brest was a Jewish town, the tradesmen and skilled artisans were all Jewish.

Not only in the sphere of commerce and industry did the Brest Jews show remarkable talents.

They also established welfare institutions which lightened the load of the poor and sick.

In 1838, before the new city was built, there was already an institute for the poor and sick which was called 'Hakodesh' (The Holy). This institution had a pharmacy, 40 beds for the sick, and was maintained wholly by donations.

The second important institution which was founded in during the cholera epidemic of 1865, which caused a great loss of lives, was Bikur Cholim – the visiting of the sick, founded by the Rav Hersh Orenstein. This society had the following aims:

To support widows and the destitute.

To distribute food and medicine to the poor and sick at a very small charge.

In 1876 an old age home was founded which had a hospital ward and a synagogue, and later in 1906, a 'welcome visitors' hostel was founded for travellers passing through. Wandering destitutes came to this house, and in the time of W.W.1, this house played an important role as a refuge for the homeless.

Another institution was the Woman's Society, which was established to provide poor women with milk and nourishing food, also this organization established an orphanage in which both boys and girls received an education, and later training in a trade to help them in later life.

There was also a 'Righteous Fund' where the poorer business people could get an interest – free loans.

In 1906 a Talmud Torah was established where many children studied, subsequently there were 1200 pupils aged 6 – 18. There were 24 teachers for 26 classes, besides Hebrew and religious studies, pupils were taught in Russian, on the orders of the Russian government.

Special teachers had to be hired to teach Russian, so special taxes were raised for this by taxing kosher meat, and donations.

As well as the four communal Jewish schools, which were attended by 800 boys and 900 girls, there were seven State Schools, in which Jews also studied – 10% of these students were Jewish. There was a Business School (Handelschule), a Technical High School called Realschule, and a High School (Gymnasium) for boys and girls.

At the pre- Gymnasium level, 50% of the pupils were Jewish.

Fire and Pogroms

The terrible fires that broke out in 1895 and 1901 have destroyed almost all the city – many people perished, and the damages amounted to tens of millions of roubles. Interestingly, the fires occurred at the same time of year and in the same street, although six years apart.

The great fire of 1895 destroyed half of the city; the second fire of 1901 destroyed the other half. Ten people perished in the first fire. In the second fire, the fire spread to a beautiful and large part of the city, wreaking wide-scale destruction and damages. Jews from abroad sympathised with Brest's plight and rushed to help the victims of the fire – sending aid, money and food. Also the Tsar, Nicholai 11 donated 300,000 roubles towards the victims. The railways provided free transport to all the victims of the city and vicinity. The second fire caused a great exodus from the city with masses of people fleeing, many returned, but many settled elsewhere.

Until the fire of 1901, almost all the whole town had been built of timber, because of the frequent fires, it became forbidden to build houses of wood, and in time Brest was rebuilt with buildings of brick and one and two storeys high.

The wide waves of pogroms that spread over the country in 1905 did not miss Brest. The anti Jewish propaganda and hatred was spread through the "Organization of King Michael"

(Soyuz Mikhael Arkangel). This organization caused the excesses of the 29th May, 1905. This was after the disastrous Russo-Japanese war when the returning soldiers and reservists came to Brest, which served as a transit station and camp to the army.

At the time there were clashes between the Jewish self-defence and the hooligans who were assisted by police patrols. Amongst the Jewish self-defence force there were many dead and wounded. A Jewish doctor, Ksaveri Shteinberg, showed great heroism in saving lives, giving medical assistance to those in need. Running around in his colonel's uniform, he showed great skill in evading the hooligans and the police.

During the Revolution

The role of Brest in the general revolutionary movement was significant. Exactly as in other towns, there was in Brest and underground revolutionary movement. Which subsequently built the movements that led to the formation of revolutionary parties – the largest of which was the Bund. The head of the Bund was Moshe the'Weisser', the teachers Schmaltz, Weinstein and others. Later they were arrested and sent to Siberia. Besides the Bund, a large role was played by the Russian Socialist Revolutionary Party, known as "Iskrah'. On the Jewish scene there were also active smaller parties such as Poale Zion and S.S. and the Polish Socialist Party (P.P.P.S.), which existed in Brest.

After the failure of the 1905 revolution Brest returned to it's quiet normal everyday life. The city's commerce and industry was almost entirely in Jewish hands -70% of the population was Jewish. In 1913 there were 57,000 inhabitants in Brest, 40,000 were Jews, 10,000 were Russian, and 7,500 were Poles. However, there were only 3 Jewish representatives in the city administration., whereas the Christian community had 29 representatives.

The outbreak of war in 1914 hit the Jews like a thunderclap, and deeply shook the community's existence as the city was on the Russo-Polish border, and at times the Russo-German border. As well as that, Brest was a fortress and the military powers gave special attention to the city, and made great efforts to fortify it. To this purpose, the inhabitants of Brest, especially the Jews, dug trenches and erected wire-fences around the outside of the city.

The issue of the mobilisation of the civilian labour force was like pawns in the power-play of the authorities, men were forcibly taken to work whether they were needed or not. During 1915, thousands of men were taken and conscripted for forced labour, they were detained all night by the police and the Cossacks, they were held in the city gardens, and in the morning they were marched on foot towards Wlodawa, driven by clubs and truncheons, hungry and thirsty, arriving beaten and exhausted at night to the village of Kostamalitz, near Klodny.

From there they were expelled as they were forbidden to stay in the village. There they spent the night in the forest, stiff with cold, trying to warm themselves around bonfires.

The next morning they were walked to Wlodawa, there they were welcomed by the local military leaders, who gave a speech about how important it was to protect the Fatherland. From Wlodawa these 'workers' were taken to work and distributed around the surrounding villages to dig trenches, however, suddenly the order came to send them home, as the Germans were approaching Brest and their work was all unnecessary.

On the 1st August, 1915, the city authorities ordered the city's inhabitants to evacuate, over the next 3 days, the 3rd, 4th and 5th August, the exiled inhabitants received free train tickets, but there were not enough trains sent, so many had to leave on foot or on carts and wagons.

In the city there were large supplies of bread, but they were forbidden to take food or belongings with them. Many left their entire fortunes behind, it was heartbreaking to witness the Cossacks and Russian soldiers ransacking and looting the abandoned homes.

On 25th August, the Russian army withdrew and set fire to the town, and if not for the German army which arrived the next morning and extinguished the fire, there would not be a trace of the city left.

The New Brest

The Russian military power depended on the fortress, with the evacuation of the city's inhabitants, the military began an all-out assault on the Germans and they held up the advance of the Austro-German army for a lengthy time, but in the end, on the 25th August, 1915, they retreated, setting the city alight with inflammable material and grenades. On the entry march of the German army, a terrible scene was revealed to them – the whole city was ablaze, the German fire fighters began extinguishing the fires and saved a quarter of the town's houses.

There was not a living soul to be seen in the city. When the fire subsided, amongst the clouds of smoke, there appeared the first inhabitant of the city, a crazy man. He spoke a good German and came from the old city dressed with a prayer shawl and a book under his arm. His behaviour aroused the suspicions of the Germans who took him for a spy, arrested and shot him. Afterwards, several others of Brest's inhabitants who had hidden from the Russians in the cellars appeared. Over the next days, the slow return of the expelled inhabitants who had fled the city and had found shelter in the surrounding towns and villages began.

The returnees formed a city committee to assist the rights of the returning Brest citizens, and provide them with food and shelter.

This was not the end of their wanderings and trials. The Germans, according to their methods carried out the second expulsion of the Brest Jews. One day, trumpets were heard in the street, the people went outside and were surrounded by German soldiers, who stopped them from returning to their homes, and marched them to the train station. From there they were sent by special trains into the towns and villages of Congress Poland. After this expulsion, the Germans declared the city as an exclusively military town and a military camp designated for Russians prisoners of war.

The Great Synagogue

The Interior of the Great Synagogue

The Orphanage

The Town Hall in Brest before World War I

The Expulsion Order From Brest Litovsk 2nd August 1915
Signed by General Leeming, the German Commander of the Brest Fortress.
In 1913 there were 57,068 residents of Brest Litovsk.
Amongst them 39,152 Jews, 10,042 Russians, and 7,336 Poles

[Page 105]

The Self-Government of the Kehilla

By A. Ludski
Translated by Dr. Samuel Chani and Jenni Buch

During the Tsarists reign there existed in Brest a city Duma (council), whose members were elected through a limited small number of voters from restricted categories, or they were nominated through the Government in Grodno (Brest-Litovsk belonged to Grodno Province).

The Jews who were representatives in those times were the Rabbi of the Minyan, and the sons of the town's community who were represented in the Duma by 2 or 3 delegates. These were wealthy merchants and rich landlords who had close relations with the ruling powers. However, they had no close local contacts with the kehilla (the Jewish community council), and their function was, in the best case, as emissaries for specific individuals, or for specific cases close to their hearts. In their position, they saw their role as the supporting basis for social and political Jewish day-to-day activities. The majority of Jews were robbed of their basic civil rights as citizens, as they were in the whole of Russia.

The national rights of a unified Jewish community collectively had never been claimed, as no one had ever had the courage to demand it. The Tsarist powers saw the Jewish kehilla only as a religious entity that satisfied their religious needs and served as an institution, formed by the Gabbeys (synagogue deacons). The authorities charged these Gabbeys with the responsibility of overseeing the collection of the Karafke (meat tax), the schools and the houses of learning, sacred matters and other religious institutions. They ruled over the community with a strong hand and with arrogance, not taking into account the real needs of the community, and doing as they pleased.

Because the town of Brest and it's fortress were on the frontline in World War 1, in August 1915, before the German took it over, the city was forcibly evacuated, especially the Jewish residents. The Jews were scattered over the surrounding towns and villages, which subsequently also became occupied by the Germans. The majority of the Jewish inhabitants were deported into Greater Russia. At the end of 1918, the Jews who were refugees in Poland and neighboring towns returned to the destroyed and damaged city, as well as the refugees who escaped back from Russia. Brest soon developed back into the typical Jewish town. The city also received a great amount of aid from American Jewry. The renaissance and rebuilding of the city took 6 years. When Poland occupied the city in 1919, many Poles were settled in Brest, taking over all the key government positions and sinecures. The Polish authorities did not however, alter the character of Jewish Brest and the composition of it' representative organizations. Although Jewish Brest by far had the majority of numbers, they were not represented in the administrative and municipal powers of the city.

The main influence was retained by the older, original residents, the White Russians who had lived there previously, as well as those who came from the neighbouring villages to settle in the city, and who intended to take from the Jews their economic livelihood – (their shops, market stalls and small factories). These aims were embedded in the city council, which was led by the spirit of Polish nationalism without any connection to the broader community.

Circled around these 'representatives' were several Jewish landlords and businessmen, as before, under the Russians, they simply represented the Jewish inhabitants, they did not represent any Jewish institutions. During the years 1922-1925 Greenbaum, established a division of the Jewish national council, and the fully elected member of the above council who represented it was a Mr. H. Milner. He was very much involved in the restructuring the official representation to the district government of the Polesie region, of which Brest was the capital.

The abovementioned period saw a blossoming of Jewish community activities. The local populace founded political parties, economic, cultural and educational institutions. Amongst the workers various movements arose – those were all connected to the activities of the American Jewish community and welfare organizations, which affected all Jewish life in Poland. Especially in Brest, a town who had accepted many refugees and with the help of American aid, was helping to rehabilitate them. Thanks to the great economic assistance from overseas Jewish communities, their positions strengthened and they were able to accommodate the refugees who came from Russia, providing medical help, soup kitchens, housing, schools, pre-schools, religious schools and clubs.

Following World War 1, in an environment of economic upheaval and development, the majority of the Jewish 'street' turned to left wing politics and extreme left political parties.

From within the community, there arose factions amongst the economic sectors - merchants, small businessmen and tradesmen, who saw the importance of guarding their professional and economic interests. These factions were under the influence of the 'Peoples Movement', they had their own means of dealing with the Polish authorities, and they behaved and acted quietly, so as not to antagonise the ruling powers.

The Zionist parties represented the national identity. In the front line was the organization of the general Zionists, led by L.Winnikoff and his supporters, who came from 'El Hamishmar'. There was also a Mizrachi organization - in general the ordinary Jew in Poland leant towards the rabbinical movements, which were affiliated to the 'Agudat Israel'.

The Jewish intelligentsia circles in those days had not shown a great inclination towards community activity. The majority were not involved with and had no agenda for social reform, with some exceptions, they were isolated from the general community – they would meet in social clubs and were occupied with the activities of daily life.

Amongst the prominent (Herschaftnikes) there were extreme left circles – in the forefront were the Jewish communists, then the Poale Zion (leftists) and Tzirei Zion who later formed the Poale Zion party, and the Bund. These parties all conducted cultural and propaganda activities, and obtained important positions in all the communal institutions.

In 1926, at the beginning of the Pilsudski upheaval, the demand grew for new elections; there was talk of nominating a Jewish deputy to the town's president. To this aim, H. Wilner was appointed. Together with the Polish military takeover, which resulted from the Polish victory over the Soviets, they announced that there would be new elections held for the Brest City Council, with democratic overtones.

Then the Brest Jews had an opportunity to take part in an active manner in democratic elections for the 1st time. These elections stirred the Jewish community and shook them out of their apathy. The Jews received a proper representation according to their proportion of the local population. In 1922, the Brest Jews were part of the 2nd Polish Parliament of the Polesie Province. On the general list of national minorities, they elected a Jewish member, H. Minzberg of the Agudat Israel Party. They elected representatives of the townspeople, Zionists, and also trades and artisans, and representatives of all the Jewish workers' groups that were active in Brest. However, because the Poles did not get number of votes that they had expected to, or because of the groupings of the persons on the Polish lists, the district governor (Vovoide), cancelled the results and called for new elections that took place two months later. The second elections did not alter the ratio of Jews to Poles. This was then followed by a change in the Polish representative system. The government accepted the newly elected and the election results were ratified, and the first meeting of the city council was called.

Before the elections, the Senatzia Party (Pilsudski's followers) were seeking contact with the Jewish representative with a view to unite to overthrow the ruling powers of the Nationalists in the city council.

At a meeting at the home of one of the Jewish councilmen, H. Zablud, (representing the artisans), several members of the provincial government participated and almost all the Jewish members of the city council. They came to an agreement to do everything possible to avoid the re-election of the former head of the city council (an articled judge), even going as far as walking out of the meeting to force the nomination of a new chairman. And so it happened. Three times the Jews and the so-called progressive Poles left the meeting, forcing the provincial governor to exert his full power and nominate Tomasz Tsalon as head of the city council. Tsalon was a locksmith by profession in the Zaglembie district, he was a member of the P.P.S., who had been accused of revolutionary activity in the past and sent to Siberia.

On the occasion of the Polish resurrection, he was elected chairman of the city council, at that time he was an outspoken man with socialist, worldly outlooks, which he later abandoned when he attained high office.

With the advent of Tsalon as Brest's representative, there began a new era in the community and of Jewish life in particular. Tsalon sought affiliation with the Jewish councilors and also with the members of the socialists groups – P.P.S., the leftist Politieren, Poale Zion, the Bund, Ukrainian Socialists, and non-party workers (Communists). He sought, and received, the support of the progressive groups in the city council, and benefited from their support, as he was therefore not beholden to the Provincial Government. Tsalon thereby created an expectation to a certain extent that the aims and demands of the Jewish councilors and the working classes represented by the socialist groups would be achieved.

Regarding the position of deputy Mayor, they were unanimous that this should be held by a Jew. Within a short time the delegate elected was H. Wilner, however, he did not hold this position long, because shortly after, he became ill and died. His sudden death hit the Jewish community hard.

To fill this position, Avraham Levinson was proposed. At the time, he was a member of the Polish parliament, and through this position was appointed temporarily as deputy mayor until the subsequent elections of the city council. With the arrival of A. Levinson there began a period of more intensive and widespread activities in the city council, and also in the Zionist movement in the city. The phenomenon of Jewish city councilors brought out and accentuated the national Jewish pride. This was an appropriate opportunity to demand the rights of the Jewish community, who were the majority in the Polesie district. These demands were aimed at enabling the participation of Jews in all the activities of the civil self-government.

For instance: the proportional employment of Jewish workers in the public works and construction projects of the city council, as well as its' bureaucracy.

Substantial financial assistance for Hebrew and Jewish classes that the government had classified as private.

Strengthening the Jewish medical and social institutions, such as hospitals, orphanages, old-age homes and youth hostels.

Subsidies for 'TOZ' (The society of public health), which was active in the Polish health institutions. As well as subsidies for the ORT trades schools, evening courses in Hebrew and Yiddish and for public Jewish libraries. The Jewish councilors never missed an opportunity to bring forward these demands and to make every effort to realize them.

The independence of the Mayor, Tsalon, made it possible to present these demands, as the ultimate decision- making was in the hands of the provincial government. The Jewish representatives were present at every city council meeting and they presented their demands in Yiddish. This had a resounding effect; each of those councilors presented his demands in the name of his organization, made clearer and more understandable, and with the correct motives. The proposers, who had the full support of the Jewish masses, often used descriptive and heart-rending terms in their speeches.

The reaction to these demands was slow and frustrating. The mayor Tsalon, tried to satisfy the basic demands, such as employment of Jewish labourers, hiring a Jewish employee in every municipal department so that Jews could communicate with them in Yiddish. He also made efforts with the provincial government not to cut the funding for the Jewish schools, social and cultural institutions in the city.

However, he did not succeed, and cuts were made in a drastic fashion. The ceiling on funds for the Jewish institutions rose from year to year - they never received their full allowance.

As the establishment of the State schools was financed by the city council and the provincial government, the Polish city councilors and the provincial government argued that the Jews could send their children to the public elementary schools and trade schools which were supported by the city administration and financed by the government. Theoretically. Jews could benefit from the government social and health institutions (the city hospitals, orphanages, etc.), but the reality was entirely different. The administrations of those institutions, the attitude of it's Polish speaking employees, the Polish language that most of the Jewish residents had not mastered, the anti-Semitic atmosphere, all these had taken away from the Jews the possibility of benefiting from these facilities, and they quickly chose the Jewish institutions. It was also possible that the government cut the funding allotted to them by the city council because it was widely known that the Jews greatly cared for their own institutions and would resist any government interference. It was revealed that at a time when the city council was greatly concerned with education, health, and social work, all which it supported and subsidized with a broad hand, that the Jews were forced to pay for their own services and be dependant on the support of the Joint, which donated generously.

It must be stressed that this relationship improved in the period 1930-1933, when the allotted subsidies have helped the annual budgets of the hospitals, orphanages and schools.

The chief element of the city's administration were the Jewish councilors from the working classes, who united in a Socialist grouping which included the P.P.S. (Polska Party Socialist), both branches of the Poale Zion, the ultra left groups and the representatives of the Ukrainian socialists. Those groups unity was not an official one, they were united by their common needs and goals at the time., and one should realise that in all the Jewish demands and needs that were incorporated into the city budget, the Jews had the support of these socialist councilors, in contrast to the attitude of the P.P.S. in the main cities of Poland and the capitol (Warsaw).

To a certain extent, this attitude of the P.P.S. councilors was the result of their identifying with the cause of Polish nationalism. Polish nationalism as a whole was imbued with anti-Semitic spirit. The P.P.S. in Brest had friendly relations with the Poale Zion and the Bund. They would march on the 1st May, they would organize public demonstrations and large public meetings at which they would appear with fiery speeches.

In 1928, when a large tract of land was given to the council for its' disposal, a Jewish plan surfaced – to employ the Halutzim (Pioneer Zionists) movement to develop the land into a village, to be used for the purpose of agricultural training (Hachshara). However, this village was transferred to the authority of the central government.

The Jews were represented in the city council's commissions and presided over important commissions such as the budget and finance, but in reality, the majority of economic decisions were not made by the city administration, but by the district government. This government governed according to the national trend against minorities in general and Jews in particular. The aim, held by both the central government and the provincial government, was to make the Jews life more difficult, and to hinder their progress and development.

All plans and projects for technical and sanitary improvements were designed in reality to eliminate the Jews from any economic advantage and to transfer their positions to Poles.

A glaring example of this was the question of the town's market. This market had always been in Jewish hands and served as the source of the livelihoods and economic income for thousands of Jewish families. All the region's peasants came there to trade; there was a flourishing trade in horses, cattle and agricultural products. The artisans and tradesmen that the peasants needed all worked there, the majority of small businesses were all in this market.

Suddenly, in 1928, the Polish provincial government that presided in Brest demanded that the city administration énact the transfer of the market to a district inhabited solely by Poles.

This demand was made on the argument of health and sanitation.

The Jewish representatives, without exception, saw in these demands an attempt to undermine the very existence of the Jewish masses – the workers and tradesmen of the small stores, workshops and factories. They delayed and obstructed the tabling of this issue on the daily agendas – and when the matter was eventually presented, they mobilized all their powers to defeat the motion. Because of this, the supervising authorities (the provincial government), several times proposed that the city council hold new elections, occasionally bringing about changes, sometimes there was an addition of several councilors to the Jewish group, sometimes to the Polish groups, but basically nothing changed because the city council did not have the required majority to reach a conclusive decision. Thus, after every two years, the city council was dismissed and reassembled after new elections, thinking that this time the situation would change – until the time that the government attained the essential majority of Poles and Jewish sycophants. This occurred after the government introduced the concept of district elections that was especially detrimental to the Jews and other minorities.

The Polish government in 1934 enacted this law for the whole of Poland.

Let's recall several positive decisions which had been adopted due to Jewish demands, and which were ratified by the supervising authorities:

1) The I.L.Peretz street. Several times, at the Jewish workers' representatives' insistence, the city council decided to change the name of Dluga St. to Peretz St. The provincial government on various pretexts never confirmed the decision (in that street there were several Polish government high schools), and they resisted the pressure to rename the street after a Jewish writer. Later the renaming was proposed for another street in the centre of town occupied exclusively by Jews. This proposition was accepted and enacted by the government so that Topolowa St. became Peretz St. The name remains until today, although there are no Jews left in Brest.

2) The department of Hebrew and Yiddish literature in the municipal library. We requested a separate department in the town's library, the majority of whose subscribers and readers were Jewish. Instead of a reply, came the excuse, that there was no librarian that would be able to manage this and that it was not possible to employ Jewish staff specifically for this purpose.

Agreement was eventually reached with the head of the city council that the city's budget would set aside a certain sum to open a separate department for Hebrew and Yiddish books.

However, because of technical difficulties in relation to opening such a department this sum was given to the Tel Chai Yiddish library that was under the leadership of the Poale Zion, and became known as the Zionist library in the city. The money was diverted to buy books on the list that had been approved by the city administration. The city budget introduced a column titled 'Judaica' without mentioning the above agreement and the provincial government later endorsed it. The sum was handed over to the Tel Chai library and new Yiddish and Hebrew books were purchased bearing the stamp of the city council.

3) In all the religious events, especially holy days, attention was given to divide equally between the Jews and the gentiles. Subsidies were handed over to the religious leaders under the supervision of a special committee of councilors. This is how, for example, the Hachshara kibbutz was able to obtain matzos for Passover, bought by these funds.

4) It remained established that amongst the delegates who assembled from all the Polish cities (which was a basic part of the government constitution), that there were always Jewish representatives – ranging from the workers groups to the general Jewish public.

5) From the first elections in 1926 until the first half of 1934 there were four elections of the city council. Every two years the provincial government had dismissed the city council and called for new elections. The last time was 1934 when it decided on a revolutionary ruling on the elections, which was directed against minorities, especially the Jews. In Brest as elsewhere, new elections were declared according to this new law with the district system.

Every district was nominated in a strongly proscribed manner with the number of mandates that belonged to it dependent on the decision of the government bodies.

The Senatzia party that existed in Poland prior to World War 11 (1934-1939) imposed their will on all the Polish inhabitants of the Kressy (the formerly Russian territories). An exemption was made for the general Zionists of the Al Hamishmar group headed by L. Winnikoff. This was not to the liking of the ruling Senatzia party and the city's Polish rulers. H. Winnikoff did not agree to appear under their patronage in the last elections in which the ruling powers embraced the methods of intimidation and fear. They did not allow the Jews to vote according to their own free will. Thus ended the chapter of independent representation of the Brest Jews in the city's self-government that in practical reality had lasted from 1926-1935. From then until the outbreak of World War 11 in 1939 there were Jewish representatives in the city council, but in reality they had no influence over the resolutions or decisions on the various issues.

At the time of the Brest pogrom, on the Eve of Shavuot 1937, the Jewish councilors were almost silenced; they also could not react later to the events that occurred as they should have at the city council's tribunal. They were suppressed by the dominating power of the Senatzia Party, which brought Poland to the brink of disaster.

The Kehilla Committee

Until 1915 there existed in Brest a council (Gorodskaya Uprava) whose members were only Russians and Poles. There were only two employees who were responsible for Jewish affairs – Yoineh Gurnreich and Gvirtzman. In addition the city administration took the advice of the head Gabbeh (deacon) of the Great Synagogue, Yeruchum Schatz, who was aggressive and stubborn. The entire community work of the synagogues' minyanim (congregations) was concentrated in supporting the existence of the hospital named Linat Zedek, visiting the sick, and a visitor's hostel.

After the expulsion order by General Leeming in 1915, the town was burnt down and only 25% of the buildings that remained were habitable. In 1918 when the expelled Brest inhabitants returned to their city, they organized a new kehilla council. The town was then under Ukrainian domination, and a Ukrainian governor was in power until 1919.

When the refugees returned they elected a reputable businessman, Reb.Zalman Tennenbaum as chairman of the kehilla council. When the Ukrainians left the city, they were replaced by Poles, and Reb. Avraham Yitzchak Bleiweis was elected as chairman of the kehilla council. He was a Jew with a good heart and the highest morals, a man of the people, and a Dayan (judge) of the rabbinical court. Among the leaders and members of the kehilla were Itzchak Winnikoff, Aaron Ludski and Shmuel Pomerantz. They were followed by Shmuel Lichtenstein who was elected as president of the kehilla; he was an orthodox Jew, a shrewd businessman and the right hand of Rabbi

Zeev Soleveitchik. Shmuel Lichtenstein was a tireless social worker who achieved much in the field of education. The fourth representative of the kehilla was Chaim Boruch Kaviatopski, an educated orthodox Jew who was burnt to death by the Germans when they entered the city.... it was said that he confronted them and was murdered.

The period of the kehilla administration under Rabbi Zelig was ended by royal patronage from Moscow. Dr. Dov Kagan was the president of the kehilla in the time of Polish rule. The son in law of Benjamin Vigdorovitch, a rich Brest merchant and landowner, he donated 25,000 with which they began to build a new hospital, which was finished in 1921 together with financial aid from the Joint. During this period the kehilla council built several buildings.

The kehilla council had no official authority but it took on the registration and issuing of birth records. It was only after the Second Sejm (parliament), that a law was passed giving the kehillas of the Kressy (former Russian territories) the full rights of an official government institution.

1917 Conference of Jewish Communists

[Page 121]

Divisions and Songs
(The Polemics between the Chassidim and Misnagdim)

By M. S. Geshuri
Translated by Abraham Muchnik and Jenni Buch

In the battle in which the Mitnagdim proclaimed against the Chassidic movement, Lithuania was in the forefront. Also the role of Brisk D'lita (Brest), which was then a vital center of Jewish Lithuania, was significant due to the efforts of its' leader, Rabbi Avraham Katzenellenbogen, then the chief rabbi of Brest.

In the year 1764 the Polish king proclaimed the closure the Council of Four Lands in Poland.

This council consisted of the leading kehillot (Jewish communities) in Lithuania and all the provinces and presided in Brest. The last committee of the five main kehillot consisted of::

Vilna, Grodno, Brest, Pinsk and Slutsk. It was in Slutsk that the last meeting was held and several rabbinical laws were introduced with the purpose of strengthening their autonomy, unaware that the Council was nearing its' demise.

It was then that the Chassidim appeared, who made concerted efforts to organize their own customs, especially synagogue services with public singing, which they introduced in addition to what had been traditionally accepted and sanctioned by the great 'Maharal' (Rabbi Loewy) of Prague. They made great efforts in reaching out and spreading their teachings to all levels of Jewish society. The old order that controlled the kehillot, and by the way, trivialized the synagogue traditions and the collective singing at weddings and other festive occasions was weakened, whilst the Chassidic movement kept on growing and strengthening.

The Lithuanian Rabbis came out to battle "the agitators and destroyers". At their head stood Eliahu, the Gaon of Vilna. The Chassidim had already extended their influence on the Lithuanian cities, in Pinsk, a city of orthodox Mitnagdim, the seeds of Chassidism were already taking hold through the great Rabbi Aharon, who was a pupil of the Mezricher rabbi and one of the authors of 'The Secret Chassidic Sect' in Lithuania and Russia.

From Karlin they pulled the thin threads that were woven into a net and spread out over many Lithuanian towns. In this town which was known for its' many Gaonim (sages) who had occupied the rabbinical seat, and it was there Rabbi Levi Yitzhak (the Magid of Mezrich) became head of the rabbinical court and head of the Yeshiva Holy congregation of Pinsk and district.

After the first excommunication ban was proclaimed by the Vilna Gaon and his followers in 1772 against Chassidim and Chassidism – the Jewish masses in Pinsk were outraged and came forward with insults and curses against Rabbi Levi Yitzhak, and attacked him in his house, which was robbed and looted.

Also in Vilna the rabbinic stronghold of the Mitnagdim, the Chassidim succeeded in infiltrating their influence. And it was in Vilna, headed by the Gaon of Vilna and other religious leaders that the community decided to make a stand. In the year 1774, after Pesach, they proclaimed an excommunication order on the 'Chassidic cult". From Vilna they sent out letters to all the main communities in Lithuania and regions towns with a 'Kol Koreh'. That everywhere the Chassidim be excommunicated. On Rosh Chodesh Iyar, a letter signed by the Vilna Gaon, and 16 Dayanim (religious judges) of the Vilna community was sent to the Brest community addressed to Rabbi Avraham Katzenellenbogen, who was a Gaon but he had no understanding of the Chassidic spirit. Therefore, he resisted and fought it with all his might.

This 'Kol Koreh' (proclamation) was spread under the name of the 'Brest letter'. After this letter there was sent from Vilna a circular in which all these accusations were repeated and more accusations added, with a list of specific details. Also in this letter the Vilna fanatics requested that all the communities drive out the Chassidim and exile them "as far as a Jewish hand could reach". To chase them out so that they could not even unite for a minyan, and especially not to allow them to pray in a minyan. In the meantime, there was published a collection of all the letters which had been sent out against the Chassidim – this booklet was called "the Songs of Tyrants and Jagged Swords". It was printed in the same year, 1776. This booklet was distributed at the request of the Vilna Gaon and the rabbis of Lithuania and Galicia.

The Chassidim bought the booklet widely, and burnt it.

It turned out that in Brest, there was no concentration of Chassidim as in other Lithuanian towns. There were several Chassidim but they did not have the nerve to publicly profess this.

The fanatical Rabbi Katzenellenbogen had already participated in the first polemic that year with the Chassidic leaders, and would often debate them. It is to his credit and should be noted that he did not follow the role of Avigdor the Informer, who was crowned rabbi in Pinsk, replacing the Chassidic rabbi. He had Rabbi Shneor Zalman of Lyady and other Chassidic rabbis betrayed to the Russian authorities, who arrested them. Only after much effort from leading personalities were the rabbis released.

Approximately nine years passed since the first excommunication order and in the month of Elul, 1781, in the days of the great market of Zelva, Grodno province, the rabbis and the leaders of the kehillot of Brest, Grodno and Slutsk, gathered in Zelva. Once again there was heard the "shofar blowing", and again an excommunication order was read out in the same fashion as had been done in Vilna:

"To chase them out and cause them troubles and uproot them like weeds" and other instructions – "to add to the great excommunication so that the Chassidim do not have a place to pray, do not allow them to stay overnight, forbid their ritual slaughter, do not do business with them, do not marry with them, and if any of them dies, do not bury them...."

Prior to this, there had been a meeting in Warsaw between Rabbi A. Katzenellenbogen of Brest and Rabbi Levi Yitzhak of Berdichev, for an open debate about Chassidism. This debate took place in the Warsaw suburb of Praga, attended by a huge audience. Rabbi Katzenellenbogen of Brest opened the debate, the majority of the audience was made up of his supporters and followers, and they encouraged him. Rabbi Levi Yitzhak answered all the questions of Rabbi Katzenellenbogen.

The Brest Rabbi then took out a proclamation, which was also signed in Zelva on the first day of Elul, 1781. And there we read these new words:

"Listen to the mountains and to godly conflicts and seek if there is a greater pain than mine, because in the house of Israel I have seen various deeds spreading out like leprosy, the recent amassing of sinners to falsify God and his Holy bible – men from the Chassidic community (may their names be struck out), who separated themselves – deviates and heretics who have cancelled the honour of the Torah and the law of the Sages. Woe! Every heart trembles, every Jewish home cries when it becomes known in the whole of the land about that argument I had in the city of Warsaw and my victory over the hoodlum, the Chief Rabbi Levi Yitzhak Zelichower over the matter of the well that was dug by the wisdom of our Sages of Torah. The most highly esteemed leaders of the nation, men of wisdom and knowledge, these are the predecessors that straightened out the paths with customs and improvements.

Now he is stuffed full of unworthiness, and the same person was silent and twisted the expression from his lips, and became like a mule that cannot open his mouth. Frightened and wounded, when I proved his guilt to all, and the masses celebrated in Gods' victory, in the synagogue in the city of Praga. And I stepped forward and objected with my civil words to the band who call themselves 'the fighters for God', so that we can tell of their shame, a small group of them and their silly and foolish deeds.... etc.

Thus spoke he that fought for our God today, Thursday, the second day of Elul, and all that witnessed were amazed".

Avraham Katzenellenbogen stayed in the Holy Congregation of Brest, mother of Israel. The book of the name 'Wars of God' of the Brest Rabbi was never printed. Apparently, the author wanted to publish the first debate but it did not work out for him. The second debate became available in pamphlets. Also Rabbi Levi Yitzhak held himself to have been the winner of the debate and let it be known to all that he answered all the questions that were put to him by his opponent. This angered and upset Rabbi Katzenellenbogen and he came forward, writing a letter to the Honourable Rabbi Levi Yitzhak of Zelichow. In this letter, he castigated the Chassidim for distancing themselves from the accepted rule of not deviating from beyond Gods' teachings. The famous Sages, the steadfast souls of this world, people of the highest morals and behaviour had set the highest standards. At the end of 1781 the Brest rabbi decreed that they would be put into excommunication – this was called for in Vilna.

But with all that, he had still not calmed himself. He endeavored to defeat the Chassidic leader in a second debate, which was to take place in the presence of important people from both sides.

In the end, he suggested that the questions be put in writing to Rabbi Levi Yitzhak, and that the answers should be in writing, so that all could see who was in the right. Rabbi Levi Yitzhak agreed to this so around 1784 – it came to a written battle (The War of The Writers).

On the 8th of Tammuz, 1784, Avraham Katzenellenbogen, the Rabbi of Brest and District, wrote from Warsaw to Rabbi Levi Yitzchak of Zelichow. After a long introduction, which contained punishing words about the 'crossings of the border' (breaking the rules) which had been delineated by our predecessors, and at the same time he included certain questions. In the second part of the letter, Rabbi Avraham Katzenellenbogen asked Rabbi Levi Yitzhak to repent of his sins and chastised him with restrained words: "That every Chassidic custom is only according to Satanic evil inclination, which forced the Sages through verbal persuasion and advice to perform these transgressions under the guise of worshipping God".

According to his opinion, the new Torah (teachings) meant to overthrow the three pillars upon which the world stood: 1. Torah. 2. Work 3.Charity.

Our Sages who wrote the Torah She Baal Peh consider the people of this new sect to be peasants and worthless people. Their prayers are tasteless and made idiotic. In particular the changes to the prayer, Tefillat Keter, which the Chassidim introduced by Tefillat Mussaf on the Sabbath, and which can be said, according to Kabbala in the Holy Land, but not in the Diaspora. He admitted that the spirit of peace had been destroyed because of this conflict that made the Diaspora into a flame of fire. At the end of this letter he appealed to the heart of his opponent and implored him to return to the righteous path, without any personal motive, and with all his efforts to avoid the desecration of the Holy One. He asked his opponent to desist from his ambitions and admit the truth that he had erred. He should endeavor to go along the path and not split the nation into two camps. According to the testimony of one who lived in those days, this letter from the Brest rabbi was delivered to Rabbi Levi Yitzhak in Zelichow.

Unfortunately, it is difficult to establish whether Rabbi Levi Yitzhak answered this letter.

The witch hunt did its' work. As the Chassidic prayer gatherings in the Lithuanian cities sprang up, they were shut down. There is no doubt that in those early days the numbers of the Chassidic prayers meetings were reduced, or held in secret. After a time, they were able to re-emerge and repair the damage; many began to support the Chassidim, seeing that they were truly Orthodox. Also Brest opened up its' gates to the Chassidic movement.

2

Who was Rabbi A. Katzenellenbogen? And what sort of character was he aside from his fanatical war on the Chassidic movement? We don't have a great deal of information on Rabbi A. Katzenellenbogen to substantiate the cause of his opposition to the Chassidim.

The Chassidic movement has been able to find writings, which have accused them wrongdoings in their behaviour and publications, and in the way they spread their Chassidism.

Many of the Misnagdim had encircled and verbally abused them. Others poured on them their wrath and frustration, and interfered with the Chassidim. We don't have much information about Rabbi A.Katzenellenbogen's personality, only what was written about him in the book 'Ir Tehila" (City of Glory) by A.L. Feinstein, published in 1886 by the printing press of Rabbi Yechiel Halter in Warsaw. This was the only book that contained material about the story of Brest. Rabbi Avraham Katzenellenbogen was the son of Rabbi David Katzenellenbogen, the head of the Beth Din in Keidani and the son of Rabbi Yehezkel Katzenellenbogen, author of the book "Knesset Yehezkel". Earlier (1746) he had been the Rabbi of Slutsk, and later wrote a letter from Slutsk to Rabbi Yonasson Eybshutz regarding the question of Kameot (amulets). When he was only 6 years old his name was mentioned in the book "Aliyah Eliahu", which was written about the Vilna Gaon. As the head of the Beth Din in Slutsk in 1752 he signed as the head of the sages of his generation his approval for the book called 'Luchot HaBrit'.

From 1760 until his death (some time after 1787) he was the Chief Rabbi of Brest. During that period, he issued many approvals for books that were published in his time including: Mayim Amukim, Minchat Aharon, Kochvei Yaakov, Beth Avraham, Seder HaDorot, and Tiferet Israel Zuta. Rabbi A.K. had 8 sons, most of who became rabbis of various cities. Their names are as follows:

1). Rabbi Joseph Katzenellenbogen who took over his father's position in the rabbinical chair in Brest.
2). Rabbi Shaul Katzenellenbogen K. of Vilna
3). Rabbi Yehezkel Katzenellenbogen K., head of the Beth Din in Swisloch.
4). Rabbi Nachum Katzenellenbogen K., head of the Beth Din in Birsz.
5). Rabbi Joel Katzenellenbogen in Komarowka.
6). Rabbi David Katzenellenbogen in Wolkowitz.
7). Rabbi Moshe Katzenellenbogen.
8). Rabbi Ephraim Katzenellenbogen.

On his tombstone in the ancient cemetery in Brest we can read the following:

"Here is buried the rabbi and Gaon, our teacher and rabbi, Rabbi Avraham, son of Rabbi David, who was the Rabbi of the Holy Congregation of Brest. The remaining details about him have been erased and are very difficult to read. "

His son, Rabbi Joseph, had taken over as the Rabbi of Brest whilst his father was still alive, according to a document signed and ratified by the King when he visited Brest. An approval was granted for the book 'Resuhe Galim' and the book ' Chidush Mahary'. From the engravings on his tombstone we read that he was head of the Beth Din and Yeshiva in Brest.

Next to his grave is the grave of his wife, Echsa, who passed away on the 2nd of Adar Bet, 1772. From Rabbi Joseph Katzenellenbogen the dynasty passed to the third generation – to his son Rabbi Aryeh-Leib Katzenellenbogen, who was crowned with the title ' Gaon and Prodigy Aryeh'. His books include: Shiloh, Midrash Tanchuma, A New Joseph, Vilna Grodno, Roar of the Lion, and Sefer Torah Or, all of which mention the name of the Vilna Gaon.

The name of the Gaon is also mentioned in these books:

Keren Shlomo, Mincha Belula, Shelot Ve Tshuvot from the Gaon Rabbi Shimon of Slonim, and the book 'Sheva Einayim'.

According to the book "Ir Tehila" (City of Glory) he was unique in his generation and his congregation. A generation of world famous righteous men owes their honour to him. From him originated the rules and regulations that every Brest Jew was obligated to give an annual donation on the eve of Passover to the value of 1/6th of their own. This money was used to distribute matzo meal - only those who donated 10 roubles had fulfilled their obligation, even if their incomes were was much higher.

Rabbi A.L. Katzenellenbogen conducted the rabbinate in Brest for almost 40 years and died on the 13th August 1837. (A great tragedy for the Jews of Brest).

We see that Rabbi A.. Katzenellenbogen established three generations of Brest rabbis, one after the other. All lived dedicated and rich lives, and each had had a great influence on the life of the city and its' surroundings. And their names were engraved amongst their congregation with love and blessings.

3

Brest was the last bastion to come to terms with the existence of Chassidism in Lithuania. For a long time the Mitnagdims city of Brest stubbornly held out against the Chassidim. The city considered itself a stronghold against the Chassidim, however, there was difference between the original Mitnagdim from the time of the Vilna Gaon and the Mitnadgdim in the generations that followed.

The original Mitnagdim obeyed all of God's laws as they were written in the Shulchan Aruch (book of laws listing all the rules and customs) according to their own interpretations and the interpretations of their commentators. They trembled at every word that had any reference to obeying the mitzvoth. Every law, every custom, everything that was permitted and forbidden, every small warning that was transmitted through their lawmakers (poskim) – this all belonged to the Torah in it's entirety and without deviation. The Mitnaged is by his nature very strict and easily offended. To say the least, he never smiled with a full mouth – to be a Mitnaged was not an easy thing to be...

In the following generations the strength of the Mitnagdim resistance evaporated.

They became more moderate in their behaviour. Brest became a city of learning and spiritual activities. The resistance to anything new and anything that needed to be renewed weakened and in the end it showed thus: between the Mitnagdim and the Chassidim the only difference was in a tzadik (a religious leader or teacher).

After all, they were very similar to each other. The Mitnagdim opposed the Chassidim with a Chassidic (messianic) fervor! With the same ecstatic enthusiasm that the Chassidim accepted and absorbed the rebbe's teachings – the Mitnagdim would annul it. Even further they were as ready to punish the Chassidim just as the Chassidim were to punish them. It was no coincidence that Rabbi Simcha Soleveitchik learned Torah from the Chassidic Rebbe Avraham Weinberg (this is before he became the Slonimer Rebbe).

There was some who remarked that the Mitnagdim showed themselves as human beings with hearts that had poetic juices instilled in them. They are dry outside and moist inside – if you delve inside them with understanding you will find warm Jews with a rich spiritual life. The Mitnagdim were in reality Chassidim who did not believe in 'Rebbes'. This is what differentiated them – the orthodox Brest was divided into kinds of Chassidism, those with a rabbi, those without. And because of that, it was not too difficult for the Chassidim to try their luck and occupy various influential positions in Brest.

4

The Chassidim began to organize themselves despite the entrenched opposition of the Mitnagdim in Brest. In the beginning they took over the poorer districts. Afterwards they had the nearer and further villages under their influence. Through the Rebbe's court and the many Chassidim, they opened up many prayer houses – the support was 100% in Brest, but the Mitnagdim were not fully integrated yet. There remained pockets of Mitnagdim, but the ideological debate between the two worlds was still unresolved.

In Brest, the rabbinical city of the fanatical Mitnaged Rabbi. A. Katzenellenbogen, the Chassidim opened up their own prayer houses. The Rebbe's courts of Lithuanian Poland - of Karlin, Stolyn, Kobryn, Radzyn, Niezvitch, Kotsk, Novo- Minsk and so on – all opened up Chassidic branches in the prayer halls which were led by prayer leaders accompanied by many Chassidic melodies. Prayers were led with warm soulful songs, with excitement and heart-rending melodies. Their righteous sages would visit Brest from time to time, and their followers were overjoyed to find themselves amongst these composers of their new melodies that were to the liking of their rabbis and had spread widely amongst the Chassidim. These melodies were used on the Sabbath and the high holidays, as well as in the singing of prayers and also the rabbi's prayer celebrations.

In Kamenetz near Brest there was a Chassidic composer, Reb Yisroel, who was a Kotzer Chassid, and he would compose to order. For example, he composed music in honor of the visit of the rabbi of Slonim, Rabbi Avraham to Kamenetz, to welcome him. His melodies touched the hearts of all the Chassidim who would swoon with pleasure at his melodies.

Upon the uprising of the Poles against the Russians in 1863, he wrote a special melody, a march for the victory of the Poles. Two of his marches were openly mentioned in Yehezkel Kotik's book 'Zichroines' (Memories). He also composed a Cossack march for the daughter of the Karliner Rebbe to the son of the Trisker Rebbe. This march was also sung by the Cossacks of the Stolyner Rebbe whilst riding to accompany the groom as he met his bride.

This same march was later sung in Kamenetz every year on Simchat Torah.

The influence of the Chassidim in Brest had grown, but had not engulfed all it's inhabitants, and the two streams in Brest each streamed quietly along as if there had always been an eternal peace between them. The Chassidim typified the longing for the Land of Israel, they produced loyal and community minded officials who worked for the public, occupied themselves with Zionists causes, helping pioneers make Aliyah. Those pioneers, who had been brought up in a Chassidic home and had absorbed the chassidic warmth, did much work for their communities, even far from Brest.

The stubbornness of the Mitnagdim and the warmth of the Chassidim became positive factors in bringing the people together into one national loyalty in Brest. They put their stamp upon the Brest Jewish community, the various Diaspora lands, and the State of Israel.

2. Cantors

From the collection of rules and regulations which were put into the booklet of the Land of Lithuania, which spanned from 5487 till 5581 we can get an understanding of the status of cantors, klezmers (musicians) and jesters in Brest and surroundings.

The cantor belonged to the holy class, which was included into the expression Rachash - rabbis, chazanim (cantors) and shamashim.(beadles). From the several tables of rules this existed we establish an opinion about the significance of the cantor, and his standing among the people who took upon themselves the strictness of keeping kosher. The cantor would also occupy himself with community work outside of his profession – because being a cantor would not have provided him with sufficient income for his needs.

In the regulations it is stated that there should not be any compromises when they choose arbitrators, rabbis, cantors or beadles. To protect the positions of the cantors they would use the old excommunication system from the olden times. In electing a rabbi, a cantor or a beadle, the decision making power lay with the elders, rabbinical judges (dayans) and the honorary synagogue officials – the most respected in the congregation.

Among the taxes collected through the Lithuanian Land Council, which presided in Brest, there existed a special tax, which was called the chuppah geldt - a tax was collected from marrying couples. This tax was collected as a percentage of the brides' dowry, not only from cash, but also from silver and gold items. It was agreed that these chuppah monies were to be used to support the rabbis, cantors and beadles of the town.

A poor man who married off his daughter was exempt from this tax. The cantor would receive only half of this sum as was determined by the size of the dowry.

Amongst the rules, which touch upon the activity of the cantors, it was determined by decree and law that no cantor was permitted to sing more than three melodies on Shabbat, at Shacharit and Mussaf – also on Shabbat Rosh Chodesh and at weddings....

The strivings to be stricter and more dominant in this restrictive life between the four walls of the prayer house caused conflicts between the synagogue officials and the holy men- the rabbis. Grim and unchanging was the situation of the cantor who tried to specifically please his followers, the people that had appointed him, and his critics.

In Brest it was forbidden for the cantor to sing from music notes so that he would not forget in keeping with 'Know before Whom you stand'. There were many famous Brest rabbis in whose books one could find descriptions of the conditions of cantorial singing and cantors in the synagogues, for better and worse.

The majority of these rabbis frowned upon the custom of cantors imitating Christians by using melodies taken from Christian music. Rabbi Joel Sirkis, who was a rabbi in Brest was not overzealous about this adoption from Christian melodies and did not issue warnings against it. However, he did speak out against cantors for bringing into the prayers 'children from foreign lands', which referred to theatre music.

Rabbi Shlomo Luria, known as the Marshal, who was also a rabbi in Brest, mentions in his book 'The Two Tablets of the Covenant' "the cantors who took on other jobs such as teachers, scribes and shochets".

Cantors were very closely associated and involved with general everyday life. The majority of the cantors came from the middle class, amongst them some exceptional individuals in whose hearts burnt with a holy flame and were blessed with great musical talents. After all, in the end, their names have been forgotten, as we don't have the most minimal information about these famous cantors of Europe. Specifically before the massacres of 1648-9 which tore at the hearts and the necessity of music to reduce people's anguish.

We hear of a cantor during the summer pogrom of 1648 from Reb Nathan (Nuta) Hanover:

"The four kehillot, men women and children, approximately 4000 people who fled to the Tartars and amongst them was a cantor with the name of Reb Hirsh Zhutov. When they neared the Tartars the cantor began to lament and sing in a strong voice 'El Male Rachamim' for their murdered brethren and the entire people with him broke out in an anguished cry. Their cry surely must have been heard in the heavens, and their captors were filled with mercy and compassion for them".

This is the first time a cantors name was mentioned in the history of our nation in this area.

The typical cantorial music in Eastern Europe was created on the foundations of Oriental music, and originated in the south, in the Ukraine, especially Podolia, Serbia, Wolyn, and the shores of the Black Sea. From there it came to Lithuania. In every single generation there were in Brest cantors who did not use written melodies and could not read musical notes. Their cantorial skills were inherited from their teachers and they created their own tunes and melodies. Because of the incomplete and inaccurate list of cantors that were in Brest, it is impossible to describe their characters and their histories over the first centuries since Jews settled in Brest.

At the beginning of the 18th century there were outstanding cantors in Eastern Europe who laid the foundations of synagogue singing and had a lasting influence on the style of prayers in later generations. The highest level of cantorial artistry was reached in the 19th century. Also in Brest there were cantors who protected these traditions and were very famous throughout Europe. The great synagogue in Brest hosted a long history of cantors, but we do not know their names or have any information about these cantors. In the book 'Ir Tehilah' by A.L.Feinstein, there is mention of a cantor who lived in the year 1690, however, there are no details of him. We should mention some of the outstanding ones:

A. Reb Shloime Weintraub (1781-1829)

Because of his red hair he was called 'Koshtan' by the masses. Born in Old Konstantin in the south of Russia, and composed for his father who was a prayer leader. He excelled with a fine and strong voice, a coloratura with which he enchanted his listeners. The warmth of his prayers touched and overwhelmed the hearts of his audience. He was a fiery Chassid in his youth, and Reb Yisroel the preacher of Kosnitz, said of him that the sweetness of his voice could bring the Messiah.

Weintraub was appointed as Cantor by the city of Zamosc, and then he came to the Great Synagogue of Brest. He had a unique and original style. His high and low notes and quavers came out of his throat with astounding clarity. He would awake a holy shiver in the congregation. The cantors of that time have remained legendary because of their great musical accomplishments. He was a man of Torah and principles. An orthodox Jew that knew his worth and position, and an artiste that valued and treasured his craft. Koshton was one of the greatest cantors in the Jewish world and the only one who understood how to unite emotion with prayer.

His book 'Shirei Shlomo' (The songs of Shlomo) contains heartrending melodies that have become famous, and there is not one cantor who has not used his beautiful creations. He was the first to write down his musical compositions on paper. He died in Durno in Kislev 1829.

B. Boruch Karliner

His surname was Kunstler but he was named after his birthplace – Karlin, vicinity of Pinsk. He was of the last cantors to sing without notes. An orthodox Jew, he was a great Talmudic scholar, and a fanatical Chassid. In his musical craft he could not read or write a note of music. Nevertheless, he was considered one of the greatest cantors of his time.

He began his career as cantor in Karlin, then went to the great synagogue in Kovno, and was later invited to Brest, where he was very highly regarded. Despite his greatness as a cantor, he remained a pauper. From Brest he went to Kamenetz-Podolsk. However, he died in Brest in 1871.

C. Reb. Noah Zlotkowski (Reb Noah Lider)

Born on Dvoretz, Grodno district. When he was only five years old he already showed his talent in singing. Already in his youth his voice rang like a silver bell. He was appointed cantor in Lida (thus his surname Lider). He applied for positions in various cities such as Lublin, Berlin, Warsaw, Moscow and others until he was appointed as cantor in the city of Brest.

Reb Noah played violin and wrote compositions that were very successful and sung in the whole Jewish world. He heft behind a manuscript in book form titled 'The prayers of Noah and the worship of Elijah'.

His Hebrew songs 'Go to Zion, Miracle and Flag', 'The Eternal Jew', 'What happened to you, My Soul, that you fell asleep', etc. were very popular with the people but the name of the composer has been forgotten. He belonged to the most important cantors in Russia who could unite prayer and emotion in the synagogue. He was not only a cantor but also a teacher of cantors and conductors. Hundreds of his students today occupy important positions as cantors and conductors in various countries. He went to live in Kalish from Brest and there he died.

D. Avraham Barkin

Avraham Barkin was born to a famous Brest family. His father Reb Baruch Barkin was the head of one of the richest households in Brest, and a music lover. His daughter also excelled in singing and this love of music was instilled through the entire family. As A child he would sing with renowned cantors who foresaw that he would be a great cantor. As an eleven-year-old he already prayed like a fully-fledged authentic cantor. When his voice developed into a strong and beautiful tenor, he went to Warsaw where he studied at the conservatory. He sang on stage with the Warsaw.philarmonic and was strongly praised by the critics. Until then, no Jew had ever trodden upon this stage. In Warsaw, he was a cantor in the Noszik Synagogue and later went to Uman, near Kiev in the Ukraine. During the time of the pogroms there he was miraculously saved and migrated to the U.S. where he became a famous singer and cantor.

E. David Gurevitch

David Gurevitch was born in Brest but never sang there as a cantor. He was a cantor in Korotch and Kremenchug. He would enchant with his singing, beautiful diction and interpretation. His voice was a beautiful lyrical tenor. The Brisker community notables were very proud of his achievements.

F. S. Tshesnik.

In the U.S. he changed his name to Chestny. Tshesnik was a ritual circumciser (mohel) and slaughterer (shochet). He possessed a beautiful baritone with a rich timbre. He was also a learned scholar and a great singer and musician. He was born in Brest and sang with many of the great cantors.

G. Reb Kalman Chazan

In Brest he was called Chazan (cantor) out of love. He was a cantor in Brest from 1890-1900. He possessed a baritone and the deepest and highest notes would come out of him strong and clear – he was twice appointed cantor in Brest where he was very sought after by the masses. But his wandering instincts, which were typical of cantors, disrupted his life. He was unable to stay in one place.

H. The Cantor Neiman (Neuman)

He was a cantor in Bialystok and then came to Brest. He had a beautiful tenor During the panic of W.W.1 he fled the city and the country. Already and old man, he went to Liverpool where he died aged over 90.

I. The Cantor Shein

He came to Brest from far away. Whilst in the Russian army, he was garrisoned at the Brest fortress. When he finished his military service, he remained in Brest as cantor and was also conductor of the Brest choir. He was invited to become the city's cantor. After Brest he went to Romania where he became conductor of the theatre in Galatz.

J. Reb Josef Tiktinski. 1857 –1934

Reb Josef was born in Mir in 1857. His father was one of the greatest emissaries of the Mir yeshiva that was called at that time in Russia: "Cedars of Lebanon, Beautiful in Torah". Reb Josef studied in this yeshiva. When he reached 18 years of age, he was ordained as a rabbi, married, and then went to Berdichev to study cantoring with 'Little Yerucham'. He was cantor in Mir, Siedlice, and after that, Brest. In Brest he also took on the task of teaching Torah to the congregation and also would eulogize when someone important passed away. He was a good looking man, and commanded the respect of all the other cantors. He did not seek fame for himself, and studied Torah all his life. Rabbi Chaim Soloveitchik was always very proud that Brest had such a learned scholar as cantor. On Hoshana Raba (the day before Shmini Atzeret) he would conduct the entire long service by heart and with closed eyes. As well as being a great scholar of Torah and rabbinical law, he possessed a great knowledge of cantorial music. He had a baritone voice, and was a great composer. He himself would conduct the choir. He lived in Brest until 1922 and died in Pinsk. After he left there were no more permanent cantors in Brest, except for the High holidays when they would hire temporary cantors. The cantors changed frequently. In 1925 after Passover they issued a cantorial tender – the cantors would try out for the position until the High Holidays, when one of them was chosen.

K. Menachem Zapovitch.

He was born in Grodno, the son of the head of the Grodno Yeshiva, Rabbi Chaim Leib Zapovitch. Menachem studied in the yeshiva as well as to be a cantor. He had a tenor voice. In 1915 he went to Odessa. Then he was cantor in the great synagogue in Vilna. He was cantor in Bialystok in 1925 when he was appointed to the great synagogue in Brest. There he sung with the choir that was conducted by Yehoshua Katz. When he stood at his pulpit to sing, the synagogue overflowed with congregants. He was cantor in Brest for three years. On one of the High Holidays, Zapovitch wanted to introduce a new custom and donned a high white cantor's hat – however, the rabbi, Zeev Soloveitchik insisted that he remove it, as he saw a Gentile (goyishe) influence in it. Only after he removed the hat was he allowed to continue praying. He moved to Bedzin and then Siedlice. At the outbreak of W.W.2 he fled to Brest and was once again cantor in his city until the Russians (1939-41) arrested him and sent him to Siberia. In 1946 he returned to Poland and was a cantor in Szczeszin and Lodz. In 1949 he made Aliyah to Israel and was the cantor in the Hapoal Hamizrachi synagogue in the Tel-Aviv suburb of Nachlat Benyamin.

The appointment of the cantors in Brest was in the hands of the gabbays – the synagogue trustees who were lovers of singing. Of them we should note the following: Shmuel Pomerantz. The last gabbey of the great synagogue in Brest.

Benjamin Padua. A gabbay of the great synagogue who was a lover of music.

Isser Gvirtzman. Chairman of the burial society (Chevra Kadisha) and a gabbey of the great synagogue. He died in Kiryat Motzkin.

In Brest there were some individuals that decided on the hiring of the cantors such as Zev Dov Begin who was the secretary of the kehilla (community council). In the synagogues there were also choirs that accompanied the cantors in their singing. The synagogue choir occupied the highest place – amongst them we should note:

Berel the bass –a second hand clothing dealer.
Meier the tenor – a shoemaker.
Yehoshua Katz the conductor – a tailor. He was occupied with training the choir between one meal to the next. Murdered in the Brest ghetto.

There were over 40 different participants in the choir including many children. The cantor would also conduct the choir. Only in the time of

Menachem Zapovitch was there a special conductor –Yehoshua Katz. The choir would perform at religious festivals such as Channuka and Purim. There were no non-religious choirs in Brest until closer to W.W.2, when the Poale Zion and the General Zionist formed the first secular choirs.

3. Prayer Leaders

Besides the Cantors in the Great Synagogue and the holy synagogues, there were also small synagogues and prayer houses in the city dedicated to certain groups, such as Chassidim. These overflowed with praying congregants. The prayers here were led by prayer leaders, who had good voices with different styles of praying. They did not possess the art of the Cantors, who had the culture of singing and the ability to read musical notes. They were the representatives of the folk congregations without the artistic format. There were distinct differences between the prayer leaders of the Mitnagdim and the Chassidim. Rabbi Nachman Breslauer described in one of his stories "A Rabbi Who had One Son", the learning and prayer methods of the Mitnagdim – "without life and without deep religious feeling". In the time when the Chassidic prayer leader would pray from the depth of his heart with a strong beautiful voice that touched the congregants. Thus they could escape the petty problems of their world and occupy themselves with spiritual thoughts. (The New Book of Generations, page 26).

Let us be reminded of the best of the Brest prayer leaders:

Kwiatkowski, he was the prayer leader at the Rabbi's prayer house, he was a Chassid.

Pollig, he was the head shammes and prayer leader in the Greener prayer house. In the same prayer house there was another prayer leader, Reb Hershel Alyenik, an oil merchant.

Reb Yakov Wishikowitz, a Stolin Chassid.

Reb Moshe der Groisser (the Tall), a Stolin Chassid.

Reb Reuven Kanel, a Stolin Chassid.

Reb Gershon who was the Shammes and prayer leader in the Koskles prayer house.

Reb Mordechai Beinish, a prayer leader in the Rabbi's prayer house.

Rabbi Avraham Yitzchak Bleiweiss, who was a Dayan (religious judge).

Zalman Hauft, the Shammes and an exceptional prayer leader in the Pauper's prayer house.

Reb Yitzchak Bruchin, a businessman – he possessed a beautiful voice. He prayed in the Ox Traders synagogue.

Reb Bobel the Shammes and Reb Itche Stoliner, who both prayed in the Funeral Society prayer house - a prayer house of the common folk where they prayed all day long without interuption –from early morning until the middle of the night.

Reb Moishe Laizerovitch, the preacher at the Tailor's prayer house. (He was the father of the journalist Laizerovitch of the "Heint" newspaper).

Reb Alter, the proprietor of a soap factory, he was an outstanding prayer leader on the High Holidays at the synagogue of Reb Yitzchak Malish in the Brest suburb on the Mukhavets River. There was another prayer leader there by the name of Reb Yitzchak Fisher, a fish merchant.

Reb Zuske Pollak Rashkes, in the Novominsker synagogue.

Reb Baruch Hirsh, famous prayer leader of the Israel Wolf synagogue, and many more that are difficult for us to recall through the passage of time.

4. Folk Singers (Klezmer)

Since the middle ages Jewish society possessed folk singers, which took upon themselves the responsibility of fighting the darkness of Diaspora life, to bring light and joyous moments to the High Holidays and celebrations such as weddings. To stimulate and bring enjoyment with their playing of the violin and other instruments. In the beginning the numbers of folk singers was small – over time they got together in small and larger collective groups under the name of Klezmer. The Klezmer originated from the deepest poverty, blessed with talent, they were not forced to the difficult task of earning their living, and singing became the source of their livelihoods. But they were of a very low social standing and earned very little. They would wander from town to town, settlement to settlement to earn their bread playing at weddings. Just as the cantors became the musicians and founders of Jewish religious music, so the Klezmers founded Jewish folk music.

Also in Brest, a centre of Lithuanian Jewry, there were groups of Klezmer who were popular with the Gentile population of the city, inviting them to play at aristocratic weddings and celebrations. Not seeking fame, their individual names were never renowned. In the period before the Second World War, Brest was famous for it's Klezmer of which there were two groups:

1). Anschel and his son, both born in Brest. Anschel was the premier violin player.

2). Shedletzki and his sons who played wind instruments.

At Chanukah they would play in the synagogue. They were invited to play at weddings in Brest and the neighboring areas as well as further away. They were so popular with their sweet music that the Chassidim made every effort to benefit from the Brest Klezmer who they would use together with their own musicians and entertainers at weddings of wealthy people. They would invite the Klezmer from both Kobryn and Brest. Kobryn had a "Shapses Klezmer Group" which became renowned for it's beautiful music. The Russian Governor, Paskievitch, was made aware of his talent, and sent for him. Shapse played his violin for him. Paskievitch then proposed that Shapse convert to Christianity. Shapse became enraged and said that he would not forsake his religion, even if he made him a Count. For three days Shapse stayed at the home of the Governor who invited guests from the highest society to hear him play. Shapse would not eat the non-kosher food so Paskievitch ordered that food be brought to him from a kosher restaurant. In the end the Governor gave him 1,000 rubles and proposed that he introduce him to the Tsar, but Shapse declined. With the money Shapse bought himself a house and kept on playing at wealthy weddings, travelling all over Grodno Province..

In Brest there were very popular melodies and folk songs about various events, even about the Chmelnitski pogroms (1648-9) as well as songs specifically about Yeshiva students and their lives – sadly these were not preserved and over time have been forgotten.

[Page 143]

The Great Fire of 1901

By Nachum Sokolov
Translated by Dr. Samuel Chani and Jenni Buch

Yesterday, Sunday, I was rushing to the train that leaves from Kiev at 3pm. From Saturday night until now we had been busily searching for bread and all kinds of edible foodstuffs.

This matter was very difficult because most people had not stored more than their immediate urgent needs, but because of the efforts of several volunteer friends a lot was collected that had been stored away. The first transport had already left at midnight on Saturday, and I wanted to take the second transport with me on the above-mentioned Sunday. Dr. Bichowski, H. Zezinski, M.Shereshevski, and Luria had all donated to the food collection. An especially a large amount was brought in by Michael Shereshevski.

The train passed through many small stations at which it did not stop, all around it was a refreshing spring – on the trees were already white sprouting flowers. The countryside did not vary much; the land around outside was flat and wide, steeped in quiet reflection. In Mrozi we stopped to take water for the engine. We arrived past 9pm. at the Brest railway station. Before our arrival, the passengers looked out the windows and could see the burnt out city. Nearing Brest, one of the passengers remarked that he could smell burning - this was not exaggerated.

The wind carried the smell over many miles, as we approached Brest we could already see flames, no-one believed it possible that Brest could still be burning. The fire had begun Saturday afternoon and on Sunday, 9pm, the city was still burning. As we neared the fires, the flames on the horizon became larger. There was no doubt that the fire was not yet extinguished. Also the smell was very distinct, almost tearing at the throat.

No one awaited me at the station. In fact, a telegram had been sent advising of my arrival, but those to whom it was sent never received it. In general there were very few people at the station.... I thought that the townspeople were more likely to come to the trains that departed rather than arrive. I didn't know the streets and lanes of the city. However, I did remember the name Burshtein and that he lived on Topolowa St. I walked through the station, which was larger and more attractive than our stations. I took a droshky (horse and cart) that was much lighter than the ones we had but a lot more speedy, and requested that the driver take me to Burshteins' house on Topolowa St.

How could this fire happen? These were my first words. In the houses I passed I saw confusion and disorder. The reason was simple – all household goods had been gathered together in order that they could be taken outside as soon as the fire threatened the house. The private home to which I came had become a public meeting place. An elderly Jew sat at the table, his eyes red and face swollen. He was not an exception, just one of the burn victims of the fire yesterday (Saturday). He was an honest businessman with a store and goods worth several thousands of roubles – now he was left without any income. Who would give him a piece of bread?

The Present fire (1901) destroyed half of city, the most important part, and the part that had been left untouched by the previous fire. I was tired and exhausted by dragging my feet and the unnerving sights I had seen – I needed to have a rest. Where was a place to stay overnight? Burshtein hosts visitors, but in his house there was no room to insert a needle. After a great effort and for more money then the grandest hotel or the most luxurious apartment I just managed to obtain a room in a guesthouse untouched by the fire. It was already 1.a.m.but who could sleep after such a panic? At the guesthouse I met a Mr. Horodiche, he was burnt out in the best way, he had managed to take with him his promissory notes and expensive belongings. He had fled with his with and children, leaving everything else he owned behind – utensils, clothing, papers, and all the superfluous things that were in his beautifully arranged and elegant house – everything was destroyed. He knew the city well and the possessions of its' inhabitants. He told me in great detail the extent of the damage, 1000s of people have lost their entire fortunes, the frightening situation and difficulties in obtaining aid. One wanted to help, but one is not sure how. It was he who had sent out the first telegram about bread. In reality we all thought the same way now that it was clear that the fallen must be helped to their feet. For this purpose, it was obvious that a huge amount of money needed to be raised.

The matter was hugely complicated; the majority of the fire victims were not insured with the insurance companies. Those who were insured had large debts to the banks, and the banks wanted to take those insurance monies and leave them with nothing. After the previous fire, the banks of the landowners had lent money to all that wanted to rebuild. This time the banks would not lend much. The banks sat on their money, their rules set firmly to a stalemate. Their doors were closed to those who needed to borrow. An enormous amount of aid was needed, for risky loans for new building. Here darkness and shock still reign. We still don't know whom or where to ask for help, but the situation is far worse than 6 years ago, this was obvious.

5

With those reflections, both with friends and alone by myself, the night passed and when I arose it was still dark. The first person that came to see me was B.Z. Neumark, he was known as an advocate and teacher of Hebrew, he was a social-activist man and active in the Zionist organization. On the day of the fire he was in Kovel, where he received the news... he immediately rushed home to find his wife and children and nothing else remaining. Whatever he had owned was burnt and destroyed, also, his Zion Bonds.

That was his entire belongings, also his books. With bitter irony he said: "also my time was destroyed". He had been a teacher in a wealthy home, and that had burnt down, so he was left naked without any means of support Later on I found out hundreds of other hitherto unknown details, Neumark knew the town well, as he had lived there for many years, he knew the political parties, the people and the social issues, he saw everything from a Zionist point of view, and from the point of view nation building. They attack the Zionists and say that the society "Linat Zedek" has been infiltrated by Zionists", and say that Jews should not mix charity organisations with the volunteer firefighters. They say that Jews should not be involved with the volunteer firefighters – that they are hotheads that have mixed everything together. The firefighters, the Zionists, the Linat Zedek society, the religious gabbeys (synagogue officials), and the bureaucrats don't feel that they have to fulfil their obligations. They fantasize and the religious fanatics put their heads together with the opponents of Zionism. Also the social activists did not do their duty - the community was full of fighting and conflicts and yet it all began to unravel. They were rich, middle class people with incomes and all of a sudden – the fire. What will happen now? All was destroyed and in ruins. Whilst chatting an old man came to see me. He came in the name of many, they wanted me to go to the district Gaon (Rabbi), only he could oversee the relief work of the committee....

6

I went out and began my work – I set myself two goals: First, to collect as many facts and figures as possible. Second, to find some organized system of help. With both of these goals, I had to speak to as many people as possible, and with limited time (until 6.30 pm), my guide from yesterday stuck by me. We are going to Rabbi H. Nadel who was on the relief committee of the previous fire, and was an obvious choice to be on the present committee. At present, one could not assess the extent of the damage or the number of afflicted families. As to the overall situation, we all agreed that it was dire - much worse than the previous fire.

The whole of the commercial/business district was damaged, the entire foundations of the city were shaken and falling down. Rabbi Nadel spoke in an official style; he had already been present at yesterdays meeting with the Governor and other high-ranking officials. They had sent various telegrams informing of a new committee, it is even now formed, and Nadel was taking a count of the Christian and Jewish members. As Rabbi, he was a permanent member; besides him there were four more Jews. My guide, together with Rabbi Nadel, undertook to scrutinize individually the character of every member – who was competent and who wasn't? Perhaps they would have to add several advisors. The second committee had already sent telegrams to the administrations of all the major cities

Nadel reported that there was already loud talk about those Jews who lit the fire with their own hands; possibly, during the fire there were such criminals. But it was proved that the fire did not originate this way, those who were suspects were proven not to have done so. On the other hand, according to general opinion, it later became clear that the accused arsonists were exploited, because of the opportunity and didn't cause the fire. These were additional tragic events, but not of great importance. About an organized relief system, the rabbi knew nothing. The committee would investigate, establish facts and make its' findings...

From there we went to Dr. Steinberg, he was standing in the grounds of his home, amongst his broken and damaged belongings. Here was an expensive Venetian table with exquisite workmanship and here was a cupboard with volumes of books and manuscripts.

Here was a booklet that I had written about the previous fire. "Soon you'll write a book about this fire". He invited us inside to the empty rooms. In addition to the burnt house he has suffered unheard of losses. We tell him that he was nominated to the new committee. He said that he would not take up this position, as he has not got the time or patience for community affairs, he has too much to do by himself. We knew that he would take up the position, but it was not possible to spend time with him in those distant moments, and we agonized with his dilemma. Zion was not burnt down, he said, and took out from a cupboard a container in which there were writings relating to Zion, there also were some bonds. Other people's bonds were burnt and destroyed. Brest generally was a big spender on bonds and shares to the sum of 25,000 rubles. Dr. Steinberg takes out from his garden wrapped copies of East and West (Ost and West), "this I rescued with danger to my own person" he said laughingly. This victim of the fire consoled us that maybe we would see each other again in better situations.

We meet Dr. Sherechevski, and active and pleasant man – it's a pity that he was not elected to the committee. He himself was not amongst those who suffered, but was very close to many that had – he stepped down from his carriage to talk to us and we converse with him in the middle of the street. I take note that he has very good intentions and that he aims the critics in the right direction of order. He is a person close to the people, a type of community worker, and an intelligent and intellectual man who was a social activist through and through. He speaks emotionally and one can see that his words come from the heart. With not a moment to lose we proceed to the local Sage and Rabbi, we pass by a synagogue of which there is a legend – it was built according to the design of Tsar Nicholas.

I like to ponder about the old synagogues and think of the new social institutions.

We are received by the Rabbi, a man in his middle years, short of stature and with large beautiful eyes, burning intensely – a sign of a man with a good memory. His clothing was very modest. Without any excessive preliminaries he led us from one room to another. At the table sits one of his best pupils, his right hand, they say he is a prodigy. If it enters the Rabbi's thoughts and attitude about city affairs, then he is the living spirit of the planners.

I immediately approach the matter at hand. I ask the Rabbi about how to organize help for the present tragedy. I must admit that I approached the rabbi with certain misgivings. Already a long time ago, I had heard unpleasant stories about him that sounded not productive, his opposition to Zionism and his extreme piousness. But even those who talked about the Gaon's religious fanaticism at the same time added in hindsight that he had absolutely no interest in money matters. Some added that he was clean and uncorrupted, but that there was a possibility that he would be influenced by others close to him. There was a possibility that when he had the means in his hands that he would only support the pious Jews and not those whose religious opinions he does not agree with.

I do not want to comment here on what sort of relationship I have had with the system of extreme religious fanaticism in general, and with this system of this group of rabbis in particular. I made it clear a long time ago in my treatise "Lemarnen VeRabbanim".

But in the instance of my meeting with one of these rabbis, I could not avoid telling him of what I had declared openly in print. But there are pressing matters where there is no place for antagonism and quarrelling. Where those in need request full assistance. This is why I went to the local Rabbi with mixed feelings, which I did not hide my attitude.

I must confess that I was pleasantly impressed with my conversation with the Brisker Rabbi. I have personally seen the rabbi's look of sincere concern about the situation of those who were burnt and affected by the tragedy. When others said to me that the fire affected mainly the rich and middle classes, I felt that they were wrong in their observations. I felt that something was missing from these remarks – they did not understand the causes and they did not understand that even indirectly the fire would directly affect the poor, no less and perhaps more than the rich. This came out specifically in the conversation between the rabbi and myself. He pointed out that assistance was needed for the masses – the tradesmen and laborers that were left without food. He also understood well the close relationship between the Jewish merchants/ shop owners and those tradesmen who did not own their own businesses – only small-shared places where they could work and support themselves financially in the Jewish traditional manner. He also stipulated that the delivery of the bread was to be properly distributed 'there are those who are ashamed to take, but later they will not be ashamed to take' the rabbi said. "One should deliver the bread to their homes'. The rabbi did not speak of the usual complaints about the previous committee. In his opinion, the previous committee handled what it inherited. We informed him of the new committee. The individual members did not interest him, the vital point being that there was a need for money and a huge aid operation to help the victims back on their feet. Bit by bit we were surrounded by many different types of people with various requests. Some burn victims, a rabbi from a neighboring town. The comments that were made there were not bureaucratic or formal, I recognized that they came from genuine people. During our conversation telegrams arrived for the rabbi inquiring about his health and wellbeing, and about what was happening in the city. There was no doubt that to some extent the rabbis' house was the center for lots of people. The rabbi did not have specific details, but he knew a great deal. He was knowledgeable and traditional. I regretted my previous conversation with him and before taking my leave I reminded the rabbi that I had known his father, the previous

Sage.... Yes, he had also seen me in Goldman's' printing shop, this was the truth, he remembered far more than I did....

It was a hot day, the air was full of smoke and dust – it was difficult to breathe, the pressure and tumult were frightening. Here and there were still burning pieces of timber with flickering flames. People were digging and searching, jostling and quarreling.

At every step passed by a cart with broken goods. Feathers flew through the air, metal was melted, but the feathers were not burnt. One couldn't even collect a sack of coal; all was burnt and gone with the wind. At every step, one asked the other "what's with you?"

"As you can see I came out empty". At every corner-weeping women stand. They tell of a man carrying the injured from a ruin, he panicked and fled to his village, when he arrived home, he collapsed and died. We went out from the marketplace to the avenues, the young trees were burnt, some half burnt, a terrible picture. We were not far from Finkelsteins house, we hesitated, to go to him or not? Over the course of one day, there has been havoc and chaos for him, we approach him, his face is pale and drawn, but he is braves and smiles at us: " only the manuscripts and copies have been burned. Who knows if one will ever find a copy?"

Overall, the estimated value of the damages was in the vicinity of five to six million rubles. The total population of Brest was about 50,000, of which 32-33,000 were Jews.

Apprentices would not suffer less than the shop owners and businessmen.

As far as we can detail the information in some order, the fire destroyed the following streets: Politzina, Topolowa, Bialostowka, Meadowa, Kshiva, etc. etc. The public high school burnt down, as did the nearby Jewish school. Various bureaus, both royal and military. From the Bank Vysaminikredit (managed by Finkelstein) all the money and promissory notes had been saved.... Close by was the branch of the Moscow Bank, and the trading houses of Winograd and Soloveitchik and the merchant house of the Nadiesta Company, shops and trading houses whose annual turnover was over 150,000 roubles.

The Jewish 'Hakdash" the destruction of which one can hardly complain because it was very old. About 10 Jewish religious schools, offices to the southwest, the prison – the prisoners had been transferred to the fortress. Three pharmacies, four bookshops, four large printing presses, five photographic studios and twelve hotels.

The Colonels' two beautiful houses and widespread damages suffered by the following merchants: Winograd, Halperin, Kantrovitch, Rosenberg, Berlin, Barlas, Nierdevski, etc.etc. In the park we recognized many faces, we met and talked to Finkelstein and Neumark, my companions pointed out many details that a visitor like me would not notice. I wanted to meet the old man Rabbi A.L. Feinstein but it was impossible to find him. I was told that his home and large collection of books had been burned. Also the booklet that was in his possession was destroyed. Not long before David Yellin was in Brest and had implored Feinstein to give him the booklet in the 'Name of the Faithful'.

He refused and thus was lost the most important of memoirs; one cannot describe the worth of things until they are fully lost.

15ᵗʰ May 1901

[Page 157]

The Mirror of the Press

By N. Chinich
Translated by Dr. Samuel Chani and Jenni Buch

The lives of Jews of the last generations in Europe – their strivings, customs and way of life. Battles and wranglings, the pogroms saga, the bitter cup of sorrow that spills over with a few cups of joy and consolation is mirrored in the following pamphlets and newspapers. In the following the readers will find a mirror of the press – chapters of the life of Brest from before the Holocaust. We read in these excerpts short accounts of the day-to-day events and the extraordinary events, about organizational matters, political infighting, and the problems of the community and about and those who suffered from fires, destructions, and those who sought happiness in distant lands. We read of charity and education, institutions and their branches, of the first attempts to unify the opposing aid organizations. The efforts of our elders and brethren, of entire generations of Jews to protect themselves in their birthplace not knowing that the enemy lurked and the perils ahead.

The Economic Situation
7th Febuary, 1889

The number of Jews in the town is close to 25,000. The majority are tradesmen; they sit with idle hands because trade is at a very low level. The competition is very strong. Because of the shortage of bread the number of emigrants to the U.S. is increasing and those who emigrated complain of the difficulties of establishing themselves in their new land.

Rentals have been reduced because the poorer sections have left the town and the big houses have been left untenanted – not taking into account that half the town had been burnt down. The rich have dropped their hands (stopped activity) and commerce is not flourishing. Competition is growing within the small shops. One feels a great spiritual need, there are no library reading rooms for books.

The Emigration Overseas
Hamelitz, 1888

In the last two months over 100 people migrated to the U.S. and in the previous week 18 girls have left Brest.

Hamelitz, August 1888

50 families are ready to return to Brest from America. What has strengthened is the emigration to Argentina. 116 families are ready to leave – the Consul in Warsaw assured them that the first twenty men would be sent out to see the land and of those four would return at his expense. Those who agreed to this were Rabbi H.Z. Slonimski and the "Sphirah". But Jews are an impatient race and not waiting for the reports, they all went to Argentina.

The Security Situation
Hamelitz, May 1888

There has been talk in the city about organized pogroms against the Jews. It was requested of the city's president to send guards. The peasants from the surrounding areas arrived armed with shovels and sticks. When they saw the guards, they turned back. Returning to their homes, a storm broke out, and in the village of Raveyevitch 400 sheep and cattle were killed because of the thunder and lightning – the Jews saw in this God's marvel.

Institutions
Hamelitz, Elul 1892

Witnesses are talking of the great undertakings that have been established and developed over the last few years. For example: the house of the Talmud Torah in its great glory where hundreds of poor boys from the surrounding villages and towns are studying; the hospital with its clean spacious rooms and run with wonderful efficiency.;the houses for the Bikur Cholim (hospital); the Old Age home, the Visitor's Hostel; and various other houses whose purpose was to help those who have fallen.

August 1860

The expenses of the city's Birkur Cholim reach eighty roubles weekly, therefore the Tsar has donated a thousand roubles yearly. The rest comes from the charity of the town's wealthy. There are separate rooms for men and women, a specialist doctor - a Jew from Vilna, visits daily, and almost every sick person leaves the place healthy.

The synagogue board members who managed the hospital were Rabbi Leib Landau and the famous wealthy Reb Baruch Lieb. The Rabbi, the Righteous Genius, had in his own lifetime established a new Bikur Cholim Society for everybody that became ill – whether poor or rich. If two people came to his home and wanted a bed for the night, he would give one the bed for half the night, and the other the second half of the night.

The doctor would go to the homes of the poor sick patients; the funds of the Society would pay the doctor and pharmacists. For all their other needs the sick could apply to the Society funds for payments. The Rabbi, blessed be his memory, paying attention to the smallest detail organized this. Following in his footsteps were his children – the famous teacher Wolf Padua and his brother-in-law the famous rabbi and teacher Rottenberg.

Hamagid, 5th Kislev, 1878

Who is capable of describing the praises of the modern hospital where good order reigns?

There we find help and healing for the sick. It is already two years since it was founded in our city, saving the lives of our less fortunate brethren, weakened and without hope.

They receive food and clothing there. The Bikur Cholim Society supports all the poor people in their sickbeds. The Society sends a doctor to visit the sick in their homes daily, and authorises the pharmacists to dispense the medicines without money. Every month they dispense 1000's of prescriptions. How large is the charity of this society – widows, orphans and the poor costs 80 roubles per week. In the house of the Talmud Torah there are about 600 poor children, some learn Torah and some are being taught a trade.

The establishment of the "Gemilat Chassidim Society"
Hamelitz 1880

The leading citizens of the city: Rabbi Tzvi Hirsh Orchov, Myer Schwartz, Peretz Gordon and Tzvi Chaim Burshtein collected donations from the businessmen of the city and founded the Gemilat Chassidim Society which loaned money to poor people when they were in need. They managed to collect 4,000 rubles and on Tuesday at the rabbi's house they assembled the landlords and important people of the city to form a good and useful constitution and charter for the society. This valued society will bring relief to the poor especially when expenses are rising and earnings are small.

Soup Kitchen for Children
Hamelitz 1882

The women of Brest organized an institution whereby poor children received   food.
These ladies: Sina Breindel, W. Haftig and Chava Salkind organised aid for the poor and pregnant women for whom there was also formed a free midwifery service. A doctor, medicines and food to strengthen them were also provided.

The New Society
Hamelitz 1887

A refuge for poor pregnant women. It has been over 2 years since the esteemed ladies founded a society whose aim is to provide speedy help and support for poor pregnant women. The expenses came to 30 rubles a month. Because of the difficult economic situation, donations have decreased. The heads of this society got together and appealed to the Governor of Brest for a deduction of a 1000 rubles a year off the meat tax – this was to help with the above cause. The Governor delivered this message to the City Council with the proviso that every month the council should receive an account of the society's income and expenses.

The society is called "Safehouse for Poor Pregnant Women" and the founders and administrators are: Chava Salkind, Liebshe Gvirtzman and Gitel Achavi.

The manager of the enterprise is M. Rubinrat.

Linat Tzedek Hostel
Hasphira

This undertaking is a branch of Birkur Cholim. Linat Tzedek does a great deal of charity work for all the sick, without differentiation between rich or poor. They sit at the bedside of the patient, straighten the bedclothes at night – this is also a voluntary institution including aid for widows and orphans. This society is conducted in the most orderly fashion supervised by dedicated people who give their hearts and souls to assisting poor widows and orphans. Before the High Holidays they distributed about 400 roubles amongst the poor.

All these voluntary institutions are grouped together under the common name of: The Society for the Support of the Poor in Brest.

Shomrei Shabbat
Hamelitz 1883

Our religious brethren wholeheartedly support the worthy society of Shomrei Shabbat to which about 100 members belong. They have much satisfaction every Shabbat eve when they do their duty – going and calling out to shut the shops, chasing out the women who sell vegetables and rotten apples in the market – so that they can prepare for the sanctity of the Sabbath and rest from their labors. If it happens that these guards/police work was not polite and oversteps their limits – if they damaged the merchandise – if they were cursed by the shamed indignant red cheeked repeat offenders, they are still are our brothers - also David in the desert did not want to come to the land of milk and honey.

The Trial on the Question of reading Shir Hashirim
Hamelitz 1888

In Brest there took place a trial over the fighting which broke out over the question of reading Shir Hashirim. Some demanded that Shir Hashirim not be read in public on Shabbat Chol Hamoed Pesach, and a part demanded that it should be read. It erupted into blows until the intervention of the police; all the prepared sweet food was trampled upon.

The verdict was 8 days incarceration for the rioters and that Shir Hashirim had to be read.

A Dispute between Chassidim
Hamelitz 1888

Already three months have passed since the death of the Slominer Tzaddik. The Chassidim quarreled. They said let's follow the grandson of the Old One (the Slominer Tzaddik), because the honor (birthright) belongs to him. The others said let's serve the Tzaddik Rabbi Noah from Kobryn. A fight broke out on the eve of the Sabbath and the Shteibl (prayerhouse) was turned into a battleground. 60 windows were broken and the wives of the Chassidim also took part in the holy war. The men ripped the headscarves covering the heads of the women – in the end the matter went to court – to our shame.

Talmud Torah
Hamagid 1860

The Rabbi the Sage the righteous teacher Yakov Meier from Padua was the first founder of the Talmud Torah. The distinguished and learned Rabbi Nachum Neumark came to assist him. He bought a large piece of land and built a magnificent house on it with 25 classrooms. In every classroom there is a special teacher who teaches the students from early morning until late evening – each one in a different manner. Over them is a Head of Yeshiva who studies with the best pupils commentaries and chapters. In the court yard there is a separate prayer house where the teachers pray with the students. The teachers and students receive food from the management. Those who missed out on places in the Talmud Torah receive food 3 times daily from the Talmud Torah fund.

The 2 officials that head the Talmud Torah are the famous rabbi and teacher Rabbi Eliahu Menachem Birman and his deputy the learned and virtuous Chassid, Rabbi Lipa.

Over 400 students are in this establishment, which has no steady income and is maintained by donations of 100 rubles monthly. To this is added the 150 roubles yearly for light, which is supplied by the wealthy Moshe Feivelstein, and the famous rich benefactor Halperin supplies wood throughout the year.

A Proposal to Establish a Trade School
Hamagid 1860

Yitzchak Berenblum proposes to establish in Brest a trade school. "To learn a trade so that they can earn". Every year the synagogue officials select several students from the Talmud Torah to become apprenticed to tradesman. The decision was difficult because there was no one to watch over the tradesmen that they should not abuse or overwork the children. The children were assigned to common tradesmen who often did not know their trades too well. When they finished this training period they were often not tradesmen and could not read and write in the language of the land. Several people have undertaken to form a special trades school, but the opposition is growing and there is a shortage of funds for the soup kitchen for the poor and visitors.

The Opposition to the Trades School
Hamelitz 1884

In our town which is outstanding for its' excellence and pious God-fearing Jews, there are also sinners amongst them who throw dirt on us from their accursed education. Over the last days there have been calls from our 'friends' to collect money to establish a trade school for poor children – who are our entire hope and from whom future teachers will arise ....

During the last Passover ruffians posted on the school walls large banners with the following words: 'The matter of posters for the establishment of a trades school.'

Brother Jews! You are all familiar with great suffering and frightening troubles which have come to us in the last four years in all the towns of our land. Our peace is disturbed and we are constantly hounded. Our friends have been transformed into our enemies – from all the corners of the land like sprouting grass in the field – our enemies who want to drive us out of here. They say that our existence is a burden on the country, and even if all that they proclaim is not correct, we cannot deny that we are not without these sins:

Usury. Deceit. Disgusting amounts of income.

We know that this is the result of bad upbringing – we have the opportunity to correct these faults. If we follow in the steps of the enlightened Jewish community in our land and establish a trade school in which the students will also learn holy teachings from pious and wise Jews who will pay attention to the moral standards and teach them the Russian language, arithmetic, etc. Through this our children will thereby reach a standard and will not have to, unlike their parents, resort to improper and dishonest means. We have enough money that we can also help those children from neighboring shtetls.

The tax (meat tax) that gives good incomes to those who are occupied with it will this year bring in 55,000 rubles. Of the three partners there is one who embodies a full European. On the High Holidays a liter of meat costs about 30 kopecks, the majority of the taxes goes to those whose have the controlling power and close the community doors without the payment of the 10 kopeck per liter levy. Our town derives little pleasure from that, although we are short of intelligent and courageous people who would come out in battle. Therefore we ask all the citizens of our town, whether small or great, merchant or tradesman to come out and lead the citizens of this town.

Zionism in Brest
Hamelitz Elul 1908

In this famous city there are 'Chovevei Zion' (Lovers of Zion) and in no small number, but what have they done for the purposes and success of Zion? In this city that belongs to Zion, in which there are 30,000 Jews is there not even a small number who will sacrifice for this high ideal? Can there not be found at least one in the city and at least two in the family who will support the society and help those Jews in the Holy land?

Zionist Organizations in the city
Hamelitz 1884

Yitzchak Berenbaum informs us that the youth assembled and formed a group that was called Legs of the Messenger, which is a branch of Chovevei Zion. The number of members reaches 500 and each pays no less than 2 kopecks a week, for every 10 members there is an allotted collector. At the beginning of each month these collected monies are brought to the chairman of the society or his deputy and transferred through the hands of trusted people. On the past Erev Hoshana Raba, the members went to people's homes and over 50 rubles was collected.

The protest against the people of the colony of Zichron Yakov
Hamelitz September 1888

The frightening news of a disgusting deed, which the inhabitants of the colony Zichron Yakov have done against the officials of the Commissar who organized them, caused great heartache to those noble people who showed great courage, our unfortunate brothers. This news hit our hearts just as it hit the hearts of every righteous man who follows the path of truth. Not only because it was from the land of our forefathers whose names and memories are etched on every living person of our religion and nation, but also because of the ungratefulness which the inhabitants of the colony have shown to their supporters. Such a thing has never happened to Jews before. For all that has been done for the settlement in Eretz Israel and for our nation, and when we take in account the stones that were planted on this road – we cannot hold ourselves back and must come out with an open protest and declare that all our hearts are embittered by this lawless deed.

We cannot rest; the criminals must listen and be ashamed of their wrongdoings. Perhaps they will learn from this example and not return to this silliness and there will be peace amongst the Jews.

Signed: Rabbi Zev Wolf son of the Sage and Rabbi Yakov Meir Arieh Leib Finkelstein, Benjamin Finkelstein, Yitzchak Meislich, Avraham Mordechai Finkelstein, Yakov Duber finkelstein, Shmuel Finkelstein, Benjamin Vigdorovitch, Mordechai Rottenberg, Aharon Eliezer Ravnitsky, Israel Leib Sulkes, Yosef Chesda, Alter Bocharsky, Joseph Eliezer Berlin, Betzalel Yakel, Avraham Tzvi Minc, Mordechai Podva, Avraham Moshe the sage and rabbi, Baruch Pearlman, Yakov Asher Feinstein, Tzvi Hirsh the rabbi, Rabbi Mordechai Gimpel, head of the Beth Din of Ruzhany, Ben-Zion Neumark, Meir ben Yitzchak Goldstein, Yehuda Leib Zalkiner, Mordechai Sheinerman.

List of monies collected for Eretz Yisroel on Erev Yom Kippur 1888
The Opening of the Hebrew Club
Hasphira no. 266, 1899

In this year the Zionists celebrated the opening of a Hebrew Club. About 1000 people assembled in the Great Synagogue. The chairman of the society, L.Horoditz and the distinguished chazan (cantor) have made speeches to celebrate the occasion and a lot of bonds were sold,

The Society "Tifferet Zion"
Hasphira 1900

A year has passed since the formation of the Zionist society of Tifferet Zion. Its 50 strong membership consists mainly of workers and artisans, who meet for lessons that are conducted weekly. Five young and good teachers who teach without pay teach them . Each one teaches a chapter of Tanach for that week. They also teach various other subjects. Special praise must go to the teacher Volovelski who has spared no effort in establishing this society.

The Fire of 1858
Hamagid

We also, the citizens of Brest, have drunk deeply from the cup of sorrows. In one of our houses there broke out a fire that destroyed 70 houses full of goods and 130 wooden shops. In the morning, the whole community had assembled in the synagogue to pour out their hearts in prayer for the delayed rains. All of a sudden, the noise of the burning fire could be heard. If not for the city guards and their leaders who risked their lives in order to extinguish the flames, there would be nothing left of the city. The elders of the local fortress whose hearts were steeped in love for their local brethren battled to deny the Devil his victory.

The Fire of 1881
Hamelitz

On the 28th July 1881, a fire broke out in the pharmacy. Within 6 hours 600 buildings had burnt down, shops, houses and one synagogue.

The Fire of 1888
Hamelitz

Yesterday at 10 in the morning, a large fire suddenly broke out in the city near the river, which destroyed 100 houses. The inhabitants rushed to try and save their belongings, but were not successful – they were surrounded on all sides by flames and were forced to abandon their homes. The entire efforts of the firefighters were in vain... after 2 hours the whole district and part of the street adjoining the Great Synagogue were destroyed. A woman died of the terror. Hundreds of homeless families wander around under the open skies.

The Fire of 1901
Hasphira 134, June 1901

Over 500 beautiful buildings went up in smoke, leaving about 20,000 people without a roof. The commerce and assets of millions of rubles also went up in smoke. The rich and well to do are putting out their hands for help.

Thanks to the efforts of the respected people of our city, a committee fully authorized by the Governor Pashkov was formed, consisting of 5 high ranking Christian officials, with nobles standing at their side to oversee the aid to the victims of the fire. The following were the Jewish members of this committee:

> Rabbi Nadel, Shteinberg, R, Shereshevsky, the banker Horodice, Finkelstein and the following businessmen: Hirsh, Chaim Birshtein, Yosef Eliezer Berlin, Schatz, Fineberg, Morgenstern, Temkin, and Vigdorovitch.

Within 5 weeks that this committee has existed, they have not shown much helping activity. Only 8,000 rubles are lying in the communal funds, apart from the subsidy from the Tsar, which has not as yet been collected.

R. Shereshevsky has proposed to make strenuous appeals to the ruling powers to revoke the ban on building factories and industrial plants with machinery, because the city abuts the fortress, which was of the highest military significance. Therefore it is not worthwhile for the residents to build buildings that will be empty of people (without employment).

2). After the first fire which broke out in our city 6 years ago (1895), all were convinced of the absolute necessity of buying water wagons in order to avoid such tragedies.

3). The committee found it essential to divide the city into 13 districts with 2 respected supervisors who will investigate and establish those who most urgently.need our help and support. This list was to be handed over to the committee who will determine the amount to be given.

Help for the Fire Victims
Hasphira 134, 15th June 1901.

Last Thursday there arrived in our city an important and respected guest – the Governor

He arrived in order to distribute amongst the victims the sum of 50,000 rubles that his Majesty the Tsar had personally donated.

The city dignitaries together with the Rabbis gathered in the main synagogue to bless the Tsar and the Governor, from the synagogue they then went to the town hall. Shereshevski took the position of treasurer in the kehilla without pay. From that sum, 15,000 rubles were given to soldiers and gentiles, the rest to the fire committee.

5,000 rubles were allocated for annual loans to businessmen without interest.

Help and Loans
Hasphira, 183, August 1901

The monies that the fire committee received came to 49,000 rubles, apart from the 10,000 rubles donated by the Tsar. The number of people registered for help and loans came to about 2000. 50 of these will get a loan of between 150 –500 rubles

These loans will be given to homeowners and merchants. Many small manufacturers will receive assistance of 10 –18 rubles each.

Those people who need housing will get it at cheap rates. The houses of the Society of Jewish Poor and those who live in the Talmud Torah school will get houses to rent for 25 –35 rubles a month per person.

Letter from Dr. Shershevski to the Editor of Hasphira July 1901

Esteemed editor,

Your letter containing the 1500 rubles was given to the committee for the fire victims.

Of this money, a sum of 500 rubles was given to a special committee consisting of the following members: Finkelstein, Horodice, Feinberg, and myself. This money will be divided between the teachers and pupils afflicted by the fire. I shake your hand for the honor and trust you have bestowed on me.

With care,

Dr. Yehuda Leib Shereshevski, 27th July 1901.

[Page 169]

The Last Rabbis of Brest

By Menachem Berisha
Translated by Abraham Muchnik and Jenni Buch

Rabbi Joshua Leib Diskin
a poem by Menachem Berisha.

The rabbi sits in the house of the rabbinical court, flicking through the pages of a book – but he can't concentrate on the issue at hand. Several times he takes it in his hands, but each time his ideas become jumbled.

The book " Be'er Yitzchak" was written by a friend from his youth "Dear friend" he calls him in his letters. His father's sharp mind had inspired both of them – they had sharpened their minds on the same book by the Maharam – Rabbi Menachem Schiff.

Today his friend Rabbi Yitzchak Elchanan sits on the rabbinical chair of Kovno (Kaunus) where he himself had previously sat. But the other was not just the rabbi of Kovno, but also the head rabbi of he Diaspora – and his name rings far and wide. From all the corners of the land they come to him for his judgements, the Greats of Volozhyn and Mir. His word is also accepted by royalty, and his book is world famous .He is a great facilitator; he finds a solution to every problem. He lightens the fast of Tisha Be Av and allows the use of chickpeas for Passover in a famine year.

But Joshua Leib is a strict judge and will not move a hair's breadth from the letter of the law. Would he have not allowed Passover to be in the month of Av? For whom did he suffer? Not for honor or greatness, but for justice. For the poor and underprivileged.

A wealthy and insolent man obtained the rights to collect the meat tax. As a result, the paupers could not afford to even buy a piece of offal. The rabbi called his gabbehs (synagogue deacons) and ordered them to throw out this vulgar person. But the Governor threw out the rabbi within 48 hours, not the guilty party. That's how Joshua Leib lost the rabbinical chair of Kovno and wandered in the diaspora until he was appointed to Shklov. From Shklov he came to Brest. Was he guilty of occupying his friend's seat? God forbid!! If Yitzchak Elchanan did occupy the rabbi's seat, he would have ruled over the world as a rabbinic authority. He had earned his good name, although Joshua Leib did not fall behind him in his Torah knowledge and sharpness...

One would have to look through the book; it is not enough just to ask the question. Once again he looks through the pages and immerses himself in the contents – but as many times he looks at "Be'er Yitzchak" his ideas continually become muddled...

Rabbi Joshua Leib Diskin was born in Grodno in 1817. His father, Rabbi Benjamin was a Great in Torah and was the Rabbi of Grodno, then Wolkowitz, and later Lomza. Joshua Leib already was known as a prodigy in his youth – he was knowledgeable in both the Babylonian and Jerusalem Talmuds, in the rabbinical laws, both ancient and later.

Aged 25, he inherited the rabbinical chair from his father in Lomza. But as he was a fanatical, uncompromising and very pedantic person – never trying to win favor with his congregants – he therefore could not remain in the rabbi's seat for long...

It happened that Joshua Leib suspected one of his congregants, a very wealthy man, of desecrating the Sabbath, for which he openly and publicly castigated him. The wealthy person was extremely offended. The community leaders and the other rich people of the town witnessed this and banded together in defense of their fellow townsman – and ousted the rabbi from their town. From there he became the rabbi of Mezrich, and after Mezrich there he came to the large Lithuanian city of Kovno (Kaunus) with much honor. This was a city where even the simple folk had great Torah scholars amongst them.

A stormy dispute broke concerning the one who collected the meat tax – the rabbi was unhappy with his greedy practices. But he himself was banished by the authorities from the city. He then became the rabbi of Shklov and after that rabbi of Brest.

After his first wife passed away, he married Sarah Hotner, a divorcee who brought with her a dowry of 40,000 rubles. This woman became the famous Brisker Rebbetzen. She was a very capable and educated woman and she spoke many languages. However, like her husband, she was very uncompromising and confrontationist. She was his greatest supporter, faithfully assisting him in all his community work. The Brisker Rebbetzen became famous in Lithuania and abroad; and was the subject of many articles in the Jewish press of many countries.

After the Rabbi and his wife went to the Holy Land and settled in Jerusalem, they began battling with the inhabitants of the new settlements. It was said of his wife that she ruled all the community affairs – that she was very knowledgeable and learned and that she also wore a small prayer vest (Tallit katan).

To recite another incident in Brest – it happened that a young couple came to Rabbi Diskin and asked for a divorce. The husband agreed to grant his wife a divorce on the condition that she grant him a large sum of money, to be deposited with the rabbi. This was done. After the divorce was granted, the Rebbetzen took matters into her own hands and saw to it that the agreement was nullified, and quietly returned the money to the wife. Her irate ex-husband refused to forego this payment and took the rabbi to a civil court claiming a breach of trust. The rabbi was found guilty and about to be sentenced to Siberian exile, but the Brest community saved him, and the rabbi and his wife hastily left for Israel.

From the time of his arrival, his name was amongst the signatories that demanded excommunication for the educated secular intellectuals and the atheist unbelievers. He was against modern education and the rebuilding of Israel by establishing new Jewish settlements. However, he considered the act of settling in Israel as holy. In 1881 he agreed to be the Jerusalem representative of the Society of the Founders of the Settlement, which founded to build Petach Tikva. He also gave this society his support by sending emissaries to various countries in the Diaspora to collect monies for this cause.

He founded the large Orphanage home in Jerusalem, where unfortunate and abandoned children could learn both Torah and a trade. He was the director of this institution until his death.

He left behind many manuscripts with revisions of the laws and illustrated examples, which were preserved in the library of the orphanage - these revisions were called "the Questions and Answers of Rabbi J.L. Diskin" (Jerusalem 1911). Also published after his death was the book "Yalkut Amarim" (Satchel of Sayings) which was a collection of commentaries on the Torah.

He died in Jerusalem on the 29th Tevet 1898.

The Brisker Rebbetzen

Rabbi J.L. Diskin's second wife Sarah was famed as the Brisker Rebbetzen. She was learned and knowledgeable in all the laws. She was very strict in the matter of orthodoxy and mixed into all the community affairs. She had very strong mind; she came from a very prestigious family – she was the granddaughter of the rabbi "Nodah BeYehudah" – and she also came from the wealthy family of Joshua Zeitlin. When she married Joshua Diskin she brought with her a sum of 40,000 rubles (a huge amount in those days), with which they built the J.L. Diskin Orphanage in Jerusalem.

Although she had very strong opinions, she was very knowledgeable in the laws of what was forbidden and what was permitted – she would even at times give her opinion in front of her husband the rabbi. And it would happen that she sometimes disagreed with her husband's rulings. Joshua Lieb's method was to try and make things easier for people – the Rebbetzen was far stricter.

Once, on the eve of Passover, a Jew came and asked a question - a kernel of corn had fallen into the soup.... Rabbi Diskin considered and decided that the soup remained kosher for Passover. When his wife the rebbetzen heard this, she jumped into the conversation and said:" Although I'm not allowed to give my opinion in front of my husband the rabbi, if we should follow Rabbi Diskin's verdict, then God forbid, the whole city would eat Chometz during Passover!"

After the writing of the marriage contract, she said to her husband the groom Joshua Leib: " Mazal Tov! Don't take your brides blessing lightly...."

On the eve of Passover she would even scour the door handles, afraid that there was a residue of Chometz on them.

It was said that she was responsible for the majority of disputes and fights between the Neturei Carta and the leaders of the new Zionist settlements.

She passed away in Jerusalem in 1907, and was accorded much honor after her death. She once asked her husband: " why did the sages create the blessing that is said every morning by males thanking God for not making me a woman? Is the shoemaker who can't learn the Torah or Gemarra better then me who is educated and learned? Or is it because I am I woman that I am inferior? "

The rabbi replied: "every man says this blessing, but only in regards to his own wife. The rabbi thanks God that he is not his wife the Rebbetzen! The shoemaker thanks God that he is not his wife...."

One Passover eve, after the burning of all the Chometz, the rabbi said: "I have already cleaned all the Chometz that is in my property, except this Chometz (pointing at his wife) which I can't get rid of....". " You are wrong" she answered her husband, "this Chometz doesn't have to be cleaned out because my father already sold it long ago to a Gentile!

[Page 175]

Rabbi Joseph Dov Ber Soloveitchik

Translated by Abraham Muchnik and Jenni Buch

Rabbi Joseph Dov Ber (Yoshe Ber) was a relative of Rabbi Chaim Volozhyner. In his youth he studied in the Volozhyn yeshiva and became renowned as a prodigy for his outstanding and keen intellect. It was said of him that as a child he already knew entire tractates by heart. As he grew into adulthood, he became famous for his penetrating insight and incisive understanding of universal dilemmas. He was close to the common man and also strove for a close relationship with learned men. He became very eager to meet Rabbi Shlomo Kluger of Brody and to become close to him personally, feeling that he would benefit from his pure wisdom and great knowledge of the Torah. The long journey from Volozhyn to Brody at that time was however fraught with difficulties and risks, and also great expense. What did Rabbi Yoshe Ber the son of a pauper do?

He hired himself as a teacher to the son of a wagon driver, traveling with him until they reached a town near Brody. In that town he again hired himself as a teacher to a driver, thus he went from one wagon driver to the next until he reached Brody and was privileged to study there for a time with Rabbi Kluger. During the time that he worked for the wagon drivers as an assistant, he collected the experiences and stories that later reflected his astuteness and sharp observations of people – the relationship between the uneducated and the learned scholars and rabbis. In reality, his wanderings were concerned with the miserable horses and their owners who walked them slowly, step by step, stopping at steep difficult hills. Rabbi Yoshe Ber witnessed the day-to-day existence of these poor folk – he combined what he had witnessed with his great learning in his writings that later became an integral part of the treasure of our folk wisdom.

Upon the death of Rabbi Eliezer Yitzchak (the son in law of Rabbi Volozhyner) the head of the Volozhyn yeshiva, they searched for a replacement. There were differences of opinion whether it should be Rabbi Naphtali Tzvi Yehuda Berlin who was known as the "Natziv", or Rabbi Yoshe Ber. For along time, the debate raged as to who of the two was better... The "Natziv", the quiet achiever, the Mt Sinai, or the mover of mountains? Finally they decided to go to a rabbinical court of four rabbis for a decision. The rabbis decided in favor of the "Natziv".

Rabbi Yoshe Ber left Volozhyn and took the position of rabbi in Slutsk. However, not only was he great in Torah and the problems of the world, he was also resolute and unwavering in his opinions. He never sought favour with the synagogue officials and would make no exceptions for the wealthy. He punished the lawbreakers and confronted he hypocrites in his congregation. It was not long before a bitter dispute broke out within the congregation because of him and he had to resign his position as rabbi of Slutsk. For several years he earned no income - when the position of rabbi of Brest became vacant he humbly recommended that Rabbi J.L. Diskin was more suited to the position and personally intervened on his behalf to the Brest community.

When Rabbi Diskin was forced to leave Brest, only then did Rabbi Yoshe Ber occupy the rabbinical seat of Brest – occupying this high office until his death in 1892. He left behind him a large volume called "The House of Levi" which contained much sophistry and writings about Jewish laws. He possessed a strong allegorical talent. His writings about the weekly Torah chapters were presented in an attractive style, containing clever reasoning and ethics. He included short stories with details intended to enlighten and uplift the soul. From these stories we can see that Rabbi Yoshe Ber was not only a genius instilled with the highest morals and ethics, he had listened and learnt from those select and talented scholars who had both understanding and emotions combined together with enthusiasm and alertness, learning with compassion. Because of these personality traits, Rabbi Joseph Dov Ber Soloveitchik occupied a very important position in the gallery of great rabbis of the world.

As well as the books he left us, and his famous name, he also left us his son, the famous Rabbi Chaim Soloveitchik, whose skill was as strong as his father's, if not greater.

[Page 185]

Rabbi Chaim Soloveitchik

Translated by Abraham Muchnik and Jenni Buch

Rabbi Chaim Soloveitchik was born in the town of Volozhyn in 1853. His father, Rabbi Joseph Ber was the Rosh (head) of the Volozhyn Yeshiva. Whilst still a child Chaim already excelled in his intelligence and sharp intellect. At the age of twenty he married the daughter of Rabbi Raphael Shapiro who was the Rosh Yeshiva at that time. In 1880 Chaim was appointed as head of the yeshiva – his name was already famous as a genius and sage of the Torah. Over the next twelve years he taught thousands of students amongst whom were some of the greatest Torah scholars. In 1892 the Russian authorities closed down the Volozhyn Yeshiva, and Rabbi Chaim went to his father's home in Brest. In the same year his father passed away and Rabbi Chaim became the Rabbi of Brest.

After the expulsion of the Jews from their city in 1915, Rabbi Chaim arrived in Minsk and lived there until 1918. On his doctor's orders he settled in the town of Otwotsk, and on a Tuesday the 21st of Av, he passed away.

Rabbi Chaim's strength was not only in the Torah, but also in his quest for truth. With his sharp intellect, he would analyse every detail. He would delve into the sea of the Talmud and discover pearls. His teachings possessed the greatest power of clarity and giving understanding by explanation. He would say " the inability to explain a matter shows in itself, that you don't understand it".

With his methods of analysis, Rabbi Chaim was able to explain clearly the commentaries of the Firsts –the great sages of the Torah – the Rambam (Maimonides), and the Ravid (Rabbi Avraham Ben David). His book: "New

Commentaries of Rabbi Chaim the Levi" (Brest 1896) was published many times with additions and clarifications about the writings of the Rambam.

His great love of truth was expressed not only in his style of teaching but also in his personal behaviour. This brought him great respect and honor – also from people who did not grasp his greatness in Torah. He was described by everyone as "Man of Truth". His ideas, speeches and actions were completely intertwined with his honesty.

Rabbi Chaim would not seek favor with anyone, and would not concede his opinions, even if it meant displeasing someone influential. On the occasion of Professor Kwalson's 50th birthday, all the Jewish towns sent congratulatory telegrams; even some famous rabbis found it proper to congratulate him due to his defence of Beylis against the blood – libel accusation, and his great influence with the ruling powers of that time. When the Brest officials came with the telegram to Rabbi Chaim and suggested that he also sign it he refused, saying: " I don't send telegrams to converts".

On another occasion he refused to sign a petition to the Tsar that was sent by a rabbinical assembly saying: " why should I send a petition to this cruel king?" When there was no reaction and result to this petition, only then did the rabbis admit that Rabbi Chaim had been correct.

In matters of Torah and the public interest Rabbi Chaim was very conservative and a zealot who would not give in at all. He opposed the new methods of education and the new administration and resisted any changes or reforms. However, his opinion was accepted by all different sections of the community who followed and obeyed him. In 1905 there were waves of unrest and strikes in all the cities of Russia. The factory workers in Brest also petitioned their employers and went out on strike. The workers were keen for Rabbi Chaim to intervene on their behalf in this matter. Rabbi Chaim got involved and influenced the employers to concede to the workers demands.

Rabbi Chaim was an opponent of the Zionists, but without malice and did not fight them as aggressively as some others did. On the other hand, he did much to help the settlement in Eretz Israel in that time. Certain yeshivas and establishments in Jerusalem were under his supervision. He was a Mitnaged and the son of a Mitnaged, but very few attained the respect and were as treasured – even by the Chassidic followers in Brest. Also the Chassidic rabbis respected him and valued his opinions. We cannot say that Rabbi Chaim ever recognized the Chassidic movement, but he never denied that it was a creative power in Judaism.

It was said that anyone who witnessed Rabbi Chaim's self sacrifice and compassion after the great fire of 1895, would never again see such utter compassion in their lives. After the fire, Rabbi Chaim would not sleep in his home, but went to the synagogue and slept on the floor there – when his family tried to convince him to sleep in his own bed he said:" I cannot sleep in my own bed, when so many others here have no roof over their heads".

Rabbi Chaim's home was a home to the Sages, to the talented students, learned men and others who passed through Brest. His doors were open to every pauper and everyone in need, to every troubled and embittered man. He did not possess riches and did not own any assets. No one hated corruption, extortion and dishonesty more than he did. He gave generously to the poor and the charities.

Two wealthy Brest Jews came to Rabbi Chaim and gave him an envelope containing bridal monies for a couple that he was to marry. At the same time, a beggar came to his door and asked for a donation – Rabbi Chaim did not hesitate, took the envelope, and gave it to the pauper.

The Funeral Of Rabbi Chaim Soloveitchik

In a correspondence to the Yiddish newspaper "Warheit" in New York, we find an interesting and detailed account of the last tributes and honors given by the Jews of Warsaw to Rabbi Chaim Soloveitchik, blessed be his memory:

The funeral was most impressive – the entire city was engulfed in deep sorrow when the death notices were pasted throughout the city saying: Today at 4.35 in the afternoon in the town of Otwotsk, a Great of our generation has passed away, the Rabbi of all the diaspora Jews, the Sage Rabbi Chaim Soloveitchik (blessed be his memory), of Brest.

The Jews of Otwotsk would not allow the honor to be taken away from their community and would not allow the Warsaw community to remove Rabbi Chaim's body from their town. In the presence of all the rabbis a ruling was issued that the Jews of Otwotsk would perform the purification ceremony, but that he would be buried in Warsaw.

A large crowd - representatives of all the neighboring communities – amongst them many Rabbis and Rebbes assembled in Otwotsk to participate in the funeral procession. Later in the evening, his coffin was brought in a special train to Warsaw. People streamed from all over the city to accompany the train. Hundreds of youths from various organizations (with the exception of the Bund), restrained the crowd. Amongst those who accompanied the coffin were the leaders of the Brest Aid Society with Shereshevski the spokesman for the Jewish community, as well as L. Davidson, Dr Poznanski, and Rabbi Kahane as the representative of the rabbinate together with other famous rabbis.

An honor guard took over the train at the station and entered the carriage where the coffin lay accompanied by the family of Rabbi Chaim and the dignitaries of Brest. Official authorization was given for the burial of Rabbi Chaim Soloveitchik. The coffin was carried out by a select group of rabbis and officials, and an entire delegation of cheder youths and yeshiva students filed past the coffin, row by row. His entire family followed behind the coffin, and behind them were thousands of mourners accompanying them through the Jewish quarters where all the businesses and shops closed as a sign of sorrow and mourning.

Tens of thousands of Jews walked to the cemetery to pay their last respects to the deceased. Then the eulogies began with the Chief Rabbi of Warsaw, Rabbi Perlmutter, followed by a eulogy from Rabbi Chaim's best student, Rabbi Gutshechter. When they began to dig the grave in the tomb of the

"Natziv" - Rabbi Naftali Tsvi Judah Berlin of Volozhyn, the group of prominent Brest residents announced to all that they had decided to appoint Rabbi Chaim's son, Rabbi Ze'ev Soloveitchik, as rabbi to their community. Everyone said "Mazel Tov". After the grave was filled with earth, everyone broke out sobbing.

Published in New York 13th November 1918.

[Page 199]

Books By the Greats of Brisk D'Lita

Translated by Dr. Samuel Chani and Jenni Buch

Even Moshe by Rabbi Moshe Bar Aharon of Brisk	Warsaw	1858
Letter from the Gaon Rabbi David Oppenheim	Nicklesburg	1698
Letter from Yehosetah the Righteous from the land of Israel. By Rabbi Simcha son of the Holy Rabbi Pesach of Brisk	Mantova	1675
Four Cups by Rabbi Avraham Yitzchak-Josef from the other side of the River Brisk	Altona	1781
Ha-Aroch Mesach with an explanation from his grandson Rabbi Aharon of Brisk	Berlin	1765
Bayit Chadash by Rabbi Joel Sirkis	Krakow	1630
Bet Yakov by Rabbi Yakov Schor (Av Beth Din in Brisk). Tshuvot (Responsa).	Venice	1652
Birkat Hazevach by Rabbi Shmuel Kaidanover.	Kaf Taf Yud Amsterdam	1669
Birkat Shmuel by Rabbi Shmuel Kaidanover.	Frankfurt Am Main	1771
Gedulat Shaul by Rabbi Tzvi Edelman.	London	1853
Chai Ariel by Rabbi Zundel of Bialystok	Vilna	1837
Zichron Moshe by Rabbi Moshe Livshitz (Av Bet Din in Brisk).	Lublin	1611
Zerah Avraham by Rabbi Avraham ben Benyamin.	Willsbach	1724
Chidushei Halachot by the Gaon Rabbi Heshel.	Warsaw	1891
Chidushei Ha Resh Yud by Rabbi Yakov ben Levi.	Grodno	1672
Helkat Mechokek by Rabbi Moshe Lima	Krakow	1670
Yad Eliahu - Tshuvat – by Rabbi Eliahu ben Rabbi Shmuel.	Amsterdam	1711
Likutei Dinim (Collection of Laws) Questions and Answers by Rabbi Moshe of Brisk.	Kaf Taf Yud	
Perush HaMeir – printed by Rabbi Moshe son of Rabbi Shmuel of Brisk	Berlin	1758
Manginei Shlomo by the Gaon Rabbi Yehuda son of Rabbi Yosef (Av Bet Din of Brisk).	Amsterdam	1714
Minchat Yehuda By Rabbi Ovadia Ellenberg.	Lublin	1589
Meshiv Nefesh by the Gaon Joel Sirkis (Ha Bach)	Lublin	1616
Mayim Amokim by Rabbi Mordechai the son of Rabbi Nachman.	Zalkady	1745

Minchat Aharon by the Gaon Rabbi Aharon ben Rabbi Meir	Novy Dvir	1811
Mefaresh Hatarim by Rabbi Moshe son of Rabbi Yitzchak of Brisk	Amsterdam	1705
Mekor Mayim Chaim by Rabbi Meir Podva	Priklev	1811
Seder Halitzah by Rabbi Zalman of Brisk	Oppenheim	1702
Porat Yosef by Rabbi Yosef -Yossel of Brisk.	Wanovek	1626
Perush Al Eser Atarot by Rabbi Avraham son of Rabbi Benyamin	Frankfurt Am Main	1698
Penei Yehoshua by Rabbi Yehoshua son of Rabbi Yosef.	Amsterdam	1715
Pilpul Hacharifta by the Gaon Rabbi Yakov Shor.	Amsterdam	1672
Perush al Sefer Eser Ma-amarim by the Gaon Rabbi Mem Shin	Kaf Taf Yud	
Pesher Davar by Rabbi Yitzchak the son of Rabbi Yoef-Yossel.	Altona	1675
Petach Ha Dvir by Rabbi Yosef Meir Yona (Av Bet Din of Brisk),	Vilna	1875
Shaagat Arieh by Rabbi Leib (Av Bet Din of Brisk and Krakow),	Neivit	1692
Questions and Answers – Bayit Chadash by the Gaon Joel Sirkis	Frankfurt Am Main	1616
Questions and Answers – Bach Hachadashot by the Gaon Joel Sirkis	Koretz	1784
Questions and Answers – by Rabbi Mordechai Ziskin Rotemberg	Hamburg	1690
Shaarit Yakov by Rabbi Yakov son of Rabbi Yoel of Brisk.	Altona	1725
Shar Chadash al Haltur by the Gaon Rabbu Meir Yona	Vilna	1873
Shiftei Ha Chamim by Rabbi Yakov ben Moshe Trichash of Brisk	Frankfurt Am Main	1711
Tvuat Shemesh by Rabbi Meir ben Aharon	Berlin	1783
Toldot Aharon by the Gaon Rabbi Heshel	Frankfurt Am Main	1725
Tvuat Shor al Haturim by Rabbi Ephrsim Zalman Shor	Lublin	1615
Kutonet Passim by Rabbi Yakov Meir Podva	Warsaw	1905
Tshuvot Macharim by Rabbi Meir Yona Podva	Warsaw	1896
Nachalei Mayim Ve Ein Hamayim by Rabbi Yakov Meir Podva	Warsaw	1883
Bet Halevi by Rabbi Yosef Ber Soloveitchik	Warsaw	1865
Bet Halevi by Rabbi Yosef Ber Soloveitchik	Warsaw	1866
Ezrat Yehuda by Rabbi Isser Yudel	Warsaw	1876
Nechamat Yehuda by Rabbi Isser Yudel	Warsaw	1883
Can-Can Bossem by Rabbi Yudel Epstein	Koenigsberg	1866
Minchat Yehuda Al Shas By Rabbi Yudel Epstein	Warsaw	1876
Or Hatzvi by Rabbi Tzvi Hersh Barlas	Lublin	1874
Maagalot Or by Rabbi Lipman ben Rabbi David	Warsaw	1867
Meorei Bet Yitzchak by Rabbi Uri Eizik	Jerusalem	1865
Beur al Midrash Tehilim by Rabbi Aharon Moshe Podva	Warsaw	1864
Beur al Psiktah D' Tuvia by Rabbi Aharon Moshe Podva	Vilna	1851
Talpiot, Beur Al Hagadah By Rabbi Arieh Leib Feinstein	Warsaw	1870
Ir Tehila by Rabbi Arieh Leib Feinstein	Warsaw	1886

[Page 203]

Brisk D'Lita - A Poem

By Menachem Berisha
Translated by Dr. Samuel Chani and Jenni Buch

Where the smaller Mukhavets and the wider Bug rivers meet. Three nations met and formed a settlement on its flat shores. When did this happen? Its beginnings are shrouded in the early kings of Poland and have been eradicated by the German monster.

Three nations – Lithuania, Poland and Wolyn. Forests stretching over 100s of miles, green gardens, hives with honey, and cottages with weaving looms.

The wagons roll by and the Jews conduct their business on land and over water, and they pay their taxes and tithes for Torah and charity.

They pay the king a part of their revenues – he gives the Jews good protection.

So live the merchants, the arendars, and the tradesmen.

The Ukrainians break out in a period of robbery and violence.

Cossacks are rushing in with a brand of slaughter, rolling in blood and destruction.

Rolling around in blood of Brisk D'lita. Standing up and not waiting for the pain of the Shloshim (mourning period).

On the old road, the old wheels will make noise. The gentiles are buying salt and alcohol.

Powers fall, the Moscovites come, already having put in their pockets Wolyn and Lithuania – now he goes after Poland. To put fur on his back, along comes the Moscovite and says: 'here it is necessary to build a fortress on the Bug'.

And the town forcibly moved backwards. Is there any point of arguing with such a storm? The old city shifts towards the banks of the Mukhavets.

They carry and drag the carts, pull the baggage with utensils and dishes. Where there was a cemetery, there is now a fish market. From the small woods, a church with a large cross was constructed. In the big houses, with pockets full of gold, the Moscovites are building on swamps, building and paying. Employed are the merchants, the tradesmen, the painters and carpenters. Also came the barracks and shops. Breaking from the warmth, in the churches ring the silver in the bells. From the port every day sound the guns. Streets, shops, markets are full of soldiers. And the mothers and fathers click their tongues.

The soldiers need kasha (buckwheat) and uniforms. And the officers like to have a drink and if woman walk past, they don't stop from making acquaintance.

Knowledge of Russian - not without curses – a stamp is required for everything.

The butcher's shops and the street of red lights, the poor cook berries during the week

There is enough as not to scrimp every penny so they built here a big synagogue and school and a mikvah for women.

One can hear the Brest heavens rain with poppy seed. Drawn towards Brest are tradesmen, middlemen, and the poor that arrive on foot, or train or covered wagon.

For every rich person there are 10 poor people, and the poverty grows between rags and silks.

_____

MEMORIES AND DESCRIPTIONS

What My Memory Reveals

By Rabbi I.Y.Unterman, (Chief Rabbi of Tel-Aviv)
Translated by Dr. Samuel Chani and Jenni Buch

In the small synagogue in which my father prayed (The synagogue of Shamai Weint) as they called it, there also prayed one of the leading teachers of the city.

Rav Moishe Aharon Weitzblum was an exceptional Jew. In the town they called him Moishe Aharon Hamotzeh. He was famous as a brilliant pupil, expert in rulings governing disputes between a man and his friend; he did not belong to the usual type of Dayan (religious judge). He did not have any children and in his old age he made aliyah to Israel. He rests permanently in Jerusalem.

Besides his great knowledge of Torah and instruction, he was known as a practical person, a fox with a shrewd intellect in complicated matters.

The local rabbis involved him in the matters of Din Torah, the law of the Torah.

In the synagogue, his influence was demonstrated by how he knew to attract the young people. They were drawn closer to the Torah and were guided by his sound methods of understanding life His entire demeanor commanded respect. Everything that he did was thought through with great attention to detail. He modeled himself on the Vilna Gaon and oversaw everything in the Beth Hamidrash (prayer house and school) that it should be according to the law. He gave special attention to the reading of the Torah so it should remain clear according to the principles of grammar (this was not the custom in our region). He warned against Mileh and Milrah, which was the emphasis on the first and last syllables and pronunciation of each word.

In his home, cleanliness and order reigned.... although his income was limited.

The young men had the special pleasure of going for walks with him and listening to his conversation, from which one could always learn.

Blessed be his memory.

B

In the rabbinical school, they always called on Rav Tzvi Orenstein, who had by his own efforts, opened a school for youths, without a head of Yeshiva, without an office and without an administration. From Brest and surroundings, as well as distant towns, good youths streamed to his school and with enthusiasm they learnt Torah. This began in about 1873 and lasted for several years. The force that attracted students from afar was the desire to be close to Reb Chaim, blessed be his memory, who taught the older youths.

There were also younger boys present, who did not participate in the lessons but were drawn by the atmosphere of the Great Yeshiva. It was is this same Yeshiva that I myself began to learn in as a child a year before my Bar Mitzvah. The older boys were very dear to me, I want to tell here of the exceptional people who have remained in my memory.

In the Beth Hamidrash there were the notable businessmen who were famed in Torah and also everyday matters and needs. I can visualize one of them, Reuven Aharaka, a flour merchant. With all his heart and energies he found financial support for the pupils who came to learn from outside the city – he himself supported the great sages because this was his only aim. In the evenings he could be seen walking around between the rows of students, observing them and taking pleasure in their diligence, (not having had the opportunity himself to reach this level of learning). This pleasure gave him the drive and energy for his work.

Until today, I cannot understand how a single person managed to find such large sources of income (donations). He influenced the public with his simple sincerity, and managed to fund and support the pupils over some years – amongst them were those who later became famed in the whole world and became the great teachers of sages.

I remember that for a very short time, the Sage, the author of "Hazan Ish" was sitting on a bench engrossed in an open Gemarrah, and studying in a quiet voice without raising his eyes. I did not dare question him, but I had the feeling that this youth would become a great man. I remember also that all of a sudden appeared a diligent pupil whom they called the 'Setzer Matmid', later I found out that he was as successful in his studies as they thought he would be -he slept only a few hours a night –he became a great scholar.

Reb Reuven Aharaka would stand hour after hour, entranced by the melody of the learning, his face shining with joy. This simple Jew, he by himself supported the entire institution, finding supporters and organizing everything with an inner strength driven by love for the Torah. Let us remember him with love.

C

There was a smaller synagogue that was called the 'Beth Hamidrash of Natan Tishper'. It was said that this name stemmed from the time of the old city, (before the city was moved west at the time of the building of the fortress). It stood on the side of the road that led to Kobryn. There, I saw many outstanding people of whom I will only mention two:

Hirsh Beilin – a great student who could recite a lesson in Gemarrah with rare depth and extraordinary clarity.

Rabbi David Feinsilber – who after W.W.1 shifted to Wolkowitz to take up the position of Dayan.

The former I only knew from a distance, the latter however, I met years later and then corresponded with him about matters of Torah. His occupation was as a supplier of goods to the Russian army. Every morning he would travel to the fortress outside the city, but he made great efforts not to cut himself off from his Torah studies. This is how he conducted himself – every morning he would rise early and study together with a gifted student who came to his house, the friend always brought something new which he had spotted in a book – an interesting question or topic, a matter to be debated over or reflected upon on his way to the fortress. The next morning he would tell his friend what his thoughts and discoveries were about the matter. Thus, I was told, he conducted himself for years.

He knew very well of worldly matters and was also a very pleasant person. In my memories, these people were personified as having many worthy attributes and participated with dedication for the good of the community. Feinsilber also needs to be remembered of a fine example of a courteous, genteel Jew.

D

The synagogue of the 'Elite' was the name given to the Mishmar synagogue that was on the banks of the Mukhavets River. There were people there who achieved a place of greatness in Torah. The best known of then was Reb. Zalman Lifshitz, Reb Tzvi Hirsh Yaffe, the son of Mordechai Gimpel Yaffe and others. In my childhood, I listened to a lesson from Rabbi Simcha Zelig, and sometimes I would sit 'guard'. My heart was particularly attracted to two youths who were studying together and there were always heated debates among them. Rabbi Moishe Sokolovsky who later became a Sage of Torah and the second, Rabbi Henoch who later became the rabbi of Malorita, and returned to Brest to become Rosh Yeshiva (the head of the yeshiva).

These two friends had various abilities and talents – the first did not distinguish himself with a quick grasp but he possessed a rare strength of concentration.

He would preoccupy himself for a long time over one sentence and would tackle the matter from all sides without interruption.

In his books (Omerei Moshe and Malchat) one can indeed see that his intellect was very developed and that his lessons were undertaken with wonder and awe. The second one had a lighter grasp and one could see how he advanced his friend by introducing relevant matters and their debates were very interesting,

The former did not have any children; his students remained loyal to him and spoke of his greatness. He was head of the yeshiva in Brest for many years and had a lasting influence on his students.

The fate of the latter in unknown to me –he was brilliant, there were not many like him.

Blessed be their memories.

Rabbi I. Y. Unterman

[Page 211]

CHAPTERS OF LOCAL LIFE

In My Parents' Home

By Michael Pochachevski
Translated by Dr. Samuel Chani and Jenni Buch

My mother was of short stature, but a handsome and wise woman, gentle and modest in her demeanor. Only deep in her heart she prided herself on her prestigious origins.

She was the daughter of a famous teacher who had wandered in towards the east from Western Europe, seeking refuge in the Torah, after the sun was setting in the west.

My mother was orphaned as a child and was brought up by a stepmother, a woman who disgraced her piety; she had married my grandfather with the hope of procuring a good place in the coming world. Despite her status and righteousness, she was a difficult person who really gave her stepchildren a very hard time, to the extent that my grandfather married my mother off at a very early age.

My father's parents were well off - my grandfather was socially active and owned a factory that he had established without means or money, but by a lot of hard work and skill. He was also distinguished himself - he was descended from the author of 'Tiferet Israel", a commentary on the Mishnah, but because he was orphaned since childhood, he had to work and had no time to give himself up to studies. My grandmother married him after he had already established himself. She was a woman of valor with extraordinary skills – she helped him in business until her good name was known in the whole area – the business was conducted with an open generous hand. At the same time she was a great housewife and brought up and married her children to famous families.

My grandmother was a clever woman with a good heart – she would take the food out of her mouth to share. Her financial situation being excellent, she decided that all her children, grandchildren, and great-grandchildren should surround her like a queen in the beehive. Her four married sons and two daughters ate at her table, which was usually set in readiness for all the workers in her factory – drivers, porters, and everyone who was connected with the business. All those men were counted as sons of the house. Also, the woodchoppers and water carriers from the district would come and eat their midday meal as if in their own home, and every beggar who came at mealtimes would receive his share.

When I was a small child a fire broke out in our street and this patriarchal house was burnt to the ground. It did not last long and in place of this house a two-story brick house was built. My grandmother gave instructions to the architect to draw plans to build the house in the form of a beehive to accommodate all of her children. And so it was. The entire family shifted into the new house. They ate together and gathered collectively in the spacious dining room, which adjoined the rooms for the aged relatives. Until today, I have never forgotten the Sabbaths and high Holydays, when the children, small and large, sat around the table with the Queen at its head, how much pleasure and enjoyment she derived!

When Succoth came in the year 1866, the beehive buzzed with the expectation of the coming holidays – all slaved feverishly – also I was amongst the grandchildren that was busy preparing the Simchat Torah flags, the celebration was disturbed however, in the middle of the holidays there was an outbreak of a cholera plague which claimed thousands of victims ... also our house was not spared and grandmother fell victim in the middle of Simchat Torah. This was a tragedy that I had to face front on in my young life – the sorrow permeated every corner of the house. With the death of the Queen the beehive emptied of all its contents. The first sign of the disintegration of the house was the separation of the main common dining table from the previously held and honored tradition of communal dining. My grandfather, seeking consolation from his grief, threw himself into business and community affairs and the private family matters he handed over to his elder sons to watch over "the tribe of brothers together...."

The first to leave the house was my father –he could not come to terms with the collective structure of the household – because he believed that it caused laziness in many members of the family. Regretfully, not all the children had inherited their mother's love of work and the spirit of love thy neighbor as thyself in which my grandmother was outstanding. She had excelled as the head of the family and the management of the household.

My father's exit was a revolt against holy tradition in the eyes of my grandfather.

He was enraged and in great anger disinherited my father. Only years later, when he had quietened down in the last years of his life, did he repent and return his rights to him. My grandfather's great love of work was not inherited by all of his children. However, they did inherit his special qualities – a spark of the mechanic was in all of us. Nothing was too difficult to take on - they loved the business. I was four and a half years old when our town received its first railway line. When the line reached the River Bug that flows with a strong current 8 kilometers from our town, the Jews beat their brains wondering how it was possible for this railway to cross this dangerous, impudent river. This especially intrigued my father –when they started to erect the iron bridge over the river, he ignored the law on the sanctity of the Sabbath and went to look at the works.

He always loved mechanical things. He didn't wait and took me, his only son, along with him. My mother did not know that he planted a love of manual work and skills in my young heart. She cried bitter tears over the fate of her poor child that was forced every Sabbath to take the long walk to see the building works.

This seed that my father planted in my young did its work – I also developed a love of mechanical skills. Machines and constructions have always fascinated me. The reigning customs of our Jewish world were against the development of my talents. My mother, who was conforming very much to tradition, would not allow me to learn a trade. She very much wanted me to develop my spiritual side, inherited from her own father, the famous scholar. My mother, who was true to the tradition, believed that tradesmen were more lowly people, who were only born to serve the talented students. They could not expect more than to end up in Hell.

Despite this, my mother was a good-natured soul who cared very much for her children and therefore I did not have the courage to rebel against her. However, when the time came and I was fed up with the meaningless life of my childhood in our town, I developed a strong desire to do something productive. I decided to leave the family nest and go out into the greater world. A battle developed in our home and when I saw the tears shining in my good mother's eyes l could not withstand her pleading any more.

Later when I came to the age of military service, my father with great efforts and much money, obtained the exemption rights of the only son. For all my desire to leave the empty life and to take up a trade – nothing became of that.

In the Beth Hamidrash (Synagogue school)

My only place of refuge was the place where I spent most of my time as did the other children of my age, and that was the house of study. There I had the opportunity to observe people and learn about life. Here I will recall several figures:

Reb Baruch Hirsh the Blacksmith.

I remember him – despite of his 70 years he was physically healthy and had a strong voice. When the city would listen to the first prayers asking forgiveness, Baruch Hirsh would recite the prayers - old and young alike would patiently wait to have the pleasure of hearing him praying. Once, I was carried along by the crowd to go and listen to how he expressed his prayers. He did not have a sweet voice but every word that came out of his mouth was heart rending, mournful and penetrating with the pain of thousands in the Diaspora.

It is interesting how Baruch Hirsh became a blacksmith. In the past the respected merchants and businessmen of the Jewish community would go to the Heads of the Yeshivas looking for talented, clever youths – capable scholars for their future sons in law. When it came time to marry -the dowry and board were given for several years so that the son in law could sit and study in the local yeshiva. Then when the sharp awakening of "what and how will we eat?" arose, then one would get rabbinical ordination, or learn Schitah (ritual slaughtering) so that one could make a living from that profession. Not one of these 'holy vessels ' ever took to trade or business.

As for Baruch Hirsh they said that he was a learned jewel of a learned scholar. He was studying in the yeshiva of one of the neighboring towns. In our town there was a blacksmith, knowledgeable in Torah, and he had an only daughter. He wished for a learned and clever student as a bridegroom for his daughter. He went away and found Baruch Hirsh – a yeshiva student who had all these talents – in addition he could hold a melody with a beautiful sweet voice. When he would lead the congregation in prayer, he would give them great pleasure. He was even lengthening the prayers – people left his prayer house on Sabbath and the high Holydays later than from other places of prayer. This young man had a very good reputation and everybody wished for such a son in law. However, from time to time, a strange thing would happen to him. This refined young man would role up his sleeves and labor in the heavy work of the blacksmith's workshop. He learned the trade properly and took the place of his father in law. He exemplified the adage: "Leave the rabbinical and love the trade". However, he did not forsake his love of the cantorial singing. In his old age he gave up blacksmithing and became a renowned bookseller in the district. But the name of Baruch Hirsh – blacksmith, stayed with him all his life. The older people would tell stories of him and his anvil, and how he would not even perspire at the hardest of tasks. Yet when he led the prayers on the Holydays, he would be bathed in perspiration and fresh clothes were brought for him so that he could change in the special room allotted to him in his prayer house. Towards the end of his life, the doctors forbade him to lead the prayers because he would collapse and faint from his deep emotions and fervor.

At the north wall of our prayer house in Brest there was for many years a distinctive man – Reb Shmaye of the herrings. No one else would come as early as he did. He always stared intently at his prayer book – Reb Shmaye was there rain or shine, he never missed a lesson or public prayer. He would not mix into the affairs of the congregation, such as the election of new officials or conflicts within the congregation, and would always distance himself from such matters.

He was a big merchant of herrings –his business demanded much work, nevertheless, he found the time to pray and did much for charity. He would quietly walk around the prayer house every day after praying and collect donations in order to help the poor and downtrodden who were ashamed of their circumstances. At this time, he would delicately avoid those who could not afford to give anything. All donated very willingly. Those he omitted would run after him to give a donation in spite of his refusals.

Another duty that Reb Shmaye performed was – our town was next to the famous large military fortress where many Jewish soldiers were serving. Thanks to the efforts of the Head of the Jewish community, the soldiers would receive permits to come into the city and be with for fellow Jews on the Sabbath. On Friday evenings they would come to the prayer house closest to the fortress, which was our prayer house, so that we received a great share of these soldiers. Who else would look after them other than Reb Shmaye? . On Friday nights, he would cut the prayers short, he would take the soldiers to one side and allot them each to a person as his guest for the Sabbath. At the same time he would use his wisdom to match everyone suitably. The rest he would take to his own home without asking his wife if there was enough to eat...

Only once a year would this quiet distinguished man become very merry and uproarious, and that was at Simchat Torah. He would dance with the Torahs around the bimah and sing with the youngsters who would crawl all over him, pulling the skirts of his garments, and he would roister with them. Many disapproved of the behavior of the children towards such a distinguished personality, but he stuck to his own habits with his 'herd'. Hearing the baa baa baa bleating sounds from his herd would only increase his merriment and he would dance and sing with them until late.

An unchangeable custom was that the rowdy crowd of congregants would accompany Reb Shmaye through the streets with noisy singing and dancing to his home.

He would whisper into the ear of a trusted youth the secret location of the "goodies" - the delicacies that his wife had prepared for them. The thief acted very quickly, got the containers from their hiding places, and the crowd immediately began feasting.

Reb Shmaye would pretend with a stern face that he was outraged at this thieving – in the meantime, eager hands passed the containers from person to person and tore at the delicacies, making a mess and getting honey on their clothes. Reb Shmaye would again become merry and take much pleasure, laughing with a full mouth – the only time in the whole year that he laughed wholeheartedly.

The following morning at prayers, he would go about quietly, collecting donations with a subdued mood and a serious expression on his face. No one could understand this marvel –how Reb Shmaye, who carried all the sorrow of the world on his shoulders, was capable of such joy and celebration.

Reb Elyahu Hirsh was entirely different. It seemed that god himself had appointed him to seek out the sinners in the congregation. He was one of the elders at the east wall, a tall elder with white hair and a long beard. He was alert to everything that occurred inside the prayer house. It seemed like he was sitting and learning a certain chapter of Gemarrah and steeped in his book, but his eyes searched from side to side and every corner. Woe to the person who (in his opinion) transgressed! Reb Elyahu would attack immediately - loudly berating him for his lack of discipline and respect.

Because of his behavior, our prayer was crowned with the nickname "Gendarme of God".

This Jew had a hidden power – everyone was afraid of his stare. He would offend everybody, but no one took offence. Amongst those who respected him were important, wealthy businessmen and great scholars. Educated men and those who believed themselves to be educated – all of them accepted our gendarme, Reb Elyahu Hirsh's accusations - without complaints, excuses or evasions.

Etched into my memory is the persona of a great man –Rabbi Arieh Leib Feinstein, who was recognized as one of the most enlightened men in our city. In these same rooms of our prayer house he studied the history of our city. He researched and extracted for "Ir Tehilah", his famous book. The fanatics denounced this great man. They boycotted him during the elections for the kehilla and prevented him from receiving any official positions. Nevertheless, Rabbi Arieh Leib showed great resolve and energy to bring about important reforms in our city.

I'll mention one of his achievements: We had a cemetery, a wide-open field, away from the city amongst the cornfields. There were trees and bushes with happy birds in them, but when they began to build a railway line close to the graves, the whistle of the locomotive would disturb the eternal resting place. Not only that, our cemetery became open to every stray passer-by. The railway workers who were not known for their love of Jews turned the cemetery into a through- way and defiled the graves with unspeakable acts – the shame and sorrow was great. None of the community leaders could do anything about it. Only the heretic, the banned Rabbi Arieh Leib Feinstein, did not rest and defended the weakened honor of the Jews.

He sent letters with petitions and demands to the Government, and described these criminal acts as great offences against humanity. He demanded that the Government allot money collected from the kosher meat taxes to build a wall around the cemetery.

His intercession met with receptive ears, and after long negotiations and great efforts, the Government issued a permit in the name of A.L. Feinstein to build a stone fence around the cemetery with monies from the meat tax. The sworn opponents of Arieh Leib could only gnash their teeth at this affair and were greatly annoyed, but none dared oppose him openly. They consoled themselves with the argument that one man alone would not be capable of carrying out such a task. But hundreds of Jewish laborers were involved in building this wall and several months later everyone who wanted to enter the cemetery had to knock on the locked gate, and wait for the guard to let them in.

What payment did Arieh Leib receive? The fanatics were pondering on how to discredit him and they devised a libel that he misappropriated kehilla funds. He was arrested by the authorities. But through the efforts of leading citizens, the government sent a special representative to oversee the accounts and it emerged that he was innocent and was released.

From the stories that I heard in my father's home, there is etched in my memory a story of one of the luminaries of our city - Reb Yehuda Arkader. An official and treasurer of the kehilla, he administered with a strong hand. Yehuda Arkader had two sons, good-looking youths, aged 16 and 17. The youths would sit in the prayer house and study. Yehuda Arkader did not have the time to supervise their studies, and as his sons did not come to him and no one betrayed them, he was certain that they were on the right path. He saw his sons only at the Sabbath table, and when on one Sabbath hey were not there at the table, he was very puzzled and found out after questioning that his sons had gone astray. They had become Chassids and gone for the Sabbath to the famous Rebbe, the "miracle worker ", at Niezvitch.

This news hit Yehuda Arkader like a thunderbolt. He was a devout Mitnaged. He sat at his table for the whole of the Sabbath and did not speak a word. After the Sabbath, he tore his clothes, said the prayer for the dead, and sat shiveh. He was inconsolable and could not be comforted over his great loss. The heart of this diligent, hardworking Jew was broken and never healed. He went around in a depressed state until a heart attack ended his suffering. Many years later, I met those two brothers both of them renowned Chassids. Their children were of my generation with long ginger side locks, (peyes), brought up by rabbis and righteous, religious men. One of them did not fit into the mould of the Chassids and at the age of 18, he stole away from his home, taking with him gold and silver. He fled to St. Petersburg, and entered a music academy. His family blotted out all memory of him...

Over time a rumor circulated that the famous singer in the Imperial opera was the grandson of Reb Yehuda Arkader. His name was Yonaleh the Redhead.

So that the orthodox women should not feel left out – I will now recount about several orthodox women. One of them was Esterke Harkavi – her married name was Minc.

She owned several businesses and was a manufacturer of cigarettes. She also owned a beautiful shop with good wines. Her office there served as a sort of club for high-ranking government employees. Esterke was beautiful in appearance and a woman of valor. Her mouth spoke real pearls; the high-ranking officials had pleasure in conversing with her, because she was just as clever as she was beautiful. I remember her as a mother to 15 sons and 1 married daughter, but nothing had lessened of her charm and wisdom. She really worked miracles, everyone who had troubles would come to her for advice: evil deeds, disputes with the law, problems of all kinds would immediately come to her for help. She was rarely at home, even on Sabbath and the High Holydays. Also it was difficult to meet her at her shop as she was always away, traveling to meet high-ranking government officials, the authorities at the fortress, and members of the tribunals. No one could refuse her. At her request, often against their will, they would cancel unjust regulations and laws – she saved many from life imprisonment, forced labor and death.

All the Jewish soldiers called her Mama Esther. Due to her efforts, they could maintain their faith, despite the attempts of many gentiles to assimilate them. Also those arrested and held in prison were treated better thanks to the intercessions of Esterke Harkavi. Thus her short life was one chain of good deeds. This flower was cut down young. She left behind a good name and 16 young human beings who did not have the opportunity to acquaint themselves with their great mother. Let us remember that one of her sons was the first Brisker Jew to go to Eretz Israel, and was one of the leaders of BILU.

Of the women of our town, I wish to mention one more, whose memory was unforgettable – Hannaleh, the wife of Zalman. A small thin woman, who walked slowly, spoke slowly and little. Her husband was one of the wealthiest merchants in the city – a tobacco wholesaler and merchant, he was a very respected personage. Their home was one of the most impressive and distinguished in the city. Their children were beautiful, it seemed that he was the most fortunate of men – but he would say that his home lacked one essential – a homemaker.

Hannaleh was never at home. In the early morning she would leave for the dairy, buy warm milk and divide it up between the poor, the sick, and the expectant mothers for whom she cared. From there she would go to the synagogue and pray the morning prayers. Then she would go with her friend Fraidlin with a red kerchief on her head to the stores to collect donations. With that money she would buy food for the widows and orphans who would be waiting impatiently for it. In the afternoon, she would go to the houses of the wealthy to collect whatever she could get. She would put out a large cloth and collect everything that she received in it, bread rolls, bread, butter, cheese, all kinds of medicines, clothing for the poor and sick. By the way, she was also a nursing sister –she would tend to the sick, changing their dressings.

Accompanied by Fraidlin, they would visit the inns and hostels to collect donations from the guests. No one could refuse this virtuous woman. They would all give according to their means with open hearts. When it came to the evening prayers, she would run to the synagogue to hear them, and from there she would run back to the dark neglected houses of the poor. Sometimes in the middle of the night she would visit the sick, and console the fallen and downtrodden.

In the Government hospital where entry was forbidden, you could find Hannaleh at every bed. In secret she would leave every patient with something to lighten their hearts – the only one who was unhappy with Hannaleh and had a full mouth of complaints was her husband, Zalman.

The goodness of another woman should also be recalled. Beile Ruchel the Banderke – she was named after her husband's profession –he was a barrel maker in his good years. A skilled tradesman in the art of wood maturing, over time he became unemployed and a lazy layabout. Beile Ruchel supported her husband and 6 small children, carrying heavy baskets of bread and fruit with her own hands. In the morning she would leave her small children and run to deliver small warm pastries to the houses of the rich for them to snack on. She would drag her bags from house to house with an empty stomach. Could she eat before she had fed her own children?

Years went by, winters and summers; there was no improvement in her life until the following happened: on an Autumn day, the rain stopped pouring down and the unpaved streets of our city became like pools of water, the mud would rise to neck -high. Beile Ruchel went with her heavy baskets, dragging her feet through the mud, and loudly complaining to God. She could not lift her mud soaked skirt and dragged herself along. Gradually she came face to face with a carriage harnessed to five thoroughbred horses, sweating and foaming at the mouth. From inside the carriage appeared a young man in the uniform of a general. He glanced at Beile Ruchel and asked the carriage driver to top. He shouted Beile, Beile... our Beile was so preoccupied with her misery that she barely heard anything, the passers by understood and thought that the young man wanted to buy something and told her to stop. Seeing this beautiful uniform, she came closer with trepidation – he asked her in Russian "is your name Beile?" She answered: "yes, my name is Beile Ruchel". He immediately stretched out his arms and took her baskets and sat her down in the carriage. The horses went forward and everybody stared at this sight wide eyed with wonder.

As the carriage sped on, Beile Ruchel slumped in fear, her teeth chattered – who knows, maybe someone had libeled her? Woe to her children!! She calmed down as the officer began to speak. He told her that as he drove past her, he recognized her as the daughter of a teacher from whom he had learnt the alphabet. He remembered how good she had been to him – it had left a mark in his memory, and he wanted to help her as much as possible, with one condition. For the time being, he would not reveal his name to her, which would have to remain secret, as he was taken away from his home as a child. The carriage proceeded to the fortress and arrived at a beautifully built government palace. He got out and said to Beile, this is where I live, come in and meet my wife and children. Beile Ruchel stepped down from the carriage, not knowing what to do, what would happen to her? The officer took her hand and went up the stairs into a salon with expensive Persian carpets and introduced her to his wife. This is my Beile, the daughter of my first teacher, who instilled humanity in my heart. Treat her as a sister. The young and pretty wife of the general did not hesitate and said, we are actually sisters - I am a Jewish daughter. Tears of joy welled in the eyes of all three.

As they calmed themselves, the general and his wife began seeking ways to help Beile Ruchel. They agreed that from that day on, Beile Ruchel would conduct their housekeeping. She would buy everything for their household from the stores and make a living from this. Furthermore, as the general was the head doctor of the large hospital inside the fortress, and the wealthy Jews came to him asking him to treat their sick at his hospital - he would not see them directly but only through Beile Ruchel. From then on, everything changed for Beile Ruchel. Her customers wondered what had happened to her and her baskets, and the school students wandered why Beile Ruchel's children came dressed in good clothes and shoes. And one could come across Beile Ruchel in the shops and stores buying supplies.

The doors at her home are not still all day – all are asking what has happened? A real tragedy, has the doctor from the fortress gone mad? He would not admit one sick person to the hospital for any money in the world without the intervention of Beile Ruchel! Once again, Beile Ruchel is tired and exhausted at night, no food has reached her mouth. Saving lives is above everything else. She does all his without compensation. The doctor at times receives a handsome present from his patients, this money he gives to Beile Ruchel. However, she goes from house to house distributing this money. She would not sell her portion of paradise for any price.

At the officer's club in the fortress, Beile Ruchel is the subject of much gossip. She delivers many kinds of expensive jewelry that the wives of the officers desire. The sellers of this expensive jewelry give her various precious items to sell —once again she drags her bags full of foreign imported jewels worth thousands of rubles. Thus she conducted her business, without knowing how to write and not knowing how to speak Russian. She spoke with all the high officials, a kind of Esperanto – a mixture of several languages. Her honesty and charity awoke trust in everyone. From all her dealings she did not receive more than food and clothes for her and her family. She did not want to profit in this world.

**The writer Nechama Pochachevski,
wife of Michael Pochachevski**

Types of poor people in Brest at the end of the 19th century

**Two Brest Ladies
at the end of the 19th century**

Brest in Bygone Years

as told by the elderly Doba-Yaffa to N. Chinitz
Translated by Dr. Samuel Chani and Jenni Buch

Doba Yaffa aged 12 (1876)

Before W.W.1 there were about 50 schools and Chassidic prayer houses, or shteibls, in Brest. The Gerrer, Karliner, Slonimer, Stoliner, Nezvicher,Kobryner, and Bialer, etc. Amongst the chassidim there were some great scholars and prominent Jews. Brest distinguished itself with its beautiful Great Synagogue, which was burnt down in 1895 and rebuilt thanks to the initiative of Reb Yerucham Schatz, who worked for the community for 50 years. The drawings for the Great Synagogue bore the stamp of the Tsar-Nicholas 1. Yerucham Schatz had personally taken these plans to the province governor, Dimitri Nicholaievitch Batushkov, in Grodno and asked for financial support to build the synagogue. The governor fulfilled his request and the Great synagogue was built in all its glory. When the governor-general Swiatowpolski- Minsky came to visit Brest he met with Yerucham Schatz in the synagogue and later in the hospital, later again in the town hall, asking him "how many meetings have we had today?"

After W.W.1, Yerucham Schatz returned to Brest from his wanderings in Russia. With the help of various officials he built the great hospital. He received awards for his service as a city councillor for over 25 years. Once two Jews wagered how widely Reb Yerucham Schatz was known in Brest as an administrator – they went into the street and asked every Jew they met their opinion of Yerucham Schatz – all praised him.

In the Mishmar synagogue there was a yeshiva run by Rabbi Simcha Zelig Ryger and Rabbi Moshe Sokolovsky who would 'change the guard' every three days, taking turns in giving the youths lessons.

Rabbi Mordechai Dov (Alter) Grosleit was the grandson of Tzvi Hirsh Barlas and related to Pinchas Michael Antopoler. A rabbi and very wealthy man, Rabbi Grosleit was accustomed to write all his income into a notebook so that he could give tithe to the synagogue. When he travelled to Moscow to purchase goods, he received a substantial donation - 25,000 rubles from Rabbi Zelig Fersitz to build a hospital. Upon his return to Brest they immediately began the construction works. The Gaon Rabbi Chaim Soloveitchik laid the foundation stone. He looked at Rabbi 'Alter' Grosleit and asked him, "here is the list of all those who have pledged for the hospital, how much will you pledge?" Rabbi Grosleit replied, " I'm giving as much as the rabbi will write down, I have confidence in you, Rabbi." Rabbi Chaim wrote down 500 rubles, after that many others wrote their pledges, each one according to his means. Just as the construction of the frame of the building was completed, W.W.1 broke out and the work was suspended. Immediately after the war, the building was completed. Every time before his trips to Moscow, Grosleit would go to Rabbi Chaim Soloveitchik and leave him a substantial sum for charity.

Rabbi Chaim would farewell him with a blessing "go in peace and return in peace", and Rabbi Grosleit said that this blessing went with him everywhere and ruled whatever he did.

Reb Butche was a Chassid, a mohel (cicumciser) and schochet (ritual slaughterer). Although he excelled in looking after the needs of the community, he refused any awards. After the war all his time and efforts went into building a religious school. He would go to the homes of the wealthy Jews and demand donations. They would ask him, "who are you?" He would reply, " I'm a Jew, a beggar, but everything about me is kosher.

A door, a window, a piece of timber, everything and anything are useful to complete building the school." His assistant was Tzvi Ber Mordechai Gimpel Yaffe, the gabbei (deacon) of the synagogue school. Tzvi Ber in his younger days had been a businessman trading in sugar. He returned from the war a broken man and would sit and learn Torah day and night.

Amongst the renowned teachers in Brest was Rabbi Eliakim Getzel, who founded the 'Glory of Youths' society. He would give a daily lesson there, attracting large crowds who would listen to his fiery words with enthusiasm.

The head of the tailors, Laizerovitch, presided over the tailors' synagogue, and would castigate his congregation with sharp words and harsh tones; nevertheless they would run to hear his speeches. Alter Tzinneman was a caretaker of the Chevra Kadisha. A rotund Jew, he was a master of prayer and a master of reading from the Torah, he was also a Mohel (circumciser). He was a clever Jew who sparkled with wit. Before that he had been a caretaker in Rabbi Yehezkel's synagogue and school – he had corrected the handwriting of the book 'Ir Tehila' by Reb Arye Leib Feinstein.

An important and interesting man was Reb Sholem Menashe – in his youth he was a student of the Gemarra. Short of stature, thin and hardworking, he would walk around with his nephew, Reb Boruch Freidman, collecting donations for the poor.

At the Greener synagogue he would give lessons in Tanach. On the high holidays he would pray in front of a lectern and say, " I have with me the Creator of the world and I can trust Him". He had a good heart and was a learned teacher. He died at the beginning of 1904.

Rabbi Yoseph Dov (Yoshe Ber) Soloveitchik was brought to Brest in 1879 and died there in 1892. After the aliyah of Rabbi Joshua Leib Diskin to Eretz Israel, Rabbi Meir-Yona Soloveitchik was invited to Brest as head of the Beth Din (rabbinical court) and from Warsaw came Rabbi Yoshe Ber. The father of Rabbi Simcha Zelig, Rabbi Baer, was the shammes (beadle) of the rabbinical court.

Once, they wanted to photograph Rabbi Yoshe Ber, but he would not consent. Then an artist wanted to paint him, but the genius would not agree, saying " why especially me? There is Baer the shammes, he has a bigger and better beard than I do, and his shape is better than mine. Why don't you paint him?" However, he was photographed once whilst making shmeireh matzos, he was so absorbed in his task that he did not notice as they crept up on him.... The photographer sat waiting in the next room and caught him.

When the Volozhyn Yeshiva closed down, Rabbi Chaim Soloveitchik came from there to his father, Rabbi Yoshe Ber, in Brest. In Volozhyn, Rabbi Chaim had been head of the community. When Yoshe Ber suddenly died, already before his funeral, Chaim was crowned as the Brisker Rav. After the eulogy, Rabbi Shalom Menashe stood up and said, "Mazel-tov rabbi! Your son has been chosen as the Brisker Rav – one should toast him with a drink in his honour'. At that time, Rabbi Chaim did not have his rabbinical ordination. Therefore, thirty days after his father's death, Rabbi Eliahu Chaim Maizel from Lodz and several other rabbis arrived in Brest to give him his ordination.

[Page 231]

My Parents' Home

By Mordechai Yaffe
Translated by Dr. Samuel Chani and Jenni Buch

Just as every man has a destiny, our city has had a special luck, and I don't mean in olden times but her fate over the last century. She was torn out of her place and shifted because of the building of a military fortress. She was burnt twice, her residents expelled, and the city itself was destroyed both by the Russians and the Germans, and then entirely annihilated by the Nazis.

After W.W.1 the appearance of Brest completely changed. Many of its former residents never returned. A portion had settled in Poland and did not want to return. Many perished in their travels and in terrible circumstance and did not survive to return.

At the same time, many Jews from neighbouring towns and villages in the district arrived in Brest and settled there. Another change was that many Christians, bureaucrats and civil servants, arrived and settled there. The nationalities of its population changed –Brest stopped being a decidedly Jewish town. A new town had arisen, completely different, and the difference was in every aspect:

The population.

The social structures

The social activists

The traditions and the livelihoods

Contrasting with the above list, was the former Brest, before its destruction and the expulsion of its population during W.W.1 – exemplified here by the description of a house, one detail from which we can learn everything.

The street was the border; on one side was the business centre, these were the houses of the wealthy respected businessmen. On the other side, closer to the river was the tradesmen's district: blacksmiths, carpenters, wagon drivers, locksmiths, etc.etc, and a special type of Jew – the Paramshitshkes This was the district of the working class – of robust, strong, well-built Jews, here was organized and unorganised self defence

The house was a large building in terms of that time and place. The apartments that faced out onto the street – vast stores of a trading house, which had existed for generations. In these stores the majority of the employees were orthodox Jews, people of the Torah, amongst them some who had began working for my grandfather as boys and now owned their own stores. They were now elderly fathers of their own inter-related families with children, grandchildren, all God fearing Chassidim.

Some of them had already outlived their working age but none of them would retire from sitting in their stores all day – although their usefulness was minimal. There were two full time drivers employed who were distant relatives of the family – Reb Eliahu and Reb Baruch-Hirsh, who were learned orthodox Jews, observant of all the laws.

The relationship between the owners and their employees was part patriarchal, contrasted by concern and joy - they shared in all their sorrows and joys.

The nearest neighbour was the synagogue where the aristocratic Jews of the city would pray – here would pray the great men of Torah, 'relatives of royalty', and those closest to the house of the Rabbi, the father, the uncles and others.

In this synagogue was also a yeshiva under the patronage of the Rabbi, its head was Rabbi Simcha Zelig who was one of the great torah scholars in the city and the right hand of the Rabbi and who later perished in the Ghetto. The second head was Rabbi Moshe Sokolovsky, also one of the elite of the yeshiva.

The reciprocal relationship between the house and the yeshiva was strong, partly because of the proximity and the assistance given to the yeshiva people, and partly because the young members of the house were themselves were students at the yeshiva.

The melodies of the Gemarrah were heard from there throughout the day and into the evening, especially on Thursdays, also at night the chanting voices would carry from the yeshiva into the house. The noise of the commerce and trade also reached the synagogue.

There it would reach the heavens in wakefulness and full harmony.

Inside the house there were three apartments. On the first floor was the elder brother Yerucham with his household. On the floor above lived the younger brother Issar and the brother-in-law Yakov Zalman – three households, three worlds.

My grandfather, Reb Yerucham was a wealthy and privileged man. In his home there were documents from the 16th century. He was a worker for the community, a social activist with every fibre in his soul. Active and energetic, he was a handsome figure with a long beard and a thundering voice. He was a trustee of the city and the great synagogue, the hospital and the Chevra Kadisha (burial society), a city councillor acknowledged by the central and city governments. His influence was felt in all areas of the city. He spoke Russian, but wrote with errors, however, that did not stop him from knocking on all the doors of the highest officials in the state and the capitol. He had appeared before kings.

He reigned over the city; but overall his power was derived from what he received from the rabbi to whom he had the utmost loyalty. His belief and loyalty reached the highest degree, for example, the rabbi's house was against Zionism, and therefore he was also a strong opponent.

Even in matters in which the majority of the public was against the opinion of the rabbi's house – a hint from there was enough- he would oppose everything.

When Dr. Herzl died, the Zionists, an acknowledged force in the city, decided to hold a memorial service in the Great Synagogue.

The orthodox Jews were not happy, also a wink from the rabbi's house caused grandfather to order the caretaker to lock the gates of the synagogue, and bring the keys to him. He took the keys and left the city for the day. In the meantime a crowd of thousands had assembled – imagine the bitter disappointment when they faced the padlocked heavy copper gates. They raised the alarm with the old caretaker who was trembling with fear at the enraged crowd – he directed them to the correct address, The result was that part of the crowd led by Zionist officials who were usually against my grandfather paid a visit to his home and broke the windows, doors, furniture, utensils, in short they caused havoc.

The police, who were alerted by the neighbours, arrested two of the Zionist leaders – one of whom was the father of Menachem Begin. The administration sentenced them to three months. The next day grandfather returned. The families of the arrested men came to him demanding that they be released. The essence of the matter was that although the damage to his house was large - the memorial service was held the next week, because the rabbi's house had been shaken and bowed to the public pressure. Did grandfather get pleasure because he had stuck to his beliefs?

His forcefulness was not only against the Jews; the local powers also felt it.

An example of this was: some of the city officials with grandfather at their head decided to establish a pharmacy for the city's poor. The pharmacists saw this as a threat to their incomes and did all in their power to stop it from happening. The simplest way was to bribe the head of the health department in the province not to issue a permit.

After drawn out negotiations my grandfather became convinced that there was no hope of obtaining this way – he did not hesitate for long and went to St.Petersburg – there he had friends with the highest connections to senators, ministers and former governors. Through these connections the head of the health services department ordered that the required permit be issued. This cost my grandfather much money and later setbacks with the local Brest authorities. However, the pharmacy was established.

My grandfather only had one daughter, a beauty with rare qualities. She died in Israel several years ago aged 87. She was named Shaindel. As was the customs with rulers, he married her into a family of many generations of rabbis. His son in law was Reb Tzvi, the son of rabbi Mordechai Yaffe of Rashenai, one of the greatest rabbis of his generation. He was one of the first Chovevei Zion (Lovers of Zion), who in his later years went to Eretz Israel and lived in Petach Tikvah and Yehudiah.

In my opinion, the rabbi's son, Reb Tzvi, a student from the Volozhyn yeshiva and a learned expert in Torah matters did not fit easily into the household. A house that was freely open all year to all: Chassidim, Mitnagdim, religious and secular, government officials, friends and followers, a house in which there was always noise - it was hard for him to adjust to the practical, material world into which he had been dragged.

A child of a house that was steeped in the love of Zion, it was difficult for him to accustom himself to the extreme fanaticism, although he immersed himself in his traditions and deep faith and did not associate with the fanatics. He trusted every religious Jew - and more than once dishonest people led him astray. Nevertheless, he did not stop trusting them.

In time, a harmony was created in the house between spirituality and practicality, between the rooms of the great library where he spent most of his time and the world of commerce and business. By the way, the greater part of his library went to Israel and was handed over to the settlement of Rabbi Kook

In the matter of educating the children, who, by the way, all received a traditional education in cheder and yeshiva – not one attended a secular school – my father's spirit prevailed, and there was no fanaticism. He was once asked from where he knew foreign languages- he gave a strange reply," Gemarrah and poskim (rabbinical lore) you learn, but languages you know!"

The First World War had greatly affected my grandfather financially. Also the new order in society, the previous powers which had declined and been overthrown by the new powers – all this hit the elderly man who was in his eighties very hard. He was not able to come to terms with the new order, a democratic community with open government and critical opinions, and the liberation from the ruling elite. He was broken down together with the destruction of the city and it's traditions.

In a wing of the upstairs floor lived his younger brother, the esteemed uncle Isser, with the various members of his family. Another world, with different inhabitants and different upbringing. His older brother Yerucham had relinquished his share of the inheritance of a family store in favour of his brother and brother-in-law. However, his brother Reb. Isser was more preoccupied with his 'weaknesses'.

His entire life he was afraid of catching colds - he would walk around swaddled in sweaters and scarves. The jokers of the house said that when Reb Isser went through a street with open windows on both sides, he would lift his collar against the cross draft!

Despite the many servants and maids in our house, everyone had serve themselves- no one was spared from physical work. In contrast the uncle's children were very spoilt and pampered and as a result had physical weaknesses and were always sick

The second wing of the upper storey lived the esteemed uncle Yakov Zalman Lifshitz with his wife Masha. They had inherited and managed a family business. Reb Yakov was the son of the famous rabbi Baruch Mordechai Lifshitz, the rabbi of Siedlice, a man totally immersed in Torah and orthodox affairs.

They had no children of their own. Their home was full of books and learning and was open to every rabbi and passing yeshiva student, and officials of 'Mechaskei Hadat', (strengtheners of the religion) the ultra - orthodox society which had it's roots in Russia.

In their home I saw the famous Rabbi Yakov Rabinovitch the Poltava rabbi, Rabbi Yakov Lifshitz and his son Noteh from Kovno, and people from the 'Black office', Rabbi Eliezer Atlas from the 'Pales' publication, and other rabbis and officials of this society that had existed even before the Agudat Israel. This society had surpassed Agudat Israel in its struggle against Zionists and Zionism – from there were issued the directives of how to conduct the battle

Here I also met with emissaries from various yeshivas and institutions, amongst them were interesting personalities and great scholars of the Torah. All were bound and united in their negative attitude to Zionism and the new settlements in Israel. A frequent guest to their home was a Rabbi Yakov Klotzkin, he would take part in Torah discussions – my uncle ignored his fanaticism and liked him a lot.

Their home often resounded with debates and arguments about Torah issues and matters in general.

I have perhaps offended some people and have not represented the complete characters - but I have just tried to give a short picture of life in my parent's home.

Page 237]

Notes and Memories

By Israel Tzemach
Translated by Dr. Samuel Chani and Jenni Buch

I was born in 1891 and named after my grandfather Israel Oiser who was already deceased, having died at the age of 35 leaving behind a widow, 4 sons and 3 daughters.

My grandmother, Bobbe Gruneh, was left with the heavy burden of making a living in business to support her 7-orphaned children.

She was called Gruneh- Rashes in our town, which was her mother's name. We were known as the grandchildren of Gruneh- Rashes. It appears that my mother's family occupied a respected position, as did that of my father's. Bobbe Gruneh told me that when she was six years old her mother took her by the hand and led her from the old town of Brest to the new town. Each inhabitant of the old town of Brest who had owned a piece of land was allotted the same size of land in the new town. Also in this, according to her, the woman were more accurate then the men. They took off their kerchiefs and with them they measured the length of their plots in the old town, and exactly received the same as measured by the kerchief in the new town. Some had cheated on kerchief lengths and received more.

Apparently everyone claimed that their plot was in the centre of the new city and fights broke out. Also corruption was rife and there were surprises and disappointments. The centre of the city was not actually where the surveyors had set it out, but over time it had moved to the edges of the city, not far from the Mukhavets River. The ancient Jewish cemetery was allocated as a fish market; they dug up the graves and transferred the remains to the new cemetery. I recall that several times after a heavy downpour that the bones of the long dead floated. Cohanim avoided receiving plots of land in that street.

Grandmother Gruneh owned a shop of imported fabrics. I don't know whether she herself had travelled to Germany in her younger days or if someone else was her agent.

She had a lot of trouble with tax collectors - it seems that she was not punctual in paying her taxes as required by law. 'God gave me my life and fortune' she quoted, but the Tsar was not fooled and she was often reported to the authorities for tax evasion. Then several tax officers would come to audit her goods and search for unstamped (untaxed) goods. They would search everywhere -they went into the storerooms where the wood was stored for winter and threw out the wood. Grandmother stood at a distance, trembling and frightened... then a miracle occurred and the investigators suddenly stopped their searching. Had they just taken away one more layer they were have found a treasure trove of textiles without the tax stamps. Grandmother got sick of the importing foreign goods business and sold all her stock and opened up a tavern.

When they opened up the tavern in the cellar of their house the old grandmother Rashe went down from her first floor apartment and stood at the edge of the cellar entrance and said "this bar is a dishonour for me and my family, my feet will never step over the edge of the cellar as long as there is a bar there. I know that you are doing this to make a living and I hope that God will help you to get rid of this business and return to the fabric shops". Thus it happened and grandmother returned to her fabric shop.

When I was 4 years old I began to learn in cheder. One day the rabbi said to look out the window at the funeral procession - "they are taking your great-grandmother Bobbe Rashe for burial." I did not understand what the rabbi meant, only years later when I was older and heard so much praise for my grandmother did I understand the honour of being a grandchild of Gruneh Rashe.

In that thin body was a treasure of wisdom, charity and a refined heart. She knew the Siddur (prayer book) by heart. With closed eyes she would recite all the usual prayers, she also knew the 'slichot' prayers very well and was familiar with the chapters of the Mishnah. In her old age she would secretly wear a small tallis.

I never saw grandmother in her cellar bar -she almost disappeared from all her relatives and acquaintances, not wanting to be seen in these lowly circumstances. She passed on the tasks of serving alcohol to drunks to others.

When my younger brother went abroad to study my grandmother worried terribly that God forbid, he would be 'ruined'. Her grandson had, according to her, lost his Yiddishkeit.

Her moaning about the matter got louder, she came to me once to ask why Shmuel had gone abroad? To acquire knowledge and learning, I replied. Wisdom and knowledge can be acquired from our own holy books, she replied. When she asked me again, I said to her that some time ago, you were sick and they called the doctor not the rabbi because he had the medical knowledge to cure you, which he learnt from other books, not from the holy books. She replied that the Ram Bam (Maimonides) was a great scholar and a great healer. But also the Ram Bam had studied wisdom and medicine from others, I answered. She asked :"What sort of wisdom is Shmuel learning?." My reply was engineer. "Why not a doctor?" She stubbornly argued. "What difference does it make, doctor or engineer?" I asked. "The difference, my son, is that when you call a doctor to come to a sick person, he comes and sees a man in pain and troubled. The patient looks into his eyes and wants know what the healer thinks of his condition, and he takes pity on him and promises him a complete recovery. After a while he comes again and sees that he can't heal him as there is a Creator of the Universe in heaven who is healer of the sick and the doctor is only his messenger. Only thus does one become a true believer and a good Jew, observing all the mitzvot. On the other hand, an engineer, what does he do? He busies himself with stones and woods, also his heart becomes hard as stone and wood and he is not a good person."

The jewel of our family was the grandmother's oldest son, my uncle Reb. Michael Rosenberg who was called Reb Michaleh Rashes in our city. From early childhood he distinguished himself in his studies- he was very diligent. Grandmother sent him to the very best teachers - they all praised him highly. Reb Michaleh was the only Chassid in our family; he travelled to the Radziner rabbi. He married the daughter of the rabbi's schochet (ritual slaughterer), Rabbi Gershon Henoch. Before the wedding he was invited to the rabbi's court, where he was welcomed with much respect -they made him sit at the rabbi's table. The rabbi and Michaleh became close - he was much influenced by this.

Rabbi Gershon Henoch was the author of 'Hatchalat' and was known as a great scholar and also had some knowledge of medicines, natural sciences and languages. My uncle Michaleh concluded from this that one could be a great scholar and follower of God, but at the same time not distance yourself from worldly matters. He became interested in technology, natural sciences and knowledge of languages. From Torah alone one cannot make a living, so he became a merchant of confectionery, he would travel to Kiev and Warsaw, and dealt directly with the sweets manufacturers. He was successful in this business for many years.

I remember him between the sacks of sugar at his desk, a thick black cigar always between his long fingers, lost in his thoughts. We did not know whether he was immersed in money matters or if he was pondering some Talmudic matter that he was studying, because after all, Rabbi Gershon Henoch had written an interpretation on the Talmudic tract "Taharot". At night when all were asleep, an hour before midnight, uncle would take a nap, then get up and wash his hands and open the Gemarrah - one could hear the muffled sounds of Gemarrah melody until 3 or 4 in the morning. Also grandmother would arise before midnight from her bed, light the fire, take a stool and open the Siddur, put on her glasses and cry bitter tears over the destruction of the second Temple and the exile into the Diaspora she knew very well the words:' streams of water will fall from my eyes over the destruction of the house of my nation'.

Brest vanished with the fire, my uncle Michaleh returned and went back once more to the confectionery business but was not successful. He became a director of the Commercial Bank, his education and knowledge of economics suited the job but not his appearance as he was dressed in rabbinical garb with a black cap on his head and long side locks. The people around him were bareheaded and clean-shaven, two worlds far apart from each other.

During the W.W.1, my uncle Michael Rosenberg and his family first went to Pinsk then Siedlice where his son in law Yedidiah Rimon (who perished later in a car accident and is buried in Tel-Aviv cemetery) lived. In Siedlice, for the first time in his life, after many appeals from his friends, he agreed to accept the rabbinical chair. However, the Gerrer Chassidim opposed him. Together with all the other refugees that had fled Brest, he returned to Brest and became a director of the People's Bank, a position that he occupied until his death in 1931, at the age of 74.

All his children and grandchildren perished during the time of Hitler. Miraculously, one of his grandchildren survived, he lives in Israel and studies at the SloboDavid Kupchika yeshiva in Bnei Brak - the chain of torah scholarship was not broken. In the house of uncle Michaleh, nothing was spoken of Zionism, except for one daughter who was carried along by the ideals of the leftist Zionists. She would attend Zionist conferences. Her husband was one of the leaders of Mizrachi in his town. Once, I recall there was a discussion about Zionism. My uncle would not participate, but towards the end he declared:" I'll tell you a story. In a village of gentiles there was only a single Jew, a leaseholder (arendar) of the nobleman's land. On the night of Passover the overseer would come in and sit at the Seder and ask that various customs be explained to him. When it came to next year in Jerusalem, the overseer would ask what it meant. The Jew replied, "because we sinned and did not obey God we were exiled and therefore we sit in the Diaspora, until we confess that we sinned and regret our sins, then we will be granted the privilege to be in Jerusalem next year".

Next year the overseer came to the Seder table once more, and again asked the same questions. The Jew replied that we had not obeyed God's mitzvot as we should have, we will make an effort to improve our ways and God blessed be He will help us. The same thing occurred in the third and fourth years, with the same questions and replies until one day the Jew arose and said" God Almighty, I am ashamed in front of this simple overseer - You decide whether next year in Jerusalem!"

In 1914, before the German occupation, I left Brest. A military band played in the municipal gardens. A large army was assembled around the fortress and we were sure that the fortress was impregnable and would not fall to the Germans. However, as the Germans neared the city it's residents did not know what to do, to leave or not to leave the city. The order was to evacuate the city within the next three days. Those who had foreseen what would happen managed to shift their goods and merchandise to Greater Russia in time and thus saved themselves from destitution on foreign soil. The majority of residents left the city with empty hands and headed for Greater Russia.

However, the Russians did not defend the fortress, but instead set fire to the city from all sides and retreated east into Polessie. Many wandered off into neighbouring and further cities such as Minsk, Yekaterinslav and Kharkov. The Brisker Rav, Chaim Soloveitchik settled in Minsk. Rabbi Alter Grosleit told me that when prominent Brest refugees came to see the rabbi with offers of financial help, he replied "I'm not allowed to take a cent from you, if the city of Brest does not exist anymore, then I do not exist as a rabbi, and cannot accept anything". The businessmen and merchants strongly appealed to him saying:" as in the past, you are also in the present our rabbi, and we are the same flock of sheep. All the Brest refugees look to you as our rabbi -in the past, present and future".

After a long dispute, the rabbi agreed to accept income.

Those that had not managed to flee into Greater Russia, because the Germans occupied the whole of Polessie, returned to Brest. I also lived temporarily in Kobryn and was one of the first to return to the empty, destroyed and burnt city of Brest.

I can still remember the fire of 1895 and the second fire of 1901. I remember that my father's house was one of the first destroyed by the fire as it was next door to Bishkowitzes house where the fire broke out and spread to the centre of the city.

These images, which are indelibly etched in my mind, have over time become confused with memories of the First World War destruction; one could not say that the city was entirely destroyed. A few houses were still intact, many just scorched, there were some houses that remained untouched, however, the city had became empty and desolate. I was surrounded on all sides by hungry dogs and cats - I tossed pieces of bread to get rid of them. As I neared our home on Paletzisker Street, I saw that only the frame remained. I went up to the second floor through the remaining staircase - everything was burnt and broken. I then went to the Zionist library that had cost so much work and money to build. The building appeared to be almost whole, the books stood on the shelves as if waiting for someone to come and clean the dust off them. In the middle of the ceiling there was a large hole from an artillery shell. With an ache in my heart I left there and wandered the streets of the deserted city, almost the only person in the deserted city, the only sounds were my footsteps on the bridge echoing my heartbeat. I left the city, travelled to Siedlice and then to Warsaw. In Warsaw we received news about refugees streaming back to Brest and the city slowly beginning to return to normal life, about 2000 had returned but then came a new blow.

An order came from the German headquarters that all residents must leave the city. On a beautiful day, they transported them all to Lukav and the surrounding Polish villages. The excuse for the expulsion that we heard was that he first refugees were caught looting goods that were rolling around in the streets. The German headquarters received complaints about this pillaging and therefore issued an order that only Germans could benefit from this lawlessness.

The Germans had indeed looted all the treasure from the city. Afterwards, they dismantled entire buildings and whole trainloads of bricks were transported to Germany. Their motive was revenge for the destruction that the Russians had wreaked in the eastern front. The refugees spread out in the Lukov district. Every village took in several families. The German headquarters forced the peasants to provide rooms for the homeless and thus excused themselves.

In 1915 a relief fund was established in Warsaw to help the Brest refugees. The chairman was the well-known banker Raphael Shereshevski whose wife was a Birshtein born in Brest. On this committee was also Yitzchak Radevsky, Avraham Goldberg the editor of the Yiddsh daily newspaper 'Heint', Yaffe and others.

Together with P.Halperin I was sent to Lukav and district to acquaint ourselves with the situation of the refugees and give a report to the relief committee. We travelled through dozens of villages meeting with Brest families everywhere. They were living in peasant huts, under terrible conditions, both physically and morally. They all had the same lament: to take them out of this bog. They saw in us saviours. Regrettably, we could only offer financial assistance and some food. This assistance reached every village and town where the Brest refugees were settled.

Typhus had broken out and took many victims during the German occupation, especially amongst the refugees. It was vital the isolate the sick. We returned to Lukav and requested help from the German headquarters. The Germans sequestered two buildings at each end of the town and there we opened a hospital for the Brest refugees stricken by infectious diseases.

In order to obtain the necessary equipment for the hospital such as beds, linens, etc.,

I was sent to escort two gendarmes to confiscate the necessary items from the residents and within one week, the hospital was functioning. The relief committee for the refugees from Brest operated from 1915 until1921 and was dissolved after the residents returned to the city.

From the distant depths of Russia and Poland, Jews began to stream back to their hometown. Brest was resurrected and the Torah was returned to it's home. They reopened the schools and the yeshivas. The old names such as the Greener Synagogue, the Rabbi Israel Wolf Synagogue regained their past characteristics. New institutions were created according to the need of the times - such as the public schools, and the Tarbut high school.

Brest had been transferred to Poland and its name became Brzesc nad Bugiem - Brest on the River Bug from the former Brest- Litevski. The streets all acquired Polish names. Once again the Brest Jews drank the bitter drops that was their fate and passed from generation to generation

I want to recall a treasured soul, Dr Y.L. Shereshevski, one of the best doctors, and a passionate and dedicated Zionist. He died of a heart attack when he was forced to intervene in a situation where Polish policemen were beating a Brest Jew.

Brest under the short reign of the Poles was a special city. Slowly the Jews accustomed themselves to their new lives. They suffered, they continued to strive and work to secure themselves in their city until they were swallowed up by the savagery of Hitler.

[Page 247]

The Blood Libel

By B. Z. Neumark
Translated by Dr. Samuel Chani and Jenni Buch

After the sudden demise of Joseph Ber Soloveitchik, in Iyar 1897, his brother Rabbi Chaim Simcha arrived in Brest from Kovno, an eminent businessman, and a man with a deep and instinctive understanding. He came to organize the affairs of his brother's son, Rabbi Chaim Soloveitchik, who had recently been elevated to the rabbinical chair in Brest.

Several days before Shavuot, an emissary of the great leader and philanthropist Reb Chaim Cohen came to me requesting that I immediately come to him on an urgent matter.

This was on a Thursday at 10p.m. – I believe that Shavuot fell on the following Sunday or Monday that year. I found Reb Chaim in a state of great agitation. He gave me a letter in which it stated that a certain tradesman by the name of Pinchas (Paulus) Meyer was openly admitting in the anti-Semitic newspaper 'The Fatherland' that he had seen with his own eyes how the Jew called Ashkenazi, who was the Rabbi of Biala Podlaska which was in the Brest district, had slaughtered a Christian child and made matzos with it's blood, and that this had been just after Purim and before Passover of 1881. This letter came to Reb Chaim Cohen from an employee of his kerosene business in Vienna, Shabtai Kartoshinski, who was born in Brest and was a relative of mine and a member of the Supporters of Zion.

Reb Chaim told me that the first thing to do was to go to the Rabbi, Chaim Soloveitchik, show him the letter and ask him what to do in this matter which was vital to the welfare of all Israel.

We went to the Rabbi and showed him the letter; the Rabbi was very disturbed and called for his uncle, Rabbi Chaim Simcha to ask his advice. After a short meeting the Rabbi said that he would travel to Ostra to investigate the matter at its source. He asked who is actually this Rabbi Ashkenazi and who is his nephew? I pointed out that there were several towns with this name in the districts of Siedlice and Wolyn. He asked, "Where then should I travel to?" It was decided that I should write immediately to the Rabbi of Biala and tell him of this matter. I posted the letter at the railway station where they were open all night for priority mail. Because the letter would reach the Rabbi on the Sabbath, he would not open it that day. Therefore we wrote on a card stating that due to the importance of this letter, the Brisker Rabbi had ordained that he should open it and read it on the Sabbath as it pertained to all of Israel. The Rabbi accepted my advice and dictated to me what to write to the Rabbi of Biala, he himself wrote the postcard ordering that the letter be read at once and that the Rabbi decide what should be done.

The next morning, I went out to investigate and asked of the Bialer Chassidim that were in Brest if any had the surname Ashkenazi and especially if anyone knew of the nephew of the Rabbi who did not behave decently. I searched and I found. I found a youth with the surname Ashkenazi and he told me that in the Biala yeshiva several years ago there had been a youth whom they said was the nephew of the Biala Rabbi. He was a good for nothing in every respect and action. No one could stand him but out of respect for the Rabbi, no harm came to him. On a Sabbath, he hanged himself from a lamp opposite the Holy Ark to take revenge on the Chassidim. When the Shammes (beadle) saw him he let out a great cry and people came running and removed him – barely alive. He was disgraced and deservedly thrown out of the town.

As the weeks and months passed, the youth and his attempt at hanging himself were entirely forgotten. He had vanished as if into the sea. No one knew what had happened to him. Once a message came that he was sitting in prison, but no one was interested in him or his escapades.

In Warsaw, the blood libel of Paulus Meyer against the Rabbi of Biala became known during Shavuot through the anti-Semitic newspaper of Raheling. Immediately they called a meeting of the Jewish Community Council at 26 Guszivoiski St. It was decided to give one thousand roubles to I.l.Peretz who was an employee of the council so that he would go directly to Brest and conduct from there a thorough investigation of the Biala Rabbi and his nephew. He was not to stop in Biala.

At the end of Shavuot I.L.Peretz arrived in Brest, and stayed at the hotel 'Berlin'. In answer to his question of who the young energetic person was, they pointed me out and he immediately came to see me. He told me all that he knew; I in turn gave him all the details of the Kartozinski letter and the consequent letter from Rabbi Chaim Soloveitchik to the Biala Rabbi. I advised him that the best thing to do would be for him to go to see one of the leading lights of the city, Rabbi A.L.Feinstein, the noted historian and writer and that he would advise us what to do.

The bad tempered old man Feinstein received Peretz with absolute indifference and asked that he not be bothered with such matters. I advised that Peretz go to Feinstein's rival, the new Gabbeh, Yerucham Schatz. When Schatz would get to hear of Feinstein not acceding to our requests, he would do all in his power to help in this matter, just to irritate his rival. And so it was. Schatz immediately grasped the matter upon hearing of the account of the Bialer Chassidim of the hanging of the nephew of the Biala Rabbi on the Sabbath and that he had once sat in the Brest prison. He asked that we wait a while and immediately went to the Brest Prison. In return for a nice gift that he gave the chief warden of the prison, he received a document stating that Ashkenazi was imprisoned in the Brest prison from March 1881 until September 1881, as he was suspected of revolutionary actions and that he had a connection to the assassin of the Tsar Nicholas 11.

With this document in hand it was left to us to clarify one matter. Was this Paulus Meyer the same as the Askenazi who had sat in the Brest prison in 1881? Paulus Meyer was currently sitting in a Viennese prison (he was arrested on the application of a Dr. Bloch, lawyer for the newspaper Oestriche Wochenschrift).

We told Reb Chaim Cohen of all that we had done and requested that he write his employee, Kartozinski, in Vienna asking that he make an effort to obtain a picture of this character. Within 7 days we had our picture - I sent a Chassid named Moshe Pechta to Terespol, seven kilometres from Brest, where the mother of the convert lived. I requested that she come immediately to Brest on the matter of her son who was sitting in a Viennese prison accused of theft. The mother, the Terespoler Rebbitzen, came immediately. The Rebbitzen confirmed that the man in the picture was her son; I went with her to a notary, who witnessed this.

From there I went to Yakov Meier Weinholtz who was an intermediary to the police, and he drew up a protocol (document) testifying to the fact that the mother of Ashkenazi stated that her son had been imprisoned on the 10th March, 1881, not for theft, but for revolutionary activities, and that that suspicions of the Viennese police were unfounded.

I sent the entire material with all the documents to Dr. Bloch in Vienna and he proved to the court that at the very time that this Paulus Meyer claimed that he witnessed his uncle the Bialer rabbi killing a Christian child for religious purposes – he was sitting in the Brest prison. Therefore, it was not only a blood libel that besmirched his uncle, but was against the whole of Israel and consequently deserved the strongest punishment.

These disclosures by Dr. Bloch were recognized as the truth by the court and the convert was sentenced to 6 years prison. Raheling the newspaper editor had received a defeat.

I. L. Peretz was not involved in this operation, but I kept him informed of everything. He spent two weeks in Brest and then returned to Warsaw, after the matter was concluded to the satisfaction of all.

[Page 251]

A Meeting with my Hometown

By I. Finkelstein (New York)
Translated by Dr. Samuel Chani and Jenni Buch

At the end of winter the cold is over, the deep snows remained but there is already a whiff of spring in the distance. The train from Warsaw, in which my friend Kleinberg and I had spent the entire night rolling on its floors, arrived in Brest in the early morning. The city was still deep in sleep – only a corner of the sky had begun to lighten and spread over the isolated huts which seemed like orphans in the street. My heart beat feverishly as I saw revealed before me the scene of what remained of my beautiful old hometown. What's more, the more I strolled around the town the more my heart tightened until the tears came to my eyes. Was this my Brisk? Was this the town of such poetic beauty? Of such dreamy tranquility? Its long wide treed streets gave it great charm and beauty. My heart was broken and from its depths there arose on curse on all those who had brought about the destruction of this beautiful city.

In the pain and anguish of observing the city of Brest with its barracks, houses, schools, synagogues which were overflowing with masses of people, young and old all over the grounds of the town, there was only one consoling factor. This was the assistance that was sent from America from my organization the Brisker Hilfsverein, from my American comrades that never forgot their homeland and stretched their warm hands and hearts.

The last rays of the sun danced over the city's church when I went to visit the places where I had spun my youthful dreams, the places that had been full of young people and the heart of the city had pulsated there until early in the morning. Now it was full of ruins casting their fear in the darkness, like tombstones in a cemetery. During the day, pigs roamed around the formerly beautiful and bustling streets. I found only the remains of several streets where frozen branches shivered with cold.

The day was almost over when a strange sensation filled my heart. I took my friend and said to him:" let's look for the street on which my cradle stood, where I grew up and where I once planted a tree. Come with me my friend, to see if the tree is still standing."

From the tens of streets that we passed on our way, there was not a single building that remained standing on either side of the streets, as if in open fields that had never known been burdened by houses. As the darkening sky drained the last bits of the evening, the shadows of the night lengthened. On the way back I recognized the tree, small when I had planted it in front of our house. The tree had spread out its branches to full width, and it's roots had spread in the empty space around it, but it had also felt the axe of destruction.

Those branches were burnt and the tree remained only as a symbol of the whole community, representing its past growth.

This destroyed part of the city was a horrible experience for us, a curse escaped my lips against the murderers, holding back the tears, I departed the city of Brest which had been turned into a ruin.

———————

[Page 253]

Between the Two World Wars

By Dr. S. Orchov
Translated by Dr. Samuel Chani and Jenni Buch

For a person whose cradle stood in the former Jewish city of Brest, it is very difficult to speak of a Brest that does not exist anymore. The chain which was forged by over one thousand years of Jewish habitation has been torn apart and will never be mended.

The source from which Brisk D'Lita obtained its strength was the completeness of its Jewish life, which reigned there. The local folk who lived in this part of the world were not capable of assimilating the Jewish population into their midst and the Jews had surpassed them in knowledge and culture. For these same reasons there was not an especially strong pressure by the Russians or the Poles as they were minorities compared to the White Russians and Lithuanians. It seems to me that there was no other such a city in all the corners of the Diaspora where the Jewish inhabitants were free from the pressures of the outside world.

Over the generations there existed in Brest various communal schools and aid organizations. Refuges for the poor and houses of learning. These institutions changed over time according to the needs of the times, but never ceased existing.

The same applied to its financial institutions. Brest did not excel in conspicuous wealth, but was always a place of profitable revenues. The town sat on a crossroads between White Russia, Ukraine, and Poland. Situated on the shores of two rivers on which floated the timber trade to the Baltic Sea, a railway junction and a large fortress.

The military headquarters was in reality an obstacle to the development of the city. The abundance of timber that was to be found in the district could have been the basis for a large industry for the town if not for the baleful eyes of the military commander at the fortress. It was forbidden in Brest to build buildings over two storeys high and also large industrial chimneys, and as a consequence it was not possible to build modern industries. The residential areas were restricted by a ring of forts and railway lines limiting the spread of the city in various directions.

On the other hand, the military garrison was the source of income for tens of thousands of families in Brest and surroundings: merchants, couriers, businessmen, tradesmen and artisans. There were many that learned their trades in Brest and then obtained responsible positions in other places. Builders, sub-contractors and tradesmen from Brest were later in demand all over the nation. Nevertheless, as a result of its military significance, the citizens of Brest saw it as a handicap to the city's development, geographic expansion, and improvement of its cultural and economic situation.

The fortress was damaged during World War 1. As fate would have it, many homes were destroyed as well as the commercial center. To tell the truth, this destruction was not as large as that caused in the conflict during the exchange of power between the Russians and the Poles. The new Polish governing power had no intention of rebuilding the ruins of the city after the war.

These new rulers of Brest would give not loans to the returning survivors. They sucked the last dregs out of their minorities, especially the Jews. They introduced a heavy tax system and created discrimination in the distribution of jobs and work allocations. If you were to glance at a map of Poland regarding taxation a strange image is projected in front of your eyes. The eastern regions that were dominated by minorities took first place – their masses were impoverished, their agricultural and urban industries had been destroyed – the closer one went west, the smaller was the taxation burden. As to any support for the community, loans, purchase of merchandise for the government's needs, the budget was mainly allocated to the western part of Poland which had suffered much less during the war.

This policy was not limited to economic matters. The new governing powers in Brest did not look favorably upon any of the Jewish organizations. Even the activity of the Joint was not to their liking, although it would bring foreign currency to the government coffers. There was an incident with the police chief, he was asked to issue a permit to a branch of the Zionist movement that had sprung up. He got angry and said: "you've got a rabbi here, what else do you want, organizations? Only we create these and no others!"

This police official and his association, in time, changed their speech but not their attitudes.

The new Jewish and Hebrew schools were created by Jewish monies and did not get any official or municipal support. On the other hand, the government opened special schools for Jewish children that were only in the Polish language. They found it only right that the Jews would have to go begging, but most important to them was that the Jews should speak Polish.

No wonder that the Brest Jews of which many had returned from Russia after the war, had no illusions of a better future under the Poles. Many left the city and wandered far away. At that time there was a large emigration to Eretz Israel, where the number of Brest Jews was estimated to be 2000. Many went to France, Canada, Latin America and the United States in the tens of thousands.

Jewish Soldiers Brest 1919

TYPES AND CHARACTERS

Characters and Figures of Brest Jews

By M. Weisman
Translated by Dr. Samuel Chani and Jenni Buch

Moshe Weisman

The city of Brest was entirely destroyed by the Nazis, our sacred martyrs will never come back to life but they will always be indelibly etched in my memory. There is the Kobryner street, the steam mill, the small house in which we lived, the wide fields with the windmill – in this field we played war games as children. Also the Tsar's soldiers would have trained there. This whole area (Kobrynska) was called a suburb.

Here are my Jewish neighbors: Itzik Leizer the stone mason, a tall Jew with a thick beard who always carried day and night, a heavy hammer with which he split stones to surface the main roads. His face was always drawn with worry.

Reb Leib the shingle maker – a thin Jew whose house was full of small children –he worked feverishly for his bit of bread.

Susser the wine maker - he made a kind of sour mash drink from cherries with which people would refresh themselves on hot days, his main income was from the Sunday markets.

Isser the blacksmith, a deaf Jew with a pointy beard and a soot smeared face, dressed in a leather apron, the sounds of his hammer and anvil could be heard at all hours, but there was no income and if not for his wife's dairy products they would have gone hungry.

Zalman the cart driver. A humble Jew dressed in a black coat tied with a red belt. He sat on his cart seat everyday and waited for income, he did not miss any opportunity.

Hannaleh the potato-cake baker. A small emaciated woman, her entire life was spent at the oven, putting in and taking out the baking trays. For a kopek she would sell her warm tasty potato cakes with a blessing for your health added.

Who can list and remember them all? There were so many of them, they have all vanished, all my neighbors. Brest, my hometown, I spent my youth on your streets and soil. In the cheder I already recited the Torah. My eyes have seen a great deal there. Days of joy and days of disaster. I recall the images of the 'Epidemic' that raged over the city. Hundreds of dear and loved ones were taken away forever. However, their burial place was known and once a year one could go to that place and open ones heart. I remember the windowpanes when I returned from cheder and could not recognize my street. The walls of the houses had been covered with whitewash and the ground with handfuls of white chalk. The acrid odors still remind me of illness. Mother was waiting outside for my return with tears in her eyes.

Years later a new trouble came to Brest. I remember that Friday morning when I was studying in Rabbi Moshe Bererez's cheder – the Boverdlicher rabbi was pacing up and down the room, stroking his long beard with pleasure that the children of this cheder knew their lessons well and by heart. It was time to dismiss the class and he went out to collect money for the Sabbath. Suddenly, there was a scream from the street: "Fire, it's burning!"

The youngsters did not wait for the rabbi to dismiss them, we ran outside, each to his home, it was known that the fire was spreading everywhere, God have mercy on us.

I ran through Kryvier Street to the suburb, near the Yehezkel prayer house the road was blocked with wagons, horses and people. The house of Shabtai Shenker is burning and the fire had spread to the neighboring roofs that were alight. Burning timbers fell at my bare feet, the possessions that people had dragged outside turned to ashes in the blink of an eye. A Jew whose body was encircled by ropes spoke angrily to me: "why do you stand here in such danger? Quickly run home". I show him my blackened toes which I can't move from the spot... he lifts me in his arms like a sack of flour and takes me to a street where the fire is not burning and gives me directions to get to my house.

I remember the wide-open fields where entire families sat on their belongings lamenting this disaster that had struck their city in the middle of the day. Every now and then people would return with some rescued item from their homes. Soldiers were sent to guard against looting. From all sides the would come more bad news, those who had lost all their fortunes would wring their hands and cry to God in heaven to pity them. Within one day the fire had spread over half of the city. In the evening the sky looked like a sheet of fire. Fear and anxiety grew – many people were burnt alive in the homes. The fire raged all night and the next day we could only smell and see clouds of smoke emanating from the charred ruins. Dozens of prayer houses went up in flames.

Brest was rebuilt. The Jews built new homes and prayer houses and the city again became the center of Torah study for Jewish children. The new study houses were roomier with many shelves and cupboards full of books. Yeshivas and Chassidic circles also sprung up.

The Rabbi of Brest was the famous Gaon (genius and sage) Chaim Soloveitchik. Brest was rich with Jews who were people of the Torah. Amongst them was Reb Sholem Menashe – he was small in stature but a giant in intellect. Every time when it was needed to ask for money for charity, the sons of the city would not go without him. The wealthy of the city would double their donations upon seeing Sholem Menashe.

Rabbi Chaim Shimshon the Dayan (religious judge). His name was on the lips of every pious woman; they blessed their children with it. Fathers would pray that their children would be like him when they grew up. He lived in a small run down house next to the courthouse for the poor. Whist delivering his verdict, Chaim Shimshon was not swayed only by the law, but always made an effort to find mitigating circumstances to reduce the sentence with compassion.

One day my mother cooked noodles in milk, which had to sustain the five hungry mouths in the house. She was in a hurry and mixed the food with a meat spoon – I happened to have just entered the house-crying Mama I want to eat! She looked at me with tears in her eyes and could hardly speak until she said:" Moishele run to Rabbi Chaim Shimshon and tell him what has happened so that he should give a ruling on this matter." Nothing more needed to be said, I had seen the meat spoon in the milk noodles and understood. I ran to Chaim Shimshon who listened with closed eyes –he opened them and looked at me with fatherly concern and asked how many there were living in the house. He pinched my cheeks and said:" Go home and tell your mother that the food is kosher but that the spoon has to be immersed and cleansed."

In Brest there were many prayer houses and synagogues to be found on every street. This saved us from having to remember the street names, it was sufficient to know the name of the prayer house that one would find there and that would serve as an address. I f someone said that they lived near the Yehezkel synagogue, or near a certain prayer house, or next to the 'Mishmar' synagogue, this was an excellent guide –one could not err.

Besides a few pale faced Jews, yeshiva students and small businessmen, Brest also had its share of sturdy Jews – many of them horse and cart drivers, butchers, porters, well built strong robust young men who would frighten away the Gentile hooligans. Many times these hooligans would be reluctant to start an incident in the marketplace, as they knew that they would receive a bloody outcome. What has become of them? Where are these dear Jews now? What has happened to those super healthy young men?

At the beginning of the 20th century there arose in Brest an organized working class. In the boulevards where one strolled one would hear new words... Socialists, capitalists, Jewish youth, workers in black shirts, they would argue about revolutions and strikes.

Fathers and mothers would worry that no good would come from all this...

In the revolutionary years of 1905-6 the Jews of Brest changed their opinions. Together with the constitution there was an outbreak of anti-Jewish unrest. At that time the young men with their black shirts were the first to defend Jewish lives. On the Shossenaya Avenue in an attic Jewish workers with guns in their hands assembled to hear the 'orator' with a bouffant hairstyle and thunder in his voice: "Comrades, here in this city, we will not allow pogroms to take place". It seems that at that time, Jewish workers defended Jewish lives with bravery and national pride.

Brest remained a Jewish town when the new rulers, the Poles, came to power. Until the bloodthirsty 'Master Race', against which the workers of Brest had no defense to counter their murderous instincts. They did not spare anyone – young, old, women, children. Jewish Brest was totally destroyed.

[Page 261]

Two Figures

By Y. Govkin (New York)
Translated by Dr. Samuel Chani and Jenni Buch

Jewish Watercarrier in Brest

Meier the Watercarrier

The year was 1919, a cold and cruel winter descended on the residents of Brest who had returned to the destroyed city after the Germans has ransacked and burnt it. Illness and epidemics were added to the troubles of the war-ravaged city. The only source of income for most of the inhabitants was the 'Joint' committee, which sustained life in the cold damp houses, allocating flour, fat and meat. The political situation in the city was unclear. On the streets there aimlessly wandered peasants from surrounding villages with rags on their feet, caps on their heads and guns on their shoulders. During the daytime they walked about like guests at a strangers wedding, and as the sunset they would begin shooting. On the other side of the Mukhavets and Bug rivers sat the Polish military but they had not entered the city. They were awaiting directives from London but as yet, no decision had been reached about what to do with the Brest, Pinsk and Polessie districts.

On one side were the Bolsheviks, the other the Petliorvites, but neither had entered the city. In the meantime, the local peasant militias from the surrounding villages maintained law and order. By the way, the militias did not behave too badly, but the guarding was not especially effective. Thieving and looting were daily occurrences. On the roads one found murdered Jews from Brest and the neighboring towns.

I'll never forget the widow of Meier the Watercarrier and her three daughters. How they ran in the night to find that their breadwinner had been found dead on the outskirts of the city. Meier the Watercarrier had been blessed with six daughters and one son. During the German ransacking of our city he had fled with his family to Lukow, where he provided his children with plentiful income. Their house was open to every Brisker, myself included. After I fled the German's forced labor I came to Lukow, which was in a more civilized area with somewhat limited military activities. There I stayed at Meier home, a simple warm house with good standards and welcoming to guests.

His oldest daughter, Liba, was an educated girl who managed a restaurant in Lukow, she made sure that I would never be short of food. I had returned starving and racked with injuries from the German forced labor, also I was infected with malaria. I had to be hospitalized and lay for several months fluctuating between life and death. It was only thanks to the Jewish German Dr Yudah that I left the hospital healthy and returned to the house of Meier the water carrier. When the news came that Brest had been reopened to civilians, Meier the water carrier was one of the first to return. His income from before the war was ruined, so he bought horses and a wagon and started to transport passengers –he traded whatever was possible and he lived a decent respectable life until he met his death on the roads.

Before the war, if a person was found murdered in Brest, the entire community was shaken – during the war years people had been accustomed to death. Especially when news came through from the southeast about mass murders of people, now this did not make a great shock anymore. They just stood quietly on the destroyed wooden sidewalks and silently looked at the distraught widow and her daughters who were lamenting their deceased husband and father with bitter tears.

Elyahu Sini Kupchik

This was his full name but the entire town called by the name of Eliahu Sini, many thought that Sini was his family name. The name of Kupchik was used in relation to David Kupchik who was one of the first to introduce the teaching of Hebrew in the Hebrew language in his 'Cheder Metukan' (Improved Cheder). Eliahu Sini and David Kupchik were related, both were Hebrew teachers of the new modern kind. David Kupchiks school was well organized. On the table was a bell that the teacher would use to call for order when the students were making too much noise. Everyone respected this bell – there was something in it that commanded obedience. Also the courtyard of the school was sparkling clean and smelt of newness.

There were swings and a place to play ball – the schoolboys who came to this school from the old neglected cheders, breathed in the airy spaciousness and learned with enthusiasm. At David Kupchiks they did not however gain a great deal of knowledge, and after finishing his school they would transfer to the school of Eliahu Sini. To tell the truth, his school was not so spotless or clean, but at his school one would learn a lot of Hebrew, Tanach, and a good grounding and preparation for the Gemarrah. There were very good teachers there: Avraham Ber, a learned Jew who taught Chumash, Rashi and Gemarrah.

Elyahu Elyon, who taught grammar and essential punctuation in which he was an expert, and prophets and writings. A youth that finished this school would leave with full Jewish knowledge. The orthodox Jews looked upon Eliahu Sini as a frivolous person but had to admit that he could teach.

It was said of Eliahu Sini that he was a teacher of the new style, but he was not just a teacher, he was always by his nature an artist and poet. He wrote Hebrew songs and poetry with great outpourings of his soul. He could write and speak beautifully. When he would read from a chapter of Joshua, he seemed like a prophet in the eyes of his high school students, as he thundered " sons I have brought up and elevated and they have sinned against me or, "console, console my nation". We could almost see the prophet as he stood on top of the mountain, punishing and consoling. When Eliahu Sini taught us from Jeremiah, his voice would tremble and tears appear in his eyes: "on the destruction of my nation, I was broken and in the ruins of her name I prophesize". The books lay open in front of us, but our eyes were focused on the teacher - we did not see the chubby Eliahu Sini with his beautiful broad beard. Instead, we saw the starving emaciated prophet Jeremiah lamenting the destruction of his people, and we were not ashamed to let a tear fall....

We were the youngest group and when I finished Mashli and began Job, I thought that we wouldn't learn anything more after chapter three, which ends with the story of the deed, and then the reproaches from above began. The teacher excelled himself with an intense and passionate explanation. The older students and I were not capable of understanding the bitter complaints from Job and the arguments of Elipaz the Yemenite. Arriving at chapter 13 in which to his honor and alone he goes out into the storm, we were overcome by fear. The presence of the Almighty was over our classroom, his voice could be heard like thunder - we felt small and insignificant as did Job in his time, and when Job began his reply with humility - we repeated his words with trembling lips.

In our class there was also a 16-year-old youth, Davidov, a pupil of the city's trade school. He would steal away and come to be with us for a while. He was full of pride, he had read Pistorov and would pester the teacher with questions about God, and worldly matters. He would often say that he actually had little interest in school but was only fulfilling the wishes of his parents. However, Job, as taught by Eliahu Sini had impressed him. We teased him and asked him, where are all your questions now? He would get angry and say: "Leave me alone boys, if you knew the passage from Job as well as I do, then you would be silent"

After finishing school, I became a visitor to Eliahu Sini 's home. He would read me his poetry written in his beautiful handwriting and would talk a lot about the rules of punctuation. Sometimes, in his own way, he would explain the problems and difficulties that preoccupied the minds of the youth in the years before the First World War. We would discuss everything and everyone – about God and man, joys and suffering.

Righteous and evil - he who does evil and he who is good to him.

His political persuasions did not appeal to me and until this day I cannot understand how come he was a dreamer and stood against the side of the Zionist movement that had sprung up in our town in those years.

The last time I saw Eliahu Sini was in 1920 after W.W.1.I was then a teacher in the Hatechiya School where the instruction of all subjects was in Hebrew. Eliahu Sini came to see me at work; he went into all the classes, heard Hebrew spoken in all the classes, and the playground. I asked him, "Rabbi what is your opinion?" He answered, " What is this work in your eyes?" I was disappointed in his answer - I was ashamed in front of my colleagues who stood around the honored guest awaiting his opinion. The man from whom I had learned so much and who had instilled in me a deep love for the spoken Hebrew – this man was not pleased by the method of teaching Hebrew in Hebrew, and that the language lived both in the mouths of the teachers and pupils.

Today, I understand that his opposition came from the fact that he could not bear hearing the language of the prophets being taught to the common people and used in secular subjects such as arithmetic, geography, and gymnastics. Tanach and grammar, his beloved subjects, were taught according to a dry system. As every actor or folk artist that sees all his roles performed by amateurs in the theatre, but without the artistic passion, this ruled his feelings of bitterness and depression. Incidentally, he himself gave other reasons for his displeasure with the school.

[Page 267]

Brest Personalities

By M. Z. Ilin
Translated by Dr. Samuel Chani and Jenni Buch

There were great personalities and scholars in the city of Brest Litovsk who are not alive any more and have been forgotten. The remnants of the older generation who knew and respected them, remember them with nostalgic longing, whilst the new generation has no full knowledge about them. I will recall several of these personalities of Brest Litovsk, people of the Mishmar synagogue that was destroyed by the Nazis.

The Schatz Family

In 1904 I left my hometown and was privileged to go to Israel. As if in a dream, I remember the elder of the Schatz family, Reb. Boruch Leib, an older good-looking Jew, a benefactor and important businessman. Although he was a great merchant and the owner of a brandy brewery, he would spend long hours in the synagogue, praying and learning. His eldest son, Yerucham, was a trustee of the city, and was involved with many charitable institutions and large charities such as the Talmud Torah, and Bikur Cholim. He was also the Gabbeh (trustee) of the Great Synagogue, which was known for its beauty and great cantors. He was forthright in his opinions and had a pleasant appearance and great energy.

He would come to the synagogue very early for the first prayers and sit through all the minyanim. In between, he would manage to finish all his prayers and answer all those who appealed to him for charity. At first, he would become irate and refuse - then he would relent and donate very generously.

On the day of Herzl's death, the Zionists of the city decided to mourn him in the Great Synagogue. The opponent of Zionism (Schatz) decided to leave the city, taking the synagogue keys with him so that they could not hold the memorial service.

The second son, Isser, was entirely different – relaxed and approachable. He was not involved in the affairs of the community. He was a great metal merchant and had a great leaning toward knowledge and education and Zionism. This resulted in several members of his family settling in Israel.

The Gaon Rabbi Yakov Zalman Livshitz

Rabbi Yaakov Zalman Livshitz was the son in law of Reb.Boruch Leib Schatz.. His own father, Rabbi Boruch Mordechai Livshitz was rabbi in several major Russian cities, and author of the book 'Brit Yakov'. He himself was a great scholar with a deep knowledge and learning. He leaned towards rabbinical literature and published commentaries in the Torah journals. He was the Gabbey of the Talmud Torah and various yeshivas and would listen to the pupils studying. He was a good looking man and used to walk step by step by the side of others, as was the custom of the talented students – to chat amicably about the Torah and also matters of the world. He loved the yeshiva students who studied in the synagogue and would look after them – he was an enthusiastic follower of the Torah and would give Torah lessons to businessmen. He was also a strong opponent of Zionism and was a member of the 'Black Bureau' whose center was in Kovno. From there all the pamphlets against Zionism were published. He was very regretful when it became known to him that one of his yeshiva students had become a Zionist. When I left for Israel he begged me to repent and not be associated with Zionism.

Rabbi Tzvi Yaffe

Rabbi Tzvi Yaffe was different, several members of his family settled in Israel, and also his wife was privileged to make aliyah. He was the son of the famous Gaon, Rabbi. Gimpel Yaffe, a famous Zionist in his time, who made aliyah and settled in Yehud near Petach Tikvah, there he founded a settlement and many talented students from Jerusalem

Yeshivas came to study and learn from him. He passed away in Eretz Israel.

Also his son, Reb.Tzvi, had the same leanings towards Zionism but did not achieve his ambition of making aliyah. Reb Tzvi Yaffe was a Jew of splendid appearance, a talented and great student of the Torah, well versed in all its chapters as well as a deep knowledge of books and rabbinical literature. He went to Israel after his father's death and returned with to Brest with his father's large library of books that his father had left him.

I remember talking with Tzvi Yaffe when he returned from his trip to Israel. He was asked about the land and the settlers and if they were really observed the Torah, or as was being written, were they free thinkers? He was very cautious with his words and answers. His children live in Israel.

Rabbi Asher Hari

A good-looking man always dressed in silk garments, also on weekdays – he was a very learned in Torah and also a very talented businessman. He would come to the synagogue very early and already have said a great deal of the prayers before they were recited. Then he would stand and pray with great devotion. After the prayers, he would sit and learn for half of the day. In the afternoon he would come to his shop. He was honest and naïve, he believed and trusted everyone, unlike the other merchants who could use any methods to solve their problems with debtors. He was a son of the Torah who kept his integrity and was righteous in his business.

Reb Yaakov Rottenberg and Reb Shloime Poliachik

The first was born in Brest and a grandson of Rabbi Yakov Meir Padua.

The second was known as the prodigy from Meytshat. Both of them were prodigies, great students who accumulated much knowledge and learning, mainly in physics and higher mathematics. Reb Shloime was a quiet man, thin and haggard, always immersed in his thoughts, his face always drawn with worry.

Reb. Yakov was a tall and always happy man. Both were great friends and good comrades to all the yeshiva students. Reb Shloime was elected to be a department head at the yeshiva of Rabbi Yitzchak Elchanan in America. He died in the prime of his life.

Reb Yakov also reached the rank of assistant and colleague to Professor Einstein in Germany. He later became professor of mathematics at Minsk University.

Simcha Zelig and Moishe Sokolovsky

Both of them were department heads at the yeshiva in the Mishmar synagogue. The yeshiva was called 'Torah Chessed' and was founded by us, the young men of the city, later attracting young men who came there from other towns.

Reb Simcha Zelig was a skinny Jew, really a bag of bones. The holiness shone from his face. Besides his greatness in Torah, he was a master of teaching. His lessons were simplistic, he did not hold in debating the points of the Torah. His lessons made a great impression, as if the world was an ordinary page of the Gemarrah. In truth, Reb Simcha went into the depth of the issues and simplified the answers to all the questions from Rabbi Akiva and other interpretations. He taught his students a method of understanding the Talmud simply. According to Rabbi Chaim Soloveitchik, he was one of the outstanding teachers of the Volozhin Yeshivah. He was the right hand man of Rabbi Chaim in matters of instruction and in all matters pertaining to what was permitted or forbidden in kosher or unkosher food. He became renowned as an expert in this and all came to him with questions. He was also renowned as a righteous man and many came to him for his blessing. Rabbi Chaim also sent people to Simcha Zelig so that he would pray for them.

His face was always happy and radiated with goodness and compassion. We never saw him angry. His whole life was one of poverty and denial. It was said that he was amongst the last to perish, until the last moment he was consoling and reassuring the Jews in the Brest ghetto.

Reb. Moishe Sokolovsky was different. His place in the synagogue was a corner near the Holy Ark. For many years he sat and studied with great diligence. He would study the Torah for 20 hours a day. Of him it was said that he had difficulty in grasping, but thanks to his perseverance he achieved much and became a learned man. His method of teaching was argumentative, his lessons were published in a booklet called "Torat Moishe', which was warmly received in the yeshivas. In my time, he had begun to teach but not in order to receive any reward. He was also involved in the management of the yeshiva and was interested in the students and looked after their needs. He liked the students and would invite them to his home to discuss matters of Torah.

[Page 271]

Bygone Years

By Dr. A. Eisen (New York)
Translated by Dr. Samuel Chani and Jenni Buch

Dr. A. Eisen

I was born in Nissan 1886 in Brisk D'Lita. When I turned three, I remember my first cheder where my teacher was Reb Avraham. It was a large room with a long table with two benches each side where the pupils sat tightly squeezed together, learning the alphabet with a tune. On the sand covered floor in large numbers lay scattered pamphlets. And there were about 30 little Moishelehs and Schloimelehs...

After that there was my second teacher of Chumash and Rashi. In this cheder there were ten or twelve boys in a corner with a bed stacked high with bedclothes. In another corner sits the teacher's wife darning socks or peeling potatoes. The teacher, Reb Yossel was a tall thin man given to fits of coughing. His meal in the winter evenings was usually several pieces of bread, a plate of peas or beans, and to finish - a tea as pale as chalk. Reb Yossel would smoke the short cigarette stubs that he would find in the streets or in the entrance to the synagogue.

I will recall another whose holy silhouette always passes in front of my eyes – Reb Yoshualeh. He came from the small town of Mezrich. My grandfather, Reb Yehuda Leib Rubin, an honest and God fearing Jew lived there all his life, and was famous for his three trips to Israel and his assistance in establishing the colony of Yesod Hamaleh in 1884.

Reb Yoshualeh came to Brest to teach Torah already aged seventy. He had a sparse white beard and the good soft eyes of a child. When he would teach us children the Chumash or about the miracles and wonders of the Exodus into Israel, or about the great righteous men that God had sent to guide his people – his voice would be soft and trembling - tears would appear in his eyes and it would take him some time to calm himself.

After him came my Gemarra teacher. In the cheder there were four fourteen-year-olds boys. The rabbi was a red –headed Jew with a long thick red beard and rosy cheeks, as if he was just out of the bathhouse. He was known to be a wonderful teacher.

My best friend in the cheder was Velveleh who was the son of the famous Brisker Rabbi, Chaim Soloveitchik. He is now known as the Sage and Rabbi Zeev Dov Soloveitchik.

Another teacher I would like to recall was Goldberg, the famous Hebrew teacher and the father of three famous sons. One of them was the poet Menachem Berisha. The story as it happened was like this: my father Reb Moshe Michael was a great and very learned man in Torah. Besides what he had learned at the table of Rabbi Chaim Brisker and Rabbi Scholem Menashe, he was also steeped in the teachings of that time. He was not very pleased with my limited knowledge of Tanach, therefore he employed the best teacher, Goldberg, to teach me the chapters of Job, Ezekiel, Daniel, etc.etc. My father would observe with great attention the anniversary of the death of Yomtov Lipa Heller , the author of 'Baal Tosphot Yom Tov' to whom we were related. I remember that on these anniversaries I would help with cleaning the house and putting kerosene in the lamps. On this day my father would invite all my former co-students and also poor students from the Brest Yeshiva, as well as our relations.

Over time I have translated many works of the classical writers of England and America (into Yiddish). After the Great Fire of Brest (1901) I went to Vilna and prepared for study in a teacher's seminary but fate decided differently.

In November 1904 I came to America as the pioneer of our family, thus beginning a new chapter of my life. I have been involved in many newspapers and monthly publications such as – Der Oifkum, Die Feyder, Die Zukunft, Chicago Tag, Tag, Vorverds, the Frier Arbeiter Shtimme (Free Workers Voice), The Wochenblatt, Literarische Bletter, and Warsaw, etc.etc.

In the 'Amerikaner' I published over seventy biographical essays as well as extracts of my translation of the Five Scrolls. Amongst my various translations were:

The Prisoner Of Chilon by Lord Byron. 1923
essays of the Rubbiyat of Omar Khayyam by Lord Tennyson 1926
Jewish Melodies.by Lord Byron 1928
Anouk Arden by Lord Tennyson 1930

His Keys. by Lord Byron 1932
25 Songs of Henry Longfellow 1933
25 Songs of Walt Whitman 1934
Songs by Thomas Moore 1935
The Shakespearean Sonnets 1944
King Lear By W. Shakespeare 1947
Judaism by Rabbi Dr. I Lowenthal..

[Page 273]

Four Personalities

By Dr. A. Wolfson. (New York)
Translated by Dr. Samuel Chani and Jenni Buch

I was sixteen years old when I arrived in Brisk D'lita in 1897. My immediate purpose was to study Torah with the genius, Rabbi Chaim Sloveitchik. For over two years I studied diligently under his supervision in the Great synagogue. In the courtyard of Rabbi Chaim's house, I studied with about two hundred other students.

The generous benefactors of the city treated us well, each one of us would receive allotted days at the homes of the respected families, and where the food we received was the very best. The following personalities have remained in my memory:

The Famous Gaon, Rabbi Chaim Soloveitchik

His graying hair wonderfully framed his face. His slightly bent head with the penetrating eyes. His sharp observance and awesome memory are well known – he was an unforgettable personality.

The home of Dr. Shereshevski

He was a renowned Brest physician with a Jewish heart, a friend of progress and knowledge. He would assemble the 'advanced' yeshiva students every evening to instruct and prepare them for exams.

Noah Finkelstein

A businessman, he was an educated and learned man who gave much of his time and money for the education of the yeshiva students. Thanks to them, I studied hard and passed the exams as a teacher and obtained a position in the shtetl of Razitza, where there had also been a teacher called Shalom Aleichem, who had taught the parents of my students.

The Lawyer Grodzensky

He would come and inspect the synagogue only once a year. He had a warm Jewish heart and was loved by everyone. He had influence with the city authorities, and was very eager to help the yeshiva students with all their needs. His wife Yaffa was very good-natured and took care that the students should not lack for anything thanks to her there were no hungry ones amongst us. It was a great privilege to eat two meals a day in their home, and to be full.

Regardless of all this, I was totally immersed in my studies of the pages of Gemarra under the supervision of Rabbi Chaimke, and I was also totally absorbed in my secular studies to obtain a teaching diploma. I was greatly helped by Lalstein, a teacher at the Brest high school. Dr. Shereshevski and Noah Finkelstein paid for my tuition, as well as that for several other students.

In 1899, upon receiving my diploma, I obtained my first position in the town of Razitza in southern Russia with the help of Noah Finkelstein.

When I was about to be mobilized into the Russian army, I immigrated to the United States. There I studied dentistry at New York College. In my life I have endured much and suffered hardships, but I wanted to describe my existence in the period of my early life in Brest and the wonderful personalities that I encountered there – to them I owe much gratitude for their help and guidance in my life.

[Page 275]

Stolin - Karliner Chassidim

By B. Kastrinski
Translated by Dr. Samuel Chani and Jenni Buch

The shteibl (prayer house) of the Karliner Chassidim was located in a house surrounded by trees. It was an enclosed separate world - inside everything seethed with activity. The Holy Ark was made of wood in the old style, a tiled stove took up an entire wall. Many lamps, some in the old style, some in the new style, excelled in their beauty and gave a special charm to this holy place. The congregation consisted of Chassidim and ordinary Jews.

The western wall of the room was allocated to the 'sons of the city'. Reb Moshe Baruch Bishkovitz, a wealthy respected Jew, was a retired flour merchant from whom one never heard a raised voice. When the Rabbi would come to Brest, he would stay at Reb Moshe's house. Moshe Baruch was not an especially fanatic Chassid – in those days before W.W.1 he would buy Zionist shekels and contribute to the settlements in Israel.

In contrast, his son Reb Yakov Bishkowitz was a fanatical fiery Chassid who would organize the pilgrimage to the Rebbe on the High Holidays. He was a master of prayer who would distinguish himself on Kol Nidrei night in the synagogue. This same Yakov Bishkowitz was accustomed to send a sack of flour to the Rebbe for the High Holidays and festivals. Also, after W.W.1, when his financial situation worsened he continued to send the Rebbe contributions exactly as he had done in the good times. He was a warm sincere person who was genuinely interested in the welfare and wellbeing of his community. If a Chassid had a celebration, he would invite all the members of his community to participate in his simcha. Also in the days of mourning he would see to it that they would not lack for anything in their homes. He did this with his whole heart, not sparing his time or money. He was especially renowned for his dancing, he would dance for hours. If someone would stop from tiredness, he would grab them and take them into his circle and further dance with them – he was always the first to start dancing and the last to stop. He would spread every new melody of the Rebbe's amongst his community. He died in Warsaw in 1939.

Older Chassidim tell that Reb Yakov Bishkowitz was greatly influenced by Reb Chaim Mendel Kastramsky, who had introduced him into this Chassidic culture and enthusiasm. Chaim Mendel was a teacher of Chassidic children and greatly respected by all. He was famous amongst the Polish Chassids. In 1936 Reb Chaim Mendel traveled to Israel and settled in Jerusalem. He died during the War of Independence in 1948 in a shteibl of the Stolin – Karliner Chassids in the Old City of Jerusalem.

Reb Reuben Kanel

He was older than Yakov Bishkowitz, he also belonged amongst the important Chassids of Brest. A passionate Chassid, during prayers he would jump up and down and dance as if he was speaking to someone or conversing with God Almighty Himself. That was in the time when we were homeless exiles - refugees in the town of Horodetz in the Kobryn district. The town was full of refugees and soldiers who had been expelled from Brest. Every courtyard and house was fully occupied. The refugees would gather in the shteibl of the Karliner Chassids in Horodetz to pray - they were all broken and embittered.

From the street could be seen distant flickering flames – Brest was burning. It was a Friday night towards the end of summer – the air was hot and stifling. The congregation begged Reb Reuven to come and lead the prayers. He glanced at the red sky, closed his eyes and started to pray as usual, jumping and dancing with his eyes raised to heaven. Even the Russian soldiers who witnessed this marveled at him and said, 'what a holy Rabbi '.

Next to Reb Reuven always stood Reb Benjamin, a timber merchant. He was also a songwriter who assisted the chazan in writing the melodies for the prayers. Reb Benjamin was renowned for his 'Lecha Dodi' melody, which was much loved by the congregation.

He was an exceptional talent.

Reb Moishe the Tall

A painter by profession, he was an elderly Chassid who still had the strength to lead the early morning prayers. His sons, David Leib and Aaron, maintained this tradition, watched over him and helped him with his singing that came from the bottom of his heart.

Once a year, Brest would be visited by the Rebbe. Reb Israel was a good-looking Jew, astute in worldly matters. Dressed as an ordinary businessman, he would not discuss Torah at the table. He was a learned scholar and could also play the violin. He composed a series of melodies and his sons were also musicians. He would not accept written appeals (notes) or redemption money but would bless his Chassids. His Chassids would ask his advice about financial matters and health issues. He had some knowledge of medicine. When he visited Brest, not only his followers would visit him but Jews from the whole community. They would dance for long hours and during the dancing put him into a carriage. Reb Israel died in Frankfurt Germany in 1922. He was succeeded by his son, Reb Elimelech, and according to the advice of Reb Chaim Mendel, this was Reb Israel's wish.

Reb Elimelech stayed in Israel for some years, days before the outbreak of W.W.2 he left Israel and returned to Karlin where he was murdered at the hands of the Nazis.

The Chassids knew how to celebrate the exit of the Shabbath and the High holidays in an exceptional and beautiful manner. The coming week could be full of worries; the Chassids were accustomed to look forward and took the daily disappointments in their stride.

At Simchat Torah, their dancing with the Torah had no bounds to their joy and merrymaking. Rich or poor, irrespective of age or status, they would all join in the singing in friendship and brotherhood. They would go from house to house collecting all the 'goodies' that had been prepared for them for the festivals. At Purim, the Chassids would go from house to house of the wealthy lead by a musician playing melodies on a violin. I can even now visualize Shmuel Lieb the watchmaker, leading them, another playing a drum, accompanied by a crowd of children. The musician would call out a blessing and the amount of money to be donated – every household had an allotted sum and a special song.

They would all sing together and ate sweet things because it was Purim and everything was permissible. Thus the parade went from all the houses, collecting extra people along the way, taking the food and drinks to the synagogue where they would sing and dance until the morning prayers.

The donated monies would go into a death fund – to help bury the poor who could not afford a funeral and headstone. Amongst the well-known Chassids in Brest was Reb Noah the painter. A Chassid, an innocent straight and pure hearted man, he would freshly paint the prayer house every year, if the Rebbe would visit, he would paint it again as he considered this a sacred task.

Reb Moshe Boaz, Reb Noah Grushavsky who was the permanent Gabbei of the shteibl. Reb Asher the baker, the elderly Reb Yonatan who prayed at the eastern wall, my own father, Reb Avraham Chaim Kastrinski, who was a son of old style fervent Stolin -Karliner Chassids. From the old-timers, Reb Zeev Koval, Reb Yakov the baker, Reb Yossele Hari, Reb Aaron Bishkowitz, the Berenson family, and many others as well.

Between the shteibls of the Stolin – Karliner and the Gerrer Chassids in Brest there was shared a thin wall and the door was always open. Both great 'powers', Stolin and Gur, lived side by side in peace and quiet. On Sabbath and the High holidays when we made a large Kiddush, we would celebrate together. On Simchat Torah one would go to the yard of the other to dance together

One of the dear Gerrer Chassids was Reb Berl Shereshevski, an elderly Jew with high standards, a very learned man and a businessman respected in the whole city. He had ten sons - they were great scholars, among them was Rabbi Meir Shereshevski of Bialystok, Chassidic rabbi of that town.

||

Brisk My City

by Anna Margolin
translated by Jenni Buch

A.

The ancient city that is small and grey - is still today like Troy and Athens, but it makes me sorrowful in it's suffering.

Sometimes I will conjure up her magic and shadowy images from inside me.

The streets in their slow and light walks are in panic.

The months of April are eternally sudden ñ the rains are saturated by song.

The Fortress is threatening in its muteness,

The tired wings of the two mills, the oak trees escaping from the King's Garden.

The oars are fluttering over the river.

The oars are whispering secrets over the river.

And the boulevards with no people are yawning with wide mouths.

From the glistening samovars the tea is flowing vigorously.

Over the Shabbat candles - prayers of the grandchildren.

The head scarves of the old ladies are mingling in a dance, and the thin lips are whispering all the time, in the memory of the fathers.

On the table finger are playing with beads, there is an open book of Mishnah, and the melody from a thick voice of a student is mixing with the wind.

 In the gardens, the yellow flowers, the poppies, the sunflowers, and the blond plaits with ribbons.

The poets, Pushkin, Nadson, and the redness of the sunset.

Couples are hurrying to the fields, speaking quiet and soothing words, as if rushing after an unseen musician.

And the sadness of Spring is pouring around and the sparkles and scent of the lilacs wafts over.

B.

At night the young women sitting on the doorsteps and talking with great interest about their men in Germany, about evil spirits, about gypsies.

The children are sneaking in the doorways, trembling and apprehensive that a gypsy will come and kidnap them.

Small Cleopatras - girls of 15, in their gloves and parasols walk around leisurely in the boulevards pulling their scarves up and down and listening to the kissing words: ilift up my heart to the wondrous distances"....

Middays, blinded by the light the grocers are all asleep, the walkers are all sleeping - sometimes a righteous man will be carried along like a storm with frowning eyebrows.

The streets are bowing and the young men hold their breath. In the background the soldiers and officers are spoiling the Jewish scenery.

On the humpy road like a thundering subway is a solitary driver.

Oh, the soft sands of my town, the oaks and the roses of my garden.

Like the smell of good bread, the fresh morning rises in all the streets saying:

"Good morning, good morning".

[Page 281]

A City Surrounded by Shtetls

By Moshe Satoy (Stavski)
Translated by Dr. Samuel Chani and Jenni Buch

The beautiful city of Brest, the great city of Russian Jewry that was through the generations crowned with greatness in Torah and high standards, known for it's generous heart and hands. A city known in Israel and the Diaspora, it was surrounded by towns and villages that were drawn to it - warming to its light and attracted by its radiance. They would send letters of questions and receive answers from their rabbis and Gaonim (sages), whom they followed and obeyed - in contrast to the ruling powers.

From my early youth, even before I saw it with my own eyes, I felt its spirit, crowned with greatness and shrouded in legends. The cheder and yeshiva students would talk of its large buildings, theatres, schools, synagogues and yeshivas. They told of their rabbis, the greats of their generation, and the glory of Judaism. The Soloveitchiks, father and son, who with their erudition could bring down mountains and they themselves, were like mountains (see I.L. Peretz Between Mountains).

The merchants, the affluent, and the wealthy benefactors who conducted business with all the major cities in the land and abroad, still followed the laws of kashrut, and wherever they were, they would not omit learning a page of Gemarra whether on foreign soil or at home.

The ordinary Jews, the tradesmen, and laborers would say a chapter of Psalms; learn a portion of the Chumash (Pentateuch) a chapter from the Mishna, and a commentary of the Book of Legends, and the Book of Laws (Chayey Adam).

There were famous doctors, greats of medicine who would not accept money for a visit to the poor and would leave medicine for free.

The method of giving charity, openly and with generous open hands and hearts.

They would tell of one Brest businessman whose wife's jewelry would be at the pawnbrokers for the whole year in order to help marry off a poor bride. On the eve of the High Holidays she would redeem her jewelry, only to pawn it again immediately after the holidays. Just as the only Jew in Antopol that dressed in clean and fresh spotless clothes, a talented and brilliant Talmudic student was betrothed to a rich man's daughter, because the Glory of Brest influenced the rich man.

The marketplace and places of trade, which seethed with activity all week, as noisy as a huge fair, the marketplace with the shops on all four sides, full of merchandise and food products.

The King's Park, a large and well cared for park with grassy lawns, trees where birds would nest in their branches, and a stork built its nest at the top of the tallest tree. On Saturdays and High holidays the Jews would wander around this park and marvel at God's wisdom and beauty.

The river Mukhavets that in summertime swelled its waters, which flowed away to distant countries and the rest of the world. It swallowed the sins of the townsfolk that were cast into it and took them away...

The fortress was at the same time both a border and a barrier between the Jewish Mitnagdim from Lithuania and the Chassidim from Poland. It built up a dividing wall between countries and governments with established borders and different destinies.

Above all, the railway station - built broad and high and world famous. It was said that from Zashmerinke to Brest there was no other railway station to equal it in the whole of Russia.

Of all the gifts that God gave the world, Brest received a beautiful portion. There was a story about the leading nobleman of the district – his name was Sztar – would eat an entire roasted stuffed turkey at his mealtimes as if it were nothing. His weight even exceeded that of His Honor the Tsar Alexander the Third himself, who was renowned as the heaviest man in all of Russia in his time. Once, during military maneuvers conducted in the Tsar's presence, he broke the back of the horse he was riding. Maneuvers. The Tsar himself congratulated him and said:"Bravo Molodetz!"

Of the ten fires that raged through Jewish towns, nine of them broke out in Brest. A Brisker fire was an event that was mourned for generations.

Brest my Origin

I knew Brest ever since I was a boy, immediately after my Bar Mitzvah, I traveled with my father and older brother going to his military service. It was my first train journey. I stood at the window during the whole journey, marveling at the wonderful sights before my eyes, that quickly came and then quickly vanished – the telegraph poles, the signs showing the distance in versts (Russian miles), villages, wintry leafless trees, an isolated house, a shepherd boy with his covered head and stick in his hand – his flock spread over the field. A peasant in a ragged fur coat sunken in straw on a wagon pulled by a thin shivering horse.

The station was huge building that overwhelmed me and reminded me of the paragraph " and we are like grasshoppers in their eyes". The noise and tumult of the station was as if in a waterfall, a train arrives, pulls up at a platform, a bell rings, the train whistles and then disappears into the distance.

I freely wandered around the streets, looking at the city, the tall buildings, the beautiful trees and gardens and sidewalks, the droshkies, the shops and the store windows with their displays of clothes and jewelry and tasty delicacies. It seemed that the people of the city had holiday food all week... and the potato cakes – hot, warming, and melting in the mouth. They were called 'Brisker Holnikes' (potato cakes).

But above all, the Brest synagogues and schools, full of people all day long. I swear that I saw with my own eyes long lines of empty droshkies outside the Greener synagogue, without their drivers. When I asked what this meant, I was told that their owners were religious Jewish drivers who had sneaked into the synagogue and between Mincha and Maariv would study a chapter of Mishna and commentaries, and a chapter of Gemarra.

Brest and Warsaw

In my first steps in the literary circles of Warsaw, I was again reminded of Brest....

Brest and Warsaw - because to Brest, Warsaw was like a magnet, a means of achieving the aim to springboard to the wider world.

It was then Warsaw that I met Menachem Goldberg (from Brest) – later known by the name Menachem Beirisha, a good-looking young man with a moustache and a refined almost feminine soul. Blue eyes, with long eyelashes, overshadowed with mischievous chestnut brown, add to this a perceptive awareness. His early verses were immature and childish – I.L. Peretz himself remarked that they amounted to nothing much, but if the great author become close to someone, then he was worthy of it.

We were a group that had liberated itself from traditions and family, and we described ourselves as 'creativity artists'. In truth, we were learning the chain of Jewish literature - we barely amounted to ten people.

I still remember Menachem's room; it was actually a kitchen in an apartment of a coworker of 'Heint' (the daily Yiddish newspaper) in Cholodna St. directly opposite the publishing offices. The apartment was on the top floor; it took one hundred steps to walk up. There Menachem would sit and work for half the day – the room was really a kitchen, and in the afternoon they would put in a bed, stool and table...

I often traveled with Menachem to Brest his birthplace and had the opportunity to befriend him in another atmosphere and environment. His home was warm and friendly and his parents lovingly received me. His father was an educated and spiritual man, was a broad boned man, always worried that his clothes were too tight and short for him. His mother was a refined charming woman, small and thin, self-preoccupied, with an expression of love and care on her face that was a prototype of Menachems. The other brothers resembled their father.

In later years we parted ways and our friendship was severed because of love.

My love for Eretz Israel. Because of this sin he could not forgive me...

Also my Rebbe and my former fellow students could not forgive me. The manner in which they reacted to my strivings was like this. ... Several weeks before my departure to Israel, I was visited by a delegation of my friends and coworkers at the newspaper.

"We heard that you are of the opinion to got to Israel. This is simply suicide, perhaps it's because you don't have enough work." Thus I came to the attention of the editor, I went to him to explain and he appointed me as a permanent member of staff.

I left Warsaw as if running away, without farewells from my friends.

[Page 285]

In The Suburb

By Y. Heftman
Translated by Dr. Samuel Chani and Jenni Buch

In the eastern side of the city of Brest, far from the tumult of the market, shops, the large department stores and the noisy droshkies, far from the pushing and jostling pedestrians – was the suburb.

Quiet streets, single storey houses built without any planning permits - no architects ever built them – everyone did according to their own taste. In keeping with the influence of that time, there were large and empty front yards surrounded by wire fences, vegetable gardens, broken and bent fences, just ruins, a reminder of the first fire. A house behind a garden, a garden behind a house, there was no order or planning in this suburb.

In summer at noontime in the suburb, its wide unpaved streets would be deserted and empty. The narrow shops were without customers. The window shutters of the houses were closed to keep out the heat. Tired women in light dresses and uncombed hair nursing their babies sat sprawled on their balconies or doorsteps, drowsily chatting. The children played in the middle of the street, rolling in the sand and the dirty puddles with green slime. The men and the older children were all employed in the city. In the evening the suburb would come alive when the fathers and sons would return from the city. The older girls would go with buckets to the wells for water. Through an open doorway one could see the flames of the fires in the kitchen, and from the chimneys dark blue smoke would come out in waves. The women are busy; the men would sit in their shirtsleeves and trousers in the front of their homes interrupting their conversations with yawns, waiting for their dairy supper.

Yossel the carriage driver, a broad boned Jew with a gray beard tells a small group of the day's journeys and events. Some person seated himself in his carriage and asked to be taken to the station for the train to Warsaw. Yossel knew that the Warsaw train had already left at five o'clock, but what did he care? The passenger should know how to look at his own watch, but as he rushed to the station, what did the driver care? In short, they arrive at the station, the train has left, and the passenger has to wait for four hours. But what did Yossel care, just take out your wallet and pay, but the traveler was obstinate and a whole argument ensued....

The circled group listens, one of them groans, the second yawns, from the other side of the street, one can hear casual chatting. "This is Naphtali" someone said, "and he had a fare to Terespol today, two rubles there and return". The darkness grows and the green of the trees becomes a large inky mass. The dark sky deepens over the suburb and gradually silence descends.

Soon after supper, in the shadows of the fences, between the trees and the dark streets, and in the dark corners, couples meet. Youths and girls with shining eyes and racing hearts, heavy breathing - the darkness covers everything and the suburb falls into stillness...

Winnitski's Garden

In a corner of the suburb were gardens that were overrun with people on the Sabbath and the holidays. The city folk had a large park with long and wide pathways and water fountains, flowerbeds and several sculptures. It was too far for the suburb dwellers to walk there so they congregated in the smaller Winnitski Gardens.

Winnitski was a former military official. But he considered his military career as a sideline, the most important work of his life was the creation of these gardens, which he had planted and cultivated by himself. He had no wife or children and no relatives, it seemed. He lived alone and was solitary, but was very polite to the Jewish passers by who would greet him, he would sometimes put a sweet in the hands of every Jewish child.

The elderly official was very popular with the youngsters of the suburb. The Cheder boys would see him as he passed their windows, they knew this was a sign that it was lunchtime as he would always go for a walk at this time. The children in the street would touch their hats and greet him as he passed them in the street, They knew that on the Sabbath when they would come to the gardens of this nobleman, he would give them berries.

Winnitski's gardens were open to all the Jews of the suburb on Saturdays and high holidays. It was not an especially large garden, there were several walkways, some flower beds behind the house where Winnitski lived, and a large orchard, larger than the public garden. The orchard mostly was rented to a Jew and therefore, one could not walk there.

Winnitski himself would sit on the veranda of his house in his dressing gown, drinking tea, smoking and watching the crowds who had come there to stroll around. He took pleasure in watching the younger generation promenading in his gardens that he had planted and cultivated himself, and had laid out the pathways and benches. He had also built a small arbor between two oak trees, so that it should be a real garden.

A strange gentile was this Winnitski. He would hardly talk all day, but Fusia the shopkeeper and Hayaleh the trader knew enough to tell that he liked to give others a livelihood, and would not argue and bargain over pennies. Shmuelke the bricklayer had earned money from him almost his whole life. Shmuelke was an elderly Jew without any remaining strength, his hands were not as they once were. David the work supervisor would not hire him anymore, in the city there was no work for him... if not for Winnitski, Shmuelke would most likely have died of hunger.

Shmulke worked for him solely – strengthening the fencing around the gardens, fixing the roof over the storehouse, making the benches for the gardens. He erected the arbor. He worked on fixing the steps to the veranda of the house, took down the old timber shed and built a new one, bigger and better than before. What did this aristocrat need with all these 'improvements'? No one knew. The truth was that he had a lot of money, he had a brother, a general, who had died and left his entire fortune to Winnitski. It was said that it was a sum of tens of thousands of rubles. He kept the money in the bank and in stocks and shares. The people of the suburb didn't exactly know his circumstances, just that he was rich, and just that Shmuelke earned his living from him, week after week.

On Sabbath the garden was full of youths and girls from the suburb. Some of them were not dressed well enough to show themselves in the city gardens. A group of girls, seamstresses, sat themselves inside the arbor and one of them reads a novel aloud.

On a bench opposite the arbor a discussion between apprentice tailors about the proletariat and socialism. Yoske Garber, a good looking youth with a red scarf around his neck, sits with his friends and sings a song from 'Shulamit'. Yoske can sing beautifully and is handsome. The group goes over to some girls, amongst who is Raisele, the daughter of Itche-Leib Rachkes. Yoske cannot look at her without his heart thumping and blushing.

Peals of laughter break out. Yossel the carriage driver is searching for his 'jewel'; he wants to take it with him to the synagogue for prayers. The 'jewel' is found amongst his friends, youths of his age. He gets a smack and then another one, his hat falls off his head and rolls about between the flowers. Shmuelke the bricklayer, who has come over in his Sabbath clothing to admire his new bench, wants to defend his 'jewel'. Yossel gets nervous and complains in a loud voice. The groups all leave their places and come over to see the dispute. The sun sends its rays, the birds twitter in the branches of the trees. A quiet breeze blows through the grass – all around sweet scents fill the air.

Yoske Garber watches from the side as Raisele leaves with her friends, now he feels freer, and begins to sing in his beautiful resounding voice, but for whom?

The Sabbath afternoon has come to its end; the evening sky is already tinged with red, spreading red through the clouds. From the distance one can hear the mooing of a cow, returning from the field. The streets of the suburb become full of life, noise and movement. A year old toddler wants to test his strength and walk by himself; his mother follows him with open arms, ready to help him. Suddenly, a pig escapes with a fearful screech from the large yard next to the laundry. The pig just runs into the elderly Reb Leib and knocks him over onto the footpath, Reb Leib yells, the toddler is thrown onto the ground and lies spread out with a frightened wail. A group of boys chase the pig...

Winnitski's garden is emptied of people. The young men and girls go home for their evening meals Afterwards they want to walk into the city, this is the best time to stroll about the streets, past the large stores.

Old Winnitski sits on the veranda of his house in the darkness of the vanishing evening. He smokes and looks at the fully-grown trees that spread their crowns towards the skies; he is lost in his thoughts. And Shmuelke the bricklayer goes to the synagogue and raises his voice in a song and thanks God.

[Page 291]

Three Things

By Menachem Begin
Translated by Dr. Samuel Chani and Jenni Buch

I have asked myself more than once: if it would be possible to travel to Brest as it was possible to travel to Johannesburg or New York, would I get up and go back to the city in which I spent my childhood?

By asking this question a heaviness falls on my heart and an inner bitter feeling tells me that, no, you will never go back to the gates of the city in which you were born, studied, dreamed and enjoyed – because it does not exist anymore.

It is possible that a small house, in which the rays of love and the shadows of poverty were merged together, is still standing today. But the home of my parents has vanished and does not exist anymore. For what would I come "home"? To roam the streets and ask questions that cannot be answered? To seek and not find, to follow shadows that would lead me to the graveyard, but not to find, as we were children not granted even the privilege of going to the graves of our parents.

No, it would be pointless to follow these shadows because they are deep within me and never have left me since the first time I heard the most gruesome bloodcurdling scream that had ever been heard since the creation of this world. Living shadows, eternally inside me and never will leave me.

As if in a dream, I see Zygmuntowska Street, the street named after one of the Polish kings, the street in which I spent my childhood. I was a child of a generation which was thrown into universal chaos by W.W.1.

In that same street I saw for the first time the bayonet carrying soldiers of another revolution. In 1920 for the first time the Soviet soldier was illustrated to my inquisitive child's eyes – entirely different from the revolutionary guards that I encountered 20 years later when I was arrested as a Zionist.

Trotski's and Tuchachevski's soldier sat in our kitchen and warmed his feet and dried his wet leggings. He chatted to my mother in a drowsy voice about the good life victory would bring. He requested, not demanded - a piece of bread to satisfy his hunger.

Later on, Stalin's revolutionary guards knew how to proclaim that Trotski and Tuchachevski had damaged communism and were traitors to the revolution in 1920.

In Zygmuntowska Street, my childhood eyes saw gentile regimes arise and disappear.

They also saw the hardships the Jews endured under those regimes. The constant danger of pogroms cast it's shadow of fear over us. This fear influenced the activities of little children and made them serious. On one of these horrible days, my father became alarmed and was called out into a nearby street where armed soldiers were conducting their pogrom with revelry and beautifying it with an anthem for the new Poland. My father left and soon after a rumor reached our house that he would never return as he had been shot.

The truth was that a Polish soldier had turned his bayonet on him and pulled the trigger, but to his luck, the bullet did not hit my father. The news of this rumor brought my father quickly home. From that day on, I remember my father as a defender of his brethren against attacks, pogroms and oppression. As a defender on occasions of a mass slaughter or great danger, not always could he avert a tragedy, but he was always ready to act when someone was threatened, even at great danger to himself.

At that time the pogrom shadows spread out from afar and came towards us. I learnt a folk song about the Pinsk martyrs who were murdered on the order of a Polish general, an enemy of Israel. The song began with a negative invitation:" better that you don't come to the Seder night" a song that was not sung loudly but that echoed the bitter sacrifices of the screaming victims of an eternal hatred. The words were etched into my brain and have remained in my memory. The simple word pearls have bit by bit infused into my heart's memory and the drops of blood of the innocent murdered Jews.

Memories from those days remain in my mind, the waves of the same anti-Semitism, and if I'm not mistaken of General Listovski, who raised his slingshot against two others of my people. Over twenty years later, when Jewish youths stood up to battle to break the whip of another general that was an enemy of Israel, it awakened in my thoughts the Jews who were openly murdered in the Brest Park.

The house on Zygmuntowska, what terrible and sacred memories were wrapped up and imbedded in its walls. The dilapidated house where I first acquired some knowledge, learning the alphabet with the other Jewish children, chanting Kamatz,Aleph,Vav.

There stands the two-storey building with the large yard where I first began to think in Hebrew. There is the synagogue wrapped in darkness and the rabbi with his black eyes and stooped back who taught me .294

At the edge of the town stood a large, red brick house, a terrible house. There we learnt foreign literature. For the hundreds of Jew- hating Christian children there were about twenty Jewish children. We bought our knowledge for the price of daily beatings, and the same amount of insults, shoving and discrimination. All this happened, sadly, in a large school. We learnt to defend ourselves and return the blows to our attackers. Betray other betrayers. We learnt more from our 'comrades' then we ever did from our teachers.

And on the other edge of the city there was a large brick house that was also a school where there were no more Jewish students than gentiles. On the Sabbath it would change into a symbol of resistance and defense of Jewish honor. They were the offices of the Jewish Youth Committee, a youth that dreamed of a free life, a youth that carried the flag of Judah with pride, a youth that revived the building of the Jewish nation, and were steeped in the love of Zion.

Such was the youth that I knew, I have never found any better in any other place, because better than them does not exist.

No. No. I will not allow myself to go back to Brest. Yet Brest will always follow me and be with me. Because the three main things I have learnt were instilled in me in sorrow and also in joy that I have carried with me from my childhood home – with me during the nights of conflict and the days of joy. Here they are:

1. Love your fellow Jews.

2. Do not fear the gentiles.

3. Lucky is the man who carries the yoke of his childhood with him.

[Page 299]

PERSONALITIES

Writers and Academics

Translated by Dr. Samuel Chani and Jenni Buch
Dr. Yaakov Gromer

Dr. Gromer was in many aspects an extraordinary man. After his childhood in the land of his birth, where he had embraced the study of the Talmud exclusively, there then developed in him a great mathematician – and he came to Goettingen, which was at that time the metropolis of mathematics in Germany. After a short time there he had attracted the attention of the local mathematicians, and in a very short time not only did he attain a deep knowledge of this profession but had also managed to write research which was very highly regarded in order to obtain his doctorate.

He came to Berlin and worked with me as my private assistant on the relativity theory. In those days we published several works together. He remained with me until the early 1930s when he was invited to a prestigious post in Minsk.

Dr. Gromer was not only a brilliant thinker, but also a man with multifaceted interests. He would participate enthusiastically in Jewish matters and was always ready to help everyone.

Taking into account the fact that he suffered from a terrible illness that left him with an ugly appearance, and weakened his body, one can only reflect on how much this man could have contributed to the world. His predicament meant that it was not easy to live with him. Socially it was difficult to maintain camaraderie with him and therefore a productive and fruitful relationship. Because of his own suffering, he was very anxious, and his painful emotions would emanate to those around him.

Signed by Albert Einstein.

(A letter from Prof. Albert Einstein to Prof. Chinitch, 7th April 1953.)

[Page 299]

Dr.Yaakov Gromer - An Amazing Figure

By Zalman Schor
Translated by Dr. Samuel Chani and Jenni Buch

Dr.Yaakov Gromer

In a chronicle in one of the newspapers, in small print, I came across the news that the former professor of mathematics, Yakov Gromer, had passed away in MinsKatzenellenbogen For the reader who knows the personalities of our generation, this name will mean nothing. The chronicle also added that Dr.Gromer was for years a member of the scientific community of Minsk and had worked with Einstein for years – this is too little information to help understand this personality. But for the minority that actually met him, and who lived in close proximity to him, and those who knew how frightful his illness was – an illness that left him devastated - this knowledge was indelibly printed into the eyes of the observers.

In my carefree childhood, learning the first story of Genesis, I was impressed by the story of the figures of the giants, the "fallen of Israel". Even then I was not sure whether to pity or respect them. It was impossible to measure them by normal standards, the giants who are ostensibly normal people, but greater than all others and very lonely and tragic figures because of their greatness. Because I had met and befriended Gromer, I was never free of this association.

It was not only his physical appearance, which certainly was the first cause of this impression - certainly his outward appearance –the overgrowth of his body –his dangerous illness which left one shaken to see his face, legs and hands enlarging alarmingly from visit to visit. How this frightful abnormal growth brought him closer to his death. Not only children were frightened upon meeting him, but also adults and relatives found it difficult to deal with their repugnance.

However, not just because of this, in his spiritual life, and with all the power of his talent and the depth of his penetrating glance – he had something of the wonderful and marvelous in him. Just as the giants who were tragically lonely in their greatness. He was one of the best pupils of Rabbi Chaim Soloveitchik, one of the few of his yeshiva students who could interpret the Torah and give Torah judgements.

The path from the yeshiva of Chaim Brisker to the mathematics faculty in Goetingen, Germany he made with one leap, and overcame the transitional difficulties of an external student, without the different adjustments needed for a new lifestyle. Just as he was the pride of Chaim Brisker, Professor Landau of Goetingen also took pride in him....

Even the First World War did not stop him from receiving his degree in mathematics, despite the fact that he did not have the correct matriculation and was a citizen of a hostile country. From Goetingen University under Einstein's patronage – he was only one step away from the legendary shoes, (he was Einstein's assistant) he became a virtual civilian prisoner in Berlin, having to report to the police three times daily. In fact, famous mathematicians and professors would come to him – they would converse with him and spend long hours in the world of ciphers, numbers and formulas. With him, one could swim more assuredly in these seas – the oars were in his huge hands. It seemed that the mathematical circles in Berlin were the ones who told Einstein about Gromer's innovations in physics and Einstein added his opinion and proposed to publish the thesis under both names.

It was enlightening to see with how much interest Gromer accepted his proposal, and with what modesty he told his small circle of friends. Seeing that he was in difficult material circumstances, Einstein arranged for part time work in the science academy of Berlin, a position that had not been granted to more senior members of the mathematics faculty – in addition to this, it was wartime, and Gromer was a Russian Jew.

Not only in the realm of science where only mathematicians occupied themselves and ordinary mortals do not tread - but also in everyday matters more familiar to us, Gromer excelled in his erudition. Gromer held that two things were essential – a logical brain and an understanding of the abstract world, and righteousness in the material world. In these two concepts he saw the essence of Judaism. He fought for both with passionate fanaticism. It seems to me that his attitude was uncompromisingly stubborn in his struggle for justice.

During lunch in a small guesthouse, he did not feel comfortable, as there were strangers at the table that he had seen for the first time, he suddenly noticed that one of the flatterers to the rich and powerful had offended a poor man. He violently protested. His large hands thumped the table and his grotesque face became as white as chalk His eyes flamed with fire – he became incoherent with rage and looked completely like a dumbstruck prophet – in the ensuing silence there was a holy shiver.

This was also how I once witnessed Rabbi Simcha Meyer Hacohen, the Dvinsker rabbi, raging at a rabbinical assembly in St. Petersburg, which had adopted a resolution against his will. No one could understand his words, and not all his words were audible. His red scarf and clenched fists, his whole face convulsed with anger. What primitiveness from a person with great power in the silence of his rage.

However, Gromer suffered a great deal from this muteness and the inability to express himself. He also liked to clarify and listen to every speaker that was able to get an audience with him. In his later years when understanding his words became so much more difficult, he would get enraged like an offended child, and blame the listener. Also his inability to express his deep and interesting ideas in writing caused him great sorrow and distress. He strongly favored one idea that seemed very simple to him to explain. He researched and delved into this idea, which was no more or less than:" The Possession of Jewish Genius, the Highest Expression of the Specific Jewish path in the Abstract Logic".

He saw living examples in Chaim Soloveitchik and the mathematician Minkovsky, both of whom he regarded as his spiritual soul brothers- twins with one vision in two beings – outstanding personalities in their elevated fields, from one and the same source of Jewish genius.

He once told me this at great length, interspersed with ideas from Rabbi Chaim's sermons and the mathematical principles of Minkovsky. He challenged them with other mathematical analyses and formulas. I proposed that he.write down his ideas. After much imploring, he agreed. For about a week he filled a notebook in densely written Hebrew. He wrote of many deep disclosures and discoveries with very clear explanations. He could unfortunately not build and finish this work. Today it is not possible to solve what might have been and reveal his ideas. By the way, Martin Buber, who found out about this work, publicized that this research would be published in 'Science'.

Before his departure to Minsk, Gromer told me that in the meantime the notebook had grown into a book that was almost finished. It was about the methods of Talmudic studies and the methods of great mathematical advances in the last generations. In addition, he had found time to make inquiries about the existing conditions in Minsk.

With his whole glowing heart, he wanted to participate in the social and community life of his generation - he was eager to attend meetings and would listen with pleasure to political debates and participating in them. However, in this there was also the primitiveness of a giant, as his words became fewer and more meaningful:

Loyalty to the Jewish people.

The sanctity of our social inheritance.

Hatred of wars between nations and the jealousy that causes them.

A tremendous violent outburst accompanied by a fearsome rage against all the men who are falsifiers and against men who are "pleasant in appearance but not pleasant in their existence". Against anyone whose inner self was different to their outer self.

When amongst people he would be a silent observer on the side, but later in his room he would erupt in a flow of hot lava – full of hatred for his enemies and full of praise for those he agreed with. It was strange to see this giant of a man sit on a small bench surrounded by boys and girls in a community hall on Lenin St. or on Dragoner St and listen for the whole evening to speakers for the Poale Zion or the League for the Workers in Israel, of which he considered himself a loyal member. His friends and professors wanted to establish a professorial chair in one of the universities for him – there were negotiations and offers. However, nothing came of it – probably because of his illness, but he thought it was because of he was a Jew and perhaps his Russian citizenship. Anyway, his bitterness rose with what he saw as the evilness of man.

Einstein, who was most impressed with Gromer, promised to take him to Jerusalem. The idea appealed to him and after the war, when life separated us –we met several times after long intervals, in all our meetings he expressed this dream of his. In our last meeting he expressed interest, even if there was a high school position available to him in Eretz Israel. But no such opportunity presented itself.

Einstein tried to influence university professors in Kovno, also with no result. Until there was an invitation from the Bolshevik university in the White Russian capital of Minsk. Since that time I had never heard from him again. Only in an American Bolshevik newspaper did I read of a mathematics conference in Russia where Gromer's name was mentioned, accompanied by the statement that Professor Gromer was the greatest mathematician of our generation and that Einstein valued him as "a colleague who was greater than himself".

[Page 305]

A Genuine Talent

By Dr.Y.Klotzkin
Translated by Dr. Samuel Chani and Jenni Buch

I personally knew Yakov Gromer for about 25 years. I knew him in my childhood and then in Brisk. He was already a young man and renowned as a Gaon, a genius.

When I was a student at the University of Berne, Switzerland, he studied the German language under me. He had a strange difficulty. Although he could solve difficult mathematical problems, on the other hand it was very difficult for him to learn languages. He remained a stammerer even in Hebrew. Yakov Gromer, in his childhood he was called Yankele Rottenberg (after his grandfather's name) was born a genius. I strongly underline the word genius.

He was not just a boy wonder. In every generation there are prodigies of all sorts – people wonderfully gifted in certain areas. But those who deserve the title of genius are very few. One must not confuse the virtuosity that is limited to one of certain fields with the phenomenon of genius that dominates his entire personality and doesn't exclude the intricate relationship between different subjects such as language, music, and science.

I don't deny that Yakov Gromer was gifted with the many talents of a prodigy, especially with a phenomenal memory – but this was not the essence for his distinct individual genius. During his childhood his genius was evidenced in his Talmudic studies. It was said that Rabbi Yoshe Ber Soloveitchik the Brisker rabbi would say: "in the presence of this child Yankele, I have to be very careful of what I say in matters of Torah, so that he will not ask me thorny questions." Later it was evidenced by his study of higher mathematics in Goettingen and Berlin. Also, in his few last years, he was helped by Albert Einstein, whether he was willing or unwilling, because of the fact that his whole life he did not want to acknowledge that the theory of relativity. Only after much persuasion from his friends, and because of his very poor financial circumstances, did he agree to serve science and Einstein. But the differences of opinion between the mathematician and the physicist genius became ever larger and Gromer was forced to leave this work. He was appointed as Professor in Minsk University on Einstein's recommendation. Isolated, he died in Minsk at the age of 56.

His greatest attribute was depth, which was reached with genuine simplicity, and which could grasp the greatest depths without any effort. It was his manner all his life to handle complicated matters with the greatest simplicity. He could undertake the most complicated issues with simple ease. Startling discoveries and developments, which were attained after great effort and research – these would roll out of his mouth, by the way, as an aside, without much emphasis and concern. He would announce this new discovery without any fuss, as if it were self-explanatory.

Those attributes of his came as a consequence of his refined methods which had nothing to do with overstated humility. On the contrary, his humility was his main quality. This quality was of genuine simplicity. It seems that he himself was not aware of the significance of his discoveries because he reached them without effort. This genius could astound the world with the wonder of his genius. He did not possess any self-importance - a vital condition for every action – a sense of self -importance. Not only did he not possess any tendency to seek praise and glory, which he never tasted throughout his life, he did not seek honor and popularity. With him there was only a natural striving to bring his strengths to expose and express.

It is possible that his severe bone disease 'Elephantitis' was the cause of his lack of lack of ambition. He did not have a great knowledge of the ways of the world. He went about us silent and unknown. He left behind no more than a small notebook that he formulated together with Einstein and a mathematical function that was named after him. By the way, he discovered mathematical formulas and rules that ran parallel to Einstein's theory.

In January 1926, Einstein invited me to his home to discuss the matter pertaining to his assistant, Dr.Gromer. During the years that he worked under Einstein's patronage and assisted him with the foundations of the relativity theory, Gromer received a monthly allowance of 200 marks from Einstein. With the fall in the German Mark, that sum was not sufficient for his survival, even with the greatest economizing. Therefore, it was my duty to make efforts to raise his income. Einstein himself could not understand how such a sum was not sufficient for an unmarried man in Berlin. On the contrary, he argued that this sum was sufficient "see how much I give him monthly?" I told him that Gromer had additional expenses of cigarettes, the price of which had risen hugely. Einstein replied that he used to smoke cigarettes but because of the crisis he had begun using a pipe. Then I explained that Gromer had additional expenses of medicines for his terrible bone disease – then Einstein said that he now understood the situation. The doctors were capable of extracting the last penny from the sick. Einstein therefore tried to obtain a subsidy to assist Gromer but said he did not know to whom to turn. I replied that he should turn to Felix von Mendelsohn, and was certain that he would not deny his request. Einstein replied that it was exactly because of that that he could not turn to him, as he knew beforehand that he would not refuse his request, and he had moral qualms about this. He preferred to find a rich Jew with the ability to refuse him, and wanted to turn to him immediately. In the end we concluded that he should write to a special institution that was involved in supporting scientists.

We talked about Dr. Gromer, Einstein praised his mathematical abilities and his assistance to him. He regretted that due to his illness, Gromer would not be able to fulfil all the hopes that were pinned on him since the publication of the exceptional notebook with the mathematical functions "As a mathematician, he surpasses me many times over" Einstein said. I told him how much Gromer respected him as a mathematician. "I am only able to extract from mathematics what is essential for me," he said.

Dr. Yakov Gromer was blessed with extraordinary talents and abilities, his illness, however, greatly weakened him and his creative powers that were capable of great discoveries and new advancements.

[Page 309]

Professor Y. N. Halevi - Epstein

By Professor Simcha Assaf
Translated by Dr. Samuel Chani and Jenni Buch

Professor Y. N. Halevi - Epstein

Yakov Nachum Halevi – Epstein was born in Brest on the 21ˢᵗ November 1878. He studied in a cheder where he excelled as a gifted child prodigy. He went to Vienna to study Jewish studies for one year and then in 1910, he went to Berne, Switzerland.

In 1918 at the inauguration of the Hebrew University in Jerusalem, he was nominated as Professor of Talmudic Studies. He participated in the publication of the book 'Dvir' (Holy of Holies), and published the quarterly 'Tarbitz' in which he presented his research on his main body of work 'Mavoh Lenoseh Hamishnah', a large book on the subject of the Mishnah.

Professor Yakov Nachum Halevi –Epstein was born in Brisk D'Lita, the city that was in the heart of the nation of Israel. It was an ancient community upon whose seat of the rabbinate there sat great rabbis from the time of the 'Marshal' (Rabbi Shlomo Luria), until it's destruction.

His family was a distinguished one, he himself once told me about the famous genius, Rabbi Arye- Leib Epstein who was a rabbi 200 years ago in Koenigsberg, author of the book 'Sefer HaPardes' and many other important books. He was one of the great lawmakers of his generation. Professor Halevi – Epstein belonged to the 'genuine Epsteins' whose distinctive characteristic was that they were Levis. He signed his early editorials under the name of Yakov Nachum Halevi, also his major work, on the subject of the Mishnah, was signed Yakov Nachum Halevi.

He was a tremulous only child to his parents. His mother was a woman who distinguished herself by her good deeds and love of Torah. She was the daughter of Rabbi Tanchum Yosef, the Rabbi of Katelneh, a suburb of Brest. He dedicated his very important work 'Perush Hagaonim Al Seder Hataharut' to her.

He dedicated his great book on the subject of the Mishnah to his father, Rabbi Chaim, who was a great Talmudic scholar, and studied his whole life. However, Yakov Nachum Halevi was never ordained as a rabbi. He studied in cheder until he was 10 years old as was usual in those days, then he studied under his father, Rabbi Chaim.

Rabbi Chaim's method of learning was based on those of the Vilna Gaon and his great pupil, Rabbi Chaim Volozhiner. The method was simple – a deep and thorough understanding of the Talmud to begin with. And thus he guided his capable son. Yakov Nachum Halevi – Epstein regarded his father as his teacher and rabbi. He published 'His Son and his Pupil'. It was at that time I first heard of him and his impressive achievements, of which his father had provided the basis.

Before his 14th birthday, his father died aged 47, leaving the family without means. His widow became the sole breadwinner. Yakov Nachum traveled to the famous Yeshiva of Mir to study. The head of the yeshiva at that time was Rabbi Chaim – Leib Tiktinski who was famous for his teaching methods, his deep analysis and deciphering of complicated and difficult issues, so that all puzzling dilemmas became self – explanatory.

Yakov Nachum studied in this yeshiva for about 2 years, and then returned to Brest, where he personally explained and presented his studies at the yeshivas of the city.

At the same time he became more involved in the study of the original teachers of the Torah. He felt that there was a great lack of books on the subject and in 1902 traveled to Vilna where the Strashon Library satisfied his thirst for books. He studied Torah and at the same time, also studied general subjects.

In the same year he began to publish his scientific work. His first article was called 'Rabbi Baruch from Greece', which was published in Hamelitz. His second editorial was published in 1903 in Hamizach, which was then under the editorship of Zeev Yavetz. It appears that Halevi - Epstein was close to Yavetz at the time and was influenced by him.

After this came a period if 5 years where he did not publish anything. This was because of his great hunger for study. He swallowed whatever possible knowledge he could and gave up nothing in return. In those years he gave himself over to the study of Torah with great diligence and gathered research material for his future publications. Some of them were written in those 5 years. Of his great research work, he said, that was written 25 years ago. Refering to another of his works he said, that article was written at the end of 1905 in Brisk D'Lita.

In 1907 he left Russia and came to Vienna to study Semitic languages and philology under David Henrik Miller at the university. He became a close friend of some Viennese intellectuals, especially with Professor Optevitzer and Dr. Bernard Wachstein, a well-known bibliograph, and director of the Viennese Jewish community library. During my visit to Vienna in the summer of 1915, I heard much praise from Wachstein about Halevi – Epstein, his intelligence and diligence.

In 1911 Halevi – Epstein went to Berne, apparently because of a desire to limit his study time at the university. There he found a large colony of Jewish students who had been unable to obtain high –school education in the Russian school system. Amongst those that became especially close to him, were the late Dr. B. M. Levine, who founded an association of religious students in Berne called 'Tachkamoni', and Dr. Moshe Seidel.

Halevi –Epstein was partially funded in Berne by the premier scholarship prize money, which it seems that he received through the efforts of Dr. Levine. This society was based in Frankfurt, Germany, with the aim of supporting Jewish students who had come from the east to study in the western European universities.

In the winter of 1913 Halevi –Epstein received his doctorate of philosophy for his important work ' Der Gaonaisch'. This was the introduction to his prolonged research for his work ' A Commentary on the Order of Purification' and his 'Interpretation of the Sages on Purification', which was published by the society 'Mekitzei Nardmim' that existed from 1915-1924. It is here that Halevi –Epstein shows his great strength in Talmudic philology and in the literature of the Sages. His outstanding scientific interpretation about this subject is of great value to generations. It is an example and model for scientific publications and texts of its kind.

In the summer of 1913, Halevi –Epstein moved to Berlin, where his name became famous between the Jewish intelligentsia. He there began to write his life's work

'Mavoh Lenoseh Hamishnah', with which, together with all his other occupations, he worked on for 33 years. It was published in the summer of 1948 in 2 volumes totalling over 1300 pages.

Epstein resided in Berlin during the entire W.W.1 and in 1923 he became one of the editors of 'Dvir' a great scientific quarterly publication for the studies of Judaism, which was founded under the initiative of Chaim Nachman Bialik. This quarterly publication did not last very long. In the same year was nominated as a lecturer at the 'High School for Jewish Studies'. In 1925, on the very day as the inauguration of the Hebrew University in Jerusalem, Epstein arrived in Israel where he had been invited to chair the Philology Studies department.

There were many years that Epstein studied and lived in poverty. He told me that there were days when he was really hungry and had to think whether to eat his piece of bread in the morning or at night. Also, whilst living in Berlin, he had no income. For a certain time he worked on assembling a dictionary for B. Garavantski, (the son in law of K.Wissotski). The work was handed over to a publisher named H. Chernowitz and was not at all to his liking and taste.

There were instances where he could not send his articles to a newspaper because he did not have the money for postage. He lived a life of austerity and suffering and studied the Torah. He obtained knowledge by sacrificing sleep, pleasure, intimacy with others, and entertainment. With his patient and good nature and the faith of a learned man he spent his life in studying the Torah that he saw as the whole world. He gave his whole soul and genius abilities, living his life by the saying of the sages:" what will a man do and how will he live? He will die alone."

He was always immersed in the process and far removed from the noisy everyday life.

He realized that being involved worldly affairs would take away the hours he needed.

In reality he was always alert and aware of what was happening in the Jewish world –especially in Israel – but he never came down from his 'Olympus'.

Already from childhood, he had the maturity of an adult. His early works show an unusual scientific maturity – there were all the signs of his thoroughness that was evidenced in his future achievements. With all his scholarly work he embraced the study of the Mishnah, in addition to the Midrash books and the Books of the Sages and the Prophets.

His devotion to the literature of the sages and the Talmud was great. With his incisiveness he penetrated very deep and complicated problems. With his keen eyes he saw every subject correctly, with his wonderful critical senses with which he was blessed always guiding him to the correct conclusion. He never was influenced by the fantasies that flew through the air. His research was always well founded and built on solid foundations. Also his doubts, of which there were not many were mostly well founded.

Every thought he would turn over many times and the result was clear and transparent.

Every matter that he was involved with, he was ever ready to examine it several times again with a critical eye. Here is an example: In his great introduction to the "Interpretation of the Sages on the Order of Purification" he leaned towards the line of evidence that the meaning was based on the Hebrew translation of the commentary of Rabbi Saadia Gaon (Rasag) which was originally written in Arabic. Over time it was discovered and published from new sources in the archives – he studied what he had researched 30 years earlier and came up with the new conclusion that the commentary had been written by none other than Rabbi Joseph Caro, the author of 'Halachot Gedolot' and therefore it's origin was in the 19th century. His research and writings as well as the great book on the subject of the Mishnah were for a select but limited group of scholars..

However, he tried to give understanding to those with understanding hearts. He himself supposed that his reading public - or more correctly, the learned and educated world of his readers was much smaller than it was in reality.

Nevertheless, he was convinced that the fruit of his research work was not just for the children of his generation, but also for future generations who would find interest in his writings. Without doubt, everything that he published had a lasting value for future generations. Everyone wishing to acquaint themselves with the Torah, beginning with the Mishnah and finishing with the rabbinic literature, cannot ignore the work of Professor Epstein. About him one can certainly quote the words of Rabbi Tarfon to Rabbi Akiva:

"Every commentary is really commentary from Life."

Valued and precious to us whilst alive, and valued and precious he is to us after his death. In the Talmud it was said that Jacob our father did not die, so also our friend Yakov Nachum Epstein did not die. He belongs to those who after their death, will be considered as living. Because he grew and struggled and steeped himself in the Torah, he was enveloped in the spirit of his achievements. He grew up with a good name and left the world with a good name.

May His Memory be Blessed.

[Page 315]

Figures I Remember

By Yitzchak Greenboim
Translated by Dr. Samuel Chani and Jenni Buch

Noah Finkelstein

The first time that we met was during the elections for the 7th Zionist Congress. Those were the days of the great spring in the Polish and Jewish associations before the revolution of 1905. In the Zionist camp at that time there was a great battle between the Zionists for Zion and the Ugandists. Noah Finkelstein, who had excelled himself in Brest with his Zionist work, was elected as the supervisor of the election results for this organization of which I was also a member. We elected groups of 200 Shekel purchasers – nothing unusual happened and everything was quiet in those free elections in which we elected our delegates. In my memory Finkelstein remains as a quiet, calm, good-natured figure with a smile.

The youth would participate very enthusiastically in the debates before the election. At that time we did not have regular elections – the voters would put in their vote cards –that was enough. In those days the voting took place at meetings before the general discussions. If I'm not mistaken, the first to speak was the representative of the Poale Zion, Ruskin from the Boruchov faction.

He came out and opposed me vehemently in his speech. Finkelstein listened to both my opponent's and my speeches and smiled at both of us.

Noah Finkelstein was a wealthy businessman, a loyal Zionist activist who got caught up in the Uganda scheme and became a realist. In that movement he was not amongst the leaders, he did his work quietly and calmly.

About a year later, Finkelstein linked up with Yatzkagan, who had begun to publish the 'Tagenblat', a small, cheap, daily newspaper which, within a few days had captured the attention of the reading public. This public was at that time far removed from reading the Jewish and Hebrew press.

From that time on, the connection between Finkelstein and his comrade Yatzkagan was unbroken. Several years later, they founded 'Heint' (today), which was a great newspaper that went through several different stages until after the liberation of Poland (1918) when it became the main newspaper of Polish Jewry with it's' Zionist leanings.

The first years of Heint were very good with the newspaper reaching a circulation previously unknown with the Jewish reading public in any language. Many complained about the Heint's methods, due to the fact that it published cheap romantic stories modeled on the Parisian daily newspapers. Also the screaming articles over time were excessive.

But the Jewish masses liked the Heint, and I must admit that the more the newspaper became established and grew; the publication found it's style and the contents improved and became more refined in the literary and publishing sense. The education that the readers got through the Heint took them away from the influence of the tabloid press and provided them with an understanding of serious editorial and literary issues. The Heint taught them a love of Shalom Aleichem, Peretz, Frishman, and many other writers who were at the forefront of Jewish literature – they all worked for the Heint.

What was Finkelstein's role in the success? It's hard to know, he stood at the head of the Heint administration and as owner apparently did not leave the decisions to Yatzkagan alone. Hard to know how much he influenced – he would always take upon himself the responsibility for the contents and style of the paper. Never did he show that one should differentiate between the owner who carried out his work in a gentle, reasonable manner and the vulgarity and screaming curses of Yatzkagan who would easily take offence whenever he wished.

However, bad days came for the Heint, with the competition from the 'The Jewish Folk', an organ of the Zionist organization. It's staff also became leaders of Polish Jewry in the New Polish Republic –it was then that the idea arose to unite the two newspapers. Finkelstein did not try to defend Yatzkagan when the Zionist leaders demanded to sideline him. Actually, Yatzkagan was not against the idea – he probably understood that he was not capable of editing a political Zionist newspaper in the New Poland.

As far as I know, there was a real bond between the two, Finkelstein and Yatzkagan, until the end of Yatzkagan's life. In Paris they formed a partnership - a newspaper that appeared right up to the Nazi occupation of

France. Only once was there a serious dispute between the partners. It came to arbitration and I was one of the referees – I don't remember the details, but both Fadlishevski and myself managed to make peace between them, which was never disturbed again.

I further met Finkelstein at work. These were the heated days of the economic boycott, which was proclaimed against the Polish Jews after the elections to the 4ᵗʰ Russian Duma in 1912. A small committee was then formed whose aim it was to monitor the press that supported the boycott and was full of anti-Semitic hatred. After a certain time the entire work of this committee was concentrated in the hands of a smaller group, which Finkelstein and myself headed He was involved with the financial side, and I was involved with general administration. When the First World War broke out, our group's activity was justified because the same Polish groups that had supported the boycott began slandering the Jews to the Russian military powers. There was malicious gossip about the Jewish connection to the Austro – German regimes and the outrageous accusations that they were involved in espionage.

The effect of this activity, together with other factors helped the Russian military command find a scapegoat for it's military defeats. The results were executions by hanging of innocent Jews, the exiling of entire Jewish communities, arrests and imprisonment. The only possibility to avert the continued expulsions was to collect factual evidence to present to the Russian opposition and the United States in order to convince the Russian authorities. Our committee tried to fulfill these objectives. The money required to fund this activity was given by individuals, especially Finkelstein. He covered all the expenses that were lacking, and did it simply, as if it were a self-explanatory thing. Never did he complain about this situation, although I would bring up the subject frequently – he would always pacify me. This situation lasted until the Germans occupied Warsaw in 1915.

Finkelstein only lived for a few years in the liberated Poland. Der Heint became an organ for the Zionist movement, and he felt superflous. His brother Nechemiah ran his business; the Zionist central committee with its representatives in the Sjem (Polish Parliament) determined the direction of the newspaper and it's attitude to day to day problems. It is possible that there were other personal reasons unknown to me. However, for almost the entire period between the two World Wars, Finkelstein lived in Paris.

Once again he founded a daily newpaper together with Yatzkagan called the 'Parisian Heint'. This newspaper was unlike the other rather miserable and poor quality daily newspapers that appeared in Western Europe to cater for the Jewish emigres from Eastern Europe. It was closer to the Polish press, its contents, however, were poorer because of the poorness of Jewish life and culture in Paris and France. The Parisian Heint did not succeed overnight, it had to struggle hard to justify it's existence, and to achieve growth. It struggled to assemble a good group of writers and staff to reach the Jewish society who would read it – they were not usually to be found in Paris in those years before World War Two.

Moreover, Finkelstein and Yatzkagan seemed to lack the drive. From its first years the newspaper suffered from the fact that the émigrés had assimilated into the local language and were not interested in the Yiddish language. The numbers of Jewish migrants from Poland and other Eastern Europe countries to France was not sufficient to fill the spirit of the times and create a greater circulation for the pro Zionist newspaper.

In France, the fault lay in the following factors: A large part of the Jewish immigrants brought with them an opposition to Zionism, even enmity - learned from the Bundist and communist schools. It became immediately clear to Finkelstein and Yatzkagan that without the support of the Zionist organization, they would not be able to maintain the newspaper. All their efforts in this direction were met with a wall of misunderstanding by the Zionist leaders who did not appreciate the value of a Zionist newspaper in Yiddish, in Western Europe. Above all, they did not see the value of day-to-day contact between the organization and the movement and activity of the many sympathizers that were interested and carried along by the growth and success of the Zionist movement.

Finkelstein and Yatzkagan did not resign their positions –they held out until the end. They found a wealthy Jewish benefactor who invested in the newspaper, he saw it as a business that was potentially profitable and tried to oust the original owners more and more.

Thus Finkelstein lived until the outbreak of W.W.11 – Yatzkagan had died earlier. During the war, I did not hear anything of Finkelstein; I assumed that he had met the fate of the Parisian Jews who were sent to the extermination camps of Poland.

When I came to Paris in 1947, I discovered that Noah Finkelstein was alive bit mortally ill – he was living with a relative in the south of France. He had cancer and was not aware of the gravity of his illness. Not long after, I received a friendly letter from him, which in those dark days when I had been left all alone, was a great consolation to me. With a few considered words that told me little, he conveyed his sufferings – I did what I could to help him – I wanted him to know that he was not forgotten and abandoned by those that knew him and appreciated his work.

One day, I was told that he had come to Paris as his health had improved and he believed that he would recover and be able to work. I immediately visited him and found him lying in bed. I saw in front of me the same Finkelstein with his good-natured smile, a man with strong faith, he was sure that his weakness came because the doctor had ordered him to bed. He was certain that this would pass and that he would be able to return to work. And what was his work? His new efforts to publish the Heint!!

I explained to him the emerging opinion in our circle to publish a Zionist newspaper – its purpose would be to maintain a daily contact with the Zionist supporters that had greatly increased during and after the war years. But these opinions were divided, some wanted a weekly newspaper and some demanded a daily newspaper. I wanted to help with the establishment of a daily newspaper for as long as I was in Paris. Finkelstein was overjoyed and immediately made plans to return to work in a few days when he rose from his sick bed.

Leaving the room, I spoke to his French sister-in-law. She had converted and gone with his younger brother to Warsaw and there had undergone all the sufferings and troubles that he and his family had to endure, but her French nationality had saved her from the concentration camps and gas chambers. She had nursed and looked after Noah during the war until he went to Nice, and presently she once again had come to look after him. She told me that his operation in Nice had been successful, but without a doubt that he still had the cancer and his days were numbered.

I visited him several times –we spoke of this and that. I gave him details about his daughter who had survived in Poland and married a Jew who was a prosecutor on the Lodz courts. She wanted to come and see him, but was unable to get the necessary visas. I had already written him of this when he was still in Nice. I did not ask him about his life in Paris during the war. It was difficult for me to talk to him, as he was unaware of the death sentence hanging over him and only felt weaker all the time. He merely said that he would walk around the streets of Paris without fear and nothing happened to him during the war. I did not press him for details. He participated in my joy when I was able to leave for Israel. I promised that I would do all I could to bring him to Israel. It did not take long before I received the sad news of his death.

Noah Finkelstein was an exceptional man. In the days when he was at his peak, when the Heint was the premier Yiddish newspaper with the largest influence and circulation in Poland, he did not possess a shred of the arrogance of the newly rich who arose and chased honor. He was always modest and besides that, he was refined, good natured and loyal. A typically cultured wealthy Jew, he was involved in the period of the development of Zionism and the national awakening. He pulled them out of their corners and assisted them with the width of social and community works in various areas. Those were enlightened and soul searching days.

Noah Finkelstein was one of those that I.L. Peretz accurately called Sabbath and Holydays Jews.

Avraham Goldberg

Born in 1881 in Brest. His father was a noted scholar and one of the original Chovevei Zion. His literary efforts began in 1902. He was a co writer of Hatzofeh and Hamelitz, then an editor in Warsaw at 'Morgenblatt' and 'Lezten Post'. From 1908, he was one of the editors of the daily newspaper, the 'Heint'.

It was during the elections to the Polish Sjem (parliament) – not in the great days of the 1922 elections, when the Polish Jews voted en masse, secure in their power and their allliance with other national minorities – but in the elections of 1928, when the cracks in the united wall of the Jewish vote and that of the minorities was noticable...

The Pilsudski government had already thrown its entire weight of administrative sanctions against the minority bloc. At this time, Avraham Goldberg was nominated as one of the candidtates to Congress Poland, where his chances of being elected were very weaKatzenellenbogen Generally Jews or the other minorities were not represented there.

Together with Goldberg we went on a propaganda (publicity) campaign through the towns of this electorate, to all the shtetls in the electorate where the majority of the population was Jewish.

Only a short time before, the local Zionists were people from the 'shteiblach' (prayer houses), who would travel to their Rebbes on High Holidays. Their brand of Zionism cost them dearly, as they had to overcome opposition from their parents and environment. It was also noticeable in the chassidic fervor expressed in the behaviour of their leaders and orators. Avraham Goldberg was already known in the shtetls through the 'Heint', the majority of those people were his loyal readers. Until this time, they had never heard him speak from a platform. At public assemblies, he came face to face with his readers for the first time. In his words, they sought not only information, but also advice and guidance.

In this relationship there was also something of Chassidism – instead of the rebbe, came the publisher who declared an awakening and called them to action. In Avraham Goldberg they saw one of their leaders who would show them the way.

His meetings were warm and heartfelt, not only in the popular assemblies, but also in official receptions and in the homes of the Jewish community leaders from the Zionist camp in the towns and villages that we visited.

Goldberg found the days of traveling one long festivity, full of light, love and loyalty. As I observed his radiant face I understood the great value of face-to-face meetings for the journalist with the masses. "We came to the Jewish press, not for an income or profession, but as a means to of realizing our lives' ideals." A newspaper that uses its power for a great goal must first of all be above reproof. A newspaper that preaches a great ideal must not deteriorate into an instrument of trivial information and entertainment. Each edition must be an awakener and reminder.

Goldberg understood that this was the purpose of his editing the Heint, where he was both a journalist and editor. From the very first edition, he tried to accomplish this aim.It was not long before the Heint became the central organ for the national Zionist movement in Poland – providing an awakening and guiding direction

He rose to the top, conducted and involved himself in all the important issues on a day to day basis. Goldberg would also not wait for certain important questions to arise – he would raise these issues by himself and catch the attention of the reading public, stirring them to demand a solution.

This was Goldberg's manner as editor of a newspaper. He did not see the Heint as a school for talented beginners. He was not involved with their articles and stories and did not show them how to progress in their pursuit of writing and publishing literature. In the end, he was indeed transformed into a reformer, awakening and demanding change. Goldberg only really felt well when conducting his journalist duties, when he would appeal for candor and openness in the articles that he printed in his second and third columns of his paper. There he acted as a commander who allocates positions, searching and caring about articles that would upset the peace of the readers. In quiet times when there were no pressing issues that demanded reading, debate and polemics, in the press and on the street, Goldberg would walk about nervously, complaining of the quiet and boredom and the lessening of the reader's interest in the newspaper. About the lowering of its contents, and complaining about the lack of stimulating and rousing elements. Then, half in earnest and half in jest, he would pose the question to his coworkers "what sort of problem can we invent for the newspaper? Why does it exist?"

The result of all these questions and debate was that he would create a new plan of action, a campaign in which Goldberg could mobilize and allocate tasks amongst his assistants and systematically stir them up.

Avraham Goldberg was a publisher who lived in the moment and day. If I'm not mistaken he never attempted to delve deeply and immerse himself in the problem, analyze, research it from all sides and give it a fundamentalist treatment. Instead, his articles identified problems that demanded instant reading and could not be put off. Moreover, his articles were a call to action. However, his style was not belligerent, rather a discussion and disclosure of his proposals, which were realistic and practical. He was by no means a propagandist or demagogue – he was far from polemics and divisions.

His chief strength was editing and managing the newspaper. He was closer to the kind of editor who almost never writes by himself, but his spirit, ideas and initiative filled the newspaper. He put his imprimatur on it. He totally dedicated himself without limit, selflessly living for the newspaper, as if he wanted to merge with it as one body.

Goldberg was still young and full of fresh strength at the time of his demise. His death was keenly felt at the Heint, because in his family of writers there was no one to replace him.

It was not long after that the great cataclysm befell Polish Jewry and the Heint was also annihilated. Those shtetl Jews who had brought into Zionism their Chassidic fervor, their naiveté and freshness which he loved and strove for – almost entirely went up in the smoke of the gas chambers and extermination camps. The Heint, the arouser and demander, ceased to exist after Hitler occupied Poland. It ceased forever, the place it occupied in Jewish society in the years of struggle and achievement. The role it had occupied and fulfilled as awakener and Avraham Goldberg, deeply etched in the memory of those remaining Polish Jews that survived as the Zionist movement reformer.

[Page 325]

Michal and Nechama Pochachevski

By Moshe Smilanski
Translated by Dr. Samuel Chani and Jenni Buch

A. Michal Pochachevski.

He was born in Brest in Ellul 1863. His father was a merchant and manufacturer. His grandfather was Reb Israel Lipshitz the author of "Tiferet Israel" (Glory of Israel). Michal went to a modern cheder where he studied Hebrew called 'Cheder Metukan'. He was one of the six students sent to Israel in 1885 by Chovevei Zion to study agriculture. He worked as an employee of Baron Rothschild in Be-er Tuvia. As an expert in fruit plantations, he became a member of the agricultural committee of the then government. From 1889 he worked the land at Rishon Letzion. His articles about agriculture were published in Hasadeh and Bustane (memories) He also lived in Zichron Yaakov, Yesod Hamaale, and Rosh Pinah.

The youth Michal Pochachevski was one of the "flowers of Zion" in his hometown of Brest. Together with his friends he would prepare 'hoshanot ' on the eve of Hoshanna Raba, on the eve of Channuka he would prepare cups so that he could sell them for the benefit of Chovevei Zion. This he did for three years, dreaming of the time when he would plant greenery on the banks of the Jordan and trees on the mountains of Judea with his own hands.

Thus it was on one beautiful day, a rumor spread that Baron Rothschild had requested that Chovevei Zion send six young men to study agriculture in Israel at his expense. The young man said a prayer deep in his heart "dear God make me a gardener", and his prayer was heard in the heavens. He was beloved by the Zionist delegates in his city.

Dr. Yasenowski in Warsaw and Dr. Pinsker in Odessa accepted the positive opinion the delegates had of Pochachevski, and the matter was decided. The soul of the young man fluttered between hope and despair, until one day the postman knocked at his parents home and said loudly enough for the whole street to hear: " telegram".

The happy news that came from Odessa evoked fear and sadness in his mother. With a cry she bemoaned all the important people of the city, ' why has my son been chosen to be sent away to a foreign land?" His father, on the other hand, took him to the rabbi who prayed and warned him not to go to the colonies where one could obtain rabbinical orders to desecrate the Sabbath. The young man argued and said:" I will go and now give me a blessing, rabbi" The rabbi blessed him with "go in peace and return in peace".

Michal Pochachevski left and never returned. In the Jewish hostel in Constantinople he and his friends were warned that they would barely escape with their lives and would flee from the land (Israel). However, he thought that even if all of them would flee, he alone would remain. On the 8th Elul 1885, the old ship Lazerow brought the future Jewish gardener to the shores of

Haifa. The sea was very stormy on that day; the Arab sailors came onto the deck of the ship with their ladders and ropes and thus the young man, tall and slim, with one shoe on and one foot bare, his other shoe having fallen into the sea introduced himself to the crowd that awaited on the shore.

The group was taken to Rishon Letzion. Pochachevski was given a room in which the landlord was lying in bed moaning with a malaria attack. Pochachevski went outside and slept on the ground, he put a stone under his head, and thus spent his 1st night. With two wagons that belonged to a German from Sharona, they went to Zichron Yaakov. The drivers were Arabs and for two days and nights they blundered around so that they were barely alive when they arrived in Zichron. Quarters had been prepared for them there, a building and a storeroom with provisions provided by the Baron's official. The building was saturated with strange smells and riddled with mice. There they erected 6 wooden sleeping bunks.

The manager of the colony, Warmesser, was good to them. However, the French gardener cast an evil eye over them. A drunk and an enemy of Israel, he had a score to settle with what he considered Russians and Nihilists at Rishon Letzion. This gardener, Degour, was supposed to begin training them in gardening. Four of the group he sent to be porters to the German wagons that brought building materials from Haifa to the colony. The other two he sent to be assistants to the cook in his own home.

The rains came late in that autumn, causing the mosquitoes in the neighboring marshes to multiply terribly. The hard physical work that the six endured, plus the bad food and living conditions had weakened them, and the terrible tropical malaria began to attack them. Pochachevski, however, did not give up. The blackest was white for him as this is how he wanted to see it. He wrote his parents from Zichron: "I can assure you that I have never had better days in my life. Since we arrived here our aim is to become good gardeners and our aim will be achieved. I myself bless the past and ask for mercy in the future"

Of the six there now remained four and to those were added two sons of the settlers. Their working conditions improved and they began to form the famous plant nursery and plant gardens in the settlement. The four youths were sent to Rosh Pinah where better conditions awaited them. The people of the remote colony received them with joy and their attitiude to them was warm and friendly. The youths began to learn their trade in earnest. The gardener gave them books to study and organized evening classes to teach them both theory and practice. They were taught how to plant - how to make wine from grapes and how to make perfume from the flowers of the fields. Then joy of the young men was great when Baron Rothschild sent them seeds of tropical plants. For this purpose they were sent to Yesod Hamaleh to organize a school of planting for these plants. The four young gardeners settled in the house of Fishel Solomon.

Things began to go well for Michal. He built a house in Rishon Letzion, and brought Nechama Feinstein, his childhood girlfriend from Brest to Rishon. There he tended his home and trees for 55 years. He labored stubbornly and subsequently with talent, concentration, loyalty, faith and above all, love. Michal Pochachevski loved trees and through that love he learnt to understand their secrets.

He was also a founder of Be-er Tuvia in it's first days and brought into existence it's tradition of the "building implements in one hand and the gun in the other". During the days he would build the sheds and at night would guard the materials with a gun in his hand.

In 1896, Michal Pochachevski left the employ of the Baron Rothschild and became a landowner. He joined the colonizers, excelled in his work and watchfulness over the national treasures – it's trees. He was one of the settlers of Rishon Letzion who paid the Baron's officials the first installment on account for the vines that were planted that day. That day was a great celebration in his life. His land and his home he had bought with money that he had earned from his own work. The day of his house warming was a day of great joy for him. In the 1880s the Zionist executive selected a committee to visit all the agricultural settlements of Keren Kayemet (the Jewish National Fund) and assess their value. One of the assessors chosen was Michal Pochachevski. During this work he fell in love with the objects he was assessing – the settlements and their inhabitants.

He was a good communicator, but after he would explain verbally, he would explain with his hands. Those hands were used to all kinds of work. Although he was a teacher, he never ceased being a pupil. In his old age, he still had an alert mind and heart. His brain was always open open to new agricultural concepts. His eyes, which were good (until his old age he could write and read without glasses) could focus into the future.

(From an article written in 1943 on his 80th birthday).

B. Nechama Pochachevski.

"Nefesh" (soul) was her literary name. This pseudonym exactly described her, as she was - a saintly soul. A young Litvish lass when she came to Eretz Israel, she had already imbibed the beauty of the Hebrew language in her childhood. The language of Yeshayahu and Avraham Mapu, the bible and love of Zion, she harbored the love of these in her heart her entire life. As if by a magic hand she was suddenly plucked from her hometown of Brest-Litovsk and taken by boat to the shores of Tzaritzin (Stalingrad) to where her parents migrated. There she studied in a Russian high school. In her old age, she added Russian poetry with its deep sorrow to the younger Hebrew poetry with which her soul was steeped.

From Tzaritzin – whilst still young and delicate - she was uprooted once again to the land of our fathers. She was kept 'hidden' in the attic of a house belonging to one of Baron Rothschild's officials in Rishon Letzion. From the attic veranda the passers-by in the street of the settlement caught glimpses of a delicate face framed by black hair, her dark shining eyes watching the people in the street with interest. She had been uprooted from her familiar world by her will to form the nation of Israel.

She married a son of her hometown – one of the six who were training to be gardeners. Her husband would usually ride his horse from one colony to another to teach the settlers how to use the tree saws and branch shears.

Even during her youth in the Russian school when all her ideas were expressed in Russian, she would stubbornly cling to the language of the Bible and the Lovers of Zion to try and express her emotions and longings. She began to speak Hebrew on the first day she arrived in the Holy Land. Influenced by the colony's teacher, her home became the first in which only Hebrew was spoken. She would send letters to 'Hamelitz' back home in which the readers could slake their thirst for the details and descriptions of the charm and beauty of the Holy Land. After some years she also sent stories and pictures of life in the new land of Israel.

Her place was not on the Eastern wall (amongst the luminaries) of Hebrew literature, but Hebrew literature was a small temple for her –her quill was an instrument that served her in times of exaltation or sorrow, she would stretch out her hand for the quill.

She was not only occupied with Hebrew literature. She was a settler and interested in agriculture –she was one of the best and brightest of the Jewish daughters of the land. She was also a pioneering founder in her colony of the cowshed, the chicken run, the vegetable garden and the flowerplanting. Her husband left the employ of the baron and became a colonist – a landowner in Rishon Letzion. He developed his farm with cows, horses, goats, chickens and most of his time in the vineyard and fields was under the control of Nechama. She added some of her flowers to the model garden, she treated the animals as her children, she brought them up the same as her son and daughter. She was an outstanding farmer and agriculturalist, mother and housewife. She baked wonderful bread in the oven and would work as busily as an ant all day long.

[Page 331]

Yitzchak (Tzvi) Lipovsky

By Asher Barash
Translated by Dr. Samuel Chani and Jenni Buch

Yitzchak (Tzvi) Lipovsky

Sadly, I never personally met my father-in-law, blessed be his memory. He died in Beirut during Hanukah 1915. He was a director of the Anglo – Palestine Bank there and died six months before I married his daughter in Tel-Aviv.

All those who knew him and came into contact with him would tell of his value as a Zionist, Hebraicist and a fine man. He was a cultured man, well educated, a lover of peace and truth. I got the more important details of his life from his family.

He was born in Drohyczyn in 1868. His father was the merchant Menachem Mendel, the son of Shmuel Lipovsky. Later his father lived for several years in Poltava and Yekaterinoslav. At the age of thirteen the young Yitzchak went to live with his wealthy grandfather Shmuel in Brest. There he received his spiritual and secular education. He befriended several of the Chovevei Zion (lovers of Zion), Feinstein, Padua, and others. He married the daughter of a merchant and businessman, Reb Moshe Kwiatkowski, blessed be his memory.

Yitzchak Lipovsky at first wanted to become a flour merchant, but his spiritual side interfered with this decision. When he was already a father of several children he had to travel to distant lands to seek his fortune. However, even in America, things did not work out with him and after several years he returned to Brest with empty hands, but enriched with knowledge of the world and the English language. After his return to Brest he was employed as a tutor in the home of the Finkelsteins. From that time on, teaching became his profession. He excelled in languages –as well as Russian and Hebrew, which he learned in his youth, he had a good grasp of French, German and English. Both Jews and Gentiles were his pupils.

In that time there were the first years of the Zionist movement, and Lipovsky was one of the few young people in the city to support and help this new movement. He participated in this work together with Noah Finkelstein, Ben Zion Neumark, Mordechai Sheinerman, Leon Horoditz and Moshe Levantin. None of them are alive anymore. Lipovsky was especially involved in the development of the Zionist movement. In the evenings he would give classes to yeshiva students free of charge.

Through Moshe Levantin he met the famous banker Zalman David Levantin who would visit Brest to see his son Moshe and son-in-law Reb Shabtai Papeh. When Zalman David Levantin was invited to run the Colonial Bank in London, he asked the language expert, Yitzchak Lipovsky to accompany him to London to work with him.

Yitzchak was very attracted to this offer, not only because of the postion but also because of the Zionist nature of the work, and that he could get closer to his ambition of living in Eretz Israel.

Therefore, he went by himself to London, and when it was decided to open the Afik Bank in Israel, he travelled together with Levantin and arrived in Jaffa in June 1903. They were to found the bank and affect all the necessary arrangements. In the spring of 1904, he brought his family to Israel. Over the next two years he worked with Levantin in Jaffa and later transferred to Jerusalem as deputy director of the bank. In 1908 he was sent to Beirut as deputy director off this branch that had been founded by Victor Jacobson.

Afterwards Jacobson was delegated as an emissary for the Zionist movement in Constantinople and Genoa, and Lipovsky became the director of the bank in Beirut until his death.

This branch of the bank was founded through economic and political reasons in the capital of the Levant, which was like a gateway into Israel. This area was under French domination and required a man with a refined appearance who knew how to conduct himself with ministers and diplomats. There was no better man than my father-in-law to serve this purpose. He indeed fulfilled this task to the highest degree as his ability and personal character perfectly suited this mission.

After the beginning of W.W.1 he became ill with cancer. Even in the heavy days of his severe illness he made great efforts that the bank should give financial assistance to the poverty-stricken settlements in Israel. At that time his oldest son and daughter were already living in Jaffa -Tel-Aviv. The son was an employee of the bank, and the daughter was employed as a teacher in the girl's school funded by the Odessa committee. Yitzchak Lipovsky was building a beautiful new home for himself in the new quarters of Tel-Aviv and intended to live there after the war. These dreams, however, were unfulfilled due to his death.

Amongst his remaining documents there was an exercise book in his handwriting that I found. He had begun to write his memoirs – from his very first days in the land of Israel. From that narrative we can see his boundless and deep devotion to the holy Zionist cause that he loyally served.

[Page 333]

The Story of My Life

By A. L. Feinstein
Translated by Dr. Samuel Chani and Jenni Buch

My birthplace was Domachevo, a small town in the vicinity of Brest. This was the hometown of my father, Meir Michael, blessed be his memory. I was born on Sabbath 1865. My parents were strictly orthodox but had a worldly education and were pratical people. They decided on all matters relevant to the kehilla (Jewish community).

At five years of age I already learnt Chumash and Rashi. I had already learnt Mashli and knew almost every chapter by heart. At the age of seven my parents brought me to a cheder where there was no shortage of good teachers to learn Gemarrah. I advanced in my studies and it was said of me that I was a great future talent. According to the advice of my parents I continued my study of the Tanach and slowly I also learnt to write beautiful and expressive letters. My good parents were pleased with me and hoped to see me sit on the rabbinical chair as one of the greatest in the land.

Higher education could not penetrate this small town that was a nest of Polish Chassidism – I would always spend time with them – I would listen to their stories and I also got to like them.

I was married at the age of 15 to the daughter of an important merchant called Michael Lipsker of Bialystok. God granted me to live with this clever woman for many years. Whilst in Bialystok I was also surrounded by Chassidim who wanted to drag me into their group. But since coming to this town, I forgot these childish dreams and my eyes were opened to a new world – the world of education and practical matters. I now saw the foolishness and aimlessness of the Chassidic customs and stories that I could no longer tolerate.

For five years I boarded with and was supported by my father in law, and was immersed in studying the Gemarra and chapters with deep debates. Over many months I wrote "Shulchan Aruch, Hoshan Mishpat" – which I knew almost by heart, and that made me very happy as I regarded it as deep wisdom for the aspects of the Torah of our Sages, Blessed be their memories.

Beside my love of expressive poetry I tried to become acquainted with the 'European' (secular) teachings but I did not have a taste for foreign languages. I regarded those merely as skills that had no connection with wisdom.

Work and a trade was a disgrace in the eyes of such wealthy sons as myself who thought that they would always live at the expense of their wealthy fathers and fathers in law, dining at their tables and living off their large dowries. But nothing eventuated of all my hopes because I finished my board at my father in laws house and became ill with a disease that was common amongst Torah students and could not be avoided – a nervous disorder. The doctors forbade me from participating in Torah study. My father in law, whose sole aim had been to anoint me with the rabbinical crown, was most unhappy about this.

At this time my father in law's material circumstances deteriorated greatly and I was forced to return to the home of my parents in my hometown. There I would sit and do nothing all day until I recovered and went into business. I had no success and lost money in bad transactions. Finding myself in difficult situation, I chose to get a job. I accepted a post with a wealthy businessman, a merchant from Bialystok who knew of me and my abilities. He treated me with respect and took me into his firm as an administrator and his agent.

Seeing my progress and because he liked me, he rewarded me generously with a good wage. I was happy with that and moved from Domachevo to Brest where my parents had once lived and built a nice house, and were respected burghers. Due to my position that demanded that I came into contact with the nobility and high officials, I had to learn Russian, Polish and German. I did not have a great flair for this, but after a certain time I learnt them. For 12 years I worked at different commercial and government enterprises. Like a bird I roamed over the nation until the years of and saw that with all my actions, all the endeavors that I had carried out faithfully and with all my abilities, my situation had not improved and I had not become rich. Then I asked myself:" when will I do something for myself?" I reminded myself of the Hebrew literature that I had abandoned. The people of the city wanted to elect me as a gabbeh - to conduct the affairs of the kehilla as an official, but the important leaders blocked me and stopped me from becoming a community worker and activist.

In 1870, after the publishing of my interpretation of the Haggada, the Jews of Brest became convinced that the campaign against me was not a righteous one and that there were no heresies in my writings. Again they wanted to elect me as gabbeh, but the well-known Rebbitzen Sarah Diskin opposed me and again I was forced to withdraw.

In 1875 there was issued a government decree to nominate an elected representative who would supervise the Jewish community affairs and I was selected. I was elected to the town council with the consent of the entire Jewish community of Brest. In vain Rabbi Joshua Lieb Diskin sent his beadle to interfere with these elections, no one would listen to him....

On the same day, they stole a great deal of money from the Rebbitzen Sarah Diskin that had been donated to her. Then the rabbi and his family left Brest. Over the next ten years I conducted all the community matters and everybody was happy with my orderly administration. It was all written in the newspapers. Everything I did was to promote the standing of the Jewish community. All the residents of Brest knew this. It was manifested in my book "Ir Tehila" (City of Glory) which was published in 1885.

However, my implacable enemies multiplied from within, and the more good I did for my people, the more they envied me and the enmity towards me grew. Nevertheless, my hands were not weakened and I finished whatever I undertook with the help of God. Except for the building of a new hospital and mikvah, which until today, they have stopped me from building. In 1885 my opponents arose once more and tried to distance me from the decision-making powers of the community. This time the Mayor of Brest, became angry and turned against me through gossip, and became my enemy. It was not enough that they demeaned me through their control over the accounts, but they also slandered me to the authorities and tried to take me to court.

Their auditor investigated me thoroughly and acknowledged my accounts as correct and without any errors. I was absolved and cleared and remained as a city councilor.

From then on I lost my pride and strength and got fed up with it all. Now that I was free of this pride, I took up the pen. As well as articles that I have written to various newspapers, I have translated several books:

New Interpretations of the Tanach

New Commentaries on the Tanach, Talmud and Midrash with Revisions.

With God's help, I will shortly publish these. These are the details of my life until now. Other experiences and stories will, with God's help, appear in a special journal or book with plenty of details.

These are the lines etched in stone on a gravestone in my memory that I have prepared for after my passing in a cemetery for which I have spent so much effort. In the free Yiddish translation, according to the tombstone, the first letters –

Aryeh Lieb Feinstein. When I was still alive I had many disappointments and pains. My enemies multiplied whilst I did accomplish some good things. There will be days when my deeds are etched on a tablet. Today I rest in peace from my sorrow and have found peace from my anger. Not for me, but for the holy people of my nation here, make an effort to build a fence and wall here. No uncivilized shall pass into it. No cattle's feet shall tread. Here then rests my body and that is my entire reward.

(The above is a portion of the article "My Life" by A.L. Feinstein, written by him alone, and published in the "Book of Memory" by Nachum Sokolov 1889).

[Page 339]

Dr. Benjamin Shereshevski

Translated by Dr. Samuel Chani and Jenni Buch

Born in Brest in 1857. In 1875 he had studied in cheder and high school. After the sudden death of his father, he left high school and became the head of his father's printing press. He only stayed there for two years. In 1878 he went to Warsaw, sat for the entrance exams and was accepted to the faculty of medicine at Warsaw University. He completed his studies and became a doctor. He practiced in Kovno (Kaunus), and then he specialized and went into scientific research and published articles in scientific works in the language of the Mishnah (Hebrew).

When Dr. Shereshevski made aliyah to Israel, he settled in Jerusalem. He was encouraged by Eliezer Ben Yehuda and David Yellin in his work and published his book "Surgical Stethoscope and Wider Implications"

Wanting to study further, he went to Vienna but could find no peace there and returned to Jerusalem. During the period of his wandering, he did not cease to perfect his scientific style in Hebrew, so that there was syntax of clarity and scientific accuracy. In 1888 he left Jerusalem and went to Russia. After further wandering he settled in Odessa. There he finished his wonderful work: 'Six Books of Science' which Bialik helped him publish in 1901. In this small booklet there is a collection of the main fundamentals of several important branches of science with details of their basic laws: Mechanics, physics, chemistry, biology, ethics and anatomy. Every subject was a treatise in itself, on the power of Gravity, the Brain, etc.

For the next 25 years Dr. Benjamin Shereshevski labored at sharpening and refining his book. With a devoted and capable hand he put down the foundations for the definition of an absolute Hebrew scientific style. In a style that was old but new, disregarding the dry scientific content, it is still a work of the high artistry and exceptional achievement. There was not one superflous word and it is a marvel how those six branches of science found their way into such a small book.

[Page 341]

Dr. Yakov Grynberg

Translated by Dr. Samuel Chani and Jenni Buch

The child of a Brisk D'lita family, his father Shabtai Grynberg was an orthodox Jew. Every morning he would rise and pray and study Mishnah. At every opportunity his nose was buried in a book. When his family emigrated from Brest, Yakov was born on the journey to Antwerp. The family stayed there for seven years before they arrived in New York. At the age of eleven he worked in the law office of A.Arndler. His duties were to open and close the doors for the clients. One day, he tearfully told the lawyer that he was leaving, as he wanted to study and not waste time guarding doors. The lawyer took him to the famous benefactor, millionaire Felix Warburg. Warburg stroked his head lovingly and said, "don't worry my child, study - I'll lend you as much as you need to become a decent human being. When you have succeeded, you can repay me in installments."

Yakov Grynberg studied at City College, New York. Then he went to Paris to study. Warburg supported him and enabled him to graduate at his expense. Returning to New York, he began working and earning income, and with much gratitude he repaid his loan.

For over 40 years he was a teacher and headmaster at schools and a writer of schoolbooks. He reformed and improved the methods of studying and teaching. He received awards and medals of distinction for his books on the subjects of History, Latin, Philosophy, Experimental Psychology, and for a time he translated French. He was an official advisor to France, Italy and Israel on educational matters. He collected a large library that he donated to the state of Israel, and the Israeli association gave him a Tanach in gratitude.

Dr. Grynberg received distinctions from the Academie Francaise. He edited pedagogic works and textbooks. He took part in editing books for schoolteachers and principals. He also organized training courses for teachers. He founded a Hebrew course in which he familiarized over 25,000 teachers with Hebrew and the State of Israel.

Yakov Grynberg founded cooperative courses for teachers through the United Nations, for China, the Atomic Energy Commission, and founded academies for Greece and Israel. He worked tirelessly for teacher's rights and introduced pensions for teachers. He was very active in the UJA for over 20 years.

For more than 20 years Dr.Grynberg was deputy chief inspector of the Schools Directory in N.Y. He was the first Jew in the history of this directory to be appointed to the ranks of Inspector of Schools. In New York City there are about 700 schools with 40,000 teachers and over one million students.

[Page 341]

Tzvi Har-Zahav (Goldberg)

Translated by Dr. Samuel Chani and Jenni Buch

Tzvi Har-Zahav

Born Kislev 1869 in Satche, Pinsk district, Minsk Gubernia (Province). He was a descendant of "Chacham Tzvi". He studied Torah with his teachers in his village. By the time he was 13, he had trained himself to study and pray at the same time. At the age of 15 he changed his name to Tzvi Har-Zahav. Thereafter he initiated writing in the Hebrew alphabet only, even for foreign words. He began speaking Hebrew with his teachers and would not answer in any other language to those who could speak Hebrew. All this occurred before he had ever heard of Eliezer Ben Yehuda.

Whilst still in his youth he made several literary advances, he translated a calendar by himself, wrote several articles and songs and studied Arabic from the book of Kaspari.

He created an eternal calendar for Jews, Karaite Christians and Moslems. In 1899 he published a large article about the necessity to use the language of the Mishnah. Later this was put into a book called "Lashon Doreinu" (The language of our generation).

He was active as a Hebraicist in Horodok in the Vilna district, and Lubachov, Minsk district, forming Hebrew associations in both towns. When he married Malka Hendler in Brest, he set her only two conditions:

1. To speak only Hebrew at home.

2. To make Aliyah to Israel.

He opened his school in Brest and founded a Hebrew association. His school was a modern one and on the walls were posters about the Jewish National Resurrection. There were placards with messages about hygiene and cleanliness, and slogans about chapters of religion, literature, and language.

When teaching Hebrew he introduced the Sephardic accent in his private lessons, but had to teach in the Ashkenazi accent in his public classes in the school. This school existed until 1915 when the Russians expelled the civilian population from the city of Brest.

Between 1917-1921 he taught at schools in Siedlice, before returning to Brest. He stayed there for two years before going to Warsaw. In the year 1925 he made Aliyah realizing his longtime dream. He studied Arabic and Semitic languages in Jerusalem that he then introduced into his work about adapting the grammar of the Hebrew language, to which he devoted all his time and efforts. In 1934 he went to Tel Aviv and became a proofreader at the Hebrew newspaper 'Hapoel Hatzair'. He edited the dictionaries of Tzvi Sharfstein, Klenitzky-Klein and the Hebrew section of the English -Hebrew Dictionary by Dr. Kaufman.

In 1930 his discoveries and research appeared in the publication of his book "Lashon Doreinu" (Language of our Generation).

On his 70th birthday a committee was formed with the participation of the Writer's Union, linguists and scientists, in order to publish his research and writings. In 1950 he finished his life's work " The Grammar of the Hebrew Language " in 5 volumes, which was published 1951-1955.

Tzvi Har-Zahav passed away on the 30th December 1956.

[Page 343]

Writers Who Originated from Brest

Translated by Dr. Samuel Chani and Jenni Buch

Dr. Avraham Eisen

He was born in 1886. From 1930 he was known in New York as the translator of the classics into Yiddish. He translated Shakespeare, Byron, Samson the Warrior, Milton, Chapters from Omer Khayyam, etc.etc. He published songs and essays in the Yiddish press in New York.

Arnold Ehrlich

Born in 1848 in Wlodavka near Brest, and lived in Brest in his childhood. Thereafter he studied in Berlin and Leipzig. In 1878 he settled in New York. He held various positions in the United Hebrew Charities. He wrote a book about the Tanach in the style of a Bible critic called " Mikreh Kepashuto " which was published in Berlin in 1901 under the pseudonym of Shabtai, son of Yom Tov the Lonely Stone. S.B. Maximan wrote an article about him in the monthly publication "Miklat".

Herman Gold (Pseudonym Hillel Gorni)

Born in Brisk D'Lita in 1888, in his youth he went to Pinsk and studied in a Yeshiva. He then worked in Warsaw on the publication 'Toshia'. In 1905 he went to the U.S, He published children's books and a book of poetry called "In my City of Brest".

Lewis M. Goldberg

Born in 1870. At he age of ten, he emigrated with his parents to the U.S. He was a journalist and published essays and articles in the Yiddish daily 'Der Tog'.

Meir Hirsh Drachleh

Born in 1880 in Brest. In his youth he went to Galicia and published poems in the 'Social Democrat' newspaper, and stories in the Yiddish newspapers in Warsaw. After W.W.1 he returned to Brest and was the editor of the Yiddish newspaper 'Polesie Shtimmeh' since 1923. At first it was a weekly, and from 1924, it became bi-weekly.

He also edited 'Polesie Nayes', followed by 'Polesie Express'. In his newspaper he wrote editorials and stories, which he signed with various pseudonyms.

Yitzchak Halperin

Born in 1826 in Brest and died in Kerson in 1901. He was a folk writer and wrote in Yiddish. His collections of songs appeared under the name 'Garland of Songs', published in Odessa in 1901. He also wrote songs in Hebrew.

Gershon Shimshon Harnfeld

Born in 1838 in Brest, and died in 1906 in Odessa. A Yiddish writer, he published in 'Kol Mevasser' depicting the lives of the Jewish inhabitants of the Crimea.

Tzvi (Harry) Wolfson

Born in 1887 in Brest. Lived in the U.S. where he was a renowned philosopher. He wrote books in English about the Chassidim of Krashkesh and a large book about Spinoza. He was Professor of Philosophy at Cambridge University (Mass.), and did a great deal to enrich the university with the library of Ephraim Dinard. After the death of Rabbi Chaim Chernovitz, he was nominated as one of the editors of the Hebrew monthly 'Betzaron' in New York.

Pauline Wengerow

Born in 1833 in Brest, and died in Germany in 1916. She published a book called 'Memoires of a Jewish Life in 19th Century Russia'. A large portion of the book is dedicated to her life in Brest.

Semyon Wengerow

Born in 1855 to Mordechai and Pauline Wengerow. He was a famous Russian literary critic. He was author of the books:

The Heroic Character of Russian Literature.

The Main Highlights of the Writings of the New Russian Literature.

His sister Zenaide Wengerow was a famous translator of foreign classics such as Heinrich Hesse and Goethe.

Dora Teitelbaum

A Brest authoress, she wrote many songs about revolutionary themes. Some of them were dedicated to her hometown such as "There was once a home…", "Melody"," My mother's hands", "I jump over the ruins of my city of Brest". Her songs were published in several books.

Israel Isser Cohen

Born in Brest in 1866. In the1880's he went to Leipzig and was occupied with his studies of bibliography and antiquities. From 1886 –1910 he was a teacher at the Judaicum Institute in Leipzig, which had been founded by Professor Franz Delitz.

In 1920 he received his professorship. He was mentioned by Professor Delman in his book "Grammar of the Aramaic Language", and mentioned by Professor Lazarus for all the assistance he gave him.

Yehoshua Yosef Kalbo

He was born in 1837 in Brest and died in Jerusalem in 1920. He was an archeologist, and was known in Jerusalem as Yehoshua Leib Brisker. From his youth he wandered through many lands –his entire life was devoted to research of the original structure of ancient Judea. He published a book called ' Binyan Ariel', which was about the destruction of the temple in Jerusalem with maps of the ruins. This was published in Vienna in 1883 under the patronage of the Austrian Imperial House, the funds donated by the Emperor Franz Josef. He carved out a model of the temple in wood based on his research at the British Museum and the Vatican. After the publication of his book, he received the title of Professor and a life-long stipend. He made Aliyah to Jerusalem and took on the research of ancient scripts.

Yakov Morgenstern

Born in 1821 in Brest and died in London in 1890. He was a folk writer and wrote in Yiddish. His books include: "The Story of Three brothers."Anti-Chassidic Satire." "Simcha Flachter","The Story of Two Partners or Two Butchers"," One Week in Paradise".

Michael Mintz

Born in 1858 in Brest and died in 1912 in the U.S. He went to Israel with BILU in 1882, and immigrated to the U.S. in 1887. In Chicago he founded a Yiddish daily newspaper called "Yiddische Courier". In 1888 he edited a newspaper called The Jewish Advocate.

Moshe Yitzchak Mintz

Born in 1860 in Brest to the prestigious Harchavi-Mintz family. He went to Kharkov University to study in 1882. He traqvelled through many parts of Russia and prepared to settle in Eretz Israel and got as far as Constantinople. In 1884 he arrived with the large BILU group in Israel. However, in 1885 he went to the U.S. where he became editor of the "Volks Zeitung". In 1889 he began as editor of the "Volks Advocate". He founded a society called "Shavi Zion" In 1892 he visited the Zionist colonies in Israel as the emissary of the American and Canadian Zionist organizations. After his return to the U.S. he became publisher and editor of the "Yiddische Courier"

(See pages 222-23 about Esterke his mother).

B. Michalevitch (His pseudonym was Josef Izbicki)

B. Michalevitch

Born in 1876 in Brest, he was one of the founders of the Bund. In 1899, he worked at the Warsaw newspaper "Arbeiter", and was assistant editor of "The Awakener". From 1916 he was the chairman of the Jewish community Administration in Warsaw. He was chief editor of the Bundist daily newspaper in Poland that was called "Lebensfrage". He published "Memories of a Jewish Socialist" in 1921 and a great deal of this book was devoted to Brest.

Menachem Berisha (Goldberg)

Born 20th October 1888 in Brest. He father was a Hebrew teacher and also taught in the state (public) school. He went to Warsaw in 1905, and published his first poems "On the Road". He was a protégé of I.L. Peretz. He came to the U.S. in 1914 and drifted into a young writer's circle called "Die Junge". As well as poems, he wrote dramas, plays and editorials. He was also a theatre critic. He visited Europe in 1926. In 1942, he received a Jewish literary prize for his book "Der Neuer". He was chief editor of the "Congress" weekly newspaper. His works include:

Poland Warsaw 1912.

A Link in the Chain -New York 1915

Velvet New York 1920

Zavel Rimmer- Warsaw 1923

The Gilgul - Vilna 1927

The Shepherd, a drama – Vilna 1932

The CrisisinYiddish – New York 1940

The Walker - New York 1943

He was also co-editor together with Y.L.Halperin of "East Broadway", a literary collection in 1916, and co-editor with S. Niger of "Tallith", as well as the weekly newspaper "Woch" with H. Levitch and L. Shapiro in New York 1929-30. "Yiddish" a weekly newspaper with H. Levick, Leder, Lubitsh, Dr. Chaim Lubsky and David Pinsky in New York 1931.

He passed away in New York in 1949.

Pesach Novick

Born in Brest in 1891. Emigrated to the U.S. where from 1907 he was active in the American Bund. He was editor and secretary of "Neue Welt", and after that the daily newspaper "Freiheit". He edited "Morgen Freiheit" which appeared in New York.

Betzalel Freedman

Born in 1897 in Brest. Pulished his poems in the "Yiddische Zammelbuch" (Yiddish Anthology) in Warsaw 1919 under the editorship of A.M. Wiseberg. After that in the anthology "Auf Dem Weg" and others. He emigrated to the U.S. and published his poems in the "Morgen Journal" and his collections "Schriften". He translated operettas and was a teacher at a Yiddish school in New York.

William (Wolf) Posniak

Born in Brest in 1884. Migrated with his family to England in 1896. Nominated as secretary of the Zionist Organization in London. Worked in the Jewish press in England. Went to the U.S. and edited the Chicago Yiddish newspaper " Chicago Late Record",."Yiddische Press" etc,etc. He published the "Black Book" that contained material about pogroms in Poland and Galicia. He also published a drama about life in during the American War of Independence.

William Zuckerman

Born in 1885 in Brest. Migrated with his family to the U.S. in 1901. He worked in factories. Published essays about faith and philosophical matters - about Bergman and his teachings. He lived his last years in London where he worked as a journalist. He published articles in English about Russian and the Russian Revolution.

Yitzachak Perlov

He was born in 1911 in Brest. He was an author and storyteller. He began his literary life by writing in "Hachalutz" and "Polessie Shtimme". He edited literary collections in Brest, " Yunge Polessie ". He published poetry and novels, one of them was "Farenze Werder," in 1932, "Untergangen" in 1934, "Theatre Songs " in 1935., "Our Warm Eclipse' 1947. "Exodus –A Poem" 1947. "The People of the Exodus" 1949. He was involved in Yiddish press both in Israel and abroad.

Avraham Karnatzki

Born in Chernigov, he lived in Brest in his youth. He died in Brest in 1889. He was the author of several books. He translated into Hebrew the book " The Jewish Triumph " by Shlomo Hirsch Openhausen and a polemic against antisemitism published by Metung in Warsaw 1873.

Avraham Kaplan

Born in 1892 in Brest. From 1912 he published articles in the "Moment" newspaper in Warsaw, the " Shtern" in Vilna and Gut Morgen" in Odessa. His articles appeared in the "Polessie Shtimme" in 1923-24, and he did a great deal of research on the history of the city of Brest.

Zeev –Wolf Rabinovitch

Born in Brest in 1829, died in 1925. He was a student of the Talmud and Jewish teachings. He published the book "Jerusalem" by A.M. Linz and his own work "songs of the Torah Eretz Israel" with interpretations. His notes and proof reading of the Jerusalem Talmud were published in Jerusalem in 1940.

Michael Rabinovitch

Born in Brest in 1856 and died in 1914. The son of Reb Israel Tzvi Rabinovitch, he was descended from the author of "Pamin Meirot". He was a businessman and an activist. He participated in the Zionist congresses He published articles in the Hebrew newspapers "Hasfira" "Ha Levanon" and "Hakol" under the pseudonym of Ben- Izchar. In 1895 his story" Or Matanah" was published in Warsaw,

Stephan Rudinski.

Born in 1887 in Brest, his father was Gedalia Rubinrat. Whilst still in high school he organized with his fellow students Raphalkes and Jurblum a student group to study philosophy and history. He published a research paper on Spinoza and Bergson in a monthly journal called "Life and Science", edited by A. Levitan. He also wrote books in Polish.

Avraham Reicher

Born in 1841 in Brest, died in Minsk in 1903. He wrote the books: "Die Yetumim" "Die Tuche" " Die Ruble" and collections of poems.

B. Shalavin (pseudonym of Benjamin Sheinman).

A writer, he was born in Brest but lived in Paris. He was the author of the Yiddish novels: " It was Yesterday", "The Family Kane", "March on Brest", "The Jews of Belville", "Grey Profiles", "Ruth and Naomi", "The House on Topolova St.", "On the Paris Bridge" "The Promised Land", and "The Golden Illusion".

During W.W.11 he served in the French army and was active in the French resistance against the Nazis.

Menachem Mendel Shapira

Born in 1891 in Brest. He was secretary of the Bund in Minsk. From 1928 he was the secretary of the editor publishing the Jewish monthly in Kharkov "Ratenbildung" (State Education).

[Page 353]

Community Officials

Reb Chaim Cohen

Dr. M.A. Eisenstadt, (Chief Rabbi of Petrograd) Translated by Dr. Samuel Chani and Jenni Buch

Reb Chaim Cohen

Reb Chaim Cohen was a wealthy businessman and benefactor in Brest. Later, although living in Petrograd, his was still involved with Brest. His son Bendet Cohen was a renowned editor and proprietor of the publication "Yalkut". His second son David, was the founder of the daily paper "HaAretz" in Tel Aviv, he was a committee member of the boards of "Davar", ORT, etc, etc.

One evening, a year or two before the war, a man whom I had never seen before came to see me. As applies to anyone who lives in a big city, I was not surprised to see a new face in my home for the first time. This visit however, was entirely different to others as he made a completely distinctive impression. "My name is Chaim Cohen", said the visitor. "I came to settle here in Petrograd in recent days – I've bought a house and therefore I've come to offer my cooperation in any philanthropic/humanitarian enterprise, as every Jew should. Whatever you ask of me, I will fulfill it. If I am away because of business, my sons will be here. If you need something, telephone them. As God has blessed me in my business, in my present situation I do not want to forget my former poverty. I'll be very grateful to you if you would act as a guide to my children in matters of charity."

I must confess that I had never heard such words in my life. It was no wonder, therefore, that this man won my heart. I did not know anything about him – who he was and what he did - understandably our first meeting was not the last. Over the passage of time I got to know the details about this man and became convinced that this Jew was a unique personality without equal.

He was an educated man and a gifted student. He was seldom without the writings of students. Not only did he help them financially, even before those in need would ask for help, he liked to be with them and learn from them.

When I say his house was open to all in the full sense of the word – a house open to talented students – so he conducted himself, this exceptional Jew, a rare individual whose doors were open to all and never closed with a lock, as was usual in a large city. When a visitor came, whether it was a rabbi, a writer, or a local from his hometown - as those were days of heavy persecutions – they all knew that the home of Chaim Cohen was a place of refuge.

His greatest pleasure was to come home in the evening after work and share his meal with rabbis and writers at his table. He took great pleasure in the brilliance of their words.

Many times I saw visitors at his home, rabbis, writers and people from the provinces. He would bring them into his rooms and invite them to his table as his guests, not feeling any strangeness. Only then did I understand the true meaning of hospitality to visitors.

His love for our people and nation had no limits. Being generally an active energetic man, he twice visited Israel. These visits increased his love for the Land of Israel. From then on, he could not find peace sitting in his house in Petrograd. Travelling to distant places which was necessary to his business, he would often think yearningly of his dream. He very much wanted to see how this wasteland (Israel) could be settled through men who had the means to build industries and factories for thousands and tens of thousands of workers, and develop commerce and trade there.

This was the essence of his correspondence with the renowned personalities of the Zionist world.

Reb Chaim did not tolerate trivialities – with a laugh mixed with sadness he would talk of the extravagances of the rich Russian Jews who spent large amounts on enlarging their communities. He would always complain to me as one who was satisfied with little in his own household, to talk to others known to us that they should spend part of their fortunes towards Israel. Incidentally, I read his letter that he sent to his sons from Kharkov.

This letter was written in the style of a testament of a holy man with a gentle soul. In this letter he reminds them that as their father all the experiences he has lived through in his life. He says that his fortune was not based on wealth but knowledge and good deeds. In this letter we found the hint that he did not intend to benefit from the fortune he had amassed during his life, but to leave it all to the land of Israel.

A year before his demise, even before his illness, he proposed that I collect ten rich Jews and request that they donate their entire fortunes to their brethren. He said without false modesty "I am one of them". Understandably, I could not find the other nine. The only one was Chaim Cohen. He became ill and did not believe that this was a fatal illness. He did not even manage to write a will, and then suddenly he died. His sons honoured him during his life and after his death. They completely fulfilled their father's wishes – and his heirs knew how much he valued the book (Torah). One evening before his death we spoke of editing the book by Dr Katzenelson,"The Talmud, the Sciences, and Medicine". He undertook to publish it at his own expense. His sons knew how much he treasured our past, which would lead us towards an easier future. They founded the "Publication of Chaim" in memory of his great soul that expired in Kislev of 1917.

[Page 355]

Israel Asher Shereshevski and His Comrades

By B. Koloditsky
Translated by Dr. Samuel Chani and Jenni Buch

Israel Asher Shereshevski was the founder of Birkur Cholim in Brest. He was the uncle of the banker Raphael Shereshevski of Warsaw. His name was provided on the insignia of Birkur Cholim and on its prescription forms because he stipulated that the pharmacists should lower their charges to the patients of Birkur Cholim. Dr. Hurwitz was the Birkur Cholim doctor and the administrator and employee of the organization was Hershel Koloditzki. Both would visit and attend to the sick.

However, in those days the houses were not numbered and the streets were difficult to find - it was not easy to find their way to visit the sick. Therefore, a building was rented and one would have to come and register with Hershel Koloditski and get on the list of home visits. The address of the patient would be written down is this manner: he lives at Velvel Fisher's, or also known as Berel at Fisher's, or Berel the fish monger... and many others with such signposts!

At the appointed time, Hershel would drive Dr Hurwitz in the buggy to the visit. Hershel was a warm and honest man, a pauper. He knew a little Latin and would stand and listen carefully to the words of the doctor, and take great heed of how he administered his medicines. Thus, in time, he acquired a great deal of practical knowledge to the extent that the doctors would often confer with him. He would also substitute for the doctor, although all knew that he had never studied medicine. After the wealthy Shereshvski died, Reb Laizer Mandelblatt, a childless, honest Jew, who became the director of Birkur Cholim, took his place.

Then the society "Linat Hazedek" was formed, and there the young people whose inclination was to help the sick and needy would register their names.

When their turn came to visit the sick, and they could not fulfill their roster, they would pay 10 kopeks to hire a substitute.

After a while the institiutions attracted directors such as Dr. Shteinberg and Dr. Leon Shereshevski. However, the landlords and businessmen were opposed to the fact that doctors headed these societies. Amongst those who opposed the doctors with great propaganda was Moshe Baruch Bishkovitch and others. Reb Laizer was a pleasant and unruffled man, they tried to infuriate him, but he would listen to his opponents and try to placate them with a smile.

One day there came to him a wagon driver before Pesach, and said "Good evening, Reb.Laizer! I wanted to honor you with a blessing, that a spirit should enter your father's father, but I won't say that, perhaps I should say that a spirit should enter you grandmother, but I wont say that either...."

Reb Laizer asked him to sit down and said," what you should not say, and the subject you should not recall are the souls of my grandfather and grandmother, neither of whom are alive. And it is better that you should leave them to lie in peace in their graves and tell me what is bothering you and why you are so angry". Hearing these softly spoken words the driver was quietened and asked for forgiveness from Reb Laizer for the ugly words that had fallen from his mouth.

A supporter of 'Chovevei Zion' (Lovers of Zion) with his name and his entire soul was Ben-Zion Neumark. He was the founder of 'Cheder Metukan', a Hebrew progressive school –the first of its' kind in Brest. He was appointed to do this by the Zionist committee in Odessa. All the monies that were collected from the Yom Kippur appeal were given directly to him – Koloditski would collect the money at Israel Wolf's synagogue – a two-storey building. He would send the sum with an additional three rubles membership payment to the Odessa committee.

Ben- Zion Neumark was one of the directors of Bikur Cholim, and also the Gabbai of the Kadosh Synagogue, which formed the co-operative "Lending and Savings Fund". All the elected directors were Zionists such as Yitzchak Winnikoff and others. The chairman was C. Shereshevski. The operation of Birkur Cholim was feeding widows and orphans (Linat Zedek), visiting the sick and the distribution of medicines to them. IN 1911-12 there was an outbreak of malaria. Bikur Cholim bought a lot of quinine and Hershel Koloditski himself distributed the doses to the needy.

Amongst the leaders of the city was Yekutiel Poliak. The secretary of the community council (kehilla) was Zev Dov Begin who was one of the leading Zionists in Brest before W.W.1. He was a member of the Zionist committee and an employee and of Lending Fund. He was dedicated with his whole heart and soul to Zionism. However, he also did many things according to his own opinions, when the Zionists requested a Zionist 'minyan' (prayer service) in a private prayer house, Begin however, determined that instead of official government permission, it would be sufficient to get an endorsement in the name of Koloditski. But it did not take long before the group was betrayed to the authorities by the landlord, who said that this was not a meeting place for the Zionists, but a synagogue and that required a special government permit.

Beinish Koloditski was fined 100 rubles or three days imprisonment by the court. He wanted to save the community money, so he sat in prison for three days. Koloditski was the representative of the Keren Kayemet and occupied this position until his departure for Israel. One day, they came to him and said that there were no facilities in the 'Slonimer Shteibl' for the Yom Kippur collection. His father in law came to him and said that he dared not send anyone to ask about this, as they would surely throw him out. Koloditski himself then went with a bowl and requested that the congregation make a donation – they actually did contribute very nicely. After prayers they told him that although their Rabbi demanded that they throw the Zionist representative out, nobody dared to.

In 1915 the Lending Fund was left with a sum of money for Keren Kayemet. When the bank stopped paying its depositors (due to the war), Josef Shereshevski took the money with him to Moscow. Koloditski wrote to him and received a reply that the money had been transferred to the Zionist Bureau in Moscow.

[Page 359]

Ben-Zion Neumark

By M. Leizorovitch
Translated by Dr. Samuel Chani and Jenni Buch

He was one of the nicest people of the Zionist movement from the BILU days. Fifty years ago in the beginning of this movement, the crucial question of Aliyah to Israel was linked to leaving a secure existence and exposing one self to hunger, poverty and malaria. Ben Zion Neumark made such a leap. As with other young people he had no plans to return. But unlike the others who returned, he did not blame the land of Israel, but himself. He was haunted by by guilty feelings his whole life Nevertheless, he had not passed the test in that fateful hour. Returning to Brest, he devoted his whole being to the Zionist cause with much fervor.

In those days it was difficult to spread the Zionist ideology. It was necessary to appear in the synagogues and penetrate the Chassidic schools. Modern secular schools did not exist then, so that when the progressive schools began to appear, Neumark opened such a school in Brest. He founded a library for the young pupils of the city. He collected subscriptions for the Zionist press - sometimes in secret, as it was against the restrictive government laws – the Russian government did not recognize the Zionist movement. Much turning and twisting skill was needed to overcome these difficulties.

Neumark printed the Proclamation of the First Zionist Congress at the military printing press of the Russian fortress in Brest. Neumark was elected to be Brest's delegate at the first Zionist Congress in Basle 1897. However, due to insufficient funds, he was unable to go to Switzerland. He was one of the Russian delegates to the conference in Helsinki 1906, and a member of the "Sons of Moshe'. He was secretary of the Zionist organization in Minsk when W.W.1 broke out. In the last years of his life, he made aliyah to Israel and died there aged 82.

[Page 361]

Rabbi Mordechai Sheinerman

Translated by Dr. Samuel Chani and Jenni Buch

Mordechai Sheinerman was born in Brest in 1870 and died in 1929. He was one of the original "Chovevei Zion" (Lovers of Zion). He would travel around the towns and villages of the area –preaching Zionism and winning people's hearts over to the movement. He was one of the best Hebrew teachers, and was a pioneer of the method of teaching Hebrew in Hebrew in Brest. His lessons in Tanach would be intertwined with facts and events from Jewish history, which awakened the Zionist consciousness of his students.

He was known as a prodigy in his youth. After being ordained as a rabbi he was invited to a position of rabbi in the U.S., but he declined the offer because he did not want to make money out of teaching the Torah. Physically he was not a strong man, but his spirit was proud and valiant. He was one of the organizers and activists of the Jewish self-defence in Brest. Their arm cache was hidden in the roof of his home, screened by a large apple tree. The Tsarist police would search his home looking for Zionist materials and arms, but he managed to evade arrest. In 1909 he made aliyah to Israel and obtained the position of teacher in Rechovot. His dream was to bring his family to live in Eretz Israel – but a severe illness stopped him from doing this, and he returned to Brest, a broken man. In 1925 he again made aliyah with all his family. A major crisis prevailed in the country at that time and he had a bitter struggle to find employment, until he was offered the secretaryship of the Literary Union, and it's monthly publication of "Mazonim". He worked there until his last day.

[Page 361]

Brest in Bygone Years

as told by the elderly Doba-Yaffa to N. Chinitz
Translated by Dr. Samuel Chani and Jenni Buch

Born in Brest in 1844, his father, Gershon Shteinberg was a lawyer. He studied in a cheder and later went to a school for children of the aristocracy. He graduated from high school in Grodno and studied medicine at the Military Medical Academy in St. Petersburg. He graduated with distinctions and was nominated as military physician to the Second Infantry Battalion. In 1878 he was posted with the rank of Colonel to the military garrison of Brest as doctor. In 1892 he was forced to submit his resignation because he categorically refused to convert. Because of this, he lost his right to a pension.

He was active in community work and in 1899 he joined the Zionist organization and was selected as delegate to the Zionist Congress.

He distinguished himself with defending Jews in Brest. The mobilization of reserves to be sent to the front in the Russo-Japanese War caused unrest and attempts to create a pogrom in Brest in June 1906. For his sympathy towards the revolutionary freedom movements he was imprisoned in the Brest fortress for one month in1906. In 1911, he became gravely ill and passed away in St. Petersburg. According to his will, he was buried in Israel.

He wrote articles in Yiddish describing the Great Fire of Brest in 1895, and a satirical monologue about a Jewish woman in Brest called "Hayele Mazal",a play titled "Hinde Eidelson" in which he described Jewish life in Romania (he had been a doctor there during the Balkan Wars). He also wrote a book about infectious diseases and an article about the Kishinev pogrom.

[Page 363]

Reb. Levi - Yitzchak Winnikoff

Translated by Dr. Samuel Chani and Jenni Buch

Reb. Levi - Yitzchak Winnikoff

Reb Levi Yitzchak Winnikoff was born in the shtetl of Surash, Chernigov district. In 1897 he married a daughter of the Brest community activist, Reb Zalman Tennenbaum. What was Levi –Yitzchak before his Zionist life in Brest? His entire life from his early youth was devoted to the Zionist ideals. He gave the greater part of his life and his material means to Zionism.

He himself was a Lubavitch Chassid, but gave the Zionist cause all his Chassidic devotion and zeal. He occupied important positions in the community life of Brest – he was chairman of the Keren Hayesod, chairman of the Zionist Tarbut, and head of the Jewish group in the City Council. He was a delegate to several Zionist conferences, etc. etc.

When he saw his son in the uniform of the Israeli army - he cried and said:" you'll never understand what it means to be a soldier in the Israeli army. Just as you could not understand my joy when I arrived in Israel and saw a tailor's sign in Hebrew..."

He was a General Zionist but not the usual conventional Zionist. There dwelt in him a constant holy restlessness, he was dissatisfied with every achievement, and it was never enough for him. He could not be comfortable with any of the powers that ruled Brest at various times... the Russians, Germans, Ukrainians, and later the Poles.

In 1923 when Greenbaum formed the 'Minority Bloc' in Poland, the Polish police arrested Winnikoff. In 1931 the security police demanded that he sign a proclamation to the Jewish community declaring that they should vote for the B.B. (government party). One had to have a great deal of courage to refuse this, but he treated it as his Zionist conscience dictated and did not sign.

As a result he suffered much discrimination. The authorities did not forget that he was born in Russia and cancelled his Polish citizenship. After much intercession in Warsaw, it was returned to him. He approached the central committee of the Zionist organization with the request that he be allowed to make aliyah to Israel.

After arriving in Israel, he still continued with several important community works, until he became ill - he suffered greatly as a result. Just before his death he said to those around him that one should pray for an easy death rather than an easy life. In spite of the terrible pain, he never complained. Fully conscious on the last day of his life, he said goodbye to his wife and children, adding that they should love their country as he did. He was known as the man who was the "Zionist Council" In Brest.

[Page 365]

Zerach Zaretski

Translated by Dr. Samuel Chani and Jenni Buch

Zerach Zaretski

Born in 1891 in Peitrikov, Minsk Gubernia. He was a member of the group "HaTechiya" (The Revival). In 1909 he went to Israel and worked in the orchards of Kfar Saba as a sentry. He participated in the founding of the Gymnasia Herzlia High School in Tel –Aviv. A year later he became very ill with malaria. He returned to Russia and became a Hebrew teacher in Yekaterinoslav. In 1921 he came to Brest and was an active participant in working for the Zionist cause. He was a member of the kehilla council, the board of the Hebrew schools, the Polessie branch of Tarbut, and the board of the Orphanage. During the split of the General Zionists he decided to join "Time to Build' during the elections to the Polish Sjem and to head this second group. This involvement meant that he was in personal danger because of the antagonism of the Polish ruling powers to the minority groups. At the outbreak of W.W.11, he was in Vilna and was active in the activities of the Joint and the kehilla committee. Terns of thousands of Jews, who were saved from the hands of the Nazis, mention his name with great reverence. Through his initiative, the Joint formed a manual workers union to employ the homeless (bankers, merchants, carpenters, etc.) In many other unconventional ways, he assisted them to flee.

Once again, in 1941, he reached Israel. There he was active in the enlistment drive for the army. In his last years he suffered from a severe illness and died in Tel-Aviv in 1947.

[Page 365]

Zev - Dov Begin

Translated by Dr. Samuel Chani and Jenni Buch

Zev - Dov Begin

ZEV-DOV was born in Brest, the son of David Eliezer Begin. In his youth he studied in yeshivas and distinguished himself with his sharp intellect. Although fully immersed in Torah studies, but even as a yeshiva student, he secretly studied medicine - but due to the circumstances of those days, he was unable to complete these studies. He was an expert in languages and one of the first public speakers of Hebrew in Brest. An expert in Jewish studies, he was also a skilled community official. He was an orator without equal, and in him was embodied fearlessness, and willingness to sacrifice himself for the good of all.

Already in his youth he entirely devoted himself to community affairs. Through his initiative, the first barracks were built to provide temporary housing for victims of the Grest Fire in Brest. He also worked for the newspapers "Heint' and "Moment" that were published in Warsaw. In 1905, when the Jews of Brest were fearful of the pogroms, Zev –Dov was one of the organizers of the Jewish self-defense. He was forced to hide from the Tsarists police who discovered a cache of arms belonging to the self-defence force. Amongst them were several revolvers belonging to he and his friend Sheinerman. Begin was the living embodiment of the Zionist youth in all it's shades and untiringly preached and was drawn to its ideals.

In 1939 when the Germans entered Brest, Begin, as usual, stood guard and saved the lives of about 300 Polish and Jewish residents of the city from the Nazi murderers...

On the bitter day in July 1941 he was drowned in the river together with 5,000 other Jews, heroic until the end. They say that when the Germans came to take him to his death, he showed exceptional strength, but his weak physical state could not hold out against them, as the Nazis took him on a truck to the river. In his last moments he shouted to his murderers "the day of vengeance will come to you".

His son Menachem Begin was the commander of the Irgun Tzava Leumi, and is leader of the Likud party and a member of the Knesset.

[Page 367]

Yakov Feinstein

Translated by Dr. Samuel Chani and Jenni Buch

Yakov Feinstein

Born in 1861 in Brest, he was one of the original Chovevei Zion. He was active in Zionist causes in Brest and participated in several Zionist conferences. He was one of the initiators of "Menucha and Nachala" which was founded in Warsaw for the establishment of settlements in Israel. In 1895 he sent his oldest son Eliezer to the agricultural school at Mikvei Israel, and also bought land in Rechovot. In 1899 and 1903 he visited Israel. After that, he came with his entire family and settled in Rechovot. The ancient well of the colony was on his land. During the excavations there were doubts about finding water. The future of the colony and its economy depended on it. The laborers did not want to dig in the dark because of fear of being suffocated underground. The old man Yonah Tzvi, the father of Yakov Feinstein, volunteered to go down deep into the well "I'm old and the sacred responsibilty lies on me". The old man said his goodbyes with great emotion and tears in his eyes and went down the well. Yonah Tzvi worked hard and sent up several buckets of soil until water appeared. He was pulled up intact and hearty. He was greeted with great joy and pleasure with his well that spouted water and watered the orchards of his son and neighbours.

Yakov Feinstein took on much community work. Through his initiative the winery in Rechovot was formed. He was a member of its committee and the first in Rechovot to plant an orchard in Rechovot. He was a member of the winegrowers association and the colony's council; also he was the Gabbey of the synagogue there. He was the brother of the writer Nechama Pochachevski.p

[Page 367]

Shmuel Pomerantz

Translated by Dr. Samuel Chani and Jenni Buch

Shmuel Pomerantz

He was born in Pruzhany, and settled in Brest in 1906. He was expelled with all his family by the Russians at the start of W.W.1 – they were amongst the first to return in 1918. He dedicated himself completely to the activities of the Joint and the Jewish self-defence that was organized by the Jews against the pogromchiks. He devoted himself to working for several institutions that were formed for the community's welfare.

The name Shmuel Pomerantz was linked with the vital institution of which he was chairman since it's establishment. This was the orphanage to which he devoted all his time and energy until his last day. With the advent of "Centrum" in Poland, Shmuel Pomerantz was elected chairman of the Brest branch. Later he was the representative for the whole of the Polessie district to its headquarters in Warsaw.

He was head of the community council and gabbei of the Great Synagogue in Brest. Together with the deputy mayor of the city council, Dr. Wilner and Avraham Levinson, he was a member of the city council administration. They struggled against the neglect of the Poles towards the needs of the city's Jews.

He was active in the Merchants' Guild and a board member of the People's Bank, which lent money to all levels of society. With his good nature and charm as well as practical good sense, he managed to solve disputes, and very much liked by the resident citizens of Brest. He made a short visit to Brest in 1937. During W.W.11 he was sent to Kovel and perished there together with the other martyrs of that city.

[Page 369]

Moshe Lubetkin

Translated by Dr. Samuel Chani and Jenni Buch

Moshe Lubetkin

Born in Brest to a prestigious family, he was a tall broad - shouldered man with beautiful eyes and a smile that usually floated on his lips. In 1913 he began his activities amongst the youths of the middle school of commerce. He set up a group called Bnei Zion (sons of Zion) He completely gave all his time to the building and enlargement of the Local Zionist library. He was an important member of the American committee (formed through the Joint) and had great responsibility and influence in providing the homeless with accommodation.

He was one of the founders of the Young Zionists which sprung up from the "Techiya" organization. He was also active in educational and social matters. He was active in the Young Zionists Bund and the Poale Zion, which were prevalent in the Jewish society after W.W.1

He made aliyah to Israel in 1924 and worked in the labor movement (Palestine Workers Fund). For the last fifteen years of his life he managed the affairs of the Workers Council in the Histadrut. He spent much time and effort on the development of the worker's archives, of which he was a member. He also negotiated a deal to build the Max Fein Trade School. He passed away in Tel-Aviv in 1942 after a severe illness.

[Page 371]

Moshe Eliezer Ben-Anat (Breinhandler)

Translated by Dr. Samuel Chani and Jenni Buch

Moshe Eliezer Ben-Anat

Born on Brest on the 16th of Marcheshvan 1903. He studied in a Modern Hebrew cheder in his childhood. He then went to middle school for about 2 years, after that he went to Warsaw University to study. He was a member of the student committee there and a member of the national council of Poale Zion. He was one of the founders of the "Hachalutz" (pioneer) movement, and was involved in the weekly publications "Polessie Shtimme", "Befreiung", and "Arbeiter Wort".

He made aliyah to Israel in 1925, and was one of the founders and the secretary of the Worker's Loan Fund. He was an active member of the United Workers that joined with other parties to form the Mapai.party. After the split in the party, he went over to the "Achdut Avodah" party and was an active member of it's central committee, and the Lands secretariat. After the union with Mapam he represented the united movement of the various institutions. He was elected as a member of the Tel –Aviv city council. After leaving Mapam, he became one of the founders of the Workers Union and a member of the Workers Council in the Histadrut and a member of the City of Tel-Aviv worker's council. He was a deputy director of the tax office of the Histadrut and a committee member of Keren Hayesod Ha-Avodah (unemployment fund).

In 1931 Ben-Anat initiated the establishment of "Mashan" and was the head of this organization. He was a delegate to the 21st Zionist Congress. He was also a member of the Haganah and in 1942 he volunteered for guard service and was one of the editors of the Hebrew language "Notar"

During the War of Independence in 1948, he was active in cultural and educational issues for the Israeli army. He was a member of the mobilization board of the Israeli army, and published many articles in the labor press:" Davar"," Pinkas", "Hapoel Hatzair", and "Lachdut Avodah".

He was one of the most recognized of the Labor movement in Israel. He was friendly to everyone who turned to him for assistance. He was always ready to help with a warm and open heart. He personified good heartedness and moral ethics. He was a fighter and demanded more of himself and was more forgiving of others.

He died in Tel-Aviv after a severe illness in 1953.

[Page 371]

Personalities and Officials

Translated by Dr. Samuel Chani and Jenni Buch

*A committee of the Brisker descendants (Yotzei Brisk) were occupied with preparing this list of Brest personalities and community officials from all levels of society. To our regret, many names have been omitted, because this committee did not receive the relevant information from relatives and friends. In the material received by this committee there were also missing details of the community lives of many mentioned in this list. The list is compiled in alphabetical order.

Hersh Archov

A representative of the Jewish community of Brest at the end of the 19th century, he was diligent and virtuous in his efforts with the Russian authorities. Through his efforts the following organizations were founded: The Old Age Home, Visiting the Sick (Birkur Cholim) and the Charity fund which gave loans without interest to many Brest residents and assisted them to recover after the two Great Fires.

His wife Dinah was known for her Philanthropic work and her untiring efforts in appealing to the Russian civil and military authorities for assistance in Jewish community matters.

Yehezkel Archov

Yehezkel Archov

He was one of the most respected merchants and industrialists in Brest. He was a confidante of Chaim Soloveitchik, the Brisker Rav. He was a Gabbeh in the Rabbi's synagogue, a member of the Board of the Jewish hospital, and other philanthropic institutions. He was the elder son of Hersh and Dinah Archov. His sister, Bertha Rassin, now lives in Israel.

Michael Archov

Michael Archov

One of the most active officials in Brest for social welfare matters. Through his initiative the Visitors Hostel was established. After the death of his father Hersh, he managed the Loan Fund. He was a founding member of the new Old Age Home after W.W.1, chairman of the boards of Bikur Cholim, Linat Tzedek, and for a while -chairman of Keren Heyesod.

His sons are now in Israel – Dr. Shmuel Archov and Tzvi Archov.

Chaim Leib Izbitzer

An active member of the Zionist organization, Keren Kayemet and Keren Heyesod. He was secretary of the Tarbut High school. He died in Russia as a prisoner of Zion.

Shimon Izbitzer

Shimon Izbitzer

Was born in Brest in 1902, the son of Chaim Leib. The family went to Yekaterinoslav and Shimon joined the Poale Zion movement there. At the time he was a student of the Burg Academy in Yekaterinoslav. He returned to Brest in 1922 and devoted all his energies to communal work. He was the secretary of ORT and a member of the city council, as well as serving on the committee of Poale Zion, Polessie district, and the national Poale Zion council for all of Poland.

In 1933 he made aliyah to Israel and worked as a construction worker. He worked in the electrical power plant in Tel-Aviv. He found it difficult to adjust to the conditions in Israel at the time. He died in Tel-Aviv.

Rabbi Yehuda Leib Eisen

Born in Mezrich in 1882. He studied in Brest, and received his rabbinical ordination from the Brisker Rav - Chaim Soloveitchik. He settled in Brest and was a member of the Rabbinate until his death. He was well liked and respected by the residents of the Grayever surburb in which he lived.

Shmuel Ashkenazi

Shmuel Ashkenazi

Made aliyah from Brest to Israel in 1907. He was a wealthy, educated and scholarly man. An energetic business entrepeneur, he was one of the pioneers of industry in Israel and one of the first builders of Tel -Aviv. He passed away in 1942 and was buried on the Mount of Olives in Jerusalem.

Asher Ashkenazi

He was Vice President of the Mizrachi organization, and a director of the "Co-operative Bank" He was very involved in the field of education and was the head of the "Tachkamoni" school. Perished together with his family in the Brest Ghetto.

Zipporah Elbaum – Grushevski

A teacher of Hebrew, she studied in Kharkov and Kiev, and was active in Zionist circles and the Zeirei Zion. Came to Israel where she was a teacher in Ramat Gan. She passed away in 1937.

Personalities and Officials (cont.)

Dr. Arieh Begun

He was the chairman of the ORT organization in Brest. A progressive community official, he was active in it's welfare institutions and especially TOZ –the healthcare organization. He was killed in the Brest Ghetto.

Dr. Shneur Zalman Bichowski

Born in Brest, in his youth he was a yeshivah student. A well –known Zionist leader, he published several interesting memoirs about Brest Jewish life. Went to live in Warsaw where he became renowned as a neurologist. He was a member of the Warsaw city council was famous as a fighter against corruption and discrimination.

Hirsh –Chaim Birshtein

A merchant, a learned scholar and benefactor. He was the grandson of the famous Rabbi David Meir, the owner of the renowned house at 12 Topolowa St. in which were located all the Zionist interests in the city, rent free.

His son in law was the banker Raphael Shereshevski from Warsaw. Birshtein died in Warsaw.

Michael Berezovski

He graduated from the Pedagogic (teaching) Academy in Grodno. He was the director of the "Techiya" Hebrew school in Brest, and founder of the Tarbut bookstore in Brest. He was killed in the Brest Ghetto.

Joseph Eliezer Berlin

He was a merchant and well-known property owner in Brest. He was a trustee of "Birkur Cholim" for decades. Was respected as an arbiter in disputes and active in community activities.

Yitzchak Brandzel

A timber merchant, he was a dedicated Zionist. Respected as an arbiter and accepted in all circles. He was the treasurer of the People's Bank He also proposed to his clients they should buy a "Shekel" and commit to Keren Hayesod for Israel. Perished in the Brest Ghetto.

Reb Moshe Yosef Barlas

Reb Moshe Yosef Barlas

The grandson of Reb Tzvi Hirsh Barlas, author of the book "Or HaTzvi". Moshe Hirsh was a scholar and an educator. He would devote himself every day to study of the Torah. He was a member of the Mizrachi organization and a Zionist activist. During W.W.1 he lived with his family in Biale, and was amongst the first to return to Brest. He was very active in the rebuilding of the city and a member of the relief committee of the Joint. He was on the boards of the Jewish hospital, Talmud Torah, Linat Zedek, and the founder of Assistance for the Poor. He was also an arbiter (judge) in family and financial disputes. His mother, Beila, made aliyah to Israel in 1894 and died in Jerusalem.

Zalman Barlas

He was one of the wealthy residents of Brest. His business was conducted abroad, and provided many jobs for Briskers from his trading enterprises. In 1905 he founded a private bank which was linked to financial capital abroad. One of his sons studied in Switzerland and was killed in a mountaineering accident there. His second son, Dov, fled into Russia in W.W.2, - went through several German concentration camps and arrived in the U.S. after the war. Zalman was a grandson of Reb Tzvi Hirsh Barlas. He perished in the Warsaw Ghetto.

Mordechai Barlas

Mordechai Barlas

He was the son of Moshe Yosef Barlas. He was active in Keren Kayemet Leisrael and one of their delegates. He was one of the Zeirei Zion (Young Zionists) and was sent to work in Israel as a cultural attache through this committee. He was a member of the Hebrew Library and other organizations. His brother Leib was active in "Hahalutz".

Chaim Bromberg

A relative of Rabbi Chaim Soloveitchik, he was the representative of the gumboot (galoshes) factory "Treygalnik". He was the permanent gabbei of the Rabbi's synagogue and a great benefactor.

Zelig Braverman

He was a timber merchant and a member of the board of ORT, and the Zionist organization. Active participant in community work. He died in Israel.

Issachar Blankstein

A repected businessman, he was a member of the board of the Brest Credit Union. He was a benefactor to Zionist and orthodox causes. He was a prayer leader in the Great Synagogue.

Wolf Ballach

He was the purveyor of food supplies to the Brest Fortress. He was a supporter of Zionist and orthodox causes. His son, Eliezer Ballach, became one of the foremost engineers in Israel in the field of Water Technology.

Emmanuel Baraks

He was born in 1907, the son of Mordechai Baraks. He was one of the pioneers of the Jewish sports movement such as:Y.S.K., Maccabi, and Nordia. One of the co-founders of Betar and the revisionist movement. Member of the Jewish academic circles and Arcad, the "El Al" corporation in Brest.

Perished in the Kowal Ghetto in 1942.

Yitzchak Baruchin

Son of the renowned merchant Yakov Baruchin and the son in law of the philantrophist Asher Radevski. Finished conservatorium, and was a member of the Brisker refugees committee in Kobryn in 1915-16. He donated his estate, "Adamkowe" for Hachshara (agricultural training) to the Hashomer Hatzair movement and other pioneer organizations. Co-founder and Gabbeh of the Oksenhendler (Ox traders) Synagogue.

Yitzchak Bodanski

He was the manager of the bank account of "Soloveitchik and Morgenstern". He was a member of the Brisker relief committee in Warsaw in 1914.

Chasia – Beile Bodanski

She was from the Zakheim family from Rozinoy. She did a great deal in assisting the sick and needy through the organization "Matan Bastar".

Yitzchak –Asher Becker

Yitzchak –Asher Becker

Born in Kobryn, from 1908 he lived in Brest. He was active in many communiy affairs. For years he was the representative of the St. Petersburg 'Nevski' soap and candle factory in Brest. He was a Chassid and close to the Stoliner Rebbe, He contributed a great deal towards the building of the orphanage in Brest. He visited Israel, returned to Brest and perished under the Nazi murderers.

His son, Aaron Becker, lives in Israel and is the head of the Histadrut.

Yehudah, the son of Yakov Baruch Breinhendler

He was born in Brest in 1882. He was the son in law of Rabbi Naphtali Tzvi Goldfarb, and the brother in law of Avraham Yitzchak Bleiweiss. The family Breinhendler was religious and Zionist. Yehudah was a member of the Jewish Community Council, the Merchant Bank and other institutions. He made aliyah with his wife Zipporah in 1936. He died in Tel-Aviv in 1943.

Issar Gvirtzman

The gabbei of the Great Synagogue, he made aliyah to Israel where he assisted in building the synagogue in Kiryat Motzkin, and was the gabbei there.

Mendel Gvirtzman

The son of Hershel Gvirtzman. One of the most influential and well-known chassdim in Brest. As an 'elder' of the Jewish community under the Russians, he greatly assisted the young Jewish men who were called up for military service.

Tzvi "Hershel" Gvirtzman

He owned an oil factory, and was one of the founders of the Mizrachi organization in Brest, and representative of this party in all the institutions. He worked tirelessly for the Joint (post W.W.1) on the committee for the homeless. Killed in the Brest Ghetto.

Nachum Govrinovski (Nachum the Slonimer)

He ran a Cheder Metukan, a modern Hebrew school, and was one of the most advanced teachers in Brest. He introduced new methods of educating his students in the Jewish nationalist spirit.

Rabbi Moshe Gottman

He arrived from the shtetl of Orleh to live in Brest in 1896 at the invitation of Rabbi Chaim Soloveitchik. He was requested to manage and oversee the supervision of the Yeshivah Torat Chaim in Jerusalem, whose directorship was in Brest. About twenty emmissaries were working under him, collecting monies for this yeshivah in all the corners of Russia. During W.W.1 he was one of the refugees in Bereza Kartuzka, who suffered greatly from hunger. He still collected his students around him and spread the Torah in abundance. He returned to Brest in 1917 and was nominated as a member of the Rabbinate. He passed away in 1933 in Brest.

Nathan Goldring

He was chairman of several of the aid institutions in the city. During the campaign for the first Polish Sejm (parliament) he was on the Zionist list. He became ill and died at a young age.

Eliezer Goldfarb

He was a member of the General Zionists and on the board of the orphanage. He was active in Keren Kayemet and Keren Hayesod. He perished in the Ghetto.

Liza Galadetz

She was active in Brest's social institutions. She was the head of the Womens Branch of the Zionist Movement. She perished in the Ghetto.

Reb Nachum Zeev Goldrei

He was born in Brest in 1864 and died in Jerusalem in 1921. He worked in the oil industry, and founded an export business - trading with Germany - with many branches in Germany and other western European countries. His sons ran the business, and he made aliyah on the advice of the Gerrer Rebbe. He built a large building in the Houses of Warsaw district in Jerusalem, which gave him the community directorship. He was a great benefactor.

David Gitelman

Active in the leftist Poale Zion and a member of the board of "Zisheh". He was active in the community institutions, and a member of the community council. Perished in the Ghetto.

Dr. Yosef Geizler

Founder and chairman of TOZ (community health organization) in Brest: He was the head doctor of the government health benefit fund. He perished in the Ghetto.

Yitzchak Gendler

Owner of a printing press. He was the editor of "Polessie Shtimmeh", a member of the city council, and active in labor circles. He visited Israel in 1935 and returned to Brest. Perished in the Ghetto.

Reb Alter Grosleit

Reb Alter Grosleit

He was a grandson of the famous Rabbi Pinchas Michael of Antopol, author of the book "Divrei Pinchas" (Warsaw 1860) "Lakat Hakotzrim" (Vilna 1867), and others. He was an in-law of Tzvi Hirsh Barlas. He gave a great amount to charity, and was a member of the board of the Old Age home and Birkur Cholim and other institutions. He purchased land in Kfar Oriya before W.W.1. He made aliyah with his wife Sheina- Rivka and settled in Bnei Brak. He died in Tel-Aviv in 1940.

His brother, Yitzchak (Itzik) Grosleit, lived in Lodz and was one of the pioneers of the Jewish textile industry. He was the chief director of the Paznitzki factory.

Dov – Ber Grosman

Property owner and manufacturer. A great benefactor to all the Jewish institutions.

Dr. Yochanan Greenstein

He was a doctor in the Jewish hospital, and a director of TOZ. He donated much medical help to the underprivileged.

Shalom Halpern

He was from an orthodox Zionist family, and active in the Zeirei Zion and Hachalutz. He was the librarian of the Brest Library from 1920-26. He came to Israel in 1927, and worked in the orchards of Kfar Saba. He was a member of the Bemaavar kibbutz in Petach Tikvah. In 1931 he moved to Kfar Azar where he was involved in agricultural activity. In his last years he worked for the Israeli Water Board. He died in 1954.

Leon Horoditch

Leon Horoditch

A banker, he was one of the first to have contacts with Dr. Theodore Herzl at the beginning of the Zionist movement. Their activities were conducted in secret because of fear of the Russian authorities. He received many letters from Herzl which were later lost. He underwrote bonds for the return of Jews to Zion, and was a delegate to the first Zionist Congress, and later participated in another 10 congresses. He died in Tel – Aviv in 1942.

Reb Shabtai (Shepsel) Haft

He was one of the best-known learned scholars of the city, and a colleague of A.L. Feinstein (author of Ir Tehila). He was the founder of the open (free) library. The ultra –orthodox banned him because of his progressive views on education.

Reb Benyamin Vigdorovitch

He was a renowned businessman. He owned properties and farming estates. He was gabbei (trustee) of the Green Synagogue He donated to all the charitable institutions and generously gave to all the needy who approached him for assistance. His granddaughter, Shoshana Persitz, was a member of the first Knesset.

He founded the large publishing house "Amanut".

Gershon Wein

One of the leading Zionists in the city. He was involved in community affairs.

Joseph Winograd

He was a member of the Merchant's Guild. A learned scholar and renowned chess champion. Settled in Israel and died in 1955 in Kibbbutz Mishmar Hasharon.

Moshe and Betzalel Winnig

They were industrialists and the proprietors of the oil paint factory in Brest. Their employees were all Jews. They donated much to the needy and to the various community causes.

Reb Yakov Meyer Weinstock

He was a well-known social activist in his suburb of Graever Slobotka. A representative in all the city's institutions, he was respected widely.

Dr. Bronislav Wilner

He settled in Brest in 1922 as the representative of the National Council in Warsaw for the Polessie district. Wilner was the Vice President (deputy mayor) of the city, and one of the founders of "Polessie Shtimmeh". He excelled in helping refugees who did not have Polish citizenship, saving many from deportation into Russia. Was a co-worker in the Joint and other institutions. Whilst still young, he became ill and died suddenly in Warsaw.

Reb Chaim Zalman Wolski

Reb Chaim Zalman Wolski

He was born in 1868, and came as a child with his family to Brest. He was a wealthy manufacturer, mill-owner, and a wheat merchant. His wife Leiba (nee Freiluk), was from one of the city's leading families. An orthodox Jew, Chaim Zalman brought up his children in the spirit of the Torah. He was a member of the Community Council and a member of the executive of the Merchant's Bank, a member of the board of the orphanage, old age home, etc.etc.

He was a gabbeh of the Oxen-traders synagogue; he would give lessons on the daily page to the praying congregation. He also resolved conflicts and disputes between parties. Perished in the Brest Ghetto.

Fanny Winnikoff

Daughter of Reb Zalman Tenebaum, wife of the Zionist activist Levi-Yitzchak Winnikoff. She assisted him in all his community work. She was active in Keren Hayesod. She passed away in Israel in 1956.

Aaron Winnikoff

Brother of the Zionist activist Levi Ytizchak Winnikoff. He was an activist and one of the organizers of the 7th Zionist Congress in St Petersburg 1917. He was a member of the Zionist committee and the board of directors of the "Tarbut " high school. He was one of the founders of "Et Livnot" (time to build) in Brest.

Before W.W.11, he went to Baranovich, where he was elected as the deputy mayor. Banished into Russia - vanished without a trace.

Mattityahu Zablud

A member of the city council, he represented the artisans union of which he was the president. He made great efforts and was dedicated to this organization. He was an amateur actor. He died in Melbourne Australia.

Eliahu – Peretz Silberschram

A merchant and a scholar. He was the son in law of Reb Asher Hari.

Reb Avraham Moshe Zisman

Born in 1878 in Zelichov. Settled in Brest. He was active in the Mizrachi organization and the Council of Yeshivas. He was a member of the board of the Merchant's Union and the Payen Bank. He perished in the Ghetto.

His sons, David Zisman, the renowned Mizrachi official, lives in Israel, Asher Zisman escaped the Brest Ghetto and died in Israel in 1957. His son in law, David Ferdman is the Cuban Consul in Israel.

Asher Zisman
(son of A. M. Zisman)

Reb Baruch Sonnenberg (Butche the shochet)

A Kotzker Chassid, he was renowned as the circumciser in Brest. He loved people, and was very encouraging to the youths in their Torah studies. After W.W.1, he rebuilt the Talmud Torah from the ruins of the city, into a building with 38 rooms. He would take only one-fifth of his income as schochet for himself –the rest he gave to the Talmud Torah. In spite of his opposition to the Zionists, he liked Israel. He died at the age of 66.

Chaim Hatz

He was active in community affairs and in various community institutions. He was popular and liked by people. A veteran Zionist, he was a member of the Jewish council. Greatly helped the suffering of his fellow brethren. Perished in the Ghetto.

Harry Arieh

Born in Brest in 1885. He was a merchant and a member of the board of the "Udzalova Bank". He was a committee member of the Merchant's Guild and the appeals committee to the tax office. He died in Brest in 1935.

Reb Moshe Scholem Hari

Proprietor of a large metal business. He was an in-law of Reb Zelig Riyer, the head dayan (judge) of the rabbinical court in Brest. He was a Gerrer Chassid, and involved in the religious and charitable institutions in the city.

Yehuda Kwianowsky (Reb Yudel)

He was a God-fearing learned man. A dedicated Zionist, he was especially involved with selling stamps for the Keren Kayemet.bonds, the proceeds of which were donated to Israel. Founder of the "Gemilat Chessed" (fund for the righteous). In 1904 he initiated the first credit co-operative in Brest. He made aliyah and lived in the Florentine district of Tel-Aviv, where he taught Gemarrah in the synagogue of that district.

Reb Gedalia Chazan

Businessman and owner of the Manufacturers Trading house. He was the Chazan (cantor) of the Kastrinski synagogue. He was one of the leading Zionists in Brest, and a member of the Zionist committee. The illegal Zionist meetings took place in his home. He was involved in the purchase of land for settlements in Eretz Israel together with the Zionist personality Y.L.Goldberg. A generous benefactor and an enlightened man.
Reb Moshe Chazan

Owner of Chazan's Barracks, which he donated to the Joint for temporary housing for the homeless that returned to Brest after W.W.1. He was a Nezvizher Chassid, and a gabbei of the Nezvizher shteibl (prayer house).

Nachman Topol

A member of the Zionist committee, he was active in the handworkers (artisans) union. He helped defend the rights of the workers against the injustices of the Polish government's discriminatory laws. Perished in the Ghetto.

Israel Tennenbaum

Leader of the Bund in Brest. He represented the Bund in the city council and was a public speaker. He was a bricklayer by profession, and he was head of the bricklayers union. Did a great deal of work towards organizing the Jewish schools. Arrested during the Russian occupation (1939-41) and sent to Siberia.

Reb Zalman Tennenbaum

A timber merchant, Reb Zalman exported wood abroad. Steeped in western culture, he was a popular man in Brest. He was the first chairman of the Jewish Community council (kehilla) after W.W.1 Reb Zalman was a city councillor, and dedicated official of various Brest charities. He was the son in law of Yitzchak Winnikoff.

Chaim Tennewitzki

He was born in Brest in 1884, the son of Nechemia Tennewitzki. A businessman he was an active participant in the administrations of ORT, HIAS, and the Tarbut High School. He was a dedicated advocate for Hebraic culture and education. He visited Israel in 1936. Perished in the Slonim Ghetto in 1942.

Rabbi Charny

He was a teacher in the "Tachkamoni" school. He was an official in the Mizrachi organization in Brest. Perished in the Brest Ghetto.

Dr. Israel Yaffe

He was a renowned doctor in Brest with much literary knowledge, especially in relation to such subjects such as Tolstoy and Dostoevski. He was the medical director of the Jewish hospital. When the Nazis proposed that he live outside the Ghetto, he refused, answering, "I would rather die with my brethren".

Benyamin Yungerman

A member of the board of the Merchant Bank, he was the proprietor of a brewery. Generous benefactor to the community causes.

Yitzchak Yerusalimski

A community activist, he was the chief accountant in the city council. He was a journalist of the newspaper "Polessie Leben". He was active in the building of residential accommodation by the Joint organization in Brest. He was the correspondent for the "Moment" in Warsaw. Perished in the Ghetto.

Aaron Ludszki

One of the leaders of the Zeirei Zion (Zionist Youth) in Brest. After the merger of this organization with the rightist Poale Zion, he was elected to the first Brest city council. He was active in the city council for eight years. After that three years in the first elected Jewish council. He was the Brest Poale Zion delegate to the 18th Zionist Congress in Prague 1933. He was always a delegate to his party conferences.

In 1934 he settled with his family in Israel. He became an active member in the Histadrut tribunal, and the chief executive of the Loans and Savings Co-operative of the Histadrut. During his 23 years service there he influenced the organization and financial development of the Histadrut. He was an active member of the Brisker association in Israel and it's secretary 1945-50. Born in 1897 and passed away in 1958.

Kadish Lubelski

An active member of the Zeirei Zion, he was a teacher in the Hatikva school for years. An ardent Zionist, he dedicated himself to educational issues and Keren Kayemet Leisrael. He worked as a secretary for the Keren Kayemet. Until the end of his life he concerned himself with the welfare of orphans, pupils of the trade schools, and assisited many of them to make aliyah to Israel.

Tzvi Lamazhevski

He was one of the founders of the Zeirei Zion in Brest in 1910. At the end of W.W.1 he was active in the rebuilding of the city. He was a member in the welfare organizations of the Jewish community. Member and director of the Joint committee. He was an employee of the Electricity Plant. Because he co-wrote an article denouncing the pogrom, he lost his position in the city council. Perished in the Ghetto.

Yitzchak Lev

A lawyer. He was the son of Moshe Lev, (a prisoner of Zion). He was one of the Zeirei Zion activists. He was very involved in the Zionist socialist movement, and general secretary of the General Zionists and "Hitachdut" from 1935-37. He was a co-founder of "Gordonia" youth movement. Perishe together with his wife Rachel, the daughter of the Zionist personality Meier Feierstein, in Ludsk in 1942.

Shmuel Lipinski

He was the Gabbeh of the Slonimer shteibl (prayer house) He was an employee of the petroleum company in Brest for 36 years.

Gavriel Lerner

Born in Brest in 1883. A merchant, he was active in the Chevra Kadisha (Burial Society), and Linat Hazedek. Perished in the Kobryn Ghetto in 1942.

Avraham Levinson

There were three vice presidents (deputy mayors) of the city under the Polish authority (1919-1939). The most popular and respected of them was Avraham Levinson. His predecessor, Dr. Wilner, had already forged a path in the wilderness of Polish municipal politics. His successor, Yechiel Mastboim, came to Brest when the Polish State was on the verge of downfall.

Avraham Levinson occupied the highest position a Jew could attain In Brest. When the government sought an understanding with the Jewish population, the Jews were not supressed anymore and demanded their rights, the majority of which were achieved. Jewish institutions, schools, libraries etc. were supported by the budget in the city's administration. After a long struglle, the name of Topolowa St. was changed to I.L. Peretz St. This was a symbolic gesture underlining the fact that the anti-semites no longer had exclusive power in the city council. Jewish taxpayers who could not meet their debts, were given discounted terms.

But Levinson was not satisfied with municipal activities. His influence on the life of the Jewish community in Brest was imprinted. During this time, all parties and organizations, professionals and workers, merchants and tradesmen, as well as the youth movements of all political persuasions developed and intensified their activities.

A vital Zionist goal was fulfilled with the Hachshara activity, where young people were trained in new trades and skills for Israel – they would immediately emigrate to Israel after training. Levinson was a driving force in these activities in Brest. His spiritual lectures awakened the Jewish youth movements. He was a personalilty who gave new content and meaning to the life of the community.

Avraham Levinson was born in Lodz and studied at Warsaw University. He was the secretary of the Jewish Democratic Society in Hadkow. He was the editor of a publication called "Land and Work". He was a delegate to the Polish parliament in Warsaw, deputy Mayor of Brest, a director of Keren Hayesod in Poland, and towards the end he was a director of the cultural department of the workers council of the Histadrut. He wrote about political and cultural subjects in Hebrew, also about the idealogical aspects of Zionism. He translated classical works and dramas from Yiddish, Russian, and Polish into Hebrew – the Tel-Aviv theatre "Habimah" presented some of these. He died in Tel-Aviv in 1955.

Zalman (Zygmund) Lutwak

A director of the Tarbut School from it's inception until it's demise. Through his efforts, the school obtained official government privileges – which very few Jewish schools in Poland could attain in Poland. The school attracted students from all the neighbouring towns. He perished in the Ghetto.

Moshe Laizerovitch

A journalist, he was the son of Eliezer Laizerovitch the well known Brest preacher, called the tailor's preacher. Moshe Laizerovitch was a member of the National Council in Warsaw. An active Zionist, he was co-editor of "Heint" in Warsaw. Perished in the Warsaw Ghetto.

Joseph Laizerovitch

Born in 1915, he was the son of Moshe Laizerovitch. Also a journalist, he wrote articles for the "Heint' and "Etzel" a military organization for Jewish self-defence. In 1939 he fled to Vilna and from there he reached Israel through Japan and India Iwith a group of Etzel members. In Jerusalem he became active in the Irgun and was arrested by the British security police in 1944.

After his release he went to South Africa where he worked for the Jewish Herald. He died in Johannesberg in May 1954. He was buried on Mt Zion In Jerusalem.

Israel Litwinski

One of the youth activists, he spread the Zionist ideals. A member of the board of the "Kadimah" and a secretary of the Zionist organization in Brest. He made aliyah to Israel in 1934 and settled in Haifa. He was an active member of the Brest migrants association in Israel. He died suddenly in 1954, aged 42.

Israel Litwinski

Reb Shlomo Lichtenstein

He was a timber and forest merchant. He was the head of the community council and a confidante of Rabbi Zeev Soloveitchik, the last Brest rabbi.

Dr. Nachman Landau

He was the son of the banker Yakov Landau, a director of the Industry bank. A chairman of ORT in Brest, and deputy head of the Judenrat in the Brest Ghetto. He did his utmost to alleviate the sufferings and troubles of the Jews in the Ghetto. Perished together with all of them.

Yechiel (Hilary) Mastboim

Yechiel (Hilary) Mastboim

After Avraham Levinson left Brest, he was elected deputy mayor of Brest, a position he held until 1939. He strove to help his Jewish brethren in their plight –was the chairman of the Polish War Veterans in Brest. He was energetic in assisting the charitable institutions. Sent to Siberia by the Russians, where he vanished without a trace.

Leizer Muller

A teacher, he was a Bundist and secretary of the Central Jewish schools organization.

Reb Aharon Matetski

Reb Aharon Matetski

A member of the city council, and a member of the kehilla council in Brest. He was on the aid committee for refugees after W.W.1. he was one of the oldest residents of the city. Dedicated and active in city affairs and a supporter of the needy. A man of the people and a friend of the people.

Reb Shmuel Dziencol

The proprietor of the first bookstore in Brest before W.W.1. He published A.L. Feinstein's book "Ir Tehila" in 1884. He was a learned scholar and a talented man.

Betzalel (Tzalke) Minivitski

A city councillor, he was one of the founders of the public school named after Boruchov. He was the head bookkeeper of the health fund. A member of the Joint committee, he fought for support for the workers organizations and the Jewish schools. An activist for the leftist Poale Zion. He perished in the Ghetto together with his wife Hadass, a schoolteacher, and his two sons, Reuven and Bunye.

Zyskind Neumark

Zyskind Neumark

Born in Brest in 1870. After W.W.1, he was very involved in the activity of the Joint (Chairman of the aid committee). He was a co-founder and committee member of TOZ, a member of the administration of the Jewish hospital, as well as the board of the Merchant Bank.

Revered and respected by every one of every faith, Jews and gentiles. He would resolve disputes between parties and would settle complicated issues and conflicts in a calm and neutral manner. He died in Brest in 1935.

Elyahu Neumark

He was born in Brest in 1900, the son of the well known Ben Zion Neumark. His upbringing was saturated with Jewish and Zionist culture. Elyahu Neumark was a partisan and active in organization within the Vilna Ghetto. The Jews who managed to save themselves and survive, arrived in Israel and testified to his bravery and actions.

Reb Zerach Nissenbaum (The Medic)

A medic, he would drive around in a wagon pulled by a pathetic horse, in order to assist the sick. Although he had no formal training, he was very much liked by the people, who regarded him as a specialist doctor.

Henoch Nimzevitch

He was a timber merchant and a great donor to charity. His daughters were active in the Zionist cause. One was a teacher at the "Tel Chai" school in Brest, and two went to Israel. Rachel Shekadi and Ruth Ratbert –a member of Kibbutz Gevah.

Aharon Netanel (Shostakowski)

Aharon Netanel (Shostakowski)

He was born in Brest in 1902. Came to Israel in the early 1920s. He went into the agricultural life in Israel. As a social activist he did a great deal, especially for the Maccabi movement in which he was involved for over 30 years. He was Chairman of the Maccabi movement in Jerusalem, and later a member of the national Israeli Agricultural Organization. Active in the World Maccabi Union. He was one of the initiators of the Maccabi Games. He died in 1957.

Shmuel Sokol

He was the son of Menachem Mendel Sokol. Born in 1897 into a Chassidic family. He was active in the communal life of the Jewish community. He was the first chairman of the Merchant's Union. Member of the Merchant's Bank and a committee member of the Mizrachi organization. Perished in the Ghetto.

Tzvi Sandlarsh

He came from the well-known Slonimer Chassids. He was of the household of Rabbi Chaim Soloveitchik and Rabbi Scholem Menasche. He would give lessons on the pages of the Gemarra in the Green synagogue.

Israel Aharon Svirinovski

He was the secretary of the American Aid Committee (The Joint). He supervised this organization with great success – and oversaw the gigantic task of relieving the plight of the returning Jews in the critical period after W.W.1.

He was popular in the city, with his polite demeanor and an honest, enterprising leader in community affairs. He married Hannah Spektor and founded a knitting factory in Lodz. Later he also set up textile plants in Israel, where he was a leading industrialist. Died in Tel-Aviv in 1954.

Shimon Savishitski

Shimon Savishitski

Born in a village near Brest. He was a businessman and the agent of the brewery "Haberbush and Shileh" from Warsaw. After W.W.1, he was the chairman of the board of the Jewish hospital and assisted that institution to overcome difficult times. Member of the city council. He died in Brest in1937.

Yosef Satir

He was a veteran of the sports movements and an active sportsman. He founded the Jewish Sports Club. Well known for many years as a footballer. The sporting circles in Poland regarded him as the representative of sport from Polessie. He perished in the Ghetto.

Yitzchak Sirota

A respected merchant. He was active in community work, especially in assisting the Old Age Home. His son, Eisig Sirota was one of the loyal Zionists in Brest, and a member of the administration of the Zionist organizations. His son, Nathan Sirota was active in the League of Workers in Israel, a loyal member of the Poale Zion in Brest. Both sons perished in the Brest Ghetto.

Shlomo Sirota

The son of the Zionist official Eisig Sirota. He went to Israel in 1933. He was an agricultural worker and a security policeman during the riots there. He traveled all over Israel as a representative of the security organizations. Active in the Haganah. He died in Tel-Aviv aged 33 in 1946.

Chaim Meier Spektor

A student at the famous Volozhyn Yeshivah, he was a textile manufacturer. A learned scholar and a spiritual man.

Itke Serlin (formerly Shiland)

He was active in welfare assistance in the community. A member of the Orphanage committee. Perished in the Ghetto.

Dr. David Sarnaker

A well-known surgeon, he was active in the welfare institutions. Active in TOZ and ORT.

Yakov Erlich

Born in Brest in 1862. His father, Elyahu Erlich was a timber merchant and community official, always ready to help people. In 1915 when the Brest residents were forced to leave the city, he traveled to Volomin, a town near Warsaw and set up a school for refugee children from Brest. He was one of the most active participants of the Brest Relief Committee set up in Warsaw (under the leadership of the banker, Raphael Shereshevski). This committee greatly assisted Brest Jews in those difficult days.

Yakov Erlich was one of the founders of the Loans Society and Old Age Home in Brest. He died in 1927. His son, Aryeh, is a well-known timber merchant in Israel.

Mordechai Padua

A director of the Jewish Hospital. He was one of the first members of the society "Menucha Ve Nachala" in Israel. He purchased land in Rechovot. His son, Tuvia, settled in Israel in 1895. The Padua family planted vineyards in Rechovot.

Yehoshua Farrer

An active member of Chovevei Zion in Brest in the 1890s. He sent his two sons Ezra and Yakov to Eretz Israel and they tilled the land of the Brisker settlement (Feinstein and others who had not yet arrived). Yehoshua Farrer came to Israel in 1905 with his whole family and conducted his affairs until his last days. He had been occupied in agricultural work even before coming to

Israel - he was the leaseholder of a large estate outside Brest. He was an advisor to the agricultural board of Rechovot in business matters.

Yakov Farrer

One of the original builders of Rechovot, he came to Israel from Brest as a young man and settled in the colony. He house was one of the first to be built in Rechovot. He took care of his farm and did not want to make changes. – he was one of the few who completely gave himself to his agricultural work. He did everything he could to develop and show his model of exemplary land management.

He died in Rechovot in 1946.

Meier Feinstein

Meier Feinstein

He was a member of the community administration – he was the last Chairman of the Zionist Organization in Brest. He was chairman of Keren Hayesod and delegate to Zionist conferences.A leader of the Zionist faction "Et Livnot" (a time to build). He was an educated, exceptional man. His father in law was the entrepreneur and benefactor Moshe Ragazhik, who built the Brest Fortress.

Noah Pozezhinski

Member of the city council, he was a director of the Merchant Bank Union. He helped small businesses a great deal. Killed in the Ghetto.

Aharon Pochachevski

He was a learned man, a scholar and official of the Agudat Israel. A director of the Jewish hospital. Killed in the Ghetto.

Betzalel Faigin

An employee of the Merchant Bank, he was a dedicated Zionist who managed Keren Kayemet affairs in Brest. Active member of the Zionist Council in Brest. Perished in the Ghetto.

Hannah Finkel

A dedicated activist in the health institutions for the poor and the orphanage. She was called the Yiddishe Mama – worked tirelessly for the Old Age home. Killed in the Ghetto with her entire family.

Godel Feingold

One of the important property owners in Brest, he was a gabbeh in the Great Synagogue together with Netanel Yokel before W.W.1.

Josef Feldman

Member of the city council –chairman of the Small Traders association and their representative in the city administration. Killed in the Ghetto.

Israel Fernik

Israel Fernik

A small trader, he was an active Zionist, member of the Zionist committee, Keren Kayemet and Keren Hayesod. A prisoner of Zion, he was sent to Russia and died there.

Reuven Pragel

Director of the Worker's kitchen in the Professional Workers Union. He was active in the Central Jewish Schools organization, named after Boruchov and the ORT organization. He was a beloved member of the leftist Poale Zion, and an active representative of the Worker's Union. Killed in the Ghetto.

Yitzchak Polani (Pollak)

Yitzchak Polani (Pollak)

Born in Brest in 1904, he was the son of Yekutiel Pollak, a gabbei of the Great Synagogue. He was one of the dedicated pioneers that went to Israel n 1922. He was a laborer and one of the first volunteers to the Jewish Police force. He served there for 17 years and was one of its first sergeants. A dedicated passionate Jew devoted to Israel and his community. He was killed in a bomb blast in April1944.

Mordechai Fein

He was a manufacturer and owner of the barrel-making factory "Finalin". A benefactor to various institutions. He was the head of the Chevra Kadisha (the burial society) in Brest. Perished in 1942.

Chaim Tzvi Fassman

An official in the philantrophic institutions, he was the co-founder of the Visitor's Hostel, and active with the Old Age home (previously named Siberska Hakadosh). A learned scholar, he studied at the Mishmar synagogue.

His son, David Fassman was a leader of the Joint and the "Malben" organization in Israel, whose aims were to provide support to the impoverished new arrivals.

Avraham Polefski

He was the son of Menachem - Mendel. Born in 1905 in Brest, he was active in the Jewish sport movement. He went to Israel in 1935 with his wife Bella, the daughter of the well-known benefactor Meier Aronson. An employee of the cooperative "Argaz", he passed away in 1950. "Argaz" allocated a scholarship in his name.

Yehuda Fachter

He was born in 1905, the son of Shmaryahu Moshe. Went to Israel in 1925. He was active in the Haganah –during the riots of 1929 he risked his life many times in the defense of his fellow Jews. In those days, he was one of the few Jews in the Mandate (British) police force. He died in 1954.

Yosef Frager

Known as Yoske the Schochet. He was the author of the book "Menuchat Yosef", on ritual slaughtering. He was close to both Yoshe-Ber and Chaim Soloveitchik. He visited Israel in 1903.

Yosef (Reb Yosseleh) Zuckerman

Active amongst the city's property owners. He journeyed to the U.S. to obtain assistance for those who had returned to Brest after W.W.1.and were suffering. He had an open house for all those who came to him seeking advice and help. He would write petitions on their behalf to the government.

Reb. Avraham David Tzemach

He was descended from the author of the book "Magen Avraham". He was an educated and learned man –he wrote articles for "Hasphirah" and "HaAsif". His business was trade, but he was deeply dedicated to the study of Torah and Hebrew literature. He was a gabbeh in the Rabbi's (Soloveitchik) synagogue. He died in Vienna in 1924.

Reb Baruch Kwiatkowski

An active community worker, he was a very good prayer leader. A member of the Mizrachi organization.in Brest. Killed in the Ghetto.

Isser Tzemach

He was one of the founders of Zeirei Zion (Young Zionists) in Brest in 1914. He was active in the Brisker Aid committee during W.W.1 for the homeless in Warsaw. He was very involved with Zionist activities and educational work. One of the Warsaw Zionist Organization representatives in the City Council. A man of the book in the full sense of the term In Israel he participated in the activities of the veteran Zionists –he was a member of the committee of the Brisk D'Lita Yizchor book. He died in Israel in 1955.

Kalman Koffberg

A scholar, he wrote articles in the "Polessie Shtimmeh" about the history and traditions of Brest.

Avraham Chaim Kastrinski

He was born in Horodetz, the son of the community leader Mordechai Kastrinski. He settled in Brest and was closely aligned with Zionist causes as well as general community issues. He was always ready to help everybody. He was a member of several companies and societies. He died in Brest in 1927. His son Baruch, was one of the active members of the Brest committee in Israel.

Shmuel Kanzevic

One of the founders of ORT. He was active in Jewish educational affairs.

Rabbi Yakov Krinski

He was the Head of the Yeshivah in Brest and a close confidante of Rabbi Chaim Soloveitchik.

Shlomo Kachel

He was born in Rovno in 1908. Settled in Brest – he was one of the leaders of Chovevei Zion in Brest. He was vice-president of the parent's association of the Tarbut School

Of his two sons in Israel, his son Zeev is a writer, the author of several books.

Sheina Kaszokievitch

She was an active members of the community –a member of Keren Kayemet, Linat Tzedek, and the orphanage. Killed with her family in the Ghetto.

Beile Klotnitzki

She was a teacher at the Jewish primary school and the Tel Chai School. Active in explanatory work for the Zionist Socialists, especially in the youth movement called Freiheit (Freedom). Killed in the Bialystok Ghetto.

Dr Yitzchak Kagan

Born in the shtetl of Grayevke. He was the Director of the Jewish hospital in Brest. For a while, he was Chairman of the kehilla (Jewish community) administration and a city councillor. He was hidden by Christian friends for 28 months and thus spared from death by the Nazis. He came to New York in 1947 with his family and obtained employment as a doctor in a sanatorium for the elderly. He was active in community work in New York. Shattered by what he had endured during the Nazi occupation he died suddenly whilst working at his post.

Chaim Baruch Kwiartowski

Chaim Baruch Kwiartowski

A manufacturer, he was a learned man and a benefactor. He was the Chairman of the kehilla administration in 1937. During the pogrom he risked his own life to help others in his community and Jewish circles in general. Killed in the Ghetto.

Reb Beinish Koloditski

A wonderful Zionist official. He was the head of the Keren Kayemet in Brest for over 25 years. He would devote himself day and night to the study of Torah and the Hebrew language and literature. Came to Israel and was happy to have achieved his ambition. He died in Petach Tikvah in 1948 aged 80.

Gelle (Genia) Konapiati –Bishkowitz

She was the daughter of the late Reb Moshe Baruch Bishkowitz. Active member of the Women's League and all the charitable institutions.

Henoch Kossovski

An official and secretary of the Mizrachi organization. He was a teacher at the "Tachkamoni" school - he was devoted to this school and Zionist causes. Killed in the Ghetto.

Eliahu Sini and David Kupchik

Hebrew teachers. Together they founded the Hebrew Modern School (Cheder Metukan) with new modern classrooms. Thousands of students received a Zionist education from them – many of them later came to Israel. Eliahu Sini was an impressive, fine figure of a man.

Yehezkiel Kopper

A community activist, he was a representative of the Joint organization in Brest and district. He was the director of the Warburg colony and built residential housing there from after W.W.1 until 1939. An active community worker, he was an outstanding personality. Killed in the Ghetto.

Yosef Kippel

Together with the teachers Fundig and Har Zahav (Goldberg), he was the founder of evening classes for adults.in Brest. During W.W.1 he found himself in Wlodavka. There he opened an evening school for adults. He was a member of the Keren Kayemet committee. He was a passionate advocate for Hebrew and Zionism. Killed in the Ghetto together with his wife and three sons.

Shlomo Kamenetzki

An engineer, he was a member of the Zionist Organization committee. He was one of the founders of "Hatechiya" and "Kadima" organizations, and the Union of Zionist Artisans. A radical Zionist, he was the leader of "El Hamishmar" and active in academic circles. Secretary of the Artisan's Union in Brest. Killed in the Bialystok Ghetto.

Berl Kandelsbrat (Berl the Medic)

A medic, he was known in all stratas of society as a folk doctor and healer. Many families benefitted from his great healing skills and knowledge. He was also active in the voluntary firefighters of the city.

Israel Kaplanski

A veteran Zionist, he was the owner of a bookstore, and a loyal supporter of the Keren Kayemet.

Reb. Mordechai Krop

A builder, he was the representative of the Artisans Union in the Polessie district. He was active in the Chevra Kadisha, (the Burial society). He was an honorary judge (referee) in the Artisans Union. It was thanks to his energy and efforts that the Chayey Adam synagogue was built. He was the gabbei there. A member of Mizrachi, he came to Israel aged 72 and lived independently. He died in Jerusalem aged 91.

Yehoshua Ramo

The Director of the Merchant Bank, he was active in the Zionist institutions and Keren Hayesod. He would grant a loan on the condition that a donation was made to Keren Hayesod.

Rachel Rokach

Rachel Rokach

She was born in Brest in 1863, the daughter of Menachem Shostakowski, a learned scholar and benefactor. She married Shimon Rokach from Jerusalem and went to live there with him. In 1884 Rachel and Shimon went from Jerusalem and settled in Jaffa, they were the first Ashekenazi inhabitants there. In the suburb of Neveh Zedek, which Shimon founded, Rachel was involved in various community activities - the hospital, she took part in guard duty, new migrants and visitors were always warmly received in her home.

In the years during W.W.1 she helped with the evacuation of Tel-Aviv – Jaffa. Rachel did a great deal for Birkur Cholim (visiting the sick) in Jerusalem and would also support the sick from her own money. She gave much to charity and helped the Invalid Home in Tel-Aviv.

Shimon, her husband was the leader of the Jewish community in Jaffa. Their son Israel Rokach was a longstanding Mayor of the Tel-Aviv. Their other sons, Yosef and Itzchak, were active members of the Israeli society. Rachel died in Tel-Aviv in 1945.

Yosef Rabinovitch

The owner of a pharmacy, he was one of the learned scholars of Brest. Active in the Mizrachi and charity institutions.

Zev (Velvel) Rabinovitch

An industrialist and a great scholar. All his days were spent in studying the Torah and working. Author of the great book about the Jerusalem Talmud, which was published in Israel. His son Michael served in the Russian army and reached the rank of General, commander of a tank division.

Fishel Rogoshik

He was the son of the renowned entrepeneur Moshe Rogoshik. He was active in the various social causes – TOZ and ORT. He was the Chairman of the Peoples Bank. A social activist and benefactor.

Reb Yitzchal Rodevski

Born in Brest in 1861 and died in Tel-Aviv in 1944. Like his father, Reb Asher, his was one of the prestigious households in the city. He was occupied in Torah study all his life and Chassidic causes.

Shimshon (Shmiel) Rodevski

An active Bundist, he was a member of the Artisan's Union. He worked with dedication and loyalty for the working classes of the city.

Reb. Henoch Rosenbaum

A man of the people. He was a good and likeable man. He was arrested several times for his pro- Zionist activities but was always freed by the authorities. No one could doubt the sincerity of this good-looking man. A passionate Zionist, he was one of the friends of Dr Yosef. Shereshevski, the famous Moscow Zionist. Killed in the Ghetto.

Reb Michael Rosenberg (Reb Michaleleh Roshes)

Leader of the Agudat Israel (Ultra - Orthodox), and their representative in the City Council. He was the Director of the "Shlomi Emunei Israel" Bank.

Tzvi Hirsh Rosenberg

A city coucillor and the Chairman of of the Merchant's Union, he was its' representative in the city 's institutions. Chairman of the Judenrat (Jewish council) in the Brest Ghetto. Made great efforts to relieve the suffering of those dark days of destruction. Killed in the Ghetto.

Zacharia Rosenthal

One of the leading Zionists in the city, together with Ben Zion Neumark and Mordechai Sheinerman. He devoted all his life to voluntary community and Zionist causes.

Reb Leib Rottenberg

A wealthy benefactor, he was one of the most respected men in the city. He was a great scholar and the gabbeh of the synagogue of Rabbi Chaim Soloveitchik. He was a grandson of Rabbi Yakov Meir Padua and the grandfather of Dr.Yakov Gromer.

Tzvi Ribatzki

A veteran Zionist. In his youth he was a Hebrew teacher and renowned as a prayer leader. He was the authorized representative of the Odessa Zionist Committee, and would stand at the entrance to the synagogue on Erev Yom Kippur and collect monies for Israel for many years. The first Zionist library in Brest was named after him. He was one of the pioneers and first employees of the Loans Society Funds.

Eisik Shostakowski

One of the most respected people of the city – a dedicated community worker. A Jew and a son of the Torah.

Helena Shteinberg

One of the city's well known activists.A member of the city council and active in all the institiutions. She was the Chairman of the Property Owners Union. She gave a great deal to charity and the "Brides Fund" (to provide dowries for poor girls). Suicided in the Ghetto.

David Shneider

He was one of the Bundist leaders of the city. A member of the community administration. He was a director of the I.L. Peretz Yiddish School at no.5 Koszciusko St., and active in professional circles. Taken by the Russians and sent into Russia.

David Tzvi Shapiro

An community elder from the time before the First World War. He was one of the founders of Bikur Cholim (visiting the sick). On a trip to St. Petersburg undertaken on behalf of this institution, he was killed in a road accident. His son is Dr Shapiro.

Yerucham Schatz

A leader of the community before W. W.1, he was acknowledged by all the ruling powers of those days. He used his position and influence towards worthwhile charities and institutions. A passionate and energetic fighter for all Jewish causes in the city for an entire generation. He was the Head Gabbeh of the Great Synagogue.

Dr. Yehuda Leib Shereshevski

He was one of the best Zionist leaders and a member of the Zionist Council until 1914. Participated in two Zionist conferences as a delegate. After W.W.1, he returned to Brest and became active as a medical specialist. Whilst attending as a doctor, he witnessed the beating of a Jew named Weisman by the Polish police. Protesting this incident, he suffered a heart attack and died.

Dr. Yosef Shereshevski

A dentist, he was one of the early Zionist activists. All the illegal Zionist activities before W.W.1 were conducted from his home. Chairman of the Zionist Organization. A great orator who spoke with emotion from his heart.

Shmuel Sharon (Sheinerman)

Shmuel Sharon (Sheinerman)

He was a son of the well-known Zionist Mordechai Sheinerman. He was an engineer and an agriculturalist. He was active in the Zionist movement in Kavkaz. He came to Israel in 1922 and settled in Kfar Millel. He taught plantation skills and land husbandry at the Mikveh Israel agricultural school at Ben Shemen. He planted orchards in Ness Ziona and Kfar Hayarok. In 1949 he participated in an international argricultural conference at the U.N. in New York. He died in 1956.

Esther Shtrickman

Esther Shtrickman

Born in 1903 in Suwalki. She settled in Brest in 1924, and went to Israel in 1934. In Israel she was active in the parent's committee of the school

"Bamerkaz" and the Working Mother's Union. During the War of Liberation (1948) she was in the soldiers aid committee. She was a volunteer worker in the military, and Hadassah hospital, as well as the children's home in Kfar Saba. She died in 1950, wife of Avraham Shtrickman and the sister of Pinchas Sapir.

[Page 407]

Rabbinical Judges and Torah Sages

Rabbi Sholem Menashe

By S. Pitlik
Translated by Dr. Samuel Chani and Jenni Buch

A small slender Jew with a creased face drawn with sorrow because of the plight of the Diaspora Jew and a smile of his resolve and faith. His place of prayer was behind the platform, near the door, in the Green prayer house. The gabbeys (synagogue deacons) asked him to sit along the prestigious eastern wall, but he liked to sit with the ordinary folk, the simple people, who struggled for their daily bread. He studied Torah with them; he was their friend and comrade. Every Sabbath, early in the morning, whether in the snow and frost of winter, the rains of autumn, or the heatwaves of summer, he would clap loudly at sunrise, waking his students. They would obey his urging and stretching like young lions, would follow him to the synagogue, where a special attic was allotted for them to study with Sholem Menashe. Sabbath mornings there was Chumash with Rashi, and during weekdays there was a page of Gemarrah between Mincha and Maariv. There were hours allotted for the study of Ein Yakov, Chai Adam, Midrash Rabah, and Midrash Tanchuma. His students especially liked Chumash and Rashi.

Sholem Menashe had a special method of teaching. His explanations were interspersed with words from the Midrash and interpretations. It all seemed like one complete explanation. The great scholars of Torah also liked to attend his Rashi lessons. After the Sabbath prayers the congregants would come to Sholem Menashe and wish him a good Shabbos. He would respond with a shining face, his face especially radiating towards the small children accompanying their parents.

On Yom Kippur he would lead the closing prayers at the lectern. In his old age, his voice was severely weakened and the congregants had difficulty in hearing his prayers. The gabbeys wanted to give him the chance to be heard, but to save his strength – but no one dared tell him that.

On the day of his death, the city was steeped in sorrow. Many cried as they followed his coffin. Masses of men, women and children accompanied him to his eternal resting-place in the cemetery, a long distance from the city. Piercing sobs were heard during the burial of this most holy and unique man. He was a symbol of the love of the Torah and a symbol of the love of Israel.

———————

[Page 409]

Rabbi Yitzchak (Itzaleh) Dayan

By Tzvi Ginat (Grynberg)
Translated by Dr. Samuel Chani and Jenni Buch

He was a teacher and a renowned judge in Brest. From all the corners of the city and from surrounding and distant villages people would come to him with questions about Kashrut, because it was known that no one was a greater expert in the laws of Kashrut than Rabbi Itzaleh was. The cost of coming from far away was worth it.

His entire life was occupied with answering questions about the laws of Kashrut, especially in the period before Passover, which was the peak time for asking questions. Every Passover Eve, masses of Jews would invade his home because the period between Purim and Passover was like a long day, with a great deal to be done before Passover.

In those days, Rabbi Itzaleh was busy all day long at the building of the rabbinical court. Men and women came to ask questions about the customs and rules of baking Matzos, and the koshering of utensils, the selling of the chametz, etc, etc. In the week before Passover, the rabbinical court supplied extra teachers to answer the questions, as Itzaleh could not manage the amount by himself. But the main burden still fell on him as he was the definitive authority on the subject and everyone wanted his blessing for the High Holidays. Itzaleh was accustomed to wish everyone a kosher Passover. Besides his blessing, he would also answer their questions to assure them that they would have a kosher Passover.

When the elderly man would return to his home on Passover Eve, there was still a great deal of activity there – one would jostle the other in order to see him first. Rabbi Itzaleh would bless those present for the holidays and ask them to be seated. He would take off his coat and put on his white robe, and this is what he was accustomed to do. He would go from one to the next, from seat to seat, from the first to the last. Everyone he approached would stand up and ask their question. Rabbi Itzaleh would judge with a wonderful skill, and after a pause his voice would be heard "kosher', "kosher", "wait, perhaps we'll be able to make it kosher, one has to think it over". "Kosher". "Ay ay ay, my children, what have you done? This cannot be kosher".

The members of his family who had been invited to his table for the Seder were sitting next door in the dining room waiting impatiently for the old man to arrive. From time to time his daughter, the widow Sheine, would open the door and look in to see if there were many questioners left. Only when they had all left would she open the wide door to the dining room. His eyes were full of joy, his face shone – he had only found two non-kosher instances. His eyes would wander over all those seated at his table, he would take a golden cup and make Kiddush. His voice carried through the stillness of the night "He who chose us over all other nations and elevated us...."

Rabbi Itzaleh was a great Mitnaged – at the time there were not many Chassidim in Brest, their righteous men had not yet settled there. In the neighbouring townships on the other side of the Bug River, there were many Chassidim and Rebbes. The nearest township was Biale Podlaska, and there lived the Bialer Rebbe.

Reb Hersh –Ber was a very learned man and a manufacturer of military uniforms. His second wife, Sloveh, was a granddaughter of the judge Rabbi Itzaleh. They were a very pious couple, who gave much to charity and donations to the poor, and prayed a great deal. However, they were not granted to have a son.

Once, Hersh-Ber was travelling to Warsaw – as was the custom, the travellers would interrupt their trip with a stay in the inn at Biale. It was the month of Cheshvan and there were heavy rains in the streets. The inn was packed with Jews who sat at long tables and ate. The noise was great and they drank toasts and shook hands on business deals.

As the renowned Brest merchant Reb Hersh - Ber sat at a table, another man from Brest sat down next to him and opened a package with a blessing for the traveller. He took out a copper tin containing smoked fish and almond cakes. At a corner of this table there was a discussion about the Biale rebbe. The man from Brest told of his visit to the righteous man, and spoke of his power with enthusiasm. At that moment, the thought flashed through the mind of Hersh- Ber that perhaps he should go go to see the rebbe, at the end of the day, he decided that there was no sin in going to say hello, and perhaps getting his blessing.... by the end of the prayer after meals, his doubts had vanished.

Hersh-Ber did not tell anyone about his trip to the Biale rebbe. Over the next few months he kept this secret and only on the eve of passover when Sloveh told him her own secret did he tell of his visit to the Rebbe and that the Rebbe had said to him: "Travel well and in good health and with the help of God your wife will have a son".

On he second cay of Passover, Sloveh took her daughters to visit her grandfather's home, as she always did. Entering as usual she presented the children to receive their blessing. Afterwards Sloveh sat quietly and asked her grandfather with a lowered head:"what sort of blessing are you giving me today?" The old man turned and looked at his granddaughter and said: "with the will of God, my granddaughter, you will have a peaceful birth". Sloveh stood up and saw that her grandfather's eyes were open, a sign that he had finished his blessing. She could not control herself anymore and appealed to him:" dear grandfather, finish your blessing with the birth of a son, and God will say Amen". The judge penetrated her with his eyes and said, "You silly fool, do you believe that a person can change an original deed? A daughter is also accepted by the Lord Almighty; because this is an addition to Jewish life."

At this she told him about the promise made by the Biale rebbe. At the door of his house she heard her grandfather's voice: " tell your Hirsh-Ber that from my point of view there is no avoiding that he should go in peace every week to Biale and there visit the Biale rebbe's table every Sabbath".

Some months later Sloveh gave birth to a boy. The rejoicing was great, but the child suddenly fell ill, his temperature rose, and one night his soul left him. The judge went to visit his granddaughter in the mourning period to console her. Less than a year had passed before Rabbi Itzaleh Dayan died.

[Page 413]

Reb Elyakim Getzel

By Tzvi Ginat (Grynberg)
Translated by Dr. Samuel Chani and Jenni Buch

Elyakim Getzel would give sermons on the Torah in the "New Prayer House" twice a year, on Sabbath Hagadol and Sabbath Shuva. Once, on a Sabbath Shuva, he castigated his audience so harshly, that the entire congregation trembled, and Reb Michael Chalfon called out "get down from the pulpit, Elyakim Getzel. Today it is Sabbath Shuva and you are harshly criticizing your fellow Jews!" The others joined in and called out "get down, get down" - Reb Getzel paled and fell in a faint.

Since that time many years had passed and Reb Getzel avoided coming to the New Prayer house. Over time a serious conflict had developed between the congregants, several of who supported the head Shammes (beadle), Moshe Chaim, who wished to lead the prayers over the High Holydays. Other congregants supported bringing a cantor, Chazan Oberman from Drochi, who was accompanied by a four-man choir. The conflict worsened until the side for the cantor won.

That Sabbath Shuva, Elyakim Getzel was invited to give a sermon in the synagogue. He began with an example about a cantor and said thus:

In a town there were two merchants that had quarreled, one had strongly offended the other, and an enmity developed between them that lasted a long time. The offended man thought that he who had offended him would come and apologize to him in the month of Elul, but it was already Rosh Hashana, then the eve of Yom Kippur, and nothing had happened. It was some time later at the final banquet, as the Jew put on his robe and blessed his grandchildren and got ready to go to the synagogue that the other showed up at his home with several youths and conducted them in song "Rabbi Joseph Chaim! Rabbi Joseph Chaim! Chaim! Chaim! Let us forgive each other!

The offended one replied sorrowfully – an entire year has passed and you did not come to apologize; now you come to make fun of me! Get out immediately!

The lesson is this my friends: the Creator of the universe stands and waits a whole year that you should apologize and reconcile with him, comes the month of Elul and nobody comes and the synagogue is empty. Rosh Hashanah comes and the synagogue is full of people but their prayers are without devotion and holy fervor. Yom Kippur for Kol Nidre they put in a cantor with a choir and he begins with a song "For everyone", and the choir echo his words, in all the prayers for forgiveness they just repeat what he sings. So I say to you my fellow Jews, that one should simply ask for forgiveness with a broken heart: Forgive us God, repent with us, console us, and help us against our enemies.

As soon as Reb Elyakim Getzel had finished his sermon, one Reb Yankeleh got up to the pulpit and begun thus:

I'll give you another example my friend, there once was a powerful king who reigned over tens of nations. He had an only son who did not go in the correct direction. They tried to influence him with good words but to no avail. They debated over what to do with him –one minister suggested that he be exiled from his father's house –in exile there was hope that he would change. The king like this advice and ordered that his heir be sent to a distant land. The minister promised to look after him. However, he mistreated the prince, so the son sent a letter to his father asking for mercy: "father save me!" The minister did not allow this letter to be delivered and wrote a letter instead saying that the king's son does not remember his father at all. The son complained bitterly, what sort of father is this who exiles him and does not reply to his letters? The king's first born complained about his father who would not answer him in front of ambassadors. The statesman replied - this is impossible; perhaps your letters have not reached him. He advised him to send a letter to his father with silly chitchat and water color drawings and between the lines write several times "father save me!" The minister would probably allow such a letter to be sent to the king. The king would surely understand that matters were not what they seemed from this letter.

The minister read this silly letter and thought that one could send such idiocies to the king. The king was offended after reading this letter and called his advisors, who said to check this letter thoroughly – it's not what it seems. They called experts who deciphered "father save me". The king was pleased and immediately ordered his son brought back to him. He also punished the minister who persecuted his son.

The moral of the story is this, my friends. The beloved son Ephraim is a sinner, and because we have sinned we have been exiled from our land into the Diaspora. The Creator thought that the Children of Israel would reply to Him. The gentiles, on the other hand, believe that they have the right to persecute Jews because there will be no one to save them. The Jews cry "father have mercy on us", but the angels do not deliver this message to the Holy throne. The Creator is angry that His children have forgotten Him and deserted Him. The angels hear the Jews cry in indistinct and incomprehensible words – but between the silly songs the words are melted together into a cry for help, and the Almighty recognizes that the Jews are appealing to the Creator of the Universe on His holy throne for help, and in that moment He has compassion for them and forgives them.

[Page 415]

Reb Tzvi-Hirsh Barlas

Translated by Dr. Samuel Chani and Jenni Buch

Reb Tzvi-Hirsh, the son of Mordechai Barlas, was one of the last of the 'old Brisk D'Lita', which was under the Council of the Lithuanian Nation. A city of Torah Sages and learned men, which shaped the character of 'Litvish' Jews of those generations. He was also one of the first of the new Brisk D'lita that was transformed from the town of his birth to a city built on trade, economic wealth and skills. He was born in 1804 and died in 1882 at almost 80 years of age.

He was a giant of Torah, and a very wealthy man. He was the grandson of Rabbi Tzvi-Hirsh Freiluker, whose children were great scholars, and exactly like him, they did not earn their living from theTorah. They were occupied in business and trade - they conducted their business abroad in foreign lands such as Austria and Germany and were very wealthy. He originated from the family of the author "Tosephet Yom Tov" – a tradition of the family was to celebrate Adar according to the book Megilat Avah – all his days he studied the Torah and researched the Talmud and Kabbalah. Reb Hirsh the Researcher they would call him. His surname Barlas - was from the initials Ben Reb Leib Sofer (The son of rabbi Sofer). His daughter married Rabbi Avraham Moshe Grosleit, the son of Rabbi Pinchas Michael Grosleit, the author of 'Leket Hakotzrim', and 'Divrei Pinchas' (Warsaw 1860), and who was the Rabbi of Antopol near Brest, and a famous ethicist in the whole region. The two families, Barlas and Grosleit, took a great part in the economic development of the city, and owned large stores and buildings in the center of the new city. After the death of Rabbi Jacob Meier Padua, they wanted to elect Tzvi-Hirsh as rabbi, but he declined. He promised to bring them a rabbi that was worthy of the position. He went to Lemberg (Lwow), and thanks to his business connections with local rabbis and learned men; he influenced Rabbi Tzvi-Hirsh Orenstein to accept the rabbinical seat in Brest. Rabbi Tzvi-Hirsh Orenstein arrived in 1861 to take up this position.

Rabbi Tzvi-Hirsh Orenstein was the author of the book 'Or Ha Tzvi" (published in Lublin in 1875). The contents were the words of the Torah and teachings, with examples and solutions and also showed his wonderful erudition and knowledge of philosophical literature from the middle Ages. The book was printed in 500 copies that were sent free of charge to libraries and synagogues and to the great rabbis of that generation. In his testament the author requested that the book should be reprinted in fifty years time.

Rabbi A.L.Feinstein who was his peer and friend, mentions in his book "Ir Tehila" the subject of the tombstone on the grave of Reb Tzvi -Hirsh Barlas - a man who was a Great in Torah, a friend of the Sages. Through his efforts the wisdom of the Torah and its teachings were preserved for eternity in the book "Or HaTzvi"

[Page 417]

Rabbi Benjamin Korman

By Leah Dagnit
Translated by Dr. Samuel Chani and Jenni Buch

I think that not many of the Brest residents knew this particular person, who for decades bent over his scrunched up pieces of paper and wrote his treatise on the interpretation of the Sabbath. I remember his figure from my childhood, and his glowing face, dreamy eyes, and soft hands that stroked my head.

I was rarely privileged to be in his presence – in my home he was spoken of with the greatest respect. When my father would mention Reb Benjamin's name, his face would light up. For thirty years his older brother Benjamin wrote his book "Helkat Benjamin" (Benjamin's Portion), a commentary on the Sabbath. Where did the title come from? Because he said that this is my entire portion of the world's effort.

For 30 years he did not look at the outside world. He had a wife and children, but they were outside the realm of his vision. My father and his brothers financially supported his household. My father was an expert in the construction of railway tracks – he wandered with his family all over Greater Russia – the steppes and remote settlements. He would set up temporary buildings and houses for the specialist workers, such as the engineers, tradesmen and the priest – and one Jewish family. My grandfather would tell me about Brest with tears in his eyes, about the synagogue of Israel Wolf, the city parks, the King's Garden. According to his description, it seemed to me that it was the most beautiful park in the world.

Arriving in Brest after W.W.1, I found a neglected garden and Israel Wolf's synagogue was no more than a wooden shack. I understood that in grandfather's eyes, longing for his hometown, they seemed thus. My father, who had always lived amongst gentiles, considered his brother Benjamin as the light of his life. On one of his visits to Brest, he built a synagogue in the vicinity of my uncle's home, so that he could sit and study in peace and be immersed in the Torah.

My uncle would not accept the position of rabbi, as he did not want to make a living from the Torah. His whole life was dedicated to writing this book, for which he had received permission from Rabbi Chaim Soloveitchik. When he finished the book, my father traveled for three days from Orenburg to Brest for the celebration. He helped edit the book and prepare it for publication.

Once, after much pleading, my uncle agreed to see the emissaries who had come to see him about becoming the Rabbi of their shtetl. By the way, they requested to see his wife the Rebbetzen, who was short and no beauty. She did not find favor with the emissaries, who did not take kindly to her. My uncle told my father of this event with great amazement: "did you know that the Rebbetzin is not good looking? "…. He himself did not know of this his whole life.

[Page 419]

Rabbi Simcha Zelig the Dayan

By Rabbi Dr. M.A. Riger (Canada)
Translated by Dr. Samuel Chani and Jenni Buch

**Rabbi Simcha Zelig
the Dayan**

My father was born in Novogrodek in 1864. In 1874 he came with his parents to Brest. He was influenced by the orthodoxy and interpretations of Rabbi Yehuda Leib Diskin, and from time to time would study Torah with him; in 1878 he was accepted to study by the head of the Beth Din, (Rabbinical Court) Yoshe Ber Soloveitchik, who was the new Rabbi of Brest. When Yoshe Ber arrived in Brest, they brought my father to him for an examination. At this time his son Chaim was the head of the Yeshiva in Volozhyn. He commented to his father:"father, why do you test his learning (erudition), better to see how he studies the page". From that day onwards there existed a special friendship between them –Rabbi Chaim would not make a move without my father's opinion in Torah and all other matters. As so it was his entire life.

In 1882 my father studied new interpretations of the Torah with Yoshe Ber Soloveitchik who was already then a famous scholar, although Brest was a famous city, full of renowned scholars and pupils. To achieve fame as a Great of Torah was no easy feat. After my father's marriage he settled in Volozhyn, which was a very famous community in the Jewish world. Amongst the hundreds of youths there were many who were prodigies and geniuses in Torah (Gaons). At that time my father was 20 years old and already known as an expert in the laws of our forefathers (the book Chidushei Rabbi Chaim Halevi) mentioned my father's innovations.

In Volozhyn at that time there were two Heads of Yeshiva: The Natzav Rabbi Naphtali Tzvi Yehuda Berlin, and Rabbi Chaim Soloveitchik. Each had his own system of teaching. The method of the first was to know the subject with all the reasonings from the Great scholars with wonderful expertise - this he also demanded from his students.

Rabbi Chaim's method was to analyze the subject for himself and to immerse himself in the originals and analyze the matter, especially the Ram Bam (Maimonides)

Most of the students were those who favored one method or the other, my father belonged to the select few that studied both methods.

When the ruling powers closed the yeshiva in 1892 and expelled Rabbi Berlin, my father was also dismissed. Rabbi Chaim proposed to my father that he come with him to Brest. Less than a year had passed and Yoshe Ber had passed away. Rabbi Chaim immediately asked my father to join him in Brest, to be the head of the Yeshiva in the Synagogue School, and to become the Head of the Rabbinical Court (Beth Din).

From that time on, he was the Head Dayan (rabbinical judge) of Brisk D'Lita and the surrounding district, and people came to him from all the surrounding towns with questions about the laws and customs.

His greatness was not only in his expertise with questions and answers, but also in knowing the laws and their original sources in the Talmud and the laws of our Forefathers. He was clear and precise about the laws as stated in Maimonides (Ram Bam), as he was about the rulings of the Sages of the last generations from Lithuania and Russia. Aside from the customs that he knew from books, he would investigate and research issues with the elders of the city, such Rabbi Scholem Menashe who had great influence with the leaders of the city, and over common folk.

His radical approach to Halacha (the legislative part of Rabbinical laws) understandably caused differing opinions and controversy. There were communities that elected preachers and officials that genuinely wanted to be in the Rabbinate, and there were some communities that elected rabbis through recommendations and connections, interestingly - amongst these were some rigorous adherents to Halacha. They caused great suffering with their rulings on deserted wives and poor people. My father recognized this when the question of a deserted wife came to his attention – he made great efforts to find a rabbinical exemption for her.

He would personally explain the laws to everyone, whether to the fanatical Zionists or to the leftist circles –when the Russians occupied Brest, Yasha the Tailor was made Commissar of the Slaughter House. At the first meeting of the Tanners it was unanimously agreed to follow any suggestion my father made. When many refugees fled across the Bug River into Brest, there were rabbis and schochets amongst them. My father organized accommodation for them in the slaughterhouse, which was controlled by the leftist workers.

By the way, the majority of learned men of his time would turn to my father with their questions, and everybody in the city honored him. He would not allow anyone to serve him. He would not don the Rabbi's hat and would not sit in front of the Holy Ark, as was the custom of the other rabbis. He did not expect others to defer to him and made it a point to be with his people. His room had no doors - that was a symbol that his house was open to all. The lowliest and the most miserable of people would spill their hearts out to him. He was loved by the people of our city – the community leaders unanimously wanted to elect him as Rabbi of Brest after the death of Rabbi Chaim in 1918 – but my father refused.

From 1894 he was the Head of the Beth Din in Brest until the bitter day in 1942 when the treacherous Nazis liquidated the city and it's residents. He was one of the first to perish in the Honor of God, in the city in which he lived most of his life. He spread the Torah to many and showed the way to his people.

[Page 421]

Rabbi Avraham Yitchak Halevi Bleiweiss

Translated by Dr. Samuel Chani and Jenni Buch

**Rabbi Avraham Yitchak
Halevi Bleiweiss**

Avraham Yitzchak Halevi was the Head of the Beth Din in Brest for twenty-five years. Born in Warsaw in 1868, he was the son of Raabi Tzvi Bleiweiss. At 18, he came to Brest. Already then he was renowned as an astute expert of rabbinical law, and of the Tanach. In 1894 he was nominated as Head of the Beth Din in Brest and for 25 years he adjudicated on Halachic law for the people of Brest. Not only did he carry the burden of the Torah, but also the burden of public office - he was selected to head all the delegations to the government. In the times of the pogroms he was oblivious to his own safety in preventing disaster.

Together with Zev Dov Begin and Rabbi Klepfish, Rabbi Bleiweiss stole into the fortress in the dark of night and rescued some Jews from hanging.

He was a goodlooking Jew, who carried himself with erect posture and commanded much respect. He wrote books and in his large library there were many old books and rare documents, which he wanted to donate to the National Library at the Hebrew university in Jerusalem.

He was a great man in Torah and great in his actions. He understood the younger generation and it's attraction to Zionism. In one of his letters to his relatives in Israel he wrote: It is said we will give speeches and learn, thanks to the efforts of the labor of their own hands, which those that went to broaden and develop our settlements in our holy land have achieved.

He died in 1936.

[Page 423]

Rabbi Eliezer Lipa Klepfish

Translated by Dr. Samuel Chani and Jenni Buch

Rabbi Eliezer Lipa Klepfish

He was born in 1880 in Warsaw. His father, Rabbi Shmaryahu Klepfish, was the brother of the famous Chief Rabbi of Warsaw, Rabbi Zangwel Klepfish. Eliezer Lipa settled in Brest after W.W.1. He was a member of the Rabbinate there, and for a time he was the Military Rabbi.

After W.W.1 the life of the city was not normalized - the warring powers changed hands several times and the people lived under great stress and fear. Rabbi Klepfish, together with the secretary of the kehilla, Zev Dov Begin and Rabbi Bleiweiss made great efforts to help and save their fellow Jews. During the time of hostilities they risked their own lives and went to the fortress in the middle of the night and rescued the three Meyer brothers (who had been charged with espionage) and were about to be executed.

His wife, the Rebbetzen Yente Klepfish, was a longstanding member of the administration board of the orphanage and she would assist children to leave the walls of the orphanage and find work when they were older. Later, in the Brest Ghetto, although she was old and sick and broken, she organized help for the poor and sick and founded a soup kitchen for them. She secretly baked matzos for them before Passover.

Rabbi Eliezer Lipa died in August 1942 and was buried in the Jewish tradition next to his friend, Rabbi Avraham Bleiweiss.

His wife, the Rebbetzen, hid in the bunkers during the Nazi liquidation of the Ghetto, where she was found and murdered by some Ukrainian murderers.

Institutions and Organizations

The Administrative Boards of the Community Institutions in Brest

Translated by Dr. Samuel Chani and Jenni Buch

Deputy Mayors: Dr. Bronislav Wilner, Avraham Levinson, Yechiel (Hilary) Mastboim.

Council of the Great Synagogue: Zev - Dov Begin, Isser Gvirtzman, Leib Nirenberg, Avraham Skarvenik, Yekutiel Pollak, Shmuel Pomerantz.

Leaders of the Chevra Kadisha (Burial Society): Shmuel Epstein, Gershon Moshe Ashkenazi, Betzalel Baron, Moshe Eliezer Begin, Reb Butche Shochet, Yeruchim Buchmal, Yitzchak Branzel, Baruch Breinhendler, Reb Moshe Yosef Barlas, Tzvi Gvirtzman, Baruch Gvirtzman, Reb Alter Grosleit, Gershon Dubinboim, Domachevski, Moshe Zisman, Shachna Landan, Leibush Landau, Gavriel Leib Lerner, Hannah Nimzevitch, Hersh Switzer, Yosef Sokol, Reb Yitzchak Eisig Sirota, Yakov Skorbnik, Meir Pochachevski, Yudel Pochachevski, Baruch Perlman, Alter Pozhinski, Eliezer Feigin, Mordechai Fein, Alter Tzinneman, Chaim Baruch Kwiartovski, Mordechai Krop, Michael Rabinovitch, Shmaye Rosenbaum, Berel Shedrovitski, Moshe Sheinerman, Eliahu –Leib Shimshonovitch, Yerucham Schatz, Yehoshua Schatz.

Jewish Hospital Administration: Reb Moshe Yosef Barlas, Moshe Menes, Zyskind Neumark, Avraham Zukerman, Shimshon Savshitski, Shmuel Pomerantz, Mordechai Krop.

Head Doctors: Dr Yaffe, Dr Zeligson, and Dr Sarnake. Head medical assistant: Yitzchak Gellenberg. Head nurse: Sarah Shapiro

The TOZ Committee: Dr A Begun, Y.Fuchsman, Baruch Kwiartovski, Dr M. Kimmel, Dr Y. Kiblitski.

Board of the Old-Age Home: Michael Orchov, Chaim Zalman Wolski, Liba Wolski, Mordechai Mullar, and Chana Finkel.

The Jewish Doctors Aid Committee for Victims: Zev Dov Begin, Shloime Belkes, Gittelman, Leah Goladetz, Nachman Glovinski, David Zusman, Moshe Yahalom, Dr Nachman Landau, Tzvi Pozezhinski, Shmuel Pomerantz, Eliezer Fein, Chaim Baruch Kwiartovski, Henoch Kronchik, Hersh Rosenberg, Shalom Shwartz.

Jewish Doctors: Dr Ukrainitz, Dr Epstein, Dr Begun, Dr Geisler, Dr Gotleib, Dr Wolfson, Dr Silberstein, Dr Sonnenshein, Dr Zeligson, DrKanat, Dr Yaffe, Dr Kagan, Dr Leibowitz, Dr Landau, Dr Leshner, Dr Manson, Dr Seigel, Dr Sarnake, Dr Perlis, Dr Kimmel, Dr Rosenbaum, Dr Shapiro, Dr Shereshevski, Dr Fruchtgarten, Dr Greenstein, Dr Gottbeiter.

The Bikur Cholim (Visiting the sick) Society:

Chairman – Alter Grosleit, Michael Orchov.

Members: Felicia Perlis, Dr Y. Yetom, L. Kolinski, M. Tennenbaum, Yakov Landau, Moshe Yosef Barlas, H. Fryman.

[Page 429]

Institutions
Hebrew Education In Brest

By Tzvi Har Zahav (Goldberg)
Translated by Dr. Samuel Chani and Jenni Buch

The method of teaching pupils in Brest was the same as in other towns. Whoever knew the interpretations and the Chumash and Rashi believed that he was qualified to teach Torah to some children. So he would collect some pupils and conduct a cheder. From the beginning of the Zionist movement, there sprang up in various cities "Cheder Metukan" – modern Hebrew schools, which had some reforms and changes to the teaching methods. In Pinsk it occurred to Yehuda Leib Berger, a bookseller, to open such a school. In Brest there was no such activist to open a modern cheder, and the old style of teaching prevailed.

Two people stood out from the other Hebrew teachers, both in their methods of teaching and of attracting students. Therefore, they were called 'teachers' and not Torah instructors. One ran a cheder and one taught at home. The first was Ben Zion Neumark, and the second was Mordechai Sheinerman.

Neumark was a Zionist activist, an official of the national Zionist movement and a journalist. When VIPs would arrive in Brest, he would make every effort to provide comfortable accommodations and lodgings. He was known in all circles and accepted – he introduced a better teaching system in his school.

Sheinerman was a community activist and dedicated Zionist. A cultured man with refined manners, he would give lessons in the homes of the wealthy. He also visited Israel, but due to an eye disease, he had to leave the country. He returned to Israel in later years and spent the last years of his life there.

After a short period of teaching in Horodok, a small town in the Vilna district, and in Lubashov a town in the Minsk Gubernia, Pinsk district - I arrived in Brest. My experiences in those places were closely connected with my transferring to Brest. A friend in Horodok had invited me to come there to teach. The town had two religious Torah instructors and one Russian teacher. Several educated men, who were not happy with the religious instructors, were seeking a good teacher for their children. I let myself be persuaded and came to Horodok. Several of the local residents asked me to teach their children – as Hebrew was since my childhood days the language that I thought and spoke in – I taught my pupils Hebrew in Hebrew, not in Yiddish as was then the custom. I would speak to the children and their parents only in Hebrew. I introduced reforms to the teaching methods: songs, exercises, and playing.

The religious instructors upon seeing these 'crazy' reforms became alarmed for their livelihoods. They turned to a petition writer and asked that he write accusing me to the Chief of Police in Vilna and requesting that he should expel me from the city. The parents of my students told me to bribe the petition writer so that he should not send his letter. But I did not want to do this. For four weeks the letter lay in his office. The police chief was busy with other matters of the day. Then I received an invitation to come to the Starosta (police chief) in the evening for a 'chat' and bring my textbooks with me. When I arrived the police chief began by asking me details, I replied and the secretary wrote it all down. The questions were; had I ever been in St Petersburg, Moscow or Kiev? If not, perhaps my parents had been there? What was I doing in this town? Who were my acquaintances and friends? For what purposes did I need the 'dry' scientific textbooks? After these questions and answers, the Starosta realized that I was not a dangerous revolutionary. He apologized to me, saying that he had received a complaint and that it was his duty to investigate the matter. However, he gave me good advice, which was to leave the town, so as not to cause complications and conflicts.

After Pesach, I came to Lubashov, and there I stayed for a longer time. A vital issue of my life caused me to leave this quiet town and transfer to Brest. Before coming to Brest I sent an inquiry about opening a Hebrew school there. I sent a letter to my uncle, Moshe Pesach Gvirtzman to permit me to print an advertisement, but his wife, Lipshe interfered in the matter and would not allow this announcement.... However, it was printed and even pasted on the walls of the synagogue schools.

Before the High Holydays I ordered benches in the modern style that I had seen in a Russian book, and with these, I furnished several rooms and the school opened. Several of the city residents entrusted me to teach their children. As soon as the school became known in the city and the religious teachers heard about its innovations, they decide that the best way to get rid of me would be to report me to the authorities, and one day a police officer came to see me at my school – the story of Horodok repeated itself, but with some differences..

The police chief came to see me, and I was not invited to his office. He came alone without a secretary and without a protocol. The questions were few, the textbooks not checked and he apologized – but said that he had to investigate according to his duty. This time he did not advise me to leave the city.

At the opening of the first class, people also enrolled for the evening classes, which were for adults and enlightened people with whom I could discuss matters that could not be mentioned openly. For example, I once remarked that it is the commentaries that suggest that King Solomon did not write his psalms by himself. This gave the 'learned scholars' the grounds to accuse me of being an 'Apicorus' (a heretic). I was cautious enough to say that this was not my opinion. They further said that it would be a sin to entrust children to me to study Torah.

New higher-level classes opened up in my school and the Torah studies became an chief part of the curriculum. The religious teachers found new deficiencies – the Torah was not studied according to the chapter of the week and not with Rashi, but with a different method – and more complaints.....

However, I was obstinate in my actions and stuck to my opinions. The school flourished and there was no lack of students as long as I was in Brest. Together with all the other residents, I was expelled from the city in 1915. Not only the school, but even speaking Hebrew was an important issue -when I arrived in Brest no one spoke Hebrew and no one had heard of speaking such a 'dead' Language. They told of a Sephardi emissary from Israel, who had arrived in the city and had great difficulty in communicating with the Jews. I turned to the more educated students of the city and proposed that we form a Hebrew-speaking Society. They agreed, and gradually also adults joined this society. I drew up a program, but none of the important officials helped me. We could not get permission for this group, so everything was conducted in secret. The meetings took place each time at a different venue. Thus the speaking of Hebrew spread through certain circles in the city. There were even parents of some of the students, themselves not members of the group, who would greet me in Hebrew on the street, and who would timidly speak to me in broken Hebrew – but nevertheless Hebrew.

This innovation was taken up, even though in mockery by some. They especially talked about my wife because we only spoke Hebrew at home "it is crazy that a woman of our city should speak Hebrew in the street and at home, whoever heard of such a thing?"

At the end of 1918 I returned to Brest for a further 18 months. The city changed and became modernized –the residents were newcomers and they were preoccupied with the worries of making a living and nobody thought of Torah study in Hebrew. All the former teachers had also vanished. My wife died, and I could barely exist from the private lessons that I gave a group of young men who wanted me to teach them Hebrew.

A year later, representatives from the Tarbut organization that had founded Hebrew schools in other Polish towns came to Brest and started evening classes in Hebrew. They invited me to join them, but I did not accept as I was preparing to make aliyah to Israel. After much preparation and difficulties, I left for Israel in Elul 1921.

[Page 437]

The Model Hebrew Primary School

Translated by Dr. Samuel Chani and Jenni Buch

The Central committee of Tarbut in Poland had designated Brest as an appropriate location to found a Model Hebrew primary school that would be a shining beacon for teachers and the educational administrators. This school, named "HaTechiya" became an example of a modern school. The headquarters of Tarbut had sent their best teaching experts. We should remember here:

The spiritually rich and talented teacher Akiva Rosenbloom, who was murdered in Kowel as one of the Nazis' first victims there.

Leah Kreinitz (may she live to long years).

Gedalia Shklarski, Zev Levana and others who now live in Israel.

Teachers of the Techiya Hebrew School in Brest 1922

[Page 438]

The Tarbut Hebrew High School (Gymasium)

Based on the foundations of the primary school, there was later founded the Tarbut Hebrew High School. It provided Hebrew and general education for those from Brest and district that had finished primary school. As with the Tarbut primary and middle schools, the standard was high. Children whose parents were Zionists attended these schools, and they had to give up the idea of attaining a Matriculation certificate because the Tarbut middle school was not entitled to grant its students diplomas.

The teachers of the Tarbut high school and its headmaster, Zev Lutwak, were concerned with a good education based on Jewishness and also general Polish studies. After a long battle with the Polish authorities the Tarbut Hebrew High School together with its sister school in Bialystok, obtained full official certification to grant matriculation diplomas.

This caused great celebration in Zionist circles. In Brest, even former opponents of Hebrew and Zionism joined in the celebrations. It was a resounding victory for the spirit of the Hebrew movement – previously the attitude towards the founders and supporters of the Hebrew schools had been one of apathy and indifference, and that the revival of Hebrew schools was only a dream.

The joy in Brest expressed itself in celebratory meetings and an open prayer Sabbath in the Great Synagogue with the participation of all the Hebrew schools' parents and students. Zev Dov Begin, the secretary of the kehilla council, welcomed them in the name of the kehilla. H.Tash spoke of the significance of a Hebrew education in the Diaspora – for such a Zionist celebration to be held in the Great Synagogue was unprecedented.

The Great Synagogue was under the direction of Rabbi Z. Soloveitchik - it was known as an opponent of Zionism – and until then it had not permitted Zionist celebrations.

[Page 439]

The Trades School Hostel

This college was founded immediately after W.W.1. There were many orphans from Brest and district who had been left homeless – their parents had been murdered, and their children wandered in the streets of the towns and villages of the Polessie district. These hungry and exhausted children found salvation in the orphanages that provided accommodation and schooling, these orphanages existed in every Jewish community, and even the smallest towns provided shelter for these abandoned children with no future. The Polish authorities did not care about its Jewish citizens.

The Jewish Society for the care of orphans in Polessie took over the responsibility for caring for homeless children.

With the assistance of the Joint, they founded a Trades School in Brest. They purchased a large three-storey building at no. 28 Third of May Street in 1924. There they opened a dormitory /hostel – the house and garden was a model of tidiness and comfort. They accommodated 80 orphans and deserted children who could study Torah and a trade there, with the aim of bringing them up as honest members of the community.

The dormitory/hostel was run on the basis of the income of self supporting youth organizations and self supporting work from skills such as locksmithing or carpentry which they had been taught in the ORT trades school. Thus the hostel served to bring up these children into their working lives and society.

Furthermore, there was an unspoken aim - the training of pioneers for Israel. That was difficult to achieve - the majority of the youths got their first education in the Tsarist pre-war Russia, where life was hard and oppressive, and did not awaken Zionist thought.

Nonetheless, the administration board managed to instill the spirit of Israel into the young people. They learned Hebrew with enthusiasm and prepared to go to Israel.

Three years later, the hostel sent its first group of students to Israel. All of them settled as pioneers. (One of them, Yitzchak Fogel – lost his only son Ben Zion Fogel in the War of Independence.1948).

Since that time, there were other groups that were sent to Israel, however, the Bund and the leftist Poale Zion reacted negatively to the activity of the hostel. According to their doctrine, the training and teaching of trades was their exclusive area and why should Hebrew "Tarbutniks' be involved with this? Especially considering that it was the Ort school that had provided them with their skilled training....

However, they did succeed in wresting the hostel away from the Zionist influence and the Zionist pioneer ideology, which had influenced the underprivileged and oppressed of the Brest and district community. But from all that involvement and greatness only dark memories remain – a broken aching heart that says in your blood and memories they will stay alive!

[Page 441]

Education and Cultural Institutions

By Nachum Chinitch
Translated by Dr. Samuel Chani and Jenni Buch

In the Old Brest there was for over 40 years a great yeshiva in the Mishmar synagogue. The heads of this yeshiva were Rabbi Simcha Zelig and Rabbi Moshe Sokolovski, they were under the patronage and supervision of Rabbi Chaim Soloveitchik.. About 100 students studied there day and night, and from this yeshiva many great and talented students in Torah graduated such as: Rabbi Meier Berlin, the genius Shlomo Politzik who was known by the name of "the Mezricher genius ", and others.

The city's Talmud Torah (synagogue school) had existed for centuries and had over 100 students, it's higher classes were preparatory to the yeshiva. In it's last years Rabbi Yakov Zalman Lifshitz was the headmaster under the supervision of Rabbi Israel and the head Gabbeh was Rabbi Butche Schochet.

In 1918-20 the concern was for the saving of lives, and the building of the new Talmud Torah. Later, Rabbi Michael Orchov took over.

In 1905 Modern Cheders appeared in Brest under the supervision of skilled teachers who worked in the system of "Ivrit Beivrit" – Hebrew taught in

Hebrew. The rooms were spotless, there were new benches and many colorful posters on the wall, like in a modern classroom.

The first to introduce these Modern Cheders to Brest were David Kupchik and Eliahu Sini. It's worth noting that Eliahu Sini was a renowned chess player and that he owned a vast library. He had spent several years as a teacher in the U.S. before returning to Brest. Important teachers of the Hebrew in Hebrew method were the elderly grammaticist Tzvi Har Zahav, who died in Tel Aviv, Rabbi M. Sheinerman, Ben Zion Neumark, Fundig, and others.

Brest also had general high schools, a commerce (business) school, state primary schools, and also two Jewish middle schools with Russian as the teaching language. After W.W.1 the Joint funded the establishment of schools for the children of Brest.

The Young Zionists (Zeirei Zion) formed the "Techiya" public school with 7 classes with Hebrew as the teaching language in all subjects – Polish, Polish History, Maths, Geography, etc. The "Techiya" had over 200 students. As well as that there were 2 kindergartens and a dormitory. The two language Hebrew/Polish school called "Tel Chai" taught Hebrew, Tanach, and Jewish history.

Over 150 poor students studied at the ORT Trades school that was under the directorship of the engineer M. Feldstein. There was also a public school established by the Bundists and the Leftist Poale Zion with Yiddish as the teaching language. Later this school split up into 2 separate schools with the Bund school headed by David Shneider and the Leftist Poale Zion school by M. Menachovski.

The Young Zionists also conducted evening Hebrew classes including the geography of Israel, as preparatory courses for the pioneer movement.

In 1924, the Tarbut High School was established with 3 classes from the Techiya school and 2 other broader classes totaling 140 students. Amongst its founders were: Chaim Tennewitzki, Izbitzer, Neumark, Winnikoff, and the headmaster Z. Lutwak.

In the Tarbut High school, the spirit of Hebrew ruled, but the general studies were in Polish. In the Polessie province, only 2 Hebrew High Schools were granted full government accreditation – the Tarbut school in Bialystok and the Tarbut school in Brest. There was much ideological debate – one side wanted to attain official accreditation at the expense of the Hebrew studies – the other side demanded that the school conduct all its teaching in Hebrew only, including general subjects. Tarbut lasted until the outbreak of W.W.2.

A separate institution was the Brest Orphanage, with over 150 children. They had a good school called "Ha Chaim" founded by the Mizrachi Organization, whose director was Rabbi Shmuel Yosef Halperin, a learned man of high standards. Also Naphtali Rabinovitch who cared for the welfare of the orphans. Later, the school enlarged and took on the name of "Tachkamoni".

The Jewish library occupied an important place in the life of Brest. From 1905 until W.W.1 it was the cultural center of the city with over 800 books, mainly in Hebrew, Russian and Yiddish. This library was under the auspices of the Zionist organization and its last directors before 1914 were Moshe Lubetkin and Isser Tzemach.

During the expulsion from the city in 1915, the library was locked and the books left inside. But the Jewish laborers that the German Army brought into the city for forced labor from the surrounding towns moved many of the books. In 1918 when the Jews returned to the city, the library committee was able to retrieve many of them.

These books formed the basis for the new library on Bialystokski St. The library committee included members of the Young Zionists and the librarian was Scholem Halperin. After the fall of Trumpeldor and his comrades in 1920, the library was called "Tel – Chai".

The Tel Chai Library Committee
From R.to L. – K. Lubelsky, M. Barlas,
S. Halperin, A. Ludski, B. Arenson, Tupak
Standing – Z. Hellman

[Page 443]

The Hebrew Tarbut Gymnasium

By M. Arazi
Translated by Dr. Samuel Chani and Jenni Buch

In accordance with the orders from the German Military powers in 1915, Brest was evacuated. Although some residents transferred to the neighboring towns and villages, the majority wandered far into Russia, away from the fighting front. Thus the existence of the Brest Community was uprooted, it had been one of the most beautiful centers of Judaism with its origins going back before the Polish/Lithuanian Commonwealth. As soon as the New Polish republic emerged after W.W.1, the remainder of the city's residents who had survived the bitter fate of homelessness returned to rebuild it from the ruins. Many of the residents, who had wandered far away at the outbreak of W.W.1, never returned and settled in new places.

Those that did return had never seen such a catastrophe.... They tried to settle into temporary accommodation in the cellars under mountains of bricks and rubble.

Many families lived for long periods like animals in their dens. But the will to rebuild was so strong that these cellar dwellers began to rebuild their homes from the ruins. There were few essentials available, but with the help of a soup kitchen and the assistance of the American funded Joint organization, many were saved from starving. The problems of poverty, food and homelessness pushed aside all other needs – it was particularly difficult to re-establish a cultural and community life.

With many difficulties new schools were created. The Tel Chai Library was opened. The orphanage with it's hostel and educational center. The first Hebrew kindergarten was formed by Esther Halperin Chinich, for the first time, Hebrew was heard and spoken by the kindergarten children.The first Hebrew public school was the "Techiya" school. Many of its teachers and students migrated to Israel.

In Brest as in other polish towns, the Tarbut organization had to fight on 2 fronts: against the Yiddishists (Bundists) and the Polish assimilation propaganda which pulled the student youth away from the wells of Jewish and Hebrew culture.

The supporters of the Hebrew language culture organized themselves – my father Ben Zion Neumark, Itzbitzer, L. Winnikoff, Gedalia Hoffman, Zaretzki, Y. Rosenblum and Zelig Braverman – Jews who were occupied with the worries of making a living, had to take on the task of building a Hebrew high school.

Together with H. Lutwak who came to us from Galicia they would spend entire nights worrying about the finances, the teaching staff, and voluntarily conducting enrolment drives for students. In 1924 the school stood erected with 3 regular and 2 preparatory classes. The first teachers were Lutwak, Liberman, Rosenblum, Shklarski, and Lehrman. They had a few textbooks and some teaching material in Hebrew. From time to time there would be a delivery of teaching material from Warsaw. This was not as much a community activity but the fulfillment of a dream, the celebration of their achievement.

The headmaster and staff naively thought that the students should occupy themselves a great deal with Polish and Polish literature and history, just as in the Polish state schools. The ambition was to reach a standard to enable the school to obtain official Polish recognition –this placed the school administration in a dilemma.

The teaching and learning of Hebrew suffered as a result of the Polish studies.

The struggle between the nationalistic Polish content and the Zionist character of the school was to be echoed between the students and in internal debates at the Hebrew middle schools. The discrimination against the students of the Tarbut School was linked to not gaining entrance to further study at Polish universities as was possible in the Polish public schools. This stopped the Tarbut administration from resting until it achieved this for the Jewish youth.

The Tarbut Hebrew High School in Brest

[Page 447]

12 Topolowa Street

By T. Govkin
Translated by Dr. Samuel Chani and Jenni Buch

Who of the Jews of Brest had not heard of the address of the Zionist center at 12 Topolowa , which later became I.L. Peretz Street? Jewish pride and efforts brought about the decision of the city council to name the street after the famous Jewish writer. Despite the name Topolowa St. the address became famous after the Jews returned to Brest after W.W.1. A square building with castle-like walls surrounded by taller buildings. In the beginning there were dozens of Jewish families without roofs over their heads living in the courtyard, because most of the city had been burnt and destroyed..The remainder of the buildings that the Russians had left standing were systematically and thoroughly destroyed by the Germans who removed the bricks from the walls and sent them into Germany.

The three-storey building always bustled with activity and children played on the stairs. One after the other the Zionist organizations and schools moved into the courtyard, until all the noise and tumult had driven the families out.

First came the Hebrew "Techiya" school with its teachers, Chinich, Bereszowski and Govkin, and its students who later became Zionist teachers. As soon as this school moved to larger premises on Bialystokski St., the organizations of Poale Zion, Zeirei Zion, and the Pioneers moved in. After they vacated the front rooms with its well-lit hall, the General Zionists occupied them with their youth branches.

Who did not occupy this building?

Zeirei Zion, Poale Zion, the Revisionists, El hamishmar, Et Livnot, Hahalutz,

Hahalutz Hamerkazi, Shomer Hatzair, Gordonia, Betar, Brit Hachayal, Keren Kayemet, and Keren Hayesod.

Who visited this building?

Itzchak Greenboim, the leader of Polish Zionism, Leon Levita, the chairman of the Zionist organization, Baruch Zuckerman, the chairman of Poale Zion, Aaron Propes, the Betar commander. Scholem Asch the writer was also a visitor to this building. The Betar members organized a celebratory reception for Zev Jabotinski there.

Some of the speeches that were held in the courtyard included,: Yosef Heftman, Moshe Laizerovitch from the "Heint" (son of the preacher and tailor Laizerovitch), A. Goldberg, the editor of the Heint newspaper, who was also a Brisker.

Avraham Levinson, the deputy mayor of Brest, whose speeches were unforgettable.

Thousands of Jewish schoolchildren would assemble there for Lag Baomer and march out of there to the city gardens with a band playing and waving blue and white flags.

In the courtyard there were scenes that reflected the hunger for aliyah to Israel. There were often fights and blows over the list for places to Israel. Jews from the Brest district would wait for days until the Zionist Organization met and allocated the certificates for aliyah to Israel for the whole region.

The great Zionist Prayer meeting, the only one in the city, was held there. They would meet on Sabbath and the Holydays – it was led by L.Y. Winnikoff, Zev Dov Begin, Zaretzki and other Zionist leaders. In the same courtyard, the Jews of Brest celebrated the establishment of the Hebrew University in Jerusalem. The orchestras of Hashomer Hatzair and Betar played all day and the street was illuminated.

Hundreds of youths and adults studied at the evening classes there which were conducted by Mordechai Yaffe.

Menachem Begin (the future leader of Israel) came to Topolowa 12, as did a series of Jewish writers such as I. Perlov. The headquarters of the Pioneer Movement for the whole of the Polessie and Wolyn districts was there. Generally, Topolowa 12 was not just a local Zionist center, but also the region's headquarters, and seethed with Zionist activities and Jewish life. This building will never be forgotten by the members of Zionist organizations of all streams – it was an integral part of their lives.

[Page 449]

Jewish Sport

By S. Rubin
Translated by Dr. Samuel Chani and Jenni Buch

The Brest inhabitants that returned to the city after W.W.1 included school-age children who after a short time began to organize the communal life of the city. They formed a football club called the Jewish Sports Club – its founding members were:

Dr. Gotlieb, Shmuel Mullar, J. Stier, and others. This club had a positive influence on the city's community life and was popular. The following were the administrators of the club: City councillor Shimon Itzbitzer, Yoshe and Chaim Youngermen, David Shedrowitzki, and Furmanovitch. This board was responsible for broadening the activities of the club, and a group was formed with the aim of developing physical education amongst the youth. The original group was: Shlomo Klein, Moshe Sarver and the chairman was Shabtai Rubin.

From 1926-7 the activities of the Jewish Sports Club strengthened and spread widely. As well as the football club that became renowned over the entire Polessie district, an athletics club, a bike riding club and a baseball club sprang up. H. Malin headed the athletics club, and the bike riders distinguished themselves at local competitions.

A national football league was formed in 1924 by the Polish government. The Brest branch of this league conducted football matches. The Jewish Sports Club participated in this league competition. They distinguished themselves and were

popular amongst the Poles. For many years this Brest group was on top of the local (Polessie) league. Representatives of this group were the lawyer Politshanski and B. Kastrinski. The matches evoked much enthusiasm from both the youth and adults alike, who attended the games en masse.

The Jewish Sports Club played against Polish clubs such as the 82nd Division (Army team), and the 9th Division, both from the fortress, and the Tanks Division team –our group defeated these teams in competition and that led to much pride amongst the Jews. These victories evoked jealousy and bad feeling from the Poles and arguments and fights would break out at the matches. The Jewish supporters would protect their players as heroes. They would leave the football ground together as a group to avoid attacks from the Poles. Outstanding players were – Bushmitz, Yoshe Youngerman, Shmuel Gelman, Moshinski, Ulman, Israel Stir, and others.

There were also other football clubs in Brest – Hapoel, Nordia, Stern and a group from the Bund. All these clubs were from opposing political movements and streams, but without exception they united in the common goal of sport and co- existed in friendly relations.

At the annual general meetings of these clubs, the question was raised as whether to join the Maccabi World Union, but no decision was reached.

The interest in sport grew, especially when in 1931, the famous Hakoah club came from Vienna to play against the Jewish Sports Club in Brest. Jews came from all the corners of Polessie to see this match. The participation of these two Jewish clubs caused much enthusiasm and pride. The Jewish Sports Club also organized a choir and a winter sports group.

At the annual general meeting in 1933 it was decided to join the Maccabi world Union, and the club adopted the name Maccabi Jewish Sports Club Brest. The chairman was the pharmacist S. Grynberg and later Janovski.

The club preserved it's non-partisan character but it had a Zionist influence and many of it's members later became active in sports movements in Israel.

I will never forget those comrades who perished, amongst them Israel Stir, who personified the spirit of Jewish sport in Brest, and was one of the founders of the Jewish Sports Club.

The Hapoel Sports Club 1934

The Revisionist Sports Club 'Nordia'

[Pages 453]

MOVEMENTS

The Zionist Organization

By B. Kastrinski
Translated by Dr. Samuel Chani and Jenni Buch

Brest was one of the first cities where the Chovevei Zion (Lovers of Zion) were popular and the Zionist ideology was discussed in the synagogues. In the newspapers of that era, such as "Hamelitz", "Hashachar", "Hamagid", and "Hatzofeh", much mention was made about the Zionist activities of the city.

As early as the BILU period (1880s), Briskers were already leaving for the land of Israel. Dr. Moshe Minc who came from Brest, was one of the original BILU group.

In 1880 he went to Israel to join his comrades in the settlement of Mikveh Israel. He later settled in Gedera. His brother, Gershon Minc, also a BILU member, built the community hall in Gedera at his own expense. Later the Brest families Feinstein, Padua, and Pochachevski made aliyah to Israel.

In 1884 the ' Bnei Zion Society' was founded in Brest. It's officials were: Mordcchai Padua, Ben Zion Neumark, and Mordechai Sheinerman. A. Mushkat and Mordechai Sheinerman were the Brest delegates to the conferences of Chovevei Zion in Odessa.

The first Zionist Society was formed in Brest in 1897 – the same year as the first Zionist Congress. The Brest delegates to this congress were Leon Horoditche (who died in Tel-Aviv), and Noah Finkelstein (the editor of the "Heint"). They presented a report on what they had seen and heard at the Congress upon their return to Brest – it evoked a great deal of interest and many Briskers joined this movement.

At the Russian Zionist Conference in Minsk in 1902, the Brest delegates were Ben Zion Neumark and Mordechai Sheinerman. At Helsinki 1906, the delegates were Mordechai Sheinerman and Israel Rakov. Mordechai Sheinerman was also a member of 'Bnei Moshe'. Ben Zion Neumark was a commissioner of the Odessa Committee the entire time. In 1909 the first council of the Zionist Organization was elected in Brest: The Chairman was L.Horoditche, members were Ben Zion Neumark, Mordechai Sheinerman, Alter Grosleit, Gedalia Hazan, Nathan Goldring, Kaplanski, L.Y. Winnikoff, Chaim Leib Itzbitzer, Beinish Koloditzki, H. Rosenblum, Dr. y. Shereshevski, Zecharia Rosenthal, and Dr K. Shteinberg. The second chairman was Dr. Y. Shereshevski.

The following were involved in the selling and distribution of the Colonial Bank Bonds (for settlements in Israel) – Shereshevski, Neumark, Sheinerman and Winnikoff. Brest became famous for its achievement in this field. The

Zionist activist, Alter Hazan helped spread the Zionist ideology. His son, Yakov Hazan, one of the leaders of Hashomer Hatzair, was born in Brest and is now a member of the Knesset in Israel.

In 1911, L.Y. Winnikoff was elected as chairman of the Zionist Organization in Brest. He held this position almost continuously (with some short breaks) until he migrated to Israel in 1935. During this period the Zionist Organization grew and gained many members and became a genuine mass movement.

The Zionist activity halted during W.W.1, after the expulsion of the inhabitants of Brest. Only after their return to the city in 1918, did the movement become active again. The Brest Zionist Movement became the headquarters for all the district – it organized many branches and served as a model for other communities.

The quarrel between "Al Hamishmar" and "Et Livnot" took place in Brest, and many remember those stormy days. The Zionists were very active in the elections to the Sjem (Polish Parliament).

From 1925-1935 these were the Zionist Council members: L.Y. Winnikoff, Israel Fernig, Zerach Zaretski, Meir Feinstein, Eliezer Goldfarb, Baruch Kastrinski and the engineer Shlomo Kamenetski. After Winnikoff's departure for Israel, four members held the chairmanship: Moshe Lev, Chaim Leib Itzbitzer, Meir Feinstein and Israel Fernig who carried on with the work until the very end.

The General Zionists participated in all the affairs of the community in Brest.

L.Y.Winnikoff was their representative on the city council and he commanded great respect from all the various sections of society. The Kehilla council representatives were L.Y.Winnikoff, Zerach Zaretski and Meir Feinstein, - they did a great deal for Keren Kayemet , Keren Hayesod and Shekel Bonds. They also established the foundations for the youth organizations.

The Pioneer General Zionists (the central Pioneers) were formed in Brest in 1923 and many young people became affiliated with them. One of the founders of this movement in Poland was B. Kastrinski. He was the chairman of the Polessie/ Wolyn until 1934. The Central Pioneers established Hachshara groups which provided agricultural training for young people before making aliyah, one of these farms was at Katelneh, near Brest.

Amongst the activists for the young Pioneers were:Tuvia Gubkin, Yitzchak Tucker (who died in Berlin), the writer Y. Perlov, Elisheva Sandlarsh, Leah Moshinski, R. Neumark, Shlomo Meltzer, Sara Sapirstein, Aharon Mandelbaum, and Rosa Wolyniec.

The members of the "Pioneer Tradesmen" at the Zionist Organization were given preparation for going to Israel in groups with the aim of settling on kibbutzim – amongst the active members of this group were: the engineer Kamenetzki, Avraham Sandlarsh, Dziencol, Shor, Havaniovski and others.

The Central Pioneers had a cultural group the members of which were young people from the schools - the instructor was a teacher from the Tarbut High School – Moshe Gutentag. Many from this cultural group made aliyah to Israel, including Berel Hari, Ltvinski, and Rosenblatt.

"Hashomer Haleumi"

Was a scouting movement that excelled in public Jewish sporting performances in gymnastics and athletics, for instance on Lag Baomer.

Active members were Moshe Felhendler, Yakov Eisenberg, Piasetzki and others.

WIZO (Women's International Zionist Org.)

Participated actively in all Zionist affairs. They organized Keren Kayemet meetings, exhibitions, and fund raising of money from the various institutions. Active members were: Gelle Koniopati, Dr. Perlis, Regina Levinson, Fanya Pomerantz, Sheine Kostakevitch, Elisheva Sandlarsh, and others. The president was Mrs. Golodetz.

Kadimah

A General Zionist youth movement was founded in 1928. Its aim was to bring Zionist propaganda to the assimilated youth through the schools and student groups. This group assisted and supported the Zionist Organization in every activity.

In 1933 their group formed a 'Kibbutz' for Hachshara training outside Brest – the chairman was Shlomo Kamenetzki – a dedicated Zionist who was killed in the Bialystok Ghetto. Active members were: Litvinski, Rosenblatt, Piatkowski, Bulkowstein, Moshe Dziencol, Hazan, Deborah Tennenbaum, Batsheva Lerner, Tzvi Gruzman, Ginsburg, the majority of the members settled in Israel.

The Keren Kayemet

It's first director was Ben Zion Neumark in 1904. The second was Beinish Koloditzki, and after him Y. Shereshevski. Isser Tzemach and Betzalel Feigin were active before W.W.1 After returning from exile in 1919, they again elected B. Koloditzki. After his departure to Israel, Kadish Lubelski and Tzvi Lomarchevski were directors. The officials of Keren Kayemet worked together irrespective of any political differences they represented.

Keren Hayesod

Was formed in 1922 in Brest and occupied a respected position in the Polessie district. L.Y.Winnikoff was the life and soul of all its undertakings. For a short period its chairman was A. Levinson, the deputy mayor, whose speeches stirred the public.

Israel Fernig – for all his days he was a dedicated active official of Keren Hayesod. He would neglect his home and business for the sake of this activity. Others fully involved officials were: Mrs Fanya Winnikoff, Yitzchak Trubovitch, Meir Feinstein, Zev Dov Begin, Chaim Tennewitzki, Sarah Zaretzki, Aron

Ludski, David Sussman, Scholem Shwartz, Minkovski, and the lawyer Glovinski. The last four of the above members were sent by the Russians to Siberia.

It is possible that there are more names of loyal and dedicated members of all the parties and organizations –young and old, they worked with all their bodies and souls for the Zionist ideal of building a Jewish State of Israel. They all drank from the sacred well of the Zionist cause.

We saw these comrades and their joys and enthusiasm in their songs and dances in Topolowa 12. Members of the rank and file, they were soldiers for an ideal for which they toiled and fought - the privilege of witnessing the building of the State of Israel.

Let these words be a memorial for their dear souls.

The Zionist Council In Brest 1909

Standing from R. to L. – M. Levine, G. Hazan, N. Goldring, L.Y. Winnikoff,
M.B. Grosleit, Y. Berliner, C. Ballach, M. Kravetski, Z.Rosenthal, L. Horoditche,
B.Z. Neumark, Y. Shereshevski, C.L. Itzbitzer. M. Lederhendler, A. Oper
Seated from R.to L.- M. Zeiger, A. Nusmacher, S. Bloch, S. Mintz, H. Rosenboim,
Kurlender, B. Kolodetzki, C. Levenberg, A. Bloch

The Zionist Committee 1934

Seated R.to L. – C.L. Itzbitzer, M. Fierstein, B. Kastrinski,
Z. Zaretzki, L.Y. Winnikoff, A.Goldberg.
Standing R.toL.-Hazan, Shov, Kamenetzki, Dziencol, Litvinski

Keren Kayemet Officials 1934
Seated R.to L. – K. Lubelski, B. Hazan, l.Y. Winnikoff, Gutentag, M.Levi
Standing, Unknown, Unknown, Dziencol, Kamenetzki, Fernig, Unknown, Kalman

[Pages 458]

Members of the 'Mizrachi Pioneers' Council 1926
Seated R.to L.- A.L. Levitski, C.L. Itzbitzer, L.Y. Winnikoff, Z. Zaretzki, B. Kastrinski
Standing –Y. Tucker, Y. Kupin, N. Tucker, A. Sandlarsh, T. Govkin

The Keren Hayesod Board 1930
Seated R.to L.-Z. Zaretzki, Y. Ramah, L.Y. Winnikoff,
A. Levinson, Mrs. N. Levinson, D. Zisman
Standing – Z.Lutwak, A. Tash, A. Ashkenazi, M. Fierstein

[Pages 461]

The Underground Zionist Work

By l. Horoditch
Translated by Dr. Samuel Chani and Jenni Buch

In 1897, a few months before the first Zionist Congress in Basel, a Dr. Buchmal came to see me in Brest, in the name of the organizing committee of the Congress. He brought with him a letter of recommendation from Dr. Herzl himself. His mission was to ensure that there should be more Russian Jewish delegates to the Congress.

I immediately called several of our Chovevei Zion (Lovers of Zion) members: Mordechai Sheinerman, Mordechai Padua, and Ben Zion Neumark. We discussed how to implement this matter. As was known, in Tsarist Russia, every meeting was seen as anti-government agitation and strongly prohibited. In spite of this, 20 people met at my home to hear Dr Buchmal speak of the necessity of participating in the coming Congress.

After the meeting, I remained alone with Dr Buchmal – we discussed the future of Zionisn until 7am. Then he told me that he had been instructed by the Zionist organizing committee to print a leaflet proclaiming the coming Congress for the whole of Russian Jewry, and to send a thousand copies of this leaflet to Jews who had a Zionist orientation. Dr Buchmal asked me to print this leaflet and distribute it. The matter was dangerous and difficult to achieve in those days, but the principle of ' to do and to be heard' was vital to our cause. I immediately applied myself to carry out this task.

I approached all the printers in the city – nobody wanted to print this leaflet fearing retribution from the authorities. It was obvious that the matter could not be accomplished – then Ben Zion Neumark came to me and I asked his advice. He said that he knew of a place where this document could be printed. When I asked which printer, he replied, the Military printing press in the Brest Fortress. He knew a Russian officer there whom he hoped would do it for his own motives. The daily army orders were printed there by the lithography method. The printer was a friend and would possibly agree.

Neumark took the handwritten text that Dr Buchmal had prepared – I advised him to print this proclamation without a signature, only signed the City of Brest and the month. Neumark took with him a bottle of brandy and a few rubles and went on his way to the fortress. A new dangerous world was before him, but later I saw him returning with a large packet that contained the printed leaflets.

The military printer had laid out the proclamation on the other side of the military orders – during the printing suddenly an army officer arrived and the situation was most uncomfortable, but the printer turned over the lithograph stone and quietly worked on the military orders. He had hidden Neumark with the already printed leaflets in a large cupboard in the corner. Immediately after the officer left, Neumark was let out of his box and the two of them worked until the 1000 copies were done.

Then we had the problem of distribution – firstly, we did not have addresses because there were no Zionist organizations allowed in Russia. We therefore had to write the names and addresses of the Chovevei Zion from memory. We occupied ourselves with writing addresses and used the list of leaders of the Odessa committee – but we were afraid to send so many letters from the city post office. For a whole week we would go to the railway station twice daily and throw the letters in the post boxes of the many passing trains, so that they would not know where the letters originated.

After several days there was meeting at my place of over 50 people and it was decided to send a delegate from Brest to the Congress, and I was unanimously elected. I traveled directly to Basel. At the Congress I was appointed as a coordinator along with some other delegates –it was not a great task. I remember that David Wolfson asked me to compile a list of all the delegates in exact alphabetical order. For half a day I went around to all the delegates one by one and compiled the list.

Upon returning from the Congress the main work of spreading the Zionist ideology began. Several months later I received an invitation from the Chief of Police to come to see him about an important matter. On arrival he showed me a copy of the leaflet. I pretended to read it carefully and remarked that it seemed that this leaflet was printed in the city of Brest, France, not Brest Litovsk. I remarked that I often got letters at my bank office addressed to Brest Litovsk but with a stamp of Brest, France. The officer liked my explanation and wrote in his report to the government authorities that according to his information, and after much investigation and questioning, this leaflet was not printed in Brest Litovsk. Besides Ben Zion Neumark and myself, nobody knew the truth of this matter for the next 20 years – no one knew about the printing of this leaflet in Russian in Russia.

This was how the first Zionists had to operate in those days.

[Pages 465]

The Mizrachi

By N. Rabinovitch
Translated by Dr. Samuel Chani and Jenni Buch

Before W.W.1 a rabbi called Yakov Reines came to Brest. And so the Mizrachi organization was founded with Michael Rabinovitch at its head. I know little of its activities then, but I remember one evening in 1905 when I came into Rabbi Soloveitchik's study house and saw three bearded Jews seated there. They were studying the "Ayin Yakov", and listening to a young man who was reading it aloud and beautifully and simply explaining the commentary. I got closer and saw a young Jew, a talented and gifted student who was discussing the laws and interpretations of the Sabbath and religious customs. At the Sabbath prayers, I met this young man again; he read a lesson in Hebrew, and again for the mid-day students of the Torah.

I found out that this young man was Shmuel Josef Halperin – we befriended each other and became close. I saw and admired his greatness, his ideals and high standards, and his love of the Torah. I saw that despite his pressing need for income for his family, he gave himself wholeheartedly to the Torah and the public good.

Many years passed and he went to Israel. Later on we met again in the destroyed city of Brest. Shmuel Josef came to see me one day and asked:" why are we silent? Why don't we form a chapter of Mizrachi here in Brest?" Together we went to see Rabbi Israel Mashgiach and we decided to rent a five roomed house – I myself paid the rent for an entire year, and there we founded a school named "Chaim" after Rabbi Chaim Soloveitchik. In that school we taught Talmudic, Jewish, and general studies. Shmuel Josef channelled all of his energy into this school.

He himself was a grandson of Rabbi Chaim Volozhyner; he was religious and steeped in the Torah. He would come and listen to his students studying. At his instigation the Grayever Rabbi was appointed as the head of this yeshiva. His followers also brought the chass society into the school, and Rabbi Shmuel Josef would conduct a lesson daily, but he was far removed from seeking honor and awards. At a general assembly of over 300 particpants, the Mizrachi movement was re-established in Brest. The committee members were: Shmuel Josef Halperin, David Sussman, Asher Ashkenazi, and Naphtali Rabinovitch. The Mizrachi movement accomplished a great deal - its members participated in all community work, and worked for both the Keren Kayemet and Keren Hayesod. If not for Rabbi Shmuel Josef, Mizrachi would not have existed in Brest.

Once, he opened a meeting with the words:" as long as we are visitors in a foreign land, we must look after ourselves and our causes". He proposed to obtain a permit to build a building on the empty lot next to the great synagogue. This was to be the headquarters for the Mizrachi and it's institutions. With the assistance of Shmuel Pomeranitz, they built the one storey "Tachkamoni" school in 1923. Rabbi Shmuel Josef was not satisfied with that and asked:" what are we doing for our orthodox youth?" He asked and replied to himself. He began to form the Mizrachi Youth, which combined Torah learning with work. He demanded a joinery where the students could work and learn carpentry and woodworking skills during the day, and to study Torah in the evening classes. The students themselves made all the doors and windows for the school.

Once on a Sabbath, he came to see me and proposed that we form a society for the orthodox women. Immediately the Mizrachi Women's Society was formed. Later on he built a second story on the Tachkamoni building for a high school with 16 classrooms and a great hall that held prayer services every Sabbath and Holyday. He advocated that besides Torah studies, students should also learn general studies and naturally, Hebrew. Studying general studies and culture would not harm a young person who studies the Torah.

In 1925, Rabbi Shmuel Josef Halperin settled in Israel. He lived in Tel-Aviv, later in Kfar Saba –liked and respected by all. He was modest and retiring, he would study day and night. He gave lessons in Torah, which he himself constantly studied all his life.

[Pages 467]
Mizrachi Youth and Mizrachi Pioneers

By S.Shamir (Petrushka)
Translated by Dr. Samuel Chani and Jenni Buch

The religious Zionist movement was very active in all aspects of the community life in Brest, as well as Zionist activities and work. This included educational methods, the religious youth, and pioneer agricultural training before going to Israel.

This group attracted the best type of officials, and their influence was great in all layers of society. The Young Mizrachi and Mizrachi Pioneers were the best and most attractive movements in Poland. They had the best organization and influence over the religious youth, and contributed a great deal to the popularity of Zionism, and their concept of Torah and Work.

At the head of the movement stood Rabbi Shmuel Josef Halperin, (who died in Kfar Saba), David Sussman, N. Rabinovitch, S. Petrushka, Asher Ashkenazi, Baruch Kwiatkowski, Dov Hazan, Lieb Kravetski, Kalman Neiman (who died in Jerusalem), Ben Zion Menes, Gershon Kassovski, Josef Rosenberg, and Zelig Grynberg (killed in the Holocaust).

The first achievement of the Mizrachi movement was to build the "Chaim" school. Rabbi Shmuel Josef Halperin and Rabbi Chaim Gershon with their friends and associates built this institution where 100s of student attained knowledge and Torah learning. The Young Mizrachi and the Mizrachi Pioneers held evening courses in Hebrew, biblical studies, the geography of Israel, and had a large library, as well as a joinery workshop for the training of the pioneers in carpentry and woodwork. The movement was influential in the many Zionist activities including Keren Kayemet, Keren Hayesod, and the Shekel Bonds.

In the elections to the City Council, the Mizrachi successfully nominated David Sussman as their delegate, and Asher Ashkenazi was their representative and deputy chairman on the kehilla council. The Mizrachi Women's Organization participated in all the community and Zionist work. Especially active in this was Deborah Felsenstein.

The Mizrachi developed its educational institutions. The school at Pilsudski Square was too small for all their enrolments - after many stormy battles, they managed to obtain a block of land and a permit to build the "Tachkamoni" school, which became the definitive school in Brest.

Rabbi Shmuel Josef Halperin

[Page 467]

The Young Zionists (Zeirei Zion)

by A. Ludski
Translated by Dr. Samuel Chani and Jenni Buch

A. The first steps of the Zionist Youth movement in Brest were linked to the "Techiya" group, which was founded by them. This group was a narrow circle of dedicated idealists, who saw their future as being in Israel.

Despite the limited possibilities under the Tsarist regime, the community activity in Brest was well developed, with the Bund, Poale Zion, and active non-affiliated youth. These non-affiliated young people were attracted to the Zionist circles. There was a "Society for the Preservation of the Hebrew Language and Literature", that was dedicated to spreading the Hebrew language both orally and in writing. It had followers who were fanatical in their dedication to this goal.

The young people voluntarily took on the collection of money for the Keren Kayemet at Bar Mitzvahs and weddings, and delivered blue boxes to the homes of the community. Some of them would diligently read the Hebrew press "Hasphirah" and other newspapers. They were interested in everything that had a link to Israel. They concentrated around the Zionist library and read books and newspapers from Israel, including the "Young Worker" and "Achdut".

Several of these members of the Young Zionists traveled to Israel and their leaving made a deep impression on the other young people who began to think about going to Israel. Several of those who went, eventually returned, as they were not able to overcome the difficulties of settling in Israel.

During the expulsion from Brest in W.W.1, the youth was spread throughout the towns of Russia and wandered with all the homeless – some to Poland, some deeper into Russia...

B. In 1918-9, most of the homeless returned to Brest and a new wave of community activity began. The Zionist Youth had a very strong influence on the Zionist organization – some of them decided to form a branch of the Young Zionists that was directly linked to the central Zionist headquarters in Warsaw. The movement quickly spread throughout Congress Poland and was strengthened by the arrival of Russian refugees, especially in border areas such as Brest. The leaders of the Zionist movement in Brest were not pleased, but under pressure from the growing youth movement – the General Zionists were forced to give up their offices at Topolowa 12 to the Young Zionists. They left behind them the spacious hall and rooms, as well as the Techiya School, in the capable hands of the Young Zionists. The Young Zionists initiated compulsory cultural activities with Israel and Zionism as the central theme. They formed a link between the Zionist Brest and the awakening of the national dream of a Jewish State in Israel.

Some of the youth leaned toward the promised magic of the Russian revolution with its deep social reforms. But in truth, the majority of the youth yearned for 'Jewishness' and Jewish independence.

The economy of the whole movement and it's educational activities were founded on the financial assistance from the Joint (American United Relief Committee), in which the Zionists had representation on the board. Especially excelling themselves in their efforts were: Lamazhevski, Svirinowski, outsiders members such as Wertheim, Shneerson, Dr Wertaks and others. In the feverish activity of opening educational and cultural institutions the Young Zionists played a pivotal role. They seized the opportunity to open schools with Hebrew as the teaching language. The leftist organizations such as the Bund, Leftist Poale Zion had earlier already founded Yiddish schools. The Orphanage had a Hebrew Primary and Middle school. The students were mainly children who returned from exile without parents – homeless they lived in the synagogue schools and institutions. A battle broke out over these homeless children between the Zionist movement and the Workers groups that dominated, and the leftist parties that sympathized with communist Russia.

Intensive efforts were carried out in the offices in Topolowa 12 and the Techiya School under the directorship of Michael Berezowski, and later Nachum Chinitch. The Tel Chai School was conducted in two languages - Hebrew and Yiddish. In the education groups there were meetings and discussions about literary subjects, and specific subjects relating to Israel such as making aliyah and the problems facing the pioneers.

C. At the same time there was a stream of the young people from the working classes to the ranks of the Young Zionists, there were also "deserters" from the old party members to the extreme leftist circles. During the fighting and invasion of the Russians in 1920, many who belonged to the Young Zionists and their institutions declared themselves as against the Russian revolution, and would not participate in the anti government demonstrations under the Young Zionist banner, only as individuals with their professional group.

In 1919-1920 the Young Zionists managed to achieve a great deal in the fields of education, cultural activities, and social assistance (a community soup kitchen). At the same time several members were being prepared to make aliyah to Israel as the first pioneer group from Brest. This first group of Young Zionists made aliyah despite the difficulties. At their departure crowds of youths and adolescents formed a large demonstration to farewell them and show their support for the future workers of Israel.

With the stream of the third aliyah, the Young Zionists fully participated in the "working Fund", actively collecting money for arms and equipment for the Haganah, which was sent through the central office in Warsaw. This fund raising involved widespread adult participation – the member's parents who supported this cause saw it as a holy mission

The Young Zionists had many members from the working class youth, from the workshop benches to tradesmen and white-collar workers. This is how they gained access to the professional unions. They were able to penetrate the organizations of woodworkers, carpenters, metal workers, and tradesmen, clerical employees – where the communists, the Bund and leftist Poale Zion had previously dominated.

The Jewish workers environment was dominated by demagoguery and one had to have great courage and strength of characters to make a stand against these strong mainstream currents. Some members penetrated the professional groups, with the purpose of influencing some of them to make aliyah.

With the election of the Polish Sjem (Parliament) in 1922, the Young Zionists participated together with the right Poale Zion on one electoral ticket. Although the results of this election were not favorable to either (in Polessie and all of Poland), from that time on the members became more involved in the political side of the organization.

At the National Congress in 1923 there was a renowned split – a part of the party went to the rightist Poale Zion. At a stormy meeting in Brest, the majority of members voted for a merger with the right Poale Zion. The members who remained loyal to the central committee in Warsaw categorically opposed this merger. Many others left the party at this time and formed their own party, which clung to the Young Zionist traditions. However, the majority of the members voted for a union with the rightist Poale Zion – a fierce drive to control the Tel Chai School ensued. The remainder of the Young Zionists made a firm stand to control the Tel Chai library, which existed on the basis of a permit issued to the Polessie Branch Committee of the Polish Zionists. And so the bitter wrangling and jostling for power continued between the two groups – it was not until two years later that they agreed to re-unite.

D. In the years 1923-24 the rightist Poale Zion did a great deal for the Tel Chai School with public appeals and lectures. Active members of the Young Zionist continued to go to Israel. Young people who had newly arrived in the town joined the Poale Zion - mainly because of the chance to make aliyah through the training opportunities provided through Hachshara in a kibbutz outside Brest.

In 1925-26 after a unification conference, the two split groups re-united into one party. The united party joined in a campaign for the city council and was successful.

In 1927 several of the members who had earlier made aliyah returned to Brest because of the very difficult economic situation in Israel. But this did not affect the morale of the group. The returnees actively participated in all the party work.

In the city council, the representatives of the party took on the responsibility of the cultural work and penetrated several professional groups. They held free open debates and lectures about Zionism and social problems. They supported the Tel Chai School against the discriminatory Polish authorities. The school, which did not identify with the aims of "Zishah" in Poland (an extreme YIddish Bundist institute) was closed down. Some of the parents sent their children to Hebrew schools, others to Polish schools.

A Grodzienski and S. Orchov remained dedicated workers for the Tel Chai School.

In 1923 the Hebrew primary school "Techiya" was transferred to the authority of the "Al Hamishmar" group, under the directorship of Z. Lutwak. Lutwak had established the school on strong foundations. Several years later the school became the Tarbut Hebrew High School, with full government accreditation.

The upsurge in Zionism had somewhat waned since the end of the Pioneer Aliyah, and at the municipal elections in 1929 the united list of Poale Zion and Zeirei Zion only managed to obtain one seat. On the other hand, the collection of funds for the workers in Israel was always successful.

The unrest (riots) in Israel in 1929 caused an awakening and brought a new stream of youth to the pioneer movement. The central branch of the party in Warsaw mobilized the young people to prepare for aliyah – and Brest was very active in this activity. The results of the 1930 election to the city council brought prestige to the party that had a prominent place in the communal life of the city.

Two ideologies dominated the Workers for Israel Party - one believed that the party should direct all it's energies to the protection and benefit of the local Jewish working classes, and conduct educational Zionist programs and work for Israel. Also to stand up and fight the leftist elements (Leftist Poale Zion and the Bundists). The second adopted the position of:"our main aim is for Eretz Israel, and there we will build on sand". Opinions were divided – the workers organizations opposed this stand and had contact with socialist parties (P.P.S.- Polish Socialist Party). The supporters of building in Israel supported the League of the Workers in Israel, the issue of Hachshara, Aliyah, and raising funds through the Israel Bonds.

The Brest branch of Hapoel conducted a sports organization that attracted a large following and members from the youth circles.

On the 1st May (International Labor Day) in the early years they would hold a workers march in Brest without permission from the authorities. The Zeirei Zion (Young Zionists) did not participate in these demonstrations as they were invariably broken up by the police, with many of the participants beaten severely. After the union of the Young Zionists and the left Poale Zion there were united public demonstrations of the party that included the P.P.S. and the Bund. Years later these combined demonstrations were cancelled. Under pressure from the Bund, the P.P.S. demanded that that the united party should not come out with pro- Zionist proclamations at these rallies. Therefore the Polish Zionist party made their 1st official demonstration by themselves.

The stream of people wishing to make obtain family certificates for aliyah to Israel rose to new heights from 1931-32. In Brest the pioneer movement ran it's Hachshara (agricultural training) program from a kibbutz just outside the city – the political party was very involved with the management of this kibbutz.

With the rise of the Nazi regime, the striving to make aliyah became stronger as many decided to leave Poland. This caused a feverish quest for certificates for aliyah, and the Zionist work of the party was much strengthened. It's members were active in Keren Kayemet and Keren Hayesod and Aliyah bet and the membership grew daily.

At this time the rise of the revisionist movement began with it's various branches: Betar, Masada, Brit Hachayal and others who were active against out party. The United Zionist Party together with the general Zionists – with Y.L. Winnikoff from Al- Hamishmar and the Y. Greenboim group used all it's strength and energies to uphold the Zionist movement in Brest.

As soon as the swastikas cast their shadows and the terrible war was on the horizon –the will to make aliyah strengthened. A few members managed to leave with Aliyah Bet, but the majority had to remain in Brest against their will. They were murdered together with their brother Jews in the terrible Holocaust that followed.

The Founders of the Young Zionists in 1913
R. to L. M. Lubetkin, Y.S.Lubetkin, S. Tzemach, Rabinovitch, A. Tzemach

Officials of the Educational and Social Assistance Group

First row: H. Epstein, R. Distler, and R. Pregel
Second row: A. Shtrickman, S. Itzbitzer, M. Distler, B. Minivetski, R. Wertheim
(the Joint representative), Y. Gelerstein, L. Mular, and M. Lubetski
Third row: S. Gershboim, Y. Tennenbaum, G.Korman – Lubelski, Z. Grynberg,
G. Goldberg, Dr. Mostovianski, M. Breinhendler, and Fanaberia

The Committee of the Poale Zion in 1922

Sitting right to left: A. Becker, M. Breinhendler, M. Machlis,
N.Chinich and B.Mackron (Ben-Tzvi)
Standing: K. Lubelski, A. Ludski, V. Shedrovitzki, and L Korman (Dagnit)

[Page 477]

The Left Poale Zion

by M. Menachovski
Translated by Dr. Samuel Chani and Jenni Buch

Brisk D'Lita was one of the cities in which the Left Poale Zion (Workers of Zion) developed a strong following, where a branch was established in Brest already before W.W.1. In 1913 the Poale Zion headquarters in Krakow established the Brisk/Pinsk committee, of which I was a member. Important activists at that time were Chaim Taubensclag and Sara Bulkovstein, who was married to Israel Reichman (the leader of Poale Zion).

After W.W.1, the majority of members that had returned to Brest joined the Left Poale Zion after the split. These were the active members at that time: Reuven Pregel, Tzalke Minivetski, and myself. After that Shimon Itzbitzer, Avraham Shrickman, Alter Lustigman, Shimon Acroplanski, David Gittelman and Sarah Gittelman, joined us. There was also a strong youth movement that founded a workers kitchen (soup-kitchen) that became the center for the entire labor movement. The activities of all the Jewish worker's organizations took place there. Hundreds of workers received their hot meals there daily, in those hungry years with the entire town in ruins - many found a home there. The police disliked this soup kitchen and would conduct frequent raids and make numerous arrests. Reuven Pregel, the kitchen manager, was arrested and sent to Czestochowa for several years. Due to the police persecutions, as soon as the economic situation improved, the soup kitchen closed down.

The influence of the Left Poale Zion was also evident in the professional circles – they had control of the trade's employees, and they also had great influence over the sewing and tailoring professions, the metal workers and locksmiths, and all the building trades. The party was active in cultural affairs and the education of children.

They ran a free university with classes for adult with lectures on literature and cultural matters. The evening course attracted hundreds of young people. As the community re-established itself, the Left Poale Zion played an important role in life of the community. It's struggle against the orthodox religious movement was especially difficult.

The party's strength was visible in the political life of Brest – it ran candidates at every election for the Sejm (Polish Parliament). Thousands of supporters would show up at their election rallies and the Left Poale Zion would always get the most votes –they were especially strong in the municipal activities and the area of education.

The third Jewish primary school was part of the rebuilding network of Brest – the teaching was in Yiddish and Hebrew. The large teaching staff included the known activists: Dr. Israel Rubin, Katyn Maladovski, and others.

As soon as the city was somewhat re-established, the officials began to create school programs. The school was not only a teaching institution, but also included a children home - with the support of the Joint; the children received two meals daily. In 1919 the first school was founded with Yiddish as the teaching language through the efforts of the Poale Zion and the Bund. This school began in Topolowa 12 and grew strongly – it's students reached 500. The head of this school was David Shnider and myself. Due to internal conflicts this school did not last for long. The Bund and the Poale Zion had differing opinions on the contents of the curriculum and how it should be taught and after a year, the school was disbanded.

The second primary school was then formed in Zymuntowska 12. This was a light and warm haven for the children who mostly lived in dark cellars, and would run from one aid institution to another, until we obtained free meals, clothing and shoes for them. At this school there was also a home for children under the age of three, supervised by Esther Menachowski. Former pupils of this school have spread over many countries of the world – the United States, Argentina, Europe, the Soviet Union and Israel. The staff included Moshe Levine, Hannah Fisherman (teacher killed in the Holocaust), B. Shlevine (renowned Yiddish writer), Chaim Finkelstein, who was later director of a Yiddish school in Buenes Aires. This primary school struggled for survival due to lack of income, and legal impediments. The budget came from three sources - school fees, collection of donations, and educational taxes. This school existed solely due to the dedicated efforts of the teaching staff.

Jewish teachers and Officials 1920

1st (bottom) row R-L: B. Minivitski, Y. Gelerstein, Katya Molodowski, Gelerstein, Malka Lys, ---, Eisenstein
2nd Row: S. Gershonboim, R. Shtrickman, ---, M. Lev, Dr. I. Rubin, ---, L. Mular, S. Itzbitzer, and Fanaberia
3rd Row:,---, ---, Acroplanski, Buchstein, E. Menachowski, ---, and Gelerstein
4th Row: D. Shnider, Dr. Mastovlanski, ---, ---, ---, Distler, Distler

Teachers and Students of the Peretz School in 1922
Centre: Director David Shnider and Esther Menachowski

[Page 481]

Hashomer Hatzair

by a Brisker
Translated by Dr. Samuel Chani and Jenni Buch

The following members founded the Hashomer Hatzair organization in Brest in 1923: Meyer Freidman, Meyer Landa, and Mordechai Neumark. A year later its status was established as a Jewish Scouts Organization. The den in Brest was only the second in Poland and had full government sanction – one of the few Jewish organizations to achieve this.

The original committee consisted of Zev-Dov Begin –chairman, Tzvi Lomazhevski and Fishel Rogoszik. The inaugural meetingwas attended by: Meyer Freidman – who was the scout -master, Meyer Landau, his deputy, Yakov Loy – secretary, Akiva Kravetski, Mordechai Neumark, Joseph Levine and Rochel Begin. After the departure of the scout –master to Israel in 1925-6, Shlomo Kravetski, Meyer Fruchtgarten, Esther Rimland, Mischa Zablud and Netanel Kolodetzki headed the organization. The den operated on three levels: Level one – cubs. Level two – scouts. Level three – adults. Each level divided into units of 10 –12 comrades.

In 1925 the den numbered 200 members. After uniting with the Trumpeldor Scouts in the summer of 1925, the membership increased to 300. The Trumpledor organization was under the leadership of: Moshe Melnitski, Chaim Gelman, Mischa Zablud, and others. The units and levels had their various activities. There were the officer's group, cultural group, drama club (with Mischa Sarver as chairman), an orchestra and a choir. There was also a library, instructors department and evening Hebrew classes.

In the first years Hashomer Hatzair was the only Jewish youth movement in the city – attracting the cream of the youth. The official activities were in Hebrew, even though the meetings were conducted in Yiddish. As a branch of the central committee in Poland, Hashomer Hatzair accepted and trained it's members into the spirit of self sufficiency and independence. We created a green garden at no. 8 Unilubelska St. Later at the farm outside Brest named "Adamkovka", owned by Yitzchak Bruchin. Still later Hashomer Hatzair united with the Halutz (pioneer) movement on an autonomous basis to conduct Hachshara (agricultural training) in an organized manner for the group of the "First Aliyah " which is now in kibbutz Ein Hachovesh, and kibbutz Hanativ (in the Negev).

The members of Hashomer Hatzair participated in all the Zionist activities in the city and excelled at collecting donations for the Keren Kayemet. A member was the secretary of Keren Kayemet, and members participated in the pioneer movement, assistance for the Tarbut School, the various children's committees, and others. The Hashomer Hatzair presence in the annual Lag Ba-omer parade was very impressive.

Members also helped create dens in the neighboring towns of Terespol and Bereza Kartuza. Prominent leaders of the movement visited Brest – Meyer Yaari, Feivel Hamburg, Joseph Alster, and Yakov Riftin. Brest hosted all the district conferences and meetings. The first one was in 1925 with the participation of Shoshana Mushkat –Blatt. In 1930 and 1933 with the participation of Tzvi Luria. The den organized scout camps and participated in the summer colonies of the Polish Scout movement.

Hashomer Hatzair was formed as a scouting movement – in the beginning it was non – political. After much time and debate the group decided to unite with the Zionist Socialist camp. The Brest branch was very involved with all these deliberations and decision-making.

The Hashomer Hatzair in Brest
Standing R-L: Y. Menes, S. Fruchtgarten, and A. Kravetski
Seated R-L: B. Zigman, M. Neumark, Rochel Begin, M. Freidman,
J. Alster (central comm.), M. Landau, Z. Yungerman, and S. Chalfi
Seated on the ground: J. Levine, E. Rimland, and Z. Neuman

[Page 483]

The Zionist Revisionist Movement

by D. Meiri
Translated by Dr. Samuel Chani and Jenni Buch

A. Betar

The Zionist Revisionist movement was initiated in Brest in 1929, and became a powerful and influential mainstream force in the Jewish community. In the beginning it was formed as a Betar group that began with 150 members and eventually reached 800 members, both male and female. Betar in Brest was instigated by Moshe Rabinovitch and Emmanuel Baraks, who formed the first temporary committee together with Dr. Moshe Steiner, David Shedrovitzki, and Mordechai Neumark. Then Berl Stigman was appointed as commander with Ephraim Steinberg as secretary. The Betarists were trained in the spirit of political Zionism and educated according to the program of Ze'ev Jabotinski. The Betar instructors taught them tidiness, discipline, the use of weapons and the carrying out of exercises.

The Betar youth varied from the poorest state schools to the children of the rich, from uneducated to the academic – all of them carried out their instructions and were trained according to the guidelines of the national headquarters in Warsaw. Members who did not know any Hebrew studied the language in special classes run by the graduates of the Tarbut and Tachkamoni schools. The use of weapons and arms training were taught according to instructions of Polish army officers (Polish Army Corps of High School Cadets).

Betar in Brest was organized as everywhere else – there was a division commander, his assistant, a secretary, education officers, and a cultural officer. The cells were organized into different levels – youth and adults. A third group of adult Betar members were called Betar reservists. In the framework of the cultural activity there were lectures on Jewish history, the Bible, the geography of Israel, the history of Zionism and the revisionist movement. The division also had an orchestra.

Several Betarists participated in an instructor's course in Zelanke in 1933 under the leadership of Yerucham Halperin. Later, they taught physical education and exercises with wooden poles. The teaching was excellent – all the exercises were conducted in Hebrew.

A number of Betarists went to Hachshara (agricultural training) outside Brest in order to prepare for making aliyah to Israel. However, due to the small number of certificates allotted to Betar, there were not many who achieved this. After leaving the general Zionist movement, Betar did not receive any certificates at all. The division conducted a large number of diverse activities. They participated in the undertaking of land surveying and petitioning for free aliyah.

At the Brest district conference, attended by some 600 members, it was decided on the initiative of the Brest Betar commander Menachem Begin, and after consultation with the members, to hold a demonstration. This demonstration was impressive, with over 600 members in uniforms and arms marching. This demonstration showed the results of the Betar training methods. Despite their strong desire to go to Israel, the majority of the members did not achieve this, and they perished together with their brother Briskers.

Only a few legally came to Israel before and during W.W.2.... only a few survived from this great Brest youth movement.

Some of the commanders of the various groups of the Brest division were: Berl Zigman, Yitzchak Hocker, Menachem Begin, Shlomo Goldstein, A. Kamenetski, and Zelig Orenstein who were all active before W.W.2.

In 1936 there was a general Betar assembly in Brest, amongst them were: Shlomo Goldstein, Hannah Malin, Moshe Ramo, Zelig Orenstein, Avraham and Moshe Kamenetski, Avigdor Tennenbaum and others who did not manage to save themselves and were murdered by the Nazis.

B. Brit Hazahar

Was also founded in 1929, and consisted of adults who did not qualify for Betar because of their age. This was a very active group of over 600 members. Amongst this group were representatives who held important and influential positions in the professional and social life of the city and the municipal institutions: The city council, the kehilla council, TOZ, ORT and others.

Brit Hazahar supported an institute in Brest for Jewish education and Zionism under the directorship of Dr. Moshe Steiner and Moshe Rabinovitch. Brit Hazahar formed a cultural group called "Kadimah" for cultural activities and lectures. The chairman of this group was Dr Moshe Steiner, others were: the lawyer Kreitstein, Eliezer Fein, Dr. Israel Leschner, especially dedicated were: David Elivetski and Yehuda Rosenman. In the Kadimah club much was accomplished by Shmerel Zbar and the engineer Steinberg.

C. Masada

The branch of Masada was formed in 1934 for students and high school children, and had about 150 members. It was organized by Polish speaking circles who were studying Hebrew. Shlomo Goldstein and Borka Krantz headed it, active members were Shmuel (Mula) Pomerantz, Itta Steinberg, Leila Kiblitzka, Daitchman, and Michael Goldberg.

D. El-Al

The El-Al group was group of academic revisionists. It was headed by Avigdor Grynberg and included: Yakov Zunshine, Moshe Landau, Shamai

Fruchtgarten, Leon Katzaf, Reuven Zablud, Dov Haro and others. The founder was Dr. Moshe Steiner.

E. Brit Hachayal

This group had 300 members - adult Jews who at one time or another had had military service. Within this group were former military men, ex-servicemen who were attracted to Zionism and active in the revisionist movement. Their commander was Mordechai Lutenberg, and especially active were Boris Rogozhik and Moshe Bielarus.

F. Veref. (National Women's Group)

Was formed in 1931 by Bertha Halasz. Members were Lisa Fein, Luba Feinberg, Luba Konopita, Frania Steinberg, Fanya Miller, and Pola Molier. The Chairwoman was Chasia Shatz, and after her Dr. Fanya Zeligson.

G. Nordia

Nordia was a national sports club that participated in local and inter-city competitions in football and boxing. Active members were Weinstock, Reuven Zablud, and Leon Katsaf.

H. Brit Yeshurun (Achdut Israel)

This group was under Brit Hazahar, and led by Rabbi Moshe Reuven Golevski, who was the son-in-law of Rabbi Simcha Zelig. Rabbi Moshe was elected as delegate to the revisionist congress in Vienna. This group of orthodox Jews had previously gone under the name of Achdut Israel.

I. Keren Tel-Chai

This was the financial arm of the revisionist movement -founded in Brest in 1930. The director was Eliezer Fein. Keren Tel-Chai would organize annual exhibitions.

J. Etzel

Few people know that already in 1938 there was a secret group of Irgun Tzva Leumi on Brest. It was formed by the efforts of Fishel Bankhalter and Shlomo Goldstein. Contact was made with the national commander of Etzel in Poland - Nathan Yellin Freidman - who visited Brest himself and praised the excellence of the work of the local branch.

In 1939 two members – David Begin, and Chaim Zilber participated in a military training course at Ivaniki near Pinsk, under the instruction of an emissary from Israel. Upon their return they both worked very energetically to form a new group of Betarists who would receive secret military training for special covert operations.

Purchases of arms and hand grenades were made from the Poles for this purpose, and the members were taught how to use the weapons and ammunition. No one knew of the existence of the Etzel group in Brest – not even the local Betar commanders. Their activity was conducted in the strictest secrecy and their cache of arms was hidden at the outbreak of W.W.2.

Only four Betar members managed to reach Israel. Of them three were active in the Lehi (the Stern gang) movement. One of them, David Begin, arrived in Israel in 1941 via Lithuania and Russia. He was one of the active commanders in Lehi – in 1944 he was arrested and sentenced by the British to 12 years imprisonment. He escaped from Acre prison in 1947.

An important personality who originated from the Brest revisionists and later held important positions in Israel was Menachem Begin who was the chief commander of Etzel in Israel, and is now the leader of the Herut party and a member of the Knesset.

The Betar Conference in Brest, Lag Ba -Omer, 1929

Ze'ev Jabotinski visits Brest in 1936
This photo was taken outside the Grynberg home
on Dabrowska St. where this meeting took place.
Circled are (left) Menachem Begin, and Ze'ev Jabotinski
Photo courtesy of Jack Grynberg

[Page 489]

The Bund

by Berl Kotlinsky, New York
Translated by Dr. Samuel Chani and Jenni Buch

I was a member of the Bund in Brest since 1905. In those days great revolutionary events occurred and strikes broke out throughout the Russian empire. The strike atmosphere also prevailed in Brest. The Bund – a Jewish worker's organization, conducted agitation in the workers groups, and also amongst the Christian workers, the Bund organized and addressed a meeting of the railway workers.

One of the best agitators amongst the Christian worker's groups was Sher the watchmaker; he was the son of Anschel Sher, a violinist with the Brest Orchestra. He spoke good Russian and achieved much influence with his oratory talents

The Brest branch of the Bund numbered 800 members, but 1000's of Jewish workers were ready to support them. The Bund was purely a workers organization – even it's leaders were workers. In order to assist the local leaders in their activities, the central committee of the party sent four officials to Brest who were expert in revolutionary activities. These 'professionals' were themselves not workers, they originated from other classes, but were passionate idealists who, instead of becoming doctors, lawyers, and businessmen – had adopted the revolutionary cause.

They rotted in prisons and Siberian exile – and some of them sacrificed their lives in the struggle against the Tsarist regime. At the head of these officials was a 'David'. This 'David' was one of the most outstanding personalities that I have ever met in my life. He was the treasurer of the Bund, and he allotted every employee three rubles a week for the purpose of living expenses and rent. Newspapers and books he purchased at his own expense – every Monday morning he would wait at the railway station for the delivery of newspapers and journals from St. Petersburg. As soon as they arrived he would run and collect them and immediately return to his humble room to read them.

The Bund in Brest was also the headquarters of the Bund for the entire Brest district. We wanted to be called the Brest committee, as was the Bialystok committee, the Dvinsk committee, and so on... we thought it was our entitlement as we had the greatest number of members and were very active, but the central committee had other ideas and refused to give us this right, so we were called the District Committee.

The Bund held an important position in the community life of Brest. It organized strikes and financially supported several groups whereby they could read socialist books and pamphlets, gave instructions to agitators, and spread revolutionary information.

We provided the information that was not printed in the government press to give the workers hope for a better world. We idealized the heroes and martyrs that were willing to sacrifice their lives for their beliefs – we were ready to follow their example. The party activities were banned – all the work was done in secret, we could not hold public meetings to address the people. Therefore, we organized large meetings in the synagogues and even at the cemetery. The Bund was strong in Brest and the synagogue officials did not dare denounce us to the authorities.

One of the largest meetings took place on the occasion of Wladek's visit to Brest. The synagogue was packed full and the workers listened to every word of his fiery speech, although this was an illegal meeting and attendance could result in imprisonment, there were several prominent people present.

I remember also a large meeting at the funeral of the Bundist 'Matil' who had drowned. On the day of the funeral, almost every worker in Brest left their workshops and factories and positioned themselves in an honor guard of two rows from the length of Matil's house to the cemetery. Then there took place one of the greatest revolutionary meetings ever held in Brest. The police did not dare interfere, they did not intervene in the funeral and it was an unforgettable event.

The most beloved leader of the workers at that time was Shloime the Shneider (tailor). Besides his great intelligence and personality he was a popular and loyal comrade. His home was a meeting place for Bund members from all the provinces. When a revolutionary would arrive and had no place to stay, Shloime would take him home and share his meal with him.

At Shloime's I met a member of the Central Committee, Beinish Michalovitch (Izbitzki), who arrived with important orders from the central committee. Izbitzki himself was a Brisker and had many relatives there. Shloime the tailor was liked and treasured by all the Bundists, and also by non-affiliated people. He was a very modest man – I remember in the 1905 revolution when practically the entire city was under Bundist control – the discussion in our group was about who would be the commandant of the Brest Fortress. Shloime was suggested as a candidate, but he refused emphatically.

A Bundist who was a legend in Brest was Fessel Kotlianski. She owned a dress salon for the wealthy, and the wives of the Russian officers. The first female members of the Bund thought it a great privilege to work for her. According to Tchernichevski (his rules of what to do), this was an exemplary example of how a workshop should be run in a socialist regime. Her workers were not treated as mere laborers but as equals in her factory – this was the first workplace that was conducted on an eight-hour working day basis.

Fessel was not the only female member of the Bund –we cannot forget Grandma – that's how she was known by all. She took care of all her comrades in Brest. Whenever a worker was ill or imprisoned, Grandma would appear to give help. She watched over all her members, she knew who needed clothes or a pair of shoes, and would fix it accordingly. Grandma's wedding was a great celebration in the city. All the workers came in large masses and the evening was spent singing revolutionary songs together.

The most respected activist and leader was Reuven Salzman "Reuven the Tailor". He was the eternal optimist. With his simple and well-defined words he would give hope and courage in the worst of times. He would say:" All the tyrants will be defeated and we will win, because the truth is with us." He was a capable and talented organizer and attracted many new members. After his arrest, little remained of the party. At that time the reactionaries reigned – they conducted many arrests and raids and all the members were affected.

When Pesach Novick took over the leadership of the organization, there were only remnants left of the former Bund Party. However, there were a few stubborn revolutionaries left who were not afraid of arrest. They resurrected the party and conducted agitation through the Jewish working classes; they gave lessons in socialism and provided revolutionary material for them to read.

Pesach and I would go every Saturday to visit Reuven in prison, in order to consult with him about party matters. Beforehand, we would bring books to the head warder of the prison and request permission to bring this with us into the prison. Often, permission would be granted – even for books that were not officially sanctioned. Then there would be great joy that we had tricked them. Food was brought to Reuven almost daily. His mother would prepare the food in a pot with a double lid in which forbidden items were hidden – circulars, proclamations, forged passports, and sometimes money.

It was a hard life to be a revolutionary under the Tsarist regime, but it was even harder for a Jewish revolutionary. Aside from the persecutions of the Tsarists, there were troubles from the religious Jewish fanatics around them.

Despite all this, there were thousands of stubborn young people who were willing to sacrifice their souls for their ideals. They all participated in the overthrow of the Tsarist regime, with the revolutionaries of Brest cooperating fully in this endeavor.

The Bund Conference in 1936
In the front are the 3 leaders of the Bundist Movement
- they were sent to Siberia in 1939 by the Russians and never returned -
R to L: Shtorch, David Shneider, and Israel Tennenbaum

[Page 493]

In the Underground

by Leizor Kling, New York
Translated by Dr. Samuel Chani and Jenni Buch

I was arrested by the Tsarist police in Biala Podlaska in1909. Because I was an active Bundist, after a period of six months the gendarmerie (police) informed me that I would be sentenced according to articles 102 and 129 – which meant six years hard labor and then exiled to Siberia for a long time. As the police had not managed to build an official case against me during these six months, I was temporarily released. My parents immediately left for Warsaw to consult with a famous lawyer – Fotek of the Polish Socialist Party. Fotek had much experience defending in political trials. His advice was that I should immediately leave for abroad whilst he studied the charges and considered what I should do.

I went to Cracow – which was then Austria, and after about six months Fotek informed me that the police had not found enough incriminating evidence according to paragraph 102, but that the secret police could banish me from the country and exile me to Siberia. I decided to return to Russia, and surrendered to the police who expelled me from 10 gubernias (provinces). In Russian it was called "Bestrochniya Tzelka". My passport was confiscated and my record listed me as a danger to society.

In the beginning, I thought, well Russia is huge and I'll find a town to settle in, but I soon realized that the matter was not so simple. Wherever I went – Bialystok, Grodno, Kovno, Minsk or Vilna – I would have to report to the police and was ordered to immediately leave the town if I did not want to go to prison.

Upon arriving in Brest I was called to the office of His Honor the Grodno Chief of Police. He began to curse me, how I, a dangerous element, had the nerve to come to a city like Brest with it's large military fortress. In a great rage he grabbed me by the hair and threw me out of his office with a Russian "Misheberach" (blessing). Notwithstanding this, the Bundists in Brest were old friends, who wanted me to stay in Brest, and despite everything, stay legally.

In 1911-12 the Bundists in Brest, as everywhere else were self-supporting and had reorganized themselves. They needed useful speakers and activists. They knew that I was a veteran Bundist and a good orator, and it was decided that I should remain in Brest.

The renowned Bundist official, Shloime Shneider met with a police official of the city – A.Makorov, who registered me at his address. I would have to pay him monthly rent of three rubles. After obtaining the right of residency, I had to face the problem of earning a living. The Brest Bund was impoverished, and could not at that time cover my expenses – but just then the printing firm "Kobrynets" received an order to print a 500-page book – General Kurapatkia's memoirs of the Russo-Japanese War (1905). I received a position as a typesetter.

The Bund at that time was developing and organizing the worker's groups: bookmakers, tailors, metalsmiths, building laborers and associated trades as well as female workers. Especially active in these group meetings were: Moshe Shapiro, a student and editor of the student Russian newspaper in Brest. After the revolution, he became assistant Commissioner for Education in St. Petersburg. The brothers Chaim and Shimshon Riger – the sons of the Dayan (rabbinical judge), Simcha Zelig Riger. Shmulke Muller, who was later wounded in the Bundist self- defence force. Shloime Shneider, and others.

Our work grew rapidly and we printed daily proclamations. However, no printer would print our proclamations. We wanted to purchase printing machines and open a printing press, but no one would sell us the equipment. The party decided to simply steal the lettering machines from the Kobrynets plant, and to form a clandestine printing press.

Each day, I would take lead letters from their boxes, conceal them in a feather quilt, and pass it to a comrade who would be waiting outside to take it away. In three weeks time we had an illegal press with all the machinery. We achieved the matter in the following manner: the binder would make 20 cardboard boxes that we would fill with our pamphlets, the printing equipment we all carried in our pockets.

We rented a room from a poor elderly married couple and printed out our proclamations there. Chaim Riger was the head setter of the press. The elderly couple noticed that every evening the room would be full of well-dressed young people, and students who would stay there until late in the night, and they were most unhappy. They suspected that we were printing counterfeit money. One winter evening, they told comrade Riger, that if he didn't move out with all his boxes, they would report him to the police. All his begging to them to wait an hour until he brought boxes to move the material did not help. The couple demanded that he remove the suspect materials immediately. Riger bought an old sack from them, put all the printing tools in it and wanted to move this to a member's home until we could find an appropriate place. He put the large sack on his shoulder and began to walk, attracting the suspicions of a policeman who demanded that he stop and wanted to see the contents of the sack he was dragging. Riger stammered as he was nervous –the policeman opened a box and found lead letters. He took Riger to the police station. Several Bundist members of the boot makers group witnessed this and decided to rescue Riger from his predicament. With much chutzpah they announced to the policeman that it was a great shame for a rabbi's son to be taken to the police station. At the same time they pressed a ruble into the policeman's hand.

The policeman immediately changed his expression, returned the sack to Riger, and asked him to disappear at once, so that he would not have to share the ruble with his colleagues.

I had a lot of satisfaction from my life in Brest, beside the Bund activity I was close to my hometown of Biala Podlaska, where my family lived. At one point the Bialer Bund asked me to return secretly and make a speech there. I arrived in the morning and was given a place to stay in secret. I stayed there several weeks and was again arrested.

My fiancé exerted all her means to get only one policeman to escort me back to Brest and hand me over to the police commandant. This policeman duly transferred me to the police chief and said "have pity on your girl (fiance) and stay quiet here in Brest, if you don't want to end up in Siberia".

I should mention that the entire time I stayed in Brest, there was not one Bundist denounced by the public to the police. Yet when I arrived in Biala Podlaska for a few weeks, I was denounced by someone to the police and found myself in the Bialer prison. This is a great credit to the Bund in Brest.

[Page 489]

The First Group of Brest Halutzim

by D. Ophir
Translated by Dr. Samuel Chani and Jenni Buch

The Halutz (pioneer) movement came later to Brest than other places as Brest had no civilian population during the four years of W.W.1 It was only after the residents returned to their city, that the pioneer movement was established in Brest in 1919 and greeted with enthusiasm by the youth.

In the beginning, three young men decided to approach the youth by issuing a proclamation urging them to join the "halutz " movement. They did this in this simple manner. One of them who had a nice handwriting wrote the proclamation in Yiddish and Hebrew, and at night they posted them on the walls all over the city, asking the young people to join this movement and to enrol at Topolowa 12. In the following weeks several dozen young men signed up and one girl. It was hoped that they would immediately be able to leave for Israel. There was talk of a group who had managed to make aliyah in 1918. We undertook to build this first group of pioneers of 14 pioneers without delay. Mordechai Yaffe was the 15th – he joined them in Israel. C. Beloch who was the oldest headed the group. All of the members were working-class men who had experienced the war and occupation. They had all endured varying degrees of hell in forced labor for the German army - in forestry, metal work, agriculture and other construction work. They had also been taught carpentry and practical skills from an elderly carpenter who lived in the suburbs of Brest. Because of these skills they could independently work upon arrival in Israel and accept jobs such as building the railway line between Lod to the British Military camp at Sarafen, and the construction of barracks for the British Army there.

The ambition of these members was essentially to work in agriculture. Several members had had agricultural experience in the villages surrounding Brest during the time of the expulsion from Brest in W.W.1 They knew how the cut with scythes, thresh the wheat with poles, plough, bind the bales of hay, planting of vegetables, and milking, etc. Many of the Briskers really became agricultural experts and taught agriculture to classes in the settlements of Israel.

The most vital and important question was how to cover the costs of the journey to Israel.

They established a local emigration fund - (the word aliyah was unknown to us at that time). The sum needed to send the 14 members was realized almost immediately. These were: Gershon Halperin (Drori), Aaron Richwert (Amitai), Noah Minkovitch (Shalmoni), Israel Saptiter (Sapir), David Goldberg (Ophir), Eliezer Shapiro, Joseph Machlis (Ben-Porat), Israel Golubovitch (Agun), Joshua Melnik (Kimchi), Berl Domberg (Gorni), engineer Eliezer Balloch, Nissan Daitchman (Ashkenazi), Guterman, and Mordechai Yaffe.

There was a great celebration and demonstration of joy at the departure of the first group of pioneers. Thousands of people accompanied us to the train. In our hometowns there was still hunger and we believed that Israel was in the same situation – so we prepared much food – sacks of biscuits, sacks of rice, buckwheat and greens. The carriage was filled with food and a huge crate that the members built themselves containing a great many utensils and work tools. Saws, axes, hammers, screwdrivers and other tools. The crate was reinforced with steel corners and a large lock. We had a great deal of trouble with this crate on our journey. Every transfer from train to train, station to station involved great effort and exhausted us. We dragged it like soldiers – four strong young comrades lifted it – four of the others would occupy the compartment and would let no one inside until the sacks of food and the crate were brought inside.

After arriving in Israel, we tossed all the food into the sea because on our first day we had received a wonderful meal – we tasted white bread for the first time in five years. Before leaving for Israel the central headquarters of the Halutz movement in Warsaw had organized for us to be in Grochow – a pioneer farm with green fields, a cowshed and a garden where we got a taste of the atmosphere of Eretz Israel. In Grochow we were joined by a girl who travelled with us until we reached Israel, and then left us.

In Vienna our group was split into two due to a shortage of money. The first group went by boat to Israel whilst the second had to remain in Vienna for several weeks. Arriving at the famous port of Jaffa, we were taken ashore by the Arab porters. These port workers were familiar with heavy items – they could lift large containers or heavy passengers. However, they had great difficulty in managing the transfer of our crate to the small boat.

The office of the Young Workers had us registered to go to Betania because we had requested agricultural work. We rested at the hotel "Presov" for several days and then we travelled. There were no passenger trains at that time from Jaffa to Lod so we travelled in a freight carriage. Yehuda Almog (Kapilevitch) himself dragged our bags and packages – we ourselves dragged the crate from place to place until we arrived tired and exhausted at a place that had no trees or buildings.

At Betania there was a group called "Dror" which was the nucleus of the Kibbutz Artzi and then later the Hashomer Hatzair Party. The atmosphere of " our community" was not felt there, and the comrades from Brest did not feel welcome there. We did not know any tricks and could not understand the spirit of Betania. The isolation, the tiptoeing around - we were not able to make friends with them, as they did not allow us to make friends or become close to them. We sat there for a whole week – nobody was interested in us or told us what to do. We saw that there was no place for us there and heard that next to Tiberias there was a large workers camp. They were building a road to Tzemach – the first road built by the members of the third aliyah.

In reality we wanted agricultural work, and had arrived there for that purpose, but we couldn't sit around and not work. We sent out a pair of 'spies' who returned that night with the news that there was work on the Tiberias – Tzemach road. Without delay, the next morning we hired a boat from an Arab, piled in all our belongings and were on our way. After several hours sailing we arrived at the port of Tiberias. At the labor office we were well received, our baggage loaded onto donkeys and thus we arrived at the camp called "Hamei Tiberias" The camp had about 500 workers and was on the shores of the Kinneret (Sea of Galilee). In the front were straw huts; behind them was an old building which was the kitchen.

We were allocated two huts and slept on the ground on straw mats. The wind from the mountains blew particles of dust and sand and the huts became full of it. In the morning we arose and washed off all the dust and sand in the Kinneret.

In time our group became renowned in the Tiberias - Tzemach road project. We were considered as outstanding workers - especially excelling was Nissan Daitchman (Ashkenazi). The work was very hard and the pay very little – we had to be thrifty – we wore sandals made out of old tyres that the shoemakers from Tiberias supplied. In the first days of our road building, we all became ill. The hot hamsims (desert winds) were unbearable; the temperature was over 45 degrees Celsius. We spent several days in a temporary hospital in Tiberias. Then the heat dropped and we returned to the road building. We were becoming experienced 'old-timers'. Before the holydays an emissary visited us from the other part of our original group, who had arrived two weeks after us. They had been sent directly to Jerusalem to level off the site for the Hebrew University on Mount Scopus. They were called the Mount Scopus group. Their emissary came to consult with us on how the two groups could be reunited.

In order to reunite with our comrades, we accepted an offer to transfer to the British military camp at Sarafen to work on the construction of the camp. We rented a house at Be'er Yakov from a farmer and began to work building the barracks at the camp. We knew our craft well and earned good money for this 'lighter' work. We could afford good food and our morale lifted from day to day.

The British proposed to the labor office of Hapoel Hatzair (there was not yet a Solel Boneh) that they build a stretch of railway line between Lod and Sarafen. None of the older workers possessed these skills. Jews had never built railway tracks! But our group had several members who had worked in forced labor gangs on railway lines under the German occupation. Therefore, we succeeded in obtaining the British project.

For this work we had to live close to the railway lines – we erected huts in the open fields and lived in them for several months until the Arab riots on the Ist of May 1921. On that day - the workers holiday, the whole group had gone to Tel-Aviv except for two guards. During this unrest, one of our group was murdered and we were transferred to a larger work camp.

We began to knock on the doors of the various institutions demanding that they settle us on agricultural land. They offered us Hulda - to replace some of the locals who had accepted work at Kfar Yehezkel. We accepted this offer with joy, and transferred to Hulda at the end of 1921. However, we couldn't stay there for long, as the Hulda group was not financially viable. Water had to be brought from ancient Arab wells – an old blind Arab would supply the water in buckets. One could not reach there in winter, so all the harvested produce rotted in the sheds.

Two years later, our group, which was known for it's skilled and capable workers, was transferred to Kfar Yehezkel. We stayed there for a year until we obtained independent agricultural work in Sharona in the lower Galilee, which belonged to the 'Ahuza' company. Sharona also did not have a stable agricultural economy. Water was scarce. The land was partially occupied by Arab leaseholders that yielded a little grain because of their improper and inconsistent land use. All our fervent efforts and idealism did not succeed in establishing a good economic basis for this land.

A few years later, we looked around for possible colonization sites in the Jordan valley. Once again, we sent out 'spies' to find the land –a small hill called Tel Toreh was found in the middle of a rich agricultural district in which we wanted to settle. The members of Nachalal knew of this land, and were opposed to it because the land was too low, and flooded in water in winter. They advised us to settle in Ein Bodeh, near Nachalal – a place of light and fertile soil. We discussed it between ourselves at length until we decided to take up their proposal.

It took us a whole year to shift from Sharona to Ein Badeh. A year of troubles, hunger and pain. The land of Israel was experiencing a severe economic crisis. We bought a military hut and erected a small barracks outside Afula that we used as a dining room and sleeping quarters for 20 men. In summer we ate outdoors and in winter we sat on the beds eating our meagre piece of bread. There was little work and the pay was not enough to buy food.

Whilst in Afula, the group was offered paid work in Ganigar to build a hut. Several of the comrades went to Ganigar. During their stay a tragedy occurred there. Joseph Machlis (Ben Porat), a young dedicated comrade became ill and died within three days. Two days after his death, his girlfriend committed suicide – an eighteen-year-old girl who burnt herself to death. She died in terrible pain. This double tragedy shattered our group.

Finally, in Tevet 1927, our group transferred to our own land at Ein Bodeh, near the settlement of Nachalal. On a beautiful cool day, we went with our two heavily laden wagons on the sandy unmade tracks from Afula to Nachalal, following the shepherds' tracks through the untrodden thorny fields. The wagons dragged on with our group's few possessions – beds, straw mattresses, long benches and the famous Brisker crate. At nightfall our wagons reached a clearing with a fence of prickly pears (sabras) as tall as trees. The rains were late that year and the earth was dry, cracked and thirsty, and a cloud of grey dust followed us the entire journey from Afula to our new home.

We erected several temporary huts, made a fire in the field and cooked our evening meal. Excited but exhausted we threw ourselves onto the straw mattresses and went to sleep knowing that many troubles and great efforts awaited us.

Five years later, the farm had grown and developed – the stables were full of cattle, the yard was full of machinery and tractors, but the destiny of the Brest group seemed to be to build and develop for others. The members never involved themselves deeply in the problems of the economy of agriculture and farming, whether it was better to become an agricultural settlement of workers (moshav) or a kibbutz. There was an unspoken peaceful agreement between the members not to touch on issues that could cause a split and divide them. But with the growth of the farm the members became involved in the problems of farming and agriculture, and a shadow fell over the group. It became clear that several members wanted to establish a moshav (workers settlement) and the conflict dragged on for a long period and caused a split in the group. The members, who supported the moshav idea, left the place where they had expended so much youthful energy. However, also the members who supported the kibbutz idea did not stay there either. New members arrived and built up the kibbutz that was called Kibbutz Ayanot.

The long hard road that the Brest comrades had achieved as a group had not been in vain. The comrades all came out as strong, educated, skilled workers, with work and life skills. Many of them are, until today, dedicated social activists. They are convinced that they, the first Brest pioneer group, showed the way for hundreds and thousands of those who arrived in Israel from Brest – Briskers who lived and had influence in the nation of Israel.

The First Pioneer Members in Brest
Standing R-L: D. Kotik, Topok, A. Shalmoni
Sitting R-L: unknown, unknown, S. Swartz,
Chaya (Chantche) Yaffe, Chaya Cohen, unknown

The Brest Pioneer Group 1919
Standing R-L: S. Golubovitch,(Arnon), Y. Melnik (Kimchi), Hari, Z. Resnik (Avivi), Gorni, B.Preger, I. Saptiter (Sapir), D. Goldberg (Ophir)
Sitting: Daitchman (Ashkenazi), G. Halperin (Drori), Chava Cohen-Gratzer, Y. Govkin, N. Minkovitch (Shalmoni), Guterman
Bottom row: S. Shwartz, Y. Machlis (Ben-Porat), Chaya Yaffe, D. Domberg, A. Richtwert (Amitai)

The first Brest pioneers laying railway track between Lod and Sarafen in 1921

The Yiddish Press In Brisk D'Lita

by Mordechai Ginsburg (Montreal)
Translated by Dr. Samuel Chani and Jenni Buch

The first issue of the weekly Polessie Shtimme (Voice of Polessie) appeared on the 18th September 1923. There had possibly been previous attempts to publish an edition, but the Polessie Shtimme was the first Yiddish periodical newspaper in Brest. It appeared under the editorship of M. Drachler – the publisher was Dr. Bronislaw Wilner who later became the Deputy Mayor of Brest.

One has to add that due to the ruling powers and demands of that time imposed upon a Yiddish newspaper – that every newspaper reflected the many facets of Jewish life in Brest and dealt with all the problems confronting the community at that time.

Polessie Shtimme did not last for an entire year due to a shortage of resources. Arriving in Brest in 1924, I made contact with Dr. Wilner and the printer Y. Gendler. As a result of our negotiations, I took over the editorship from the 1st September 1924. After an interval of six months, the paper re-appeared.

We very quickly came into conflict with the administrative powers after the first editions were published. It emerged that the Brest police chief was a keen reader of our paper – as soon as my editorial would touch upon the issue of Vilna, he would politely call me the next day to his office and advise me that in the future we should not interest ourselves in how the government of Poland handles Vilna. But our paper remained steadfast and campaigned for all sorts of social injustices.

Due to inner wrangling amongst the editors the existence of the paper was interrupted once again. The paper reappeared on the 25th April 1925, under the title of "Polessie Wochenblatt" (Weekly), and quickly became very popular amongst the Jewish community of Brest and district. The community recognized that the paper was an advocate for it's rights, and would fight against injustice and for social and cultural reforms.

Again, the paper was under the leadership of established Zionist activists. The paper underwent several stages, changed owners, but essentially remained committed to the public interest and fought for the national and social rights of the Jewish masses.

We should recall several of our important activists who participated in spreading the literary and moral values of the paper: L.Y. Winnikoff, the Zionist leader in Brest. His brother the engineer Aaron Winnikoff (Aharoni), David Zisman the leader of the Mizrachi movement, Felman the leader of the small traders organization, Padwa the director of the Merchant Bank, Zablud and Grynberg of the artisans union, and the leaders of the Tarbut organization, as well as the teachers. Fanaberia and Menachowski from the

Borochow Yiddish school, and almost all of the Brest doctors such as Br. Begun who was the chairman of ORT. Dr. Reisler, who was the head doctor at the medical clinic and a social worker. Savshitski the chairman of the hospital, Rabbi Alter Grosleit, the chairman of the Linat Hatzedek (the paupers hostel), Noah Pozezinski, who was a city councilor, Skorbnik, Dr Yitzchak Kagan, who was an important social activist who recently died in New York. The employees of the old age home and others who contributed.

In the Brisker Wochenblatt also participated: Tzvi Lomazhevski, Israel London, M. Menachowski, Hershel Fanaberia, Ze'ev Lutwak, headmaster of the Tarbut school, and all those who had some literary talent.... H. Breinhendler, Izbitzer, the humorist Chune Rabinovitch, Israel Noy, Marcuze, Kaplan, and many others, including those from outside Brest.

We often would receive articles from Jewish members of parliament from Galicia, such as Moshe Prostig, Senator Rottenstreich, Dr. Joshua Tahun, Dr Jerzy Rosenblatt from Lodz and others.

The success of the Brisker Wochenblatt attracted much attention from the surrounding towns such as Pinsk, Kobryn, Pruzhany, etc. Consequently, it was through the initative of engineer Avraham Levitas of Kobryn that several other editions of the Brest Wochenblatt were printed with headings that read: Kobryner Shtimme, Pruzhaner Shtimme, etc. Every edition would contain it's own local section of news and events, written by Levitas, Noah Alcan, and Y. Faigenboim. These articles were delivered by messengers who would arrive every Thursday morning by train – they would return on Fridays with the printed editions of the Kobryner Shtimme.

The idea arose to create a special Polessie section in the Warsaw newspapers, but no one was interested beside the Red Express. It meant printing the entire Red Express leaving the heading on the front-page blank – in Brest they would then insert the "Brisker Tagenblatt" (daily) heading, and later Polessie Tagenblatt. Often the paper would not arrive at all due to technical and administrative difficulties – the page reserved for the news would appear in the following day's edition...

I must mention that the articles from the Brisker Wochenblatt would be reprinted in many other Yiddish newspapers in Poland, such as the "Heint" (Warsaw), the Lodzer Daily, and "Der Zeit" (The Times) of Vilna. "Unzer Leben" (Our Life) in Bialystok would reprint our articles and columns weekly. There were instances when an article written in the Brisker Wochenblatt would be reprinted up to 15 times in various newspapers the following week.

Standing R-L: Tzvi Lomazhevski, I. London, A. Kaplan, M. Drachler,
Dr. B. Wilner, Y. Babich, Z. Zaretski, D. Zisman
Sitting R-L: Z. Shedrovitski, N. Marcuze, Y.Gendler, Hellman,
M. Breinhendler, Rubinstein, Rabinovitch, Israel Noy

Mastheads of the Yiddish press in Brest

[Page 511]

ECONOMIC ORGANIZATION

The Jewish Population in the 19th Century

Translated by Dr. Samuel Chani and Jenni Buch

According to the 1864 census there were 19,302 inhabitants of Brest and 812 houses. By 1889 the population had risen to 41,615 and 2063 houses. The number of Jews was estimated at 27.005. The number of Jews classed by professional categories was: Tradesmen 3464, Merchants (traders) 1235, and Industrial workers 1000.

The two great fires that occurred within a short period in the Jewish quarter –17th May 1895, and the 11th May 1901 destroyed a large part of the city.

According to the mid- 19th century census of 1847 there were the following number of Jews in Brest and the district around Brest:

Community	Men	Women	Total
Brisk D'Lita	3557	4579	8636
Wlodawa	147	225	372
Wysokie Litovsk	780	695	1475
Volchin	328	558	886
Kamenetz Litovsk	645	806	1451
Total of district	**5457**	**6863**	**12,320**

Regarding the relevance of Jews to the development and growth of the city we can learn from the following population 19th century statistics. The number of Jews in Brest in 1881 was: men 3837, women 4066, total 7903. In 1897 the figures were: men 15,033, women 15,575, total 30,608. The Jews were occupied in the following professions: Tailors, shoemakers, bakers, carpenters, blacksmiths, locksmiths, and stonemasons. The Jewish footwear industry was conducted at all the markets of central Russia and Crimea.

The proportion of Jews to the general pop. In 1897 was:

Place	General Pop.	Jewish Pop.
Volchin	617	588
Wysokie Lit.	3434	2876
Domachevo	1180	1057
Zamotzche (near Kam. Lit.)	1288	976
Kamenetz Lit.	3569	2722
Malorita	1480	227
Mileitchik	1685	814
Tchernovitchik	1209	481
Tchernigov	678	85

The total count of the Jewish schools and yeshivas was 30. There were 5 libraries, and 8 printing presses. The credit institutions – the Loans and Savings Fund, the Merchant bank, and the Credit Society for Small Traders, all played a significant role in the development of the trade and business of the city and district.

(From the Jewish Encyclopedia St Petersburg 1909).

[Page 513]

The Jewish Community Council (Kehilla) in Brisk D'Lita

by Sholem Schwartz
Translated by Dr. Samuel Chani and Jenni Buch

At the beginning of 1919 a district conference concerning the establishment of Jewish community councils (Kehillas) was held at 12 Topolowa st. This street name was later changed to I.L. Peretz St.) It was decided that the elections to these councils should be democratic and that the Kehillas should be democratic and secular.

Two years later the famous Pilsudski decree was issued which allowed the establishment of religious councils. However, there was not even a religious council established in Brest – the formation was delayed for another 8 years. Only in 1929 did the first election take place due to pressure from the Jewish parties. The elected chairmen of the board were Shlomo Lichtenstein and Avraham Skorbnik from the city council. This board only met very rarely –once a year to determine the budget. The district governor (Voiyevoda) would read out the list for the council administration and Dr. Y. Kagan was nominated on the spot as chairman.

The second Kehilla was entirely different – it began it's activity in 1935.The convening of the administration of the kehilla was much more democratic. The elected head of the kehilla was Chaim Baruch Kwiartowski and the members were: Asher Ashkenazi, David Gitelman, Mattityahu Zablud, Shimon Savshitski, Englender, Meir Feinstein, Kronczek, David Shneider and Sholem Schwarz.

This new Kehilla was not only the representative organ of the community in external affairs, but also a strong influence in the economic and social affairs of the city. It participated with vigour in the battle against anti Semitism. As we know, Poland introduced a law forbidding Jewish ritual slaughtering. Our kehilla conducted a campaign against this law for weeks and collected 15,00 zlotys for the meatworkers who were suffering as a result of this ban.

The popularity of the Kehilla grew and the meetings were attended by 100s of Brest Jews.

Immediately at the outset of this new Kehilla it was determined that the Kehilla would meet 2-3 times weekly, and that this council would be very active. There were various sub committees elected: Finance, Economic, Taxation, and Social Assistance.One of the sub committees was for community welfare, which resolved that:

A. All the social institutions in the city would come under the administration of the Kehilla.

B. The institutions that could not be transferred to the Kehilla at that time would still be supported by the direct involvement of the Kehilla.

C. The assistance given by the Kehilla should be constructive.

The Kehilla achieved a great deal in those difficult times

A special chapter in the activity of the Kehilla occurred when the pogrom took place in Brest on the 13th May 1937. The formation of the OZON party, which often spoke of the destruction of Jews the relationship between Jews and Poles became more strained. Anti- Semitic riots took place in many Polish towns, and anti- Semitic leaflets were distributed amongst the Christian communities.

In this tense atmosphere the following occurred: the young Jewish butcher Tcherbowski stabbed the Polish secret policeman Kendrzara. This was soon followed by a full-blown pogrom incited and instigated by the police. The Poles began robbing and looting the Jewish stores and beating up Jews.

When I went to the Kehilla for advice and guidance in what should be done, I encountered the Polish police instead of the council members. The police were looking for the Jews who had apparently thrown stones at the Christians....

The deputy mayor, Yechiel Mastboim reported that the district governor was in no hurry to stop the pogrom. We immediately organized the Jewish carriers, wagon drivers, and meat workers - and by midday had already formed the first resistance stand. The lawyer Nachman Glovinski, Dr. Sarnake and Yechiel Mastboim the deputy mayor went to the Brest fortress to meet with the Commander of the Polish Military forces there, but did not have any success. Only after a phone call to the central police headquarters in Warsaw were police sent from Warsaw, and by nightfall had put a stop to the pogrom.

An emergency meeting of the Kehilla was convened and resolved to set up an assistance committee for the victims, as there had been great damage inflicted. A delegation from Warsaw hastily arrived: Deputy (Polish parliament member) Zammerstein, Engineer A. Reis, and Dr S. Z. Kahane. It was decided to establish a large relief program.

The Kehilla became even more popular with the Jewish community after the pogrom. However, it's days were numbered. Just before Rosh Hashana 1939, the Germans entered Brest and many of the men were brought to the site of the city council chambers. The German general called for the representatives of the Kehilla: Kwiatkowski, Begun, Ashkenazi, Englender and Schwartz. He demanded that they supply him with a list of Brest Jews who had originated from Germany, also a list of Jewish Communists, and to hand over any arms and ammunition in the possession of Jews.

We replied that there were no Germans at all in Brest, and that the communist party was banned in Poland, so that we knew that there were no members. Regarding the arms we would put out a call to the whole Jewish community. . He demanded 40,000 Zlotys and took Kwaitkowski and Englender as guarantors.

In this way the activity of the Kehilla in Brisk D'lita ended – city and people of the Jewish nation.

[Page 515]

The Census of Jewish Industry and Trade in Brest 1921

By Engineer K. Lichtenstein
Translated by Dr. Samuel Chani and Jenni Buch

The economic activity of the Jews in Brest in the period of the New Polish Republic (1921-1939) becomes clearer if we research the earlier economic situation during the years of the occupation 1915-1918, and the following Polish- Russian border wars 1919-1920.

In 1921 a new epoch arose in the history of Brest. After the treaty of Riga and the establishment of the Polish regime, Brest became part of the Polessie province. The city began to heal the deep wounds and damage inflicted on it by 6 years of war and upheavals.

There are some remaining sources that are relevant to Brest in 1921. After the economic conference held by the American Joint in April-June 1921 for the whole of Poland, a questionnaire/poll concerning industrial enterprises was issued (prepared by Engineer Eliezer Heller). This study served as a guide for the restoration of the Jewish workshops and factories – its' findings consisted of 9 volumes. Volumes 7 and 8 were dedicated to Kressy (the eastern border regions of Poland), including Polessie, Novogrudek, Vilna and Wolyn.

The enterprises researched were owned and managed by Jews, or they actively worked in production – this was done with the intent of refuting the slander and libel against the Polish Jews, claiming that they did not contribute to the economy.

In the Polessie district, research was carried out in the following cities: Brest, Pinsk, Pruzhany, Kobryn and Sarny. From the chapter dealing with Brest alone, we can draw conclusions for the averages for the whole Polessie district, as the figures for the other 4 towns were the same as for Brest.

Table 1: Industry and trade In Brest in 1921 (Figures in %)

Branch Of Industry	Percentage of the Enterprises (per 100 enterprises)	Percentage of businesses with working - owners, and their relatives	Percentage of the salaried employees	Percentage of Jewish salaried employees
Stone cement and glass industries	0.1	0.1	0.0	0.0
Metal	8.4	6.1	3.8	100.0
Machinery and parts	4.6	3.4	2.3	100.0
Timber	4.6	5.7	4.1	100.0
Leather and Tanning	2.7	3.4	4.0	57.0
Manufacture	1.1	0.8	0.7	100.0
Clothing	49.3	39.6	36.7	98.4
Paper	1.3	0.8	0.3	100.0
Food articles	8.9	22.7	31.9	95.6
Miscellaneous	1.5	2.0	1.7	100.0
Building	12.5	10.1	9.8	97.1
Printing	1.5	1.9	2.0	95.3
Cleaning and maintenance	3.5	3.4	2.7	89.6
TOTALS	**100.0**	**100.0**	**100.0**	**95.6**

1) Under Leather and Tanneries, there were 4 enterprises with 35 workers, 17 of whom were Jewish.

2) Under Food articles were included 3 Tobacco factories with 159 workers –156 of whom were Jewish.

95.6% were employed in the manufacturing industries. The figures show that in reality the production industries in Brest were entirely in Jewish hands, except for the leather industry where 57% of the workers were Jewish.

The total number of enterprises, and the total number of workers, Jews and non-Jews, are shown in Table 2, including statistics for the whole of the Polessie district. From the column of owner-workers and their relatives the true number of Brest Jews emerges – 35.8% are proprietors, 14.4% are their relatives. These figures were less than those for the whole of the Polessie district, which were 38.4% and 18.3% respectively. This smaller figure is explained by the direct participation of owner-workers and their families in the production work.

At the same time the number of salaried employees in Brest was 53.8%, which was higher than the rest of the district that totaled 43.3%. This shows more markedly that small factories and workshops had been founded in Brest and the emergence of a working-class – was distinctly stronger than the smaller towns and villages in the district.

We can reach the same conclusion from analyzing the columns "Enterprises with employed workers (Brest)", in the general statistics for Polessie. For every 100 enterprises in the district, only 50 were salaried workers (1228 to 726). In Brest the figure was 100 to 111 (323 to 359). This shows that for every 100 workshops that employed only the owner and his family – in Brest there were double as many paid employees in contrast to the rest of the district. Table 2 also shows the principal trades and branches of production in Brest according to the number of employees.

Table 2: Industry and Trade in Brest in 1921

Manufacturing Branches	Enterprises				Employees (According to the season for each trade)														
	Active and non-active	Active		Non active	Owner-workers, their families and paid workers	Owners		Family members in the enterprise		Salaried Workers									
		Salaried workers	Without salary workers			Overall number	% of all employed in the trade	Overall number	% of all employed in the trade	Jews					Non Jews				
										Overall number	% of all employed in the trade	Men	Women	Children under 15	Overall number	% of all employed in the trade	Men	Women	Children under 15
Stone, cement and glass industries	1	0	1	0	1	1	100.0	0	0.0	0	0.0	0	0	0	0	0	0	0	0
Metal	60	24	33	3	119	57	47.9	22	18.5	40	33.6	36	0	4	0	0	0	0	0
Machinery and parts	33	17	16	0	66	33	50.0	9	13.6	24	36.4	24	0	0	0	0	0	0	0
Timber	33	15	16	2	112	65	58.0	3	2.7	44	39.3	44	0	0	0	0	0	0	0
Leather and Tanning	19	11	7	1	66	16	24.2	8	12.1	24	36.4	23	1	0	18	27.3	18	0	0
Manufacture	8	3	4	1	16	7	43.8	2	12.5	7	43.8	5	2	0	0	0	0	0	0
Clothing	350	193	148	9	778	339	43.6	52	6.7	381	49.0	281	90	10	6	0.8	5	5	1
Paper	9	2	6	1	15	7	46.7	5	33.3	3	20.0	3	0	0	0	0	0	0	0
Food articles	63	32	25	6	444	51	11.5	56	12.6	322	72.5	218	94	10	15	3.4	13	2	0
Miscellaneous	11	6	3	2	39	11	28.2	10	25.6	18	46.2	17	1	0	0	0	0	0	0
Building	88	29	55	4	198	80	40.4	15	7.6	100	50.5	98	0	2	3	1.5	3	0	0
Printing	11	7	4	0	38	10	26.3	7	18.4	20	52.7	19	1	0	1	2.6	1	0	0
Cleaning and maintenance	25	20	5	0	67	24	35.8	14	20.9	26	38.8	20	5	1	3	4.5	2	1	0
Total of all branches in Brest	711	359	323	29	1929	701	35.5	203	10.4	1009	51.5	788	194	27	46	2.3	42	3	1
Figures for all of Polessie District	2028	726	1228	74	5299	2033	38.4	972	18.3	2222	41.9	1635	509	78	72	1.4	66	5	1

According to the poll:

The clothing industry was 49.2% of total industry, and employed 39.7% of all employees.

Food production 8.8% and 22.6%.   Building industry 12.35% and 10.1%.

Metal Industry 8.4% and 6.0%   Timber 4.6% and 5.7%.

Another separate volume deals with the number enterprises and the amount of paid employees – this means the small Jewish tradesmen – the tailors, bootmakers, carpenters, locksmiths, blacksmiths, weavers, builders, etc. As a rule they generally worked by themselves, and in the high seasons their wives and families would help with the work. The role of these small businesses in every trade very distinct. The ratio according to trades is shown in %. %: Building, cement and glass -100%. Metal industry – 58%. Machinery and parts – 48%. Timber - 52%. Leather and tanning - 57%. Clothing - 43%. Paper – 75%. Food articles – 44%. Mixed – 29%. Building – 65%. Printing – 36%. Cleaning and maitenance –20%.

These figures show how high the level of self-employment was, that is, tradesmen in their own small workshops and factories. The weakest economically were those who could not employ one worker, even in their busy season. This research was done according to the work seasons and for each trade separately. The figures show evidence of the difficult and miserable economic situation, in spite of the productive role that the Jewish population played. They also show the number of employees in every trade. The total of column 1 gives the percentage of paid workers. The majority of the salaried workers - 68.6% worked in the two classic Jewish trades, characteristic of all the Jewish neighborhoods in Eastern Europe – clothing and food.

In the metal, machinery and chemical industries the percentage was negligible. We can see that even on the subject of the production of the Jewish economy in Brest, it was a "Diaspora Economy'. In hindsight we can see that the results of the poll in Brest was the same as for the entire Polessie district, and even the same as those for all the border regions of Poland. The average number of employees, according to the industry and trade is given in Table 3. Study of the figures show clearly that the main manufacturing was produced in the small factories and workshops (except for food production, but three tobacco factories with 159 employees were included in this industry). The average number of paid workers was no more than three to an enterprise, and in a "Jewish trade" like clothing, even less than two workers. In the last three columns of Table 3, one can see the percentage of women and children under 15 of the Jewish workers. Amongst the paid workers it is clear that the food, clothing and manufacturing trades account for 25% of the total number of employed females. However, women did not work at all in the heavy work such as metal, timber, and building trades. In contrast we should remark on the relatively high number of children employed in the metal trades – 10%.

All these figures of the poll conducted by the Joint and relevant to Brest were Tables A and A1 published in Volumes 7-8.

Some statistics for the whole of the Polessie district which covered the five cities where this poll was conducted, are also relevant to Brest, one can accept that the differences are insignificant.

Table 3: Industry and trade in Brest in 1921 (Absolute and average)

Manufacturing Branches	Average number of salaried workers				
	Average count of workers in an enterprise	Average count of workers in an enterprise (Only with salaried workers)	Men	Women	Children under 15
Stone, cement and glass industries	0.0	0.0	0.0	0.0	0.0
Metal	0.7	1.7	90.0	0.0	10.0
Machinery and parts	0.7	1.4	100.0	0.0	0.0
Timber	1.4	2.9	100.0	0.0	0.0
Leather and Tanning	2.3	3.8	95.8	4.2	0.0
Manufacture	1.0	2.3	71.4	28.6	0.0
Clothing	1.1	2.0	73.7	23.6	2.7
Paper	0.4	1.3	100.0	0.0	0.0
Food articles	5.9	10.5	67.7	29.2	3.1
Mixed	2.0	3.0	94.5	5.5	0.0
Building	1.2	3.6	98.9	0.0	2.0
Printing	1.9	3.0	95.0	5.0	0.0
Cleaning and maintenance.	1.2	1.4	96.9	19.2	3.9
Total for all trades in Brest	**1.5**	**3.0**	**78.0**	**19.3**	**2.7**
Total for Polessie district	**1.2**	**3.2**	**73.5**	**22.9**	**3.6**

Divided into 2 groups: A. Those that already existed before W.W.1

B. Those that came into being after 1st July 1914

Until this census (1921) 74.8% belonged to group A, and 25.2% belonged to group B in the Polessie district. In 1921 33.1% of workers worked in pre – war enterprises. The average count of the workers in 1921 in the pre-war enterprises in the district was 1.1% as contrasted with 3.2% in 1914. This estimate applies to both the Jewish and non- Jewish workers, but the number of Jewish workers fell comparatively more compared to that of 1914, up to 23.9%

Enterprises that had been founded during the war employed 28% of the general work force. At the time of this poll (1921), Jewish workers made up

96.5% of the total workforce in these enterprises. The statistics show that trade and industry fell to one third of the production levels before the war. The Jewish worker in 1921 had lost 75% of their employment opportunities as compared to 1914. The facts are that despite the reduction of the population in Brest due to the occupation and expulsion, and although there were new work places established between 1915-1920, industry and trades were unable to provide full employment, and the unemployment rate in Brest at the end of the war was very significant.

[Page 523]

The Trade Workers (Artisans) Union

by Avraham Chani, Australia
Translated by Dr. Samuel Chani and Jenni Buch

A.

There were many artisans and tradesmen in Brest long before W.W.1. From Brest they would travel to other cities of Greater Russia. Brest construction workers were to be found everywhere that stations, railways and barracks were being built. They represented all the various trades: carpenters, painters, metalsmiths, and others.

Masses of shoes and boots were manufactured in the workshops of Brest for the monthly fairs and all the major Russian trade fairs, and even sent as far as Siberia. After W.W.1, Brest was absorbed into Poland and thus lost all the Russian markets – however, the number of tradesmen in the city did not decrease.

This naturally resulted in a large trade union movement in Brest, which was as important as the trade unions of Vilna, Bialystok and Lodz. In 1919, after the Germans had left Poland, the American Joint organization began an overall assistance program in all the cities and towns of Poland. The Jewish population received economic support, food and clothing, and the "American Joint Committee" was established by local officials to supervise the relief activities. At that time several delegates for the tradesmen confronted the representatives of the Joint and requested that they distribute food and potatoes specifically to poor tradesmen.

By the way, these delegates for the tradesmen had no affiliation to the working masses – one was a dairy merchant who presented himself as a cheesemaker – the other was a shoe merchant who presented himself as a shoemaker. They gathered several Jews from the synagogue, Jewish tradesmen of the old style – held a meeting in front of a homeless rabbi who was from a neighboring village and decided to form a trade union. Thus the "Trade Workers Union" was formed in Brest.

B.

As soon as several dozen tradesmen had enrolled in this union, they received from the city council a large store in Pilsudski Place and hung up a large placard with "Trade Workers of Brest Union". They received wagonloads of potatoes from the Joint to be distributed amongst the tradesmen. This union ceased it's activities in 1920 because of the Bolshevik assault. The Bolsheviks were indeed driven out in 1920, but in the midst of the tumult the chairman of the union, the formerly homeless rabbi, and his two officials – vanished. At a general assembly they elected as chairman the tailor Shoshanov. Amongst the committee members were: Candlesbroit, a medic, and a retired goldsmith, Zylberberg, who lived off rental income. The first activity of this committee was to gather a quorum in it's offices and to demand that the Joint Committee co-opt a representative from the Trade Workers Union. No real activity was carried out until the end of the Russian-Polish war.

Only after the peace treaty of Riga in 1921 (in which the whole of Polessie was annexed to Poland), and the steady stream of expatriates returning from Russia swelled the population of Brest daily - only then did the Trade Workers Union spring into action. New members joined the union and the committee was forced to increase it's membership fee. The committee was forced to create new positions for new young active members because ,according to a previous decision, the committee had to represent all trades. Two new members were co-opted onto the committee – Zablud the photographer and Chani the watchmaker. The chairman was preparing to emigrate to the U.S. and consequently neglected union affairs, so the opposition managed to push through 3 decisions: I.) To renovate the hall with a mezzanine. 2.) Establish contacts with the Central Union movement in Warsaw. 3.) Call for an A.G.M. after Passover.

Before Passover notices were posted and many invitations sent out. Immediately people began to visit the office in order to sign up as members. This A.G.M. made a strong impression in the city – it was discussed in the streets and synagogues. A day before the meeting, Hoffman, an educator from the Warsaw committee of the union arrived in Brest. Seeing that there were two camps, he made efforts to broker an agreement between the two.

An hour before the meeting, the front seats were already occupied by important dignitaries, and slowly the hall filled with the ordinary people, Jewish working folk and tradesmen. The first vote was almost unanimous – to establish a democratic list with another three new members, this new administration consisted of 14 committee members, Candlesbroit was elected chairman for the sake of peace. In reality the union was run by the deputy chairman M. Zablud, and the honorary secretary A. Chani. The new committee established 4 sub-committees: 1. Finances 2. Cultural. 3. Health. 4. Political. Mr.Chavetsky, a capable and hard-working secretary was employed. That year the membership reached 400.

The cultural committee organized a series of lectures with instructors from Warsaw. The members would gather before the Sabbath for tea with sugar. Illiterate members were be taught to read and write. The committee sent representatives to the various welfare institutions: the city hospital, ORT, TOZ, and others. The Joint allocated 2000 zlotys to a lending fund that lent interest free loans. There was a collection amongst the members of raw materials, merchandise and remnants. A lottery was held, the proceeds of which were directed to the purchase of medicines and medical equipment for the union's clinic.

C.

The Inaugural Meeting of the Jewish People's Party in Brest 1922

In 1922 during the election to the Sjem (Polish parliament), Rastner, the chairman of the central Trade Workers Union from Warsaw arrived in Brest. In accordance with his proposal, a branch of the People's Party (Socialist) was formed in Brest. The head of the People's Party, Noah Priludski, came to Brest and addressed a packed meeting of the People's Party in Sarva's hall.

There were also tradesmen with Zionist sympathies. Without the union's knowledge and with assistance from the local Zionist organization, they brought Goldberg and Bromberg - delegates from the Zionist Trade Unions in Warsaw to address the members. At a meeting in the Mizrachi hall, the assembled Zionist supporters of the Trade Workers Union heard speeches by Winnikoff and Z. Begin. They stressed the fact that the People's Party ruled the Trade Union circles at a time when the Jewish mainstream sympathized with Zionism. The truth was that the People's Party existed only on paper, as the union had no party activities. Yet many more voted for the People's Party in comparison with other cities of the Kressy (eastern Poland). Thus Brest became known as a stronghold of the People's Party.

The next A.G.M. took place in a stormy atmosphere. A new administration was elected, consisting mainly of previous members with a few newcomers: Chairman – Zablud, Chani - deputy chairman, Sussel – treasurer, Rosenshein, Labushevski, Leider, Topol, Daitch, Wapniarski, Rubin, Lev, Shpigelmacher, and Savaniuk.

The Health Committee (who administered the clinic) was: Lev, Sussel, Manker, Tepper, Mocasi, Zablud, Chani, Topol, Donovski and Weinstein.

The Cultural Committee: Zablud, Chani, Rubin, Levy and Rosenshein.

The new administration faced very difficult problems. Especially in the field of finances as the devaluation of the Polish currency meant that the membership fees did not cover the expenses. The subject of money caused much friction between the workers and employers, resulting in many strikes. The union and the professional unions cared for the interests of the poorer tradesmen, with some success, always compromising between the opposing sides.

In the summer of 1923 the union received a demand to vacate it's premises as the owner had returned from Russia. The matter came to court and the owner lost his case due to the tenancy protection laws. But the committee did not want to wrong anyone and searched for a suitable site.

At the A.G.M. of 1924, which was held after Passover, the building workers section proposed the engineer Greenberg (the founder of the ORT school), as chairman. The committee agreed, enrolled him as a member and invited him to the A.G.M. Both sides proposed a list of the former board members with Zablud and Susser instead of Greenberg and Chani – however, Greenberg was elected as chairman at this meeting. In 1924 there was also a celebratory function upon the opening of our new premises, with representatives from all the social institutions, the powers at the city council, not only the Jewish press, but even the anti semitic Polish press published favorable, if somewhat sarcastic reports of the event. At the opening meeting the following demands were formulated: 1. The union would accept the flag of the Warsaw Trade Unions. 2. That a library for union members be established.

The following actions were implemented in 1924 –5:

1. Each trade was organized into it's own section, with it's own administration.
2. A free Yiddish lending library was founded.
3. The purchase of new instruments and medicines for the union medical clinic, as well as new doctors and specialists.
4. A lawyer was hired as a legal counselor for the union, he gave free legal advice twice weekly to the union members.
5. Due to the demands from some members, an orchestra was formed.

The union developed and grew stronger under the chairmanship of Greenberg – 150 new members joined up at this time – in 1925 the membership reached over 400. The financial situation also improved as the members began to pay their fees punctually.

D.

In the summer of 1925 there was a Polish-Jewish meeting of trade unions. Five delegates were sent from Brest: Gendler, Wabnik, Chani, Rubin and Spigelmacher. They represented all the various groups at the conference.

In 1927 the Polish government introduced the new "Union Laws" which were a hard blow for the Jewish tradesmen. The central union committee in Warsaw tried to unite both of the Brest trade union organizations, for this purpose there was an executive committee elected that had full powers. This committee decided that: I. The divisional committee should disband, vacate it's premises, and the members transfer to the Trade Workers Union. 2. Both funds should amalgamate, and the funds of the liquidated division should be used to pay off any debts under the supervision of the treasurer of the executive committee. 3. All members would automatically be members of the Trade Union and pay membership fees. 4. The executive committee would run the board of both groups until the A.G.M. 5. This meeting was to be held within one month, and the previous chairmen of the two groups, Greenberg and Zablud, could not be candidates for this new committee until January 1928. 6. The A.G.M voted to annul the autonomous powers of the Brest union and affiliate it with the central union movement in Warsaw.

However, Mr. Zablud, with a group of about 20 members, did not recognize this peace agreement and boycotted the union.

On Sunday, 21st January 1928, the A.G.M. of the united Trades Unions in Brest took place with the participation of Mr.Rastner, chairman of the central committee in Warsaw. A Mr. Roisman, an ordinary tailor, was elected as chairman. The newly elected executive had representatives from all the different trades. This was a very active committee, and according to the government laws, every member was issued with a union membership card, and the various sections had to be organized for that purpose.

E.

In 1929 Dr Yitzchak Kagan arrived in Brest as doctor for the union medical clinic. He was a pleasant man with a leaning towards social justice. He accepted the proposal that he become the next chairman of the Trades Union, on the condition that the A.G.M. would endorse this by open vote. The A.G.M. of 1929 voted Dr Kagan as chairman by a large majority. The question of obtaining their own premises was debated over a long period at many meetings. An American tourist, a Mr. Berger, donated money for this purpose and suggested that all the members donate towards this building and participate in the building work. It did not take long and we obtained a plot of land at Kosciusko 41 on a ten-year lease. This land belonged to the Jewish community (kehilla), but was held in the name of Benjamin Padva, the grandson of the Brest rabbi, Yakov Meir Padva. The kehilla was reorganized in 1930 and demanded rent money. But the union stated that the kehilla should support, not hinder the union, as it was a communal institution.

Construction began after Passover 1929. That summer, the union received an eviction notice and we had to transfer from our premises to the unfinished building. At this time a famous agreement was reached with the Christian Trade Workers Union, according to which the amalgamated Trade Workers Union would consist of 60% Christians and 40% Jews. The chairman was a Christian and the deputy a Jew. The Trade Union was a section of the government ministries and the agreement was advantageous and useful for the Jews. As Brest was the capital of the entire province, an office was established for the entire district. Every town and village in the district could elect 2 delegates, one Christian and one Jewish. Voting rights were only for tradesmen who had union membership cards.

The board consisted of 5 members, 3 Christian and 2 Jews. As the administration had to be from Brest, the question of who was to be the deputy chairman arose. The suitable candidate had to speak good Polish, command respect in the community, and be clear and concise on the workers issues, as well as political skills. Mr. M. Wabnik was elected temporarily to organize the trade union movement in the Polessie district, and to collect monies for the election fund.

On the 1st July 1929, the Polish Government introduced a statute that set the 13th October as the election date. According to reliable sources, the government predetermined the list of candidates, and Wabnik was picked as deputy chairman. The board ratified Wabnik as deputy chairman, and Loy as a board member. They were unanimously accepted. On Sunday 27th October 1929, there was a celebratory inauguration with a street rally attended by all the tradesmen of Brest, Jews and Christians alike. The Jews marched with their trade union flag, and led by their orchestra. The Christians marched with their flag and 10 holy images, and at their head, the firefighters band. There was a large banquet in the evening at the Citizen's Club with representatives of both the Jewish and Christian Trade Unions, and all the social institutions. The mood was optimistic. The Trade Workers Union building in Brest achieved a great deal in the 10 years of it's existence. It had a chairman, deputy chairman and board.

The chairman, Zhuk, was a Brest barber, who lived amongst Jews and was a Christian liberal. His deputy, Wabnik, a tinsmith, was a decent Jew who knew how to co-exist with the Christians. The director was Menasovitch, a lawyer, a progressive man and friendly to the Jews. Due to his Jewish sympathies he was stood down from his position as police chief. The government officials firstly organized an examination committee for all the trades. These committees consisted of nominated union members, mixed Christians and Jews, and in some cases, wholly Jewish. The examination fee was 90 zlotys, with concession 60 zlotys. Later on the committee decide to reduce this fee for the poorer tradesmen, and in hardship cases, to waive the fee entirely. The Brest and Brest district tradesmen underwent their exams at the Brest Trade Workers building – in more distant towns such as Kobrin, Pinsk and Luninets the chairman would arrive with a board member to conduct the exams on the spot. The Jewish tradesmen felt at home in the

Trade Workers house in Brest. Yiddish was often spoken in the building as in the other Jewish institutions, the chairman was often occupied elsewhere, and the Jewish deputy represented him at the various functions. The Jewish tradesmen had no difficulty in passing the exams.

After 4 successful years of activity, several Christians conspired against the chairman and deputy chairman as not being competent. The chairman was dismissed, as there was no complaint against the deputy, he remained in his position and replaced the chairman after a year. The district governor wanted to charge him in court, but realized that the charges would not succeed, so he sacked the entire committee. According to the agreement on both sides, Christian and Jewish, it was decided to set up a new committee with a Mr. Gur as deputy chairman, a decent and honest man. However, he had no influence with the Christian circles. The conditions and times changed unfavorably for the Jewish interests.

At the end of 1929, the Jewish Trade Workers Union house was opened. The workload lessened, Dr. Kagan left the union, and he did not leave a suitable replacement. The influence of the tradesmen weakened, and in 1935 the leadership went into the hands of Zablud and his disciples. The enthusiasm and dedication disappeared and the work dragged on without success.

In the city elections the trade unions obtained 2 seats on the city council. There were also 2 representatives on the Kehilla council, but there was no real activity. The library was closed down – the orchestra disbanded and the musical instruments sold. There was no cultural/educational activity. Only the medical clinic, not longer exclusive to the ordinary tradesmen, was still active.

In 1939 after the Russian occupation, they exiled Zablud to Siberia. The trade union building was converted into a worker's club.

Of the 25,000 Jews that lived in Brest, there remained barely 150 alive. Of the hundreds of members of the trades union, four members managed to save themselves: Mattityahu Zablud, engineer Shloimeh Greenberg, Avraham Chani (now in Melbourne Australia) and Dr. Y. Kagan (died in New York).

A. Chani

Shossenaya St - The Commercial Center

The First Cinema in Brest – 'Elchayon'

[Page 535]

Technical Training and Education

By A. Shtrickman
Translated by Dr. Samuel Chani and Jenni Buch

The professional training of Jews in the various technical trades was not very developed in Poland. The only Technical Schools that existed were in Warsaw and Lodz. The ORT organization only began it's activity after W.W.1 when Poland became independent.

The Brest inhabitants that were expelled from the city in 1915 and returned in 1918 began, piece by piece, to rebuild the ruins of the city. The assistance came from the 'Joint' that established a committee to distribute tools to the tradesmen and open workshops for Technical training. This committee turned to the central ORT organization in Warsaw, and it was decided to establish a branch of Ort in Brest in1921. All the different political factions and parties co-operated in the establishment of a Technical School for the Jewish youth. The founders were: Aaron Matevsky, David Lichtiger, Shmuel Pomerantz, Manes Goldfarb, Berl Barenboim, Gershon Feinstein, Avraham Freidman, Leib Katz, Yakov Gelerstein, Dr. Avraham Epstein and Shlomo Greenberg.

The committee set the following goals:

1. Assistance for Jewish agricultural workers.
2. To provide tools, equipment and loans for Jewish tradesmen.
3. To provide professional technical training and the supervision of the existing workshops.

The Joint endorsed several subsidies for Jewish agricultural workers in the Brest district and the committee received the contract to assist them because ORT was interested in Jewish agricultural workers in Poland. The Brest branch opened workshops for technical training – these workshops were in rented halls. The carpentry school for boys was at Sadowa 37. The new school for girls was on Jagielonska St. The ORT offices were at Zygmuntowska 55 – Tiempskis building – (which also housed the Joint). The carpentry workshop was at first transferred to Jagielonska St and then to a building owned by the Joint at Kszywa 5. The carpentry workshops were recognized by the Polish government as a Technical School with Yiddish as the teaching language.

The organization registered members and on the 24th August 1924, the first A.G.M. took place. The following were members: Dr.Begun, Wapniarski, Feingold, Consevic, Glassman, Guss, Tupok, Chani, Shavtiel Rubin, Joseph Rubin, and Zablud. In addition were representatives who were co-opted from other organizations: Zara Zaretsky and Nathan Eisenberg, both from the orphanage, Kopper and Dr. Wilner from the Joint.

Another department of technical training was opened in 1924 – a mechanics and locksmiths workshop which was needed by the city. Also evening classes were established for adults and an ORT exhibition was held.

In February 1925 there was a fire in the middle of the night, the cause of which was unknown – the Technical School and all it's contents were destroyed – only a few machines were rescued from the fire. The Jewish kehilla made great efforts to rebuild the Technical School assisted by the Joint, ORT, and local volunteers who managed to rebuild the school with barracks (temporary huts) in the courtyard. The practical training sessions continued, but the theoretical lessons could only be resumed after the building was rebuilt one storey higher than before.

The new building was completed in 1929, and only then were all the branches situated in the same building at Kszywa 5.

A severe crisis for the Technical School occurred during 1930-1932. This was due to disagreements between the committee members – the national progressive members did not agree with the other members of the committee as to obeying the national guidelines. They believed that the following of national guidelines for technical training was a lowering of national standards. The Jewish community of Brest was shaken by this dispute and decided to support the nationalist officials who decided to throw away the line of the opportunists. This dispute brought the organization to a desperate financial situation. This situation somewhat improved in 1933 with the changing of the committee, and the management boards of the institutions that received financial government support and from the Jewish community council (kehilla).

The budget consisted of the following:

A. Subsidies
    1) From the ORT Central Committee in Warsaw. 2) The government subsidy for 1933. 3) Support from the local kehilla.
B. Other Income
    1) Income from the workshops. 2) Student fees. 3) Membership fees.

Nevertheless, the deficit was great and the organization struggled with financial difficulties for years.

The organization had the following departments:

Workshops for Boys - The practical work of the workshops.

The mechanical and locksmiths department.

The metal smiths department.

Carpentry department.

Mechanical joinery department.

Classroom lessons for all various trades.New departments for girls.

The count of students who had graduated from the Technical School by 1937 was 173 boys, 137 girls.

Of the active committee members one must mention: Dr. Arieh Begun – a warm folksy personality, he was the long-standing chairman of the organization. Avraham Shtrickman, secretary 1926 –1934, Dr. Ganz, chairman of the committee 1924-34, Dr. Nachman Landau, chairman of the committee 1934-1938, Zablud 1924-1929, Chani 1924-1929, Reuven Pregel 1932-1938, Shlomo Greenberg, secretary of the committee 1937-1938, Zev Dov Begin, the secretary of the kehilla council.

The department directors were: Engineer Kanevitch 1924-1928, Engineer Feldstein 1925-1932, and Engineer Charetman 1933- 1937. This report only covers the period until 1937, as we have no details of the activity of the Ort organization In Brest from then on. It is said that an extra building was built at Kszywa 5, and the activity of the organization broadened and developed.

There is no doubt that the entire community recognized and valued the ORT organization and it's departments. Brest was represented and respected in all the national and international conferences of the ORT organization, as well as having a delegate from Brest in the central committee.

The ORT organization was a very positive symbol of achievement in Jewish Technical education in our city. Our ORT officials and active members were models of dedication – excelling as national and social identities in the Jewish community of Brest.

The 1926-27 Graduation Class of the ORT Dressmaking School
The central column of photos (from top to bottom): The board of the ORT school,
the headmistress Sarah Shwartz, and the director Shimon Itzbitzer. The two white-
framed photos are the teachers, left side Batya Shedletzka, and right side Esther-
Malka Margolin. The surrounding photos are the graduating students.
Photo courtesy of Dr.S. Chani

The ORT Committee in 1934
Seated R-L: Zev Dov Begin, Dr. D. Sarnaker, Dr. Y Ganz, A. Shtrickman,
V. Sheinberg.
Standing: Engineer Rechtman, Dr. N. Landau, R. Pregel, Dr. A. Begun,
A. Deitchman, D. Adansky, Y. Itzbitzer (Secretary)

[Page 539]

Banking and Industry

Translated by Dr. Samuel Chani and Jenni Buch

One hundred years ago the Finkelstein Bank existed in Brest. It belonged to one of the prestigious families in our city (Finkelstein was the father of Dov Finkelstein and the grandfather of Nechama and Noah Finkelstein the editor of the 'Heint' Warsaw newspaper).

In 1888-90 the bank of Soloveitchik and Morgenstern was established in Brest, a branch of the Warsaw bank of this name. The Brest branch of this bank existed until 1905.

The first big bank to open was the Credit Bank of Brisk D'lita in 1901. Its director was Pinchas Kroll. This bank conducted large business deals and assisted the development of trade and commerce in the city a great deal. The first chairman of the board was Yerucham Schatz, board members were Aaron Matetski and Mordechai Baraks. The basic activity of this bank was the discounting of promissory notes and savings. Amongst the employees were Yosef Meir Padua and Asher Hari.

In 1905-6 the United Moscow/ Brest Bank opened. This bank was the central bank for industry, and conducted big business for the merchants and businessmen of Brest.

Between 1897-1907 there was a Bank Horoditche – Horoditche was a famous Zionist figure and a delegate to the first Zionist Congress. The Zionist activities were concentrated in this institution; this was in the time of Chovevei Zion. In 1908 Horoditche transferred to Warsaw and the bank was liquidated.

An important credit institution which began it's activity in a small room was the Kupec Bank (Merchant Bank), which grew rapidly. Although called the Merchants Bank, it assisted all levels of society without discrimination. The founding director was Benjamin Padua, the board consisted of: Meyer Metchik, Aaron Padua, Shmuel Hammer, Nachman Berliner, Zyskind Neumark, and others. This bank existed until the destruction of the city.

In 1924 the People's Bank (Bank Ludovi) was formed under the directorship of David Zisman, an energetic and influential official in the city council and various philanthropic institutions - (he was exiled to Siberia in the time of the Bolsheviks, but he now resides in Israel). His deputy was Shmuel Pomerantz, and employees were: Ze'ev Braunzel, Tzvi Lomazhevski, and Wolf Kirshroit.

Amongst other important banks one should mention the Shares Bank (Bank Udzielowy), which would not conduct banking operations unless the client agreed to buy an Israel Shekel. All the financial operations for the Zionist institutions were conducted through this bank. The Board was: L.Y. Winnikoff, Yakov Ramo, committee members were: Avraham Skorbnik, Chaim Zalman Wolsky, and Asher Ashkenazi. Employees were: Finkel, Gelerstein, Tennenbaum and Mrs Katz.

The last bank to be established was the Cooperative Bank in 1932, and its director was Dr. Nachman Landau. The Savings and Loan Fund that was founded in 1905-6 became an important institution in Brest for the Jewish national institutions. The founders were Zionist activists who led a fight for the management. This was the first financial institution in Russia with a higher ideal – to assist Jews with their savings and loan monies. The bank had deposits of 1,200,000 rubles, and could compete against the larger banks of the city. The interest was according to official guidelines and many Jews withdrew their money from the government banks and deposited their money in the Savings and Loans Fund. The Savings and Loan Fund enjoyed their trust and lent money to businessmen, gave tradesmen and merchants credit, as well as lending to the middle class. The first chairman of the board was Leon Horoditche and the director was Dr. Kasavery Shteinberg. In 1910 Levi-Ytizhak Winnikoff, Moshe Baruch Bishkowitz, Shmuel Mervil, Zacharia Rosenthal, and others joined the board of administration. The board members also included Dr. Leon Shereshevski and Dr. Meir Wolfson. In 1911-12 Michael Rosenberg was elected as director - a prestigious businessman, he was a learned man and talented man. However, he was not a Zionist. The bank had 22 employees including Ben Zion Neumark and Mordechai

Sheinerman, Zev- Dov Begin, Y. Ribetsky, Leizer Korlander and others. This bank existed until W.W.1.

Brest did not have a strong industrial base; because of the fortress the ruling powers had forbidden the building and development of industry. Despite this, the Jews still built and managed factories in the city. One must remember the mills of the Kwiartevski brothers and Chaim Zelman Wolski, and the large sawmills owned by the Kwiartevski brothers, Michaelson and Finkel. The large chemical factory "Feinalin" owned by Mordechai Fein. The paper mills owned by Glaser, the glass factory owned by Gdanski, Epstein and Grossman. The oil paints factory owned by Padkorene and Winnig, and the soda water and fruit essence (cordial) factory owned by Krantz and Savitshitski.

Directors and staff of the Shares Bank (Bank Udzielowy)

**Seated R-L: L.Y. Winnikoff, A. Ashkenazi, A Skorbnik, M. Zisman,
Y. Hari, Y. Ramo, Z. Ayin.
Standing: A Sirota, unknown, D. Rosenberg, Y. Gelerstein,
Finkel, and S. Tennenbaum**

Savings and Loan Fund 1906
Seated R-L: Sheinerman, Zev Dov Begin, Leon Horoditche, Padua, unknown.
Standing: Unknown, Ribetski, Korlander, and Birenboim

[Page 547]

DESTRUCTION AND HOLOCAUST

I Stride Over the Ruins of My City

A Poem by Dora Teitelbaum
Translated by Dr. Samuel Chani and Jenni Buch

I feed on the conflagration, I feed on the disaster as six million dead run after me and drag the stones out of the bridge, and count the drops of tears in the River Bug.

Bricks, bricks, bloodstained bricks. Here is a cap, there is the wheel of pram, here is a sleeve, there is a shoelace. Home, my home, you are an orphan exactly like me.

City, my city, my burnt city, your wounds and ruins are poured over with the years. The orchard - the garden where my baby carriage stood is now a ruin. The earth, the earth is now my only relative.

I lift a fistful of earth in my hands –see how many eyes peer out at me. Every grain - a grandfather, every stone - a generation. The earth is my relative for over 10,000 years.

I stride over the ruins and seek out the memories of my home, my street, and the remaining tree. There my grandfather would sit under the broad branches in the old Bereza. There in Bereza it stands with a split trunk and broken branches - the bark peels off like an old tablecloth. Bereza, Bereza, you are now my father!

Bereza, Bereza, I want to play for you, a flight of my heart which I cannot quieten. The songs of the birds that rise and will not be silenced that disturb the quiet...

Yankel the Klezmer (musician) gave his fiddle to me and swore that I should play as long as 1 live. I lost my heart, my doomed sister. I am left alone, now I am the entire orchestra.

I will stand over the ruins and play and play until my heart turns to stone, until every one of the fallen will rise from their graves, and I will greet every Jewish victim of the Holocaust that occurred in our time.

I will stand over the ruins and tear at the strings of the violin until a stream of water will fill the thirsty wells. I shall play and play about conquest and belief until my city will rise up from the ruins to heaven.

[Page 549]

Memories of an Escapee From Brest

By L. Gluzman
Translated by Dr. Samuel Chani and Jenni Buch

Early on the 22nd of June 1941 one could hear the firsts shots of the invading German army. By 8 a.m. Brest was already in the hands of the Germans.

The first victims were the Jews. The first German orders were anti–Jewish: Jews were not allowed to move house, and were forbidden from seeking employment without special permission. The Jewish population then numbered 40,000 and the leadership of the community was in the hands of several capable and talented people that the Germans immediately dealt with (executed). Hunger and fear of the coming terrors filled the city.

In the streets Nazi soldiers checked every passer by who they suspected were Jews. Despite this I risked it and went to the home of a friend of mine – a Polish engineer whom I had helped in the past. He received me in a very friendly manner and found work for me at the railway station, as the Brest stationmaster was an acquaintance of his. I went to work for him as a Pole with the name of Kalevitch. My job was to paint signs. My supervisor was a German soldier who was not happy with my work - my letters did not come out to his satisfaction. I was forced to teach myself in the evenings and my work improved daily. My fear and dread did not lessen – I was still without a passport.

Arising one morning at 6 a.m. for work, I immediately realized that I had fallen into an "Aktion" - a round up of civilians. The Germans were checking every passer by and every Jew was pushed into covered trucks. Several times the Germans pushed me towards a truck, but with great effort and wildly thumping heart I managed to extricate myself.

My family lived in the home of a Ukrainian who was a rabid anti-semite and an opponent of the Russians. Because of my good behavior during the Russian occupation – I had not denounced anyone to the Russians – I found favor with him and he hid my family and me. When the Germans went from house to house searching for Jews, he risked his own life when he assured them that there were no Jews in his house.

The German soldier for whom I worked showed more trust in me every day – wanting to please me, he called me over to point out to me how the Jews were being tortured – in front of my eyes the most terrible scenes appeared. On the station platform there were about 200 elderly Jews who were being forced to dance horas and various wedding dances. They were surrounded by German soldiers and Polish railway workers who murderously beat them with wooden clubs and iron bars. The wounded fell then and there – whoever still showed signs of life was beaten to death with an iron bar by a Polish railway worker to quieten them forever. The remaining Jews had to drag the bodies to the Jewish cemetery. Everyone was eager to perform this task to escape the ghastly terrible dance. The old Jews with bodies on their shoulders had to run quickly – stones and iron bars were thrown at them. The cemetery was close by – on the road another 2 Jews were murdered.

This "Aktion' of catching, torturing and murdering Jews lasted 3 days. During this time over 9,000 Jews of varying ages disappeared from the city.

The Brest Jewish community was forced to establish a fund to raise money for clothing for 200 Germans - later they demanded 5 million zlotys. The collectors also came to my place, my wife opened the wardrobes and begged them to take whatever they liked...later I also gave them 1200 zlotys.

Each day the Nazis thought up new provocations – at this time an edict was issued that Jews had to wear a white armband on the left arm with a 12-centimeter blue Star of David. Later one had to wear it on the left chest.

On the 13th October 1941, the borders of the Brest Ghetto were established. It was decreed that all Jewish residents of the city would have to move into the designated streets. During my work at the railway station I met a Polish building engineer from Warsaw who was carrying out building works for the Germans. I proposed that he obtain a work permit to employ Jews, he agreed, and I was one of his first workers. Later he employed my father who was a glazier, and I managed to obtain employment for other relatives.

In the ghetto the hunger and terror was overwhelming. The ghetto chief was a Major Rade, he demanded a contibution of 10 million dollars, to be paid within 3 days.

Yom Kippur arrived and despite the prohibition of public assemblies, the Jews of Brest did not desist from praying together. Rabbi Simcha Zelig and his son organized a prayer meeting in the tightly packed synagogue on the corner of Kosciusko and Pietrowski streets. The beds were taken out and packed into the courtyard of this building - responsible people posted on all sides to stand as sentries, and it was just as it was when the Marranos (secret Jews) choked on their tears on Yom Kippur in Spain long ago.

The deputy chief of police, who was also Procurator of Jewish affairs, excelled himself in carrying out the most murderous deeds, and was much hated by the Jewish population. At 10 p.m. a Jewish policeman came to him and notified him that they had caught a Jewish partisan who was conducting communist propaganda in the ghetto. They had beaten him and thrown him into the Jewish prison and did not know what further to do with him... the police deputy chief jumped up in vicious joy and immediately went to the prison which was situated in the basement of Grynberg's house. The policeman opened the door of the cellar and entered first, the deputy chief followed, immediately the door was locked from the inside by a second Jewish policeman, at the same time the first policeman threw himself upon him and cut the German's throat with a knife. These 2 policemen vanished the next day – it is not known whether they survived or not. The corpse of the

Procurator was found 2 days later – the entire population lived in great fear – the specter of bloody revenge hung over the ghetto.

On the same day the community decided to send some expensive 'gifts' to Major Rade. Four beautiful girls who had some idea of the importance of their mission delivered these gifts. They spent that whole night with the Germans and when they appeared on the streets the next day, every Jew looked upon them as Biblical heroines, who sacrificed themselves for the greater good of the community of Israel. None of these girls survived the war.

I continued to go to work every day with my father and brother in law. We would return laden with food and coal for heating. One day when crossing through the barbed wire I was caught by a Pole that knew me and worked for the German police. He beat me severely. The second time the German police thrashed me.

On the burnt out place between Ksziwa and Jagiellonska they began to erect barracks containing workbenches for no apparent reason. A German called Guss displayed brutal cruelty to the Jewish laborers. He was hated by the Brest Jews as much as Major Rade the police chief was. When the Germans demanded 900 men, everyone was too frightened to report to them. Then Guss gave up the men who worked for him to the Germans. Of the 900, only 12 returned, even my own father, who was amongst the returnees, would never discuss what had happened to the others.

In any event, my father decided that we had to begin building a secret hiding place. For an entire week the men of our family worked at building and finishing this ingenious hiding place.

At the beginning of 1942 cells of young Zionists and communists were collecting money to buy arms and send young men into the forest. One frosty evening a printer from Lublin called Arieh Schoenwald came to see me on a mission. When the Germans had invaded Brest he had left the Jewish quarters and come to see at the home of the Ukrainian. Now, he showed me that he had managed to collect money to transfer men from the ghetto into the forests. He told me how 3 young Jews, disguised as peasants were recognized by a Polish policeman on Kobryner St. With the assistance of a German gendarme he tried to stop them. The Jews shot the Pole and the German on the spot – making it look like they had shot each other.

Arieh used all his powers that no suspicion should fall on any Jew. After some days, the police dismissed several Poles and no one ever knew what happened to them ...

The day of the major "Aktion", the liquidation of the Brest Ghetto arrived. From our hiding place I saw how the Ukrainian police with howls of triumph and pleasure stormed the houses of the ghetto. Besides being armed with guns the bandits also had axes and bayonets. The streets filled with the cries of children and the frantic calls of their mothers. I heard the German commandant order that they be taken to Krutke St. The Germans knew that many Jews were hiding in the cellars and bunkers and specially built hiding places. I saw them come to a barn that adjoined my own hiding place – they found a young man who was not a native of Brest hidden under the straw. He was dragged out by the Germans and told go to the yard – they shot him in the head as he ran. In the cellar where my wife and 10-month baby were hidden, the water supply ran out in the second day. The cellar was tightly packed with people; mothers nursed their babies at the breast all day long so that they would not cry. After a falling out with my brother in law I was left alone in my secret attic hiding place – through the grille I saw how the bandits came ever closer – they closed in on the cellar, demanding that everyone come out. I saw my wife and tens of others emerge, broken and bewildered.

In the days and nights that followed I was alone and regretted that I had not accompanied them – suddenly, late after midnight, I heard a stifled groan. No one answered my whispered call. After a long search in the neighboring barns and cellars I found one of my neighbors, Yakov Barkin. The 70-year-old man was completely swollen and unable to move. He was delirious and I brought him water.

We spent several days and nights in his hiding place, alone and isolated from the outside world, not knowing what to do. No Jews were to be seen in the ghetto. Polish workers came - supposedly to load up the belongings of the vanished people for the Germans. At the same time they picked 'bones' for themselves. I was lying hidden quite close to them and I could hear their conversations, all of which concerned one subject – how to become rich. One told the other that his son Stephan had found a hiding place of Jews at Friedman's house on Dluga St. He assured them that he would not report them for the 20 gold zlotys reward. It was not half an hour before he received his reward – the German police arrived and plucked out at least 60 well-dressed people – probably aristocrats. Stephan later regretted not demanding more money. My heart ached with pain – I knew these people that lived in Friedman's house.

The second man jeered, "What would you say to the following? Last night I was with a friend (ransacking) a Jewish house on Kosciusko St. The house was clean and orderly. At the table sat a man, on the floor near him lay a woman, another woman lay on the bed. At first we were frightened but then we realized that they were dead - they had poisoned themselves." This awful scene was of dead Jews.

I listened to these terrible conversations and saw their jeering faces, my fists clenched as I prayed for revenge against them. At night I told Yakov Barkin, we agreed that this must have been Dr. Begun's house.

The next morning I prepared placards written in German and Polish. The Polish placards were a warning to those that helped the Hitlerites to destroy the Poles:

Poles, Ukrainians, and White Russians

Do not suppose that you will not receive your just rewards for divulging the hidden Jews to the Germans. After the Germans exterminate the ghetto, they will turn on you. Don't be stupid dogs that lick their masters. Whoever assists the Germans is a senseless dog. Do you want to remain idiotic senseless dogs forever?

Signed: The Fighting Democratic Party

In German I wrote:

German citizens. People of culture. Why are you so blindly carrying out the executioners' orders? Don't you know how much revenge there will be against you? Today you are the executioners, tomorrow you will be hung. Did the Jews eat your bread? Don't you have wives and children? Must you unwillingly follow your leaders and commit such criminal atrocities? Remember that you were once good honest children yourselves, and that the children that you murder are innocent of any sin. Remember also that justice does exist in the world.

Signed: The German Communist Party.

I stuck 12 such posters in various locations that night. I hung 2 near my hiding place so that I could observe the reactions of the reader.

At 7 a.m. 3 Poles passed by. They stopped to read. It was obvious that they could not read well. One of them said: "what is this?" When he saw the German signature he said: "these are Communist posters". They called on a passer-by, a German with coarse pig like features who quickly read both signs. He became pensive for a moment, then straightened up and went on his way. I saw that the words had made an impression on him and wondered what he would do if he found in my hiding place?

In the meantime a Gestapo agent and a Polish policeman arrived who tore it down and stomped on it after reading it. On the other hand the Gestapo agent stood stock still in front of the German poster. Not a muscle twitched in his face. Then he motioned to the Pole and they both left. I saw how many passers-by read my proclamation, but at the same time I knew that they would have murdered me if they had discovered me.

No Jews remained but there was much activity in the ghetto. They dragged suitcases filled with feather bedding, furniture and possessions out of the buildings. They stripped all the room and searched the cellars. Suddenly there was a noise from old Barkin. I saw a Ukrainian outside and inside there was another Ukrainian screaming at the old man to come out. The old man pointed to his swollen legs and said in a broken voice that he could not move. The outside Ukrainian shouted to the other: "What are you playing at? Finish him off! But find out from him where the money is and where other Jews are hiding". I heard several shots. From the cellar emerged a gentile, a male of medium height with a red face – not a word passed between them as they nonchalantly walked along as if nothing had happened.

My head was bursting. I lay there paralysed – only my heart beat stronger with the desire for revenge. I considered how to eliminate several of these bandits. My brain formed a plan and I waited for the next day impatiently.

Very early in the morning I left my secret hiding place in the attic. I took a heavy iron bar and stood waiting for a solitary passer-by. The iron bar would only be effective with a lone person, as another would quickly discern where it came from. The desire to live was as strong as ever - I had to survive. A policeman went past – I hit him on the head but missed and hit his shoulder. He fell down screaming; I don't know what happened next as I quickly fled back to my hiding place. Every day more workers came into the ghetto to strip it of every valuable. I saw tens of men at my father's house – the curiosity burnt in me. Without thinking of the consequences I left my hiding place and sought a convenient observation post where I could see what was happening in the courtyard of my father's home. If someone had accidentally opened the cellar door I would not have had time to escape. In such situations a man thinks of the most extraordinary things that could save him. I imagined that I would spot a familiar friendly face. A Gestapo man stood in the yard and directed the Polish workers who dragged everything out of the rooms. More police and civilians arrived. I heard the German order them to immediately kill any Jew if they were to come across one...

In this instance I felt no nervousness. I felt great peace. In no way did I want to be caught. From marks that I made on the walls I knew that it was Friday but did not know the date or month. I very much wanted to know how long I had being lying hidden.

There had already been some snow falling for several days and at nights when I foraged for food and water I had to walk backward for the last 20 meters so no one would see where my footprints came from. The days became more difficult and my food was running out. My loneliness grew and I began to think of running away from there.

At 6 o'clock in the evening I shaved myself in the dark, which was very difficult. My beard was already 3 weeks old. I washed myself and packed my suitcase. I had various items in the cellar – a suit, good underwear. I found my overcoat – my legs shook as I tried to hold back the tears that came to my eyes. My shirt became drenched with my tears – this brought me back to the reality that I must not give in and break down. I knew that I must remain strong and calm for my escape.

I remembered that my wife had hidden 10 dollars amongst the clothing – after searching for some time I found it. At that time I regretted that she had not taken it herself –perhaps it would have been useful to her. Immediately another thought came into my mind about death – wasn't it better that it came sooner? Was it worthwhile to struggle for life that is just a terrible waiting for death? I saw in these discarded objects how much effort people had made, and in order to rid myself of these sad thoughts, I began to dig a hole and put into this hole 2 barrels full of their expensive articles and belongings. I covered the hole with soil. Then I washed myself. I took the suitcase and a travel bag and went out into the street.

It was a Saturday evening – the 3rd or 4th of November 1942. The snow was falling but immediately melted turning the ground into sticky mush. It was odd, once I would have avoided going out in such bad weather. Now everything seemed large, broad and beautiful. I felt the blood pulse through my veins, and my heart beat faster. I stopped and felt the snow fall on my face, taking pleasure from its whiteness. I considered how to safely move out of the ghetto.

I remembered that the parents of my sister's husband, the Rimland family, lived on Pietrowski St. not far from where we lived. They had made a good hiding place under the floor of their shop. Perhaps they were still alive – there was not a living soul about – as I went forwards I heard Ukrainian voices from afar. The further I went the more my fear disappeared and my steps became more assured. Here was the house of which I knew every entrance well. I noticed that the rubbish bin that had covered the 50-centimeter trapdoor in the floor had been moved and that the hole to the hiding place was open. I summoned courage and went down into the hole and softly called out knowing that there would not be an answer...

Soon it would be 7 p.m when the curfew began and movement was forbidden even for the Poles. I had to get out through the gate –in the distance I saw the two white shadows of the ghetto police - about 25 to 30 meters apart, who guarded the entrance to the ghetto. I used the distance between them to sneak from yard to yard. At Fuchsman's house I waited several minutes as the policemen went further into the distance and then quietly walked out into Dabrowska St. I pretended to be drunk and came face to face with a Gestapo man - singing a Polish song and making a stupid drunken face I went right up to him - he kicked me and sternly reminded me about the curfew. I pretended that I did not understand and continued to sing loudly as I continued along Dabrowska St. I realized that I actually did not know where to go or to whom to turn for help. As it happened I knew many Poles but wouldn't they be too frightened to take me in with all my things? I entered the yard of Greenstein's house at the corner of Dabrowska and Sienkiewicza - my father's watchman lived there. I silently entered the building. The watchman's wife saw me and crossed herself. She did not ask me to sit down and told me that the Germans had caught everyone who had escaped from the ghetto. If they found a Pole hiding a Jew, he would also be arrested. The Germans often came to search for Jews and she begged me to leave immediately.

I asked her for a little water and if she would permit me to leave my suitcases containing my clothing with her. At first she was afraid that I was carrying communist literature, but when I opened the suitcases and showed her the clothes, she agreed. When I departed she begged me not to betray her to anyone if I was caught.

Again I stood lost and not knowing to whom to turn or where to go. I looked around at the courtyard I knew so well – several months ago Skorbnik had lived there – he was the head of the Jewish Kehilla, at that time I had been there almost every day. There was an open closet there – I threw myself on a bundle of straw in the closet and fell into a deep sleep.

When I awoke it was 5 a.m. –and not yet light. I had to wait until daylight. Suddenly I heard steps and the closet door opened to reveal my uncle's neighbor Petrovski, a building engineer. When he calmed himself from the shock of seeing me there, he invited me to his home. Everyone was still asleep.

He boiled some milk for me on the electric stove that really warmed me from the bitter cold of the night.

I did not get much information from him, but his humane behaviour strengthened me. He was a much more distant acquaintance than those that I hoped to get more warmth and help from. I asked him if he could get me some work away from Brest. He politely refused and advised me to try some private contractors who needed laborers. The most important thing was not to lose hope and despair.

The first visit I made after this was to the engineer Tadeusz Brzezinski. I had worked for him until the Aktion (the liquidation of the ghetto) – and he owed me a lot of money for services and materials that I had delivered to him. His office was on the corner of Zygmuntowska and Ksziwa streets. Before the establishment of the ghetto this building had been Shlomevitch's bakery. Now it stood empty, the dwelling above the engineer's office deserted. Unobserved by anyone, I entered the building, removed the shutters from the door and observed all that went on from my hiding place. Soon the engineer arrived with his assistant technician. I understood from their loud discussion that they were returning after a night of celebration and drunken revelry. I did not wait for too long and approached them – it was all the same to me – I didn't care if they would hand me over to the Gestapo. The assistant who opened the door called out "holy Jesus" when he saw me. I motioned with my head for him to be silent and asked if I could come in so that the other employees would not see me. I tried to look confident and show faith in the coming German demise. They listened earnestly to me and the engineer asked me what I intended to do next. I assured him that I had not come for what he owed me – I was only interested in obtaining work. They asked me to come back in three days time, and would not hear of my suggestion that I hide in their bathroom for the three days.

Again, as I sat in the deserted rooms of the upper storey, I felt severe hunger and for a moment regretted that I had not requested food, but when I remembered their ugly mugs I was happy that a hungry Jew had not demeaned himself by begging them for food. Every corner of the house became familiar to me – I continually walked around to in order not to stiffen up from the cold. In a corner I found a mouse bitten piece of dried up bread. I threw myself on it like a wolf and remembered the long forgotten words told to all children when they did not want to eat a piece of bread with butter: "remember that in times of war, one does not even get a dry piece of bread".

When evening came I went out into the street. I went to the offices of the Ukrainian Building Enterprises and told the engineer there that I wanted to travel to the Crimea for work. He immediately agreed, on the condition that I bring a release document from my last employer. Outside there was a gay atmosphere, the shops were busy, around the Adria cinema children were throwing snowballs and their laughter resounded over the whole street. I entered a shop and bought myself a glass of soda water with 2 cookies. Whilst eating I observed the people and their faces to see whether someone would recognize a Jew when they saw me. Nobody even looked at me – it did not occur to them that 3 weeks after the liquidation of the ghetto - a Jew would dare to stroll around the streets of Brest.

The curfew hour was approaching; I decided to walk to the house of my uncle's servant. In the courtyard, all was quiet - the shutters were closed. I stood at the door for a few minutes and listened carefully for sounds from the neighbours before I knocked on the door.

The woman reception overwhelmed me. She threw herself at me with a cry as if she had found a very dear and close friend. I quietened her - she quickly drew all the curtains shut and began to tell me that she had seen with her own eyes how they had taken my family away to the railway station in the direction of the fortress. But she did not know what had happened to them.

To stay there with her was not a possibility. She was afraid of her neighbors, and would only allow me to stay there for one night. She made me something to eat; the warmth of her home penetrated my entire body. She made up a bed for me – I tried to say something about being more careful, that I should sleep under the bed. Yet I willingly lay on the warm soft white bedding.

In the morning this Christian woman – her name was Marisha Popievska, arose whilst it was still dark outside and lit a fire in her stove. She brewed coffee for me and again I had a decent breakfast and tasted being alive. She also prepared some food for me to take with me on the road – a flask of coffee and pieces of bread that she put into my jacket.

Thanking her with all my heart, I went out into the street. It was 5.30 a.m. and still dark. But by the time I arrived back at the engineer's office building, it was already light and I could have been spotted by someone… my brain worked feverishly as I tried to recall a Polish acquaintance who lived nearby.

Suddenly I remembered the mistress of Engineer Heydul who had lived for the last six months in the neighboring street near the railway station. The last time I had visited her I brought her an expensive piece of fabric. She had boasted that her apartment was very small – it could only hold 4 people. I cautiously moved through the courtyard of her building to the cellar from where I could see everything that occurred in the courtyard from a window. At 10 a.m. the woman stepped out and locked her door behind her, from that it was evident that she lived alone. I decided to wait for her return. At 6 p.m. she returned. I waited in the damp cellar and then knocked on her door. She politely asked me to enter, and asked after me family. I told her that I was the only one left, and this simple woman cried bitter tears and said that if she had taken my little daughter away with her she would still be alive. She permitted me to spend the night there and gave me a good meal. That night I slept not thinking of any danger.

The next day, Tuesday, there were knocks at the door – the woman paled and I hid behind the bathroom door. With a trembling voice she asked who it is. The engineer entered – she was delighted to see him and immediately came to the bathroom and called me, taking me to see him. He sadly smiled as he shook my hand. I could not get any news about the fate of the Jews out of him, or what was happening in the outside world. He stayed for several hours. Upon leaving he whispered quietly to her at the door. She told me later that he had told her to get rid of me as soon as possible. Because it was already late, she decided to let me stay another night in the cellar under her staircase. I knew that my pleadings would not be of any use. This night was difficult and cold – the coat that she gave me to cover myself with did not warm me. It was still dark when I walked back to Zygmuntowska St. On the way I stopped at an acquaintance with whom I had worked for the Russians. His name was Jan Sztarnetzki, he was a communist sympathizer. He ran a locksmithing business and lived comfortably.

I knocked at his door and his wife would not let me enter. With a pleading voice she asked me to leave for the sake of her children. On Zygmuntowska St there was not a soul to be seen. The engineer's house was still sunk in sleep. I waited in my hiding place and then knocked on the door. His assistant opened the door and I immediately noticed a change from 3 days earlier. Now the engineer was angry – he said that by my coming there I was endangering not only him, but also all other Polish families. I immediately understood why he had put off speaking to me for 3 days – clearly he thought that I would have been caught in the street during those 3 days. Pretending that I did not understand his meaning, I told him that I had the greatest confidence in him, and as he could not help me, then at least he should repay his debt to me. He immediately told his assistant to pay me off and went into another room, without wishing me farewell.

Carefully, like a cat I returned to Shlomevitch's empty house. I went out into the streets in the evening, ate in a restaurant and walked along Dabrowska St to Engineer Shibulski's office. He received me cordially, and asked me for my papers, when I replied that I did not have any, he asked me what assurance did he have that I was not a Jew?

From behind him someone remarked that one could see immediately that I was a Jew. The engineer said that this didn't interest him – just to bring him a document from my previous workplace, and I would get work with him straight away.

I quickly left and promised to bring the document tomorrow. I returned to the empty house on Zygmuntowska St. That night was longer and more drawn out than usual – it was freezing cold. I ran back and forth, did exercises, but there was no way that I could get warm. In the morning a laborer arrived just behind the door where I lay frozen. He opened the door to relieve himself - when he spotted me he got a shock, but realized who I was and smiled. I proposed that he sell me a Polish document. He did not think for too long and gave me a piece of paper that stated in German that the construction company of Engineer Brzezinski employed the Pole Zenon Cholevitch of Warsaw. We agreed on a price. Then he told me that there were many Jews in the Warsaw ghetto and that it would be worthwhile for me to travel to Warsaw.

Several days later I saw Stephen Vaschuk, a driver, in the courtyard of the engineer's office. He had been a good friend of mine and was happy to see me. He also advised me to travel to Warsaw, because it was impossible to get through to the partisans to the east of Brest without a guide to contact them. That evening I went to the railway station. The way to the station teemed with spies and denouncers, who scanned and checked the faces of all the passers by. I had to walk through Unij Lubelskie St. with several detours. I entered the booth of a railway guard. A rather obtuse and dense youth was inside. It was not difficult to befriend him. I told him that I was traveling to Warsaw on business and that I would bring him useful things back from there. Suddenly steps sounded from a distance – he pointed to a bunker in which I should hide. The steps neared my hiding place and I heard voices in German. They lingered at the same place for quite a while – one even shone his electric torch in to the bunker to light it up, but I was pressed to the wall and he miraculously did not see me.

After waiting for over an hour a transport train loaded with tar arrived which stopped and then continued on to Terespol. I got into an empty wagon leaving the guard with a packet of cigarettes and a little money as well as the promise of a fine present when I returned. The night was very cold with a nasty wind that raged throught the fields and the wagon I was in. I wished that I had gone on the passenger train directly to Warsaw. The train dragged along slowly. It was already after midnight and we still had not crossed the bridge over the Bug River. Arriving at Terespol, I found out that there was no train to Warsaw and that I should have to travel on to Malchevitch, 3 kilometers down the road, where a train would leave for Warsaw at 3 a.m.

I walked 2 kilometers along the railway tracks and was stopped several times by the Gestapo. Instead of answering them, I would scream out in Polish: "Stephan, hand me the lamp". Thanks to this response I arrived at the railway station. At the station there were many people and I breathed a little bit more freely. Suddenly, a young man greeted me. His name was Alex Kerner; he was a Volksdeutche (a Pole of German ethnic background). He had once worked with me at Engineer Brzezinski's. He was a good young man and had a weakness for drink. However, I was careful and pretended to be a carefree traveler who was traveling to Warsaw on business. He believed what I said and gave me his father's address with an assurance that his father would help me with my purchases.

I tried to talk to him for as long as possible in order not to draw attention to myself. He told me that whilst traveling to Warsaw 4 weeks ago, he was accompanied by a doctor from Kobryn who promised him 200 dollars and gave him 50 dollars for introductions to his Polish acquaintances for accommodation in Warsaw. The next day when he returned for the rest of his money, he was told that the doctor had gone out for a walk and never returned, leaving his belongings there. It was then that Kerner said: "I decided that I would not help save any more Jews, even for a million." What about me? I jokingly asked. His reply was that if you were a Jew you would not be moving around so freely. Those cruel words rang like music to my ears. They gave me the courage and confidence to succeed in saving myself from falling into their hands.

We drank a glass of brandy and wished each other a speedy return and to see each other again in Brest. The train going to Brest arrived, I helped him get on board, then he turned and whispered to me that 4 weeks ago he had traveled to Warsaw and had seen how a bank teller had denounced a Jew to the Germans and that I should take care.

That meant that he knew what I was and that my rejoicing had been in vain. Once again, I was all alone and the Warsaw train would arrive in 2 hours time. The ticket window would only open 30 minutes before the train was due. How would I go up and buy a ticket?

I raised my collar and sat in a corner and pretended to doze – but from the corner of my eye I observed the people. My eye caught sight of an elegantly dressed man but his face showed barely concealed anxiety and worries. He gave the appearance of almost being in a trance but I observed his knees trembling.

The ticket window opened and the ticket seller carefully eyed all the people in the queue. If he did not like someone's face he would demand their documents. If this happens to me, I'm lost, I thought. I decided to handle it by being brazen and insolent.

I turned the large hand of my watch to ten to four o'clock., and began to agitate the crowd against the ticket seller, saying that we would miss the train because of him as it only stopped there for 2 minutes. The people in the queue became impatient and began to curse the ticket seller and urge him to hurry up. Now he did not search their faces so slowly, but he gave them all an angry glare. When it was my turn, he gave me a piercing look into my very depths. I repaid him with the same glare and added angrily that: "you don't care if people miss the train, a decent Pole would not do that." He felt that all the people were on my side and gave me my ticket.

On the platform I again noticed the elegantly dressed man saying goodbye to a woman. Coming closer to them and under the pale light of the lantern I recognized him – it was Dr. Kavaleriski, a Brest nerve specialist (neurologist). When the German gendarmes had brought him into the ghetto, it had caused a sensation because no one had known that he was a Jew before this. His wife had betrayed him to the Germans as being of Jewish origin after an argument. His priest attested that he was a true Christian but to no avail – he had to live with the other Jews of Brest in the ghetto. He did not work and received support from the Catholic Church.

At that moment I envied him, he was not alone as the woman warmly farewelled him. The thought crossed my mind to wink at him, to let him know that I recognized him, but my instinct told me not to... I sidestepped him and entered another carriage.

The closer we got to Warsaw, the greater the activity. We were surrounded by outside movement and life, multicolored humanity – but nowhere was there a trace of a Jew to be seen.

From Right to Left: The Railway Station, the Government High School, the City Gardens, and Hotel Victoria (center)

[Page 572]

My Father

A poem by Wolf Kachel
Translated by Dr. Samuel Chani and Jenni Buch

Father, where is your dust? Where do your bones rest now? Ask every wind in the world, bowing with tears. Every stone, every path, every tree and flower winks at me. The whisper of the world follows me under every sky.

You have gone and are not anymore. The secrets of your life spread in silence and in storm. Sown over a domain, somewhere at a grave only a lonely branch stands.

My father, my teacher, I see in you everything around me. In my heart there always is a light that does not flare up high and proud, but lies softly as a joyous small light until tomorrow when it will shine.

You proud Jew, faithful to your people and to your city. Your heart always pulled towards Zion, and redemption. What did you think when your home crumbled, when mankind and the world was hidden in darkness?

You have gone away, but your inheritance presses on me, and the way is difficult and forlorn. Only those who knew him would never pull back until the storm has passed and the path through the forest leads to victory.

[Page 573]

The Partisan Hannah Ginsburg

by S. Alitsky
Translated by Dr. Samuel Chani and Jenni Buch

On the 21st of October 1941 at 7 a.m. all the communications between Brest and Kowel were cut at the village of Makarne. The village was in the hands of a group of partisans that numbered about 30 people who were dressed in SS uniforms. They set up a roadblock and stopped every German vehicle, killing the people inside on the spot. This was a Jewish group of partisans who that day killed 100s of Germans.

When news of this reached the nearest German garrison, punitive expeditions were sent out from 4 directions – from Brest, Kowel, Malorita and Kobryn. The partisans put up barricades at the village of Lysechowska. The battles began the next day at 6 a.m. The partisans had surrounded the village with burning coals and set fire to many houses and trees. When the Germans surrounded the village they we repulsed by the heavy firing from the partisans. They called for support from the air force, and Messershmidt planes bombarded the partisan positions from the air. The partisans still battled to repel the German push, but eventually the Germans were victorious and the majority of the partisans fell in this battle.

Amongst the survivors was a Brest Jewess, Hannah Ginsburg. For 2 hours she stood and held back a group of S.S men with her machine gun. Suddenly the firing stopped – the Germans thought that she had fallen. When they approached her – at that instant she threw a grenade that killed the whole group of Germans.

I do not know where this heroic partisan is today, but I feel great pride and awe when I am reminded of this Jewish heroine.

[Page 574]

The Partisan Activity in and around Brest

Translated by Dr. Samuel Chani and Jenni Buch

A resident of Brest, Kandlik, describes in a letter his arrival in Brest during the horrific night of the liquidation of the ghetto. Young men would often arrive by small boats on the river, and would try to persuade the youth to organize themselves or to leave the city.

Especially outstanding amongst them was a heroic woman – Genia Eichenbaum, who was born in Poltusk. She operated in several areas blowing up railway tracks. In 1942 she took part in the destruction of the Brest –

Baranovitch line, and the Brest-Pinsk, Horodetz and Drohicyn lines. Thanks to her efforts there were no less than 13 derailments of trains full of German soldiers and their explosives.

Similarly distinguished was the partisan Zerach Kormien, who led the Kartovski partisans (a Brest group). As well as his activities in other areas, he derailed 13 trains on the Brest – Pinsk line between Febuary and June 1943. He blew up the Drohocyn – Antopol line, the Brest – Moscow line. At Bluden station they detonated a train of 25 wagons that were laden with guns and explosives. On the 23rd Febuary 1944 Kormien blew up another 4 German trains at Orenzhik station on the Brest – Moscow line.

He was decorated with the Red Star and the Order of Lenin, first and second-class.

The underground leadership provided the following description of Kormien: The fighting character of the partisan Zerach Kormien, the son of Avraham Kormien of the Brest Kartovski Group. Zerach Kormien was a member of this group from 28th June 1942 until the 10th June 1944. During this period he distinguished himself with his bravery.

As commander of the extermination group, he exploded and destroyed 22 enemy trains, participated more than ten times in battles, destroyed more than four and a half kilometers of telegraph and telephone wires, 3 military vehicles on the Brest – Pinsk road, and was very active in the detonation of railway tracks. He accomplished a great amount to the development, training and arming of the Kartovski and Stashures partisan groups. Due to his assistance the Stashures group received 18 machine guns, 10 vehicles, and 10,000 rounds of ammunition. He was much loved and respected amongst the partisans.

Signed and stamped by A Leshzhov.

Brest and District Committee Commissar 1943.

Amongst the partisans who distinguished themselves was Nathan Licker who destroyed 31 railway wagons, he was also awarded the Order of Lenin and made a hero of the U.S.S.R. He lives in Brest today.

From the book by M. Kahanovitch: 'The struggle of the Jewish Partisans in Eastern Europe'.

[Page 575]

The Days of Destruction

By S. Winograd
Translated by Dr. Samuel Chani and Jenni Buch

Yesterday my Brisker friend Shlomo Kandlik came to visit me. I will endeavor as best I can to describe what he endured from the outbreak of the war until the end, so that one can get some idea what 'life' was like under Hitler's Hell.

Shlomo was mobilized into the Polish army in 1939, where he was promoted to sergeant. In 1940 he was imprisoned in a prison camp near Berlin. From there he escaped and returned to Zamosc in Poland and smuggled himself into the Zamosc ghetto. He was recognized as a stranger by the Jewish ghetto police who handed him over to the Germans. They sent him to Lublin. From there together with other Polish prisoners they were sent to Majdanek, and forced to work on constructing this death camp – they were the original builders and the camp was so not closely guarded at this stage. He escaped and returned to Zamosc, where he fled into the forest together with several other youths, the majority of who were Russian. Wanting to get arms, they stole a cart loaded with heavy wooden poles from a peasant and placed it across the road, removing a wheel so that it looked like it had broken down. Eventually a German car with 5 Gestapo men arrived, and being unable to pass, had to get out of their car and help the "peasants" unload the heavy poles, so that they could move the cart. At that moment the peasants ambushed them, taking their revolvers and automatic weapons. They then began their lives in the forest. Their group attracted about 100 men - they were commanded by a Russian youth called Bogdan. At this time there were no partisan groups set up to fight the Germans yet in this area. This group was set up to defend their own lives. During the day they hid in the forest, at night they foraged through the villages for food from the local peasants. On a certain day they were betrayed by Polish peasants to the Germans, and all were caught. Only 3 men managed to escape, and Kandlik was amongst them, but they had to flee this part of the forest. He again returned to Zamosc – it was Passover 1942, but as the ghetto was being liquidated at this time, he decided to return to Brest.

German soldiers guarded all the roads with the assistance of Polish collaborators. Despite this Kandlik reached the Mukhavets river, which he crossed swimming with one hand in the air with his bundle of clothing - he fell into the hands of a Ukrainian guard, and barely managed to extricate himself and get into the Brest ghetto.

He got through the fence at Szpitalna St. and saw a terrible sight. People were coming from work with their heads bent; they were wearing two yellow patches, one on the front and one on the back. His 'beautiful clothes' without patches evoked suspicion from the passers by who side stepped him with fear. He was forced to hide himself until evening. It was already quite dark when he went to search for his parents whom he found living in another house as their previous home was not in the ghetto area. They told him that several days after the Germans occupied Brest; they had taken away 5000 men for "work". Amongst them was 'our' Simcha Barchasman, the son in law of Josef Winograd. The remaining inhabitants deluded themselves that these 5000 would return home after they finished their work. In reality, they had all been murdered. The remaining population lived in extremely congested conditions. He found our Bracha and Baruch in a house; they did not survive together with the 20,000 other Briskers. Unlike other ghettos such as Vilna and Lodz, the members of the Judenrat (Jewish council) behaved honorably – they did not betray their fellow Jews as in other ghettos. They requested contributions and this was collected honestly and decently.

Shlomo had witnessed the liquidation and had heard about Aktions in various other cities. He understood that the same fate would befall Brest. He called on his friends and appealed to them to escape from the ghetto into the forest. But the youths would not hear of it. Adunski's wife worked in for the authorities in the administration office of the ghetto. Adunski was one of the 5000 that were taken and murdered. She used her position to save Jews. Shlomo's plan was to prepare false papers, leave with a group of youths and organize themselves in the forest. No one would listen to him – they all believed that the ghetto was under a good commandant and that nothing bad would happen to them.

The same mentality prevailed with the Jews in other ghettos. Everywhere they were convinced that it would be different and better in their own town. On the night of the 15th Oct 1942, Shlomo was awoken from sleep, there was heavy shooting from all sides in the ghetto – it was clear that the ghetto was surrounded and that the liquidation had begun. There was panic as everyone tried to save some of their meager belongings. They still did not believe that death was imminent. Shlomo decided to flee – he packed his travel bag and ran into the street. The ghetto was surrounded by flames, the sounds of machine gun fire mixed with the cries and screams of 1000s of people. Shlomo ran in the direction of Shiroka St., he got into the canal (drain) that ran along the length of the street. He hid there for a long time, before continuing on to Kobrynska St. and then to Zygmuntowska. A veterinarian doctor who once had promised Mrs. Adunski that he would be prepared to hide her if necessary lived on Zygmuntowska. At that time she had told Shlomo of this, and that he was able to obtain Aryan papers for her. Shlomo went to the vet's house but did not dare knock on the door, as it was already late at night. He stood in a closet in the courtyard until morning. When the vet left his home alone, Shlomo approached him and mentioned Mrs. Adunski.The vet took him into his home where he and his wife showed him much kindness and concern. Shlomo became hysterical as a result and cried for two hours. When he had calmed himself, he prepared for his journey. Leaving the vet's house he stopped at the corner of Jagiellonska and Zygmuntowska streets, where he witnessed 1000s of Jews being led away to their deaths. They were pushed into train wagons that stood on railway tracks that extended from the banks of the river. The wagons contained lime and many Brest Jews suffocated during the journey, the remainder was taken to Bronnaya Gora, which lies between

Kartusz Bereza and Kossovo. There they were stood at the edge of pits that had been dug and shot into the pits with machine guns.

Many Jews were murdered in the ghetto itself. This is evidenced by the eyewitness testimony by the Katsaf sisters and the Golumbovitch brothers who survived. Boza Tennebaum gave me this account and I relate it here to you:

The Hitlerites took a large number of people and separated them – men on one side, women and children on the other. Gestapo men with automatic machine guns surrounded this mass of people and began firing after an initial order to fire. There was great panic and several people managed to flee, among them the Golumbovitch brothers. The second liquidation in the Brest ghetto was in the coutyard of Ratners building at 128 Dluga St. There they collected 4000 Jews and lined them up in rows. The Jews had to dig a long and deep grave themselves. After they finished digging, they were ordered to undress. The Jews obeyed this order without any resistance. Only the children cried out: "Mama, it's so very cold". Their mothers quietened them by saying that they would not be cold for long....

At first they shot the first row. Many were wounded and still alive. The second row was ordered to push those in front who had not fallen into the grave. This happened with each row. When the grave was filled and covered, cries were heard from those buried but still alive. This was witnessed by the two Katsaf sisters who were hidden in a stable under a pile of rubbish. I'm not certain if these 2 mass shootings occurred in those final days of the Brest ghetto – according to eyewitnesses it was in this period before October 1942. In all events the final liquidation of the Brest ghetto took place on the 15th Oct 1942.

Thus ended the existence of 20,000 Jews of Brest.

I return to the experiences of Shlomo Kandlik. Seeing the masses of people being led into the train carriages evoked in him the desire to look around the ghetto for the last time, but a hidden force prevented him from doing so. He came to Kosciusko St. and observed the final Aktion through the fence. At that moment an S.S. officer arrived accompanied by a Polish youth who recognized Shlomo and denounced him to the German. But Shlomo succeeded in merging into a crowd of Poles who were leaning on the fence and observing the ghastly scene with pleasure.

Shlomo went in the direction of the Mukhavets River. On entering the river, he swam until he reached Terespol. Going through the town in the daytime was extremely dangerous. He hid in a ditch until dark – it was already dark when he left the ditch – past the hour of the police curfew. Shlomo had to crawl very carefully to the railway station. From there he traveled to Warsaw, he did not know why, but it became clear to him on arrival that he had made a great mistake. He did not know where to go, to stay with the Poles would be to hand himself over to the Angel of Death. He decided to volunteer as a Pole for labor in Germany. He was sent to Vienna. There he met a Pole with whom he had served in the Polish army. He was the only one who knew Shlomo's 'terrible' secret. He used it to blackmail Shlomo for his own purposes – on a certain day, the worst happened. Shlomo from a window saw his Polish 'friend' approach accompanied by 2 Gestapo men. They were already on the stairs when Shlomo jumped out of the window and escaped. He got on a public bus and traveled through the streets of Vienna, seeking for a Jew that he could trust. After several hours, he found a man at a bus stop wearing the badge with Jude on his coat. Shlomo followed this man into a side street, went up to him and begged him for help.

This Jew only gave him an address of the Jewish community center and left. Shlomo was overjoyed – he had already reached the steps of this building when he met a girl to whom he told all. She quickly led him away, saying that he was lucky not to have gone inside; they would have reported him to the Gestapo. This girl brought him food and gave him the address of an editor of a Viennese newspaper editor who would help him. This editor did help; he made a plan for Shlomo to escape to Switzerland and gave him the necessary papers and money. At the border Shlomo was stopped and held down by his throat by 3 St. Bernard dogs. Immediately the Gestapo arrested him and took him back to Vienna.

On the 2nd March 1943, Shlomo Kandlik was transported to Auschwitz. Also there his luck still stayed with him. At the last moment he was ordered out of the line designated for the gas chambers. What saved him was his evidence about the escape route to Switzerland - the Gestapo was convinced that they were dealing with a highly placed political personality, and placed him under special guard and organized a special investigation.

In this manner, Shlomo was again saved from death and remained in Auschwitz until the evacuation of the camp on 19th January 1945, when the Russian army launched it's offensive on Krakow. In the same camp Shlomo found Sima Shiltezki, who had been in Pruzhany when the war broke out. But when the camp was evacuated Shlomo never saw him again.

The evacuation. This was a long march (death march) of tens of thousands of people in a westerly direction. The S.S. guards hurried the Jews along, prodding them with their bayonets. During this march, Shlomo succeeded in escaping. He fell into a ditch and stayed there until nightfall. At night he began walking east towards the direction of the battlefront. He came to a village in hid himself in a Polish peasant's barn. On the tenth day, barely alive, he felt dogs tugging at him and a Russian voice called out: "here is a spy". It was quickly established who he was as the Russian soldier was a Jew. In a pure Yiddish he told him that he was free and could go wherever he wanted. Shlomo went to Lublin and from there to Eretz Israel.

[Page 583]
The Entrance of the German Army into Brest

Translated by Dr. Samuel Chani and Jenni Buch

The bombing from the air of Brest began on the 1st September 1939. In the first few days, the bombing was limited to the fortress, the airstrip and other military targets. Masses of refugees streamed into Brest from the east, completely overwhelming us. The members of the city council were responsible for finding food and shelter for them.

A heavy bombing of the city occurred on the 8th September 1939. Within the space of 2 hours, a multitude of bombs fell on the city from 100s of German bombers. Half of the city was in flames –hundreds were killed and thousands injured. The residents of Brest and the refugees began to flee eastwards. The heaviest bombing took place on Wednesday just before Rosh Hashana; the bombs fell specifically on the Jewish quarters. This was a present for the Jewish Holydays. About 200 people perished in this bombardment and 1000s were left homeless. On the 15th September the Germans marched into Brest – it was a Friday night, the German High command immediately issued an order that all the prominent city dignitaries – bankers, merchants, rabbis, priests, and professionals such as doctors - should all report to the marketplace at 4 p.m. on Saturday.

Thousands of Poles, Jews and Belorussians gathered at the designated time. The Germans appeared and separated the Poles, Jews, and Belorussians. The Belorussians were immediately freed, the Poles and Jews thrown into the prison. Not many Jews had assembled; among them was Chaim Boruch Kwiartovski the head of the Jewish community. On the other hand several hundred Poles were imprisoned. In the prison the Jews were treated brutally and tortured to get the names of the Jewish leaders and activists who had not reported to the marketplace (I was amongst them). All held out and no one was betrayed.

Two days later several hundred Germans who formerly had been imprisoned in the Polish prison camp at Kartusz Bereza arrived in Brest. The military commandant ordered that the Jewish community provide food, clothing, accommodation and money for these freed German prisoners. A German came to my home and told me to come to a meeting at the city hall. Not finding me at home, a whole platoon of Germans came to my home that evening to search my house, cellar, and attic for me. Upon leaving they posted 2 guards outside my house - a German soldier and a Belorussian who knew me. These guards stood there the entire time that the Germans were in Brest. During this period, the Germans managed to steal much merchandise from the Jewish stores. In this task they were assisted by a lot of the local Poles, who looted the Jewish stores under German protection. A self-defence group was organized immediately to guard against the Polish looters. When they were on duty, they managed to retrieve the stolen goods, breaking some Polish bones in the process. This was effective in stopping the Polish bandits as German accomplices.

On the 22nd September 1939, the Red Army marched into Brest. At 4 p.m. there was an official ceremony with both the German and Russian armies. In front of the German Headquarters both the Russian and German flags flew – the red Russian flag with it's hammer and sickle and the red German flag with the swastika. The commanders of both armies stood on an especially constructed podium and reviewed their troops. Until this day, I can still hear the sound of the jubilant Russians celebrating their 'victory' over the Germans.

After this parade the Germans left Brest.

This description by H. Kronchik is from the Book of Horrors (1945), page 139.

The Germans handed over Brisk-Litovsk to the Soviets on September 22 1939. In the photo, Generaloberst Heinz Guderian is in the center. [Bildarchiv Preussischer Kulturbesitz]

[Page 585]

The First Fateful Day

by Bertha Karlesh – Borenstein
Translated by Dr. Samuel Chani and Jenni Buch

After midnight on the 22nd July 1941, the air bombardment of Brest began. I lived with my parents on Dabrowska St. On that very day I had read in Pravda (the Soviet newspaper) that the relationship between the Germans and the Russians had never been so good.... the massing of German troops on the Russian border was described as military exercises. But in the morning we saw the German military and tanks already on the streets of Brest. The first few days were quiet with only some sporadic robberies and beatings occurring. No one thought of fleeing the city – the possibilities were minimal - the roads were continually bombarded from the air. After the ghetto was liquidated I fled to a village and stayed there with the peasants for almost two years. They did not know I was Jewish. In August 1943, when the Bialystok ghetto was liquidated, I fled another 8 kilometers to another village. Even then the peasants had no idea about the gas ovens. The Germans cleverly managed to hide the secrets of their terrible and murderous deeds.

On the 28th and 29th June 1941, the Germans surrounded all the Jewish streets – they loaded 5,000 Jews aged from 16 to 60 onto trucks and declared that they were being taken for work....

In August 1941, 20 new members of the Judenrat (Jewish council) were appointed, among them were: Hirsh Rosenberg, Dr Nachman Landau, Dr Liberovitch, Dr Yaffe, A. Warhaftig, Dr Kagan, Pochachevski, Chaim Hatz, Dr Zeligson, etc.

It was decreed that 2 million marks was to be handed over to the Germans, and the community leaders were arrested as guarantors. It was also decreed that a yellow patch with a Star of David be worn on the front and back. Jews were forbidden to go to the marketplace and the Polish shops.

At night I smuggled myself into my Polish friends home and gave them my mother's fur coat, my husband's suits, bedding and many other items. I begged them to let me stay the night, but they requested that I leave their house. It seldom happened that a Pole would help a Jew with food or temporary shelter.

Together with Lisa Rubin, Lisa Epstein, Pira Reichenbach, Stella Adunski, Helena Szteinberg, Dudke Bloch, Tchernikovski, Bella Kuperberg and others, I was summoned to the community council. There they gave us the job of collecting underwear, kitchen utensils, and many other items for the Germans - this was in order to avoid the pillaging of Jewish homes. Bronka Katzler and I had to move furniture and clothing to the police station where an elderly S.S. major smiled at us and asked if the clothing was not lice infested, and ordered us to bring more. In the first days of the German occupation many Jews and Russians were arrested – also arrested was the mathematics teacher L. Perlis – he was beaten brutally and disappeared without a trace. Rumors abounded that one of his own high school students had denounced him to the Germans.

In November –December 1941 the transfer of all the Brest Jews into the ghetto began – a section of the city had been fenced off with three barbed wires a metre high. At the ghetto gates stood a Jewish policeman on the inside and a Ukrainian policeman on the outside. One could only leave the ghetto with a work permit or the authorization of the Judenrat. Going out to work everyone made great efforts to find pieces of wood to heat the stoves. Both the Ukrainian and Jewish police guards would not permit and food or wood to be brought into the ghetto – to get caught bringing these items in meant risking one's life. In the ghetto one had to pay inflated prices for food, a soup kitchen was set up where soup was served twice daily. This together with the additional supplement of several hundred marks monthly made life just sustainable for many Jewish families.

An order was issued forbidding Jews from walking on the sidewalks; only doctors were exempted from this in special circumstance. Only very few families were permitted to live outside the ghetto. Dr Zilberstein, Dr Kagan, Dr Zeligson, Skorbnik, Dr Grynstein, all treated people outside the ghetto but they themselves lived inside the ghetto. Dora Braverman owned a beauty salon outside the ghetto, but she had to live inside. The two daughters of Ganz the hairdresser, went to their hairdressing parlour on the Aryan side to work. Also several tailors went outside the ghetto to work. Dr Rosenberg and Dr Nachman Landau were officially permitted to live outside the ghetto; however, Dr Libovitch and Dr Yaffe refused to live apart from their fellow Jews and shared the fate of their Brest brethren.

Included in the ghetto area were the buildings that had previously been the Great Synagogue, and the Jewish Community building where the Germans decreed that a communal kitchen be set up. Part of the Jewish hospital on Listovska St, which had housed the clinic of Dr Lopata, became an emergency clinic, they transferred some medical equipment there and the doctors worked in this small space with the greatest dedication. Amongst others we should praise the efforts of the young Dr V. Mostovlanski.

Hundreds of men were brought to Brest from Biala and Mezrich, these people worked in forced labor outside the ghetto. Huts were erected for them in the ghetto on Jagiellonska St. From Malorita and other villages men and women who were working for the Germans building roads were brought into the ghetto.

The ghetto of Kobryn was liquidated in August 1942, included were many Brest families: Mullier, Sarva (Except for Mischa Sarva who was in Russia with S. Matzkevitch), Blankstein and others. There were also thousands of Brest Jews in the Kowal ghetto: Pinczuk, Pomeraniec, Baraks, his son in law Chaim Shmuel Grossberg, Kwiartovski, and Munye Baraks who was shot from behind in front of his house by a German.

On the 14th October 1942 rumours began circulating that the Ukrainian police were fully mobilized. The polite Germans reassured us - on that same evening Nirenblatt and I were with the likeable German major who assured us that nothing bad would befall us Jews.

We went to bed as usual - at 4 a.m. we were awoken by loud noises and footsteps. We immediately saw that we were surrounded - we managed to pull two heavy planks from the floorboards and went down into the cellar that was only half a metre high. There were prepared buckets of water and some food there – we squashed in with our parents and several other tenants. The same instant that we replaced the two covering planks we heard knocking and banging on the windows. We stayed silent, even the four-year-old Serling grandchild did not make a sound, he silently snuggled his pale face into his grandmother. Through the gaps and holes in our hiding place we could see what was happening outside in the courtyard. There stood Lithuanian and Ukrainian policemen in black uniforms with large badges on their sleeves and caps. They had machine guns and hand grenades. The entire day there was great fear and terror – when it grew dark, the uproar abated but the shooting from close by and further away could be heard throughout the night. The blood stood still in my veins.

We lay in this hiding place for 8 days until we ran out of water – we decided to escape at night. Our back yard had a wooden fence that was the border to the Aryan side - on Dabrowska St (opposite Ganz's hairdressing salon). We could not get out the same way that we had entered the cellar – we had to go through a small opening into a lower cellar. In the early morning I lowered myself into this cellar - the long period of lying in the damp had caused my legs to swell, I swayed and fell. I dragged myself to our house, I could not recognize it – the furniture and everything in it had vanished without a trace – the windows were all smashed, and the doors ripped off.

The scene was terrifying. I hid in a closet as others began to come out of hiding. At our neighbours the Lamanovskis who lived above us, 15 people were lying hiding in a camouflaged attic. Manya Lamanovski had been during that time on the Aryan side a few times to see her friends and acquaintances. She did not receive any help from her Aryan friends, not even a piece of bread for her daughter. There was nowhere to flee and no purpose in fleeing, she said. For us here there is no way we can save ourselves. These were the terrible words we heard after 8 days hiding in our cellar.

In the ghetto there was not a living soul to be seen. All around was a deathly silence. On the deserted streets the Lithuanian and Ukrainian police wandered around in their black German uniforms.

[Page 593]

Pages from a Diary
By Asher Zisman, Antwerp
Translated by Dr. Samuel Chani and Jenni Buch

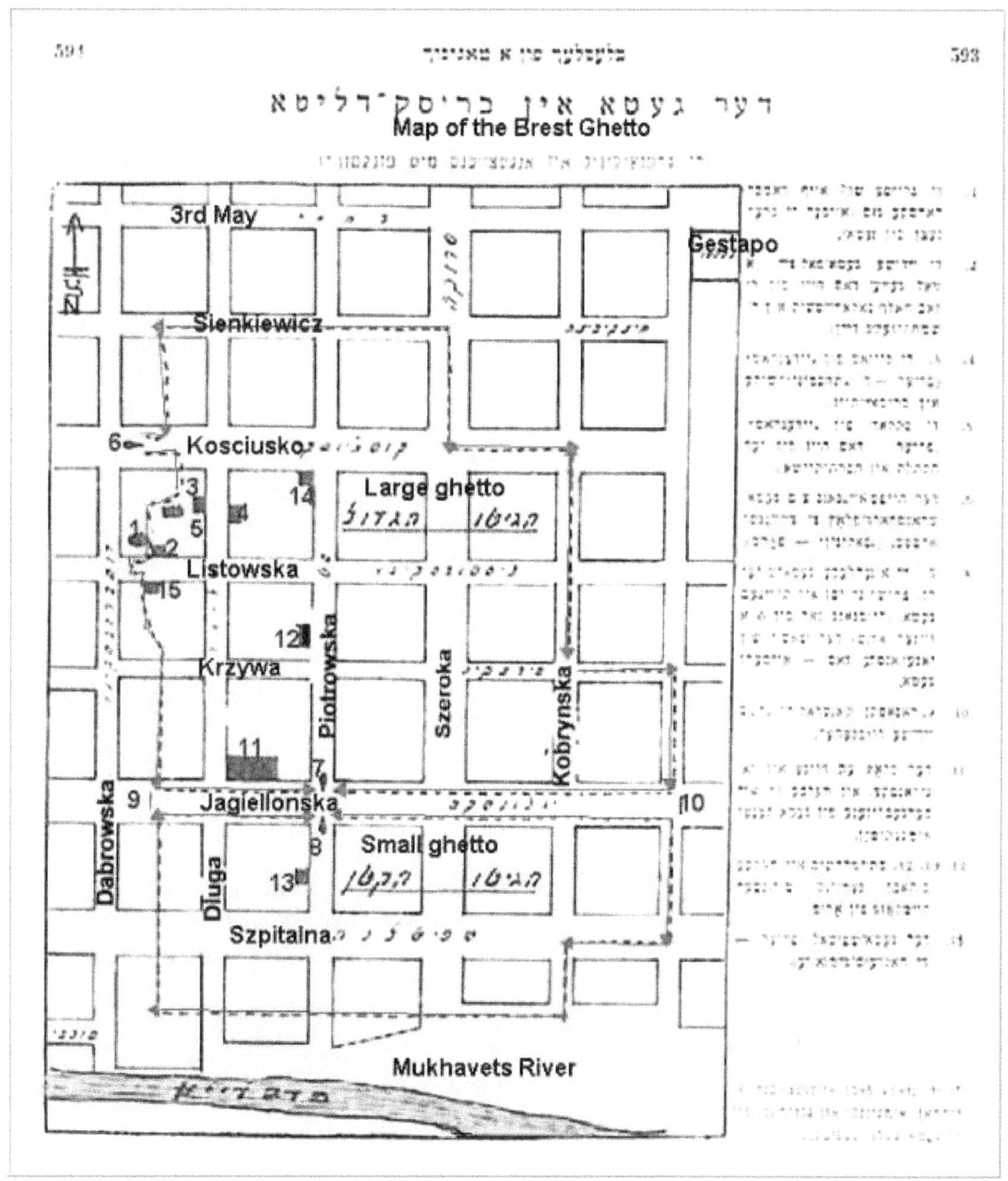

The Ghetto in Brisk D'lita

The dotted line indicates the ghetto limits. The Mukhavets River is just to the south of the ghetto.

1. The Great Synagogue on Dabrowska St. (Just outside the large ghetto).

2. The Jewish ghetto police headquarters (formerly the house of Rabbi Zeev Soloveitchik and Rabbi Simcha –Zelig the dayan).

3 + 4. The office of the Judenrat - formerly the Tachkamoni School in Borochov's building.

5. The storehouse of the Judenrat - formerly the building of the Jewish Community Council and the Burial Society.

6. The main entrance to the large ghetto. The transport place from which forced labor was assembled and taken away.

7+8. The internal fences between the 2 ghettos, large and small. Transit between them was only allowed before 6 p.m. The thoroughfare of Jagiellonska St that divided the 2 ghettos was not part of the ghetto.

9+10. Sentry gates on Jagiellonska that controlled the passage of non – Jews.

11. The place on the corner of Dluga and Jagiellonska in which the Jews that remained in the ghetto were murdered.

12,13,+14. Synagogues in which thousands of homeless people from the district lived.

15. The ghetto hospital (formerly the Business School).

December 1st 1941.

We are greatly distressed at the tragedy of 5,000 fallen innocent martyrs. Everyday brings new plagues: forced labor, savage beatings on naked bodies. The Gestapo vents it's anger on the books in the Great Synagogue and burns everything. A Judenrat (Jewish Council) was established. The German commandant is a murderer and a blackmailer, who takes away anything of any value. We return from the hard physical labor broken and exhausted – beaten and thrashed with sticks. Every limb and part of the body begs for rest.

We are inconsolable at the news from the district - they have liquidated the Jews of Kobryn, Zhabinka, Drohycyn and Antopole. The head of the Jewish community, Hersh Rosenberg, was brutally beaten – the others members of the Judenrat walk around dazed and broken. Our enemies have robbed and looted everything from us. The chairman Rosenberg and his deputy Dr. Nachman Landau said that they would not sell our lives and souls. Hirsh Lamazhevski said in the name of the community:" 5,000 Jews have been taken away and are not here with us any more. They were taken for slave labor as porters, carriers and drivers. We can make a stand if the murderers attack the ghetto, and there will be also casualities inflicted on them."

Already five months have passed. How dreadful our life is. The attacks and violent punishments, getting caught in the street. The chairman and his deputy were openly beaten in front of our eyes.

"Jews must hand in their gold and silver", thus demands the German beast. It is compulsory to wear the yellow patches. In the ghetto people die of hunger and sickness. It is forbidden to arrange funerals; only three men are permitted to bring the bodies for burial. It is forbidden to transport the dead by carts.

The German Commandant announced that Jews would be severely punished for spreading rumors about the murder of 5,000 Jews. They caught the goldsmith Nitzky on Jagiellonska St. and put him on a truck and forced him to shout;" all Jews are alive and working".

Shmuel Pomerantz met with one of the Brest community activists in Koval. There were dozens of Brest refugee families there, who were preparing to return illegally to Brest. In Koval life was even more terrible. The commandant there was a wild beats who declared that it was a waste of bullets to shoot Jews –one should beat them to death with iron bars.

I belonged to a group of tradesmen – tailors, bootmakers, carpenters, and locksmiths who were living in the yard of Rattner's building on Dabrowska St. The workers were treated like slaves from morning until night. I am working as a carpenter together with others who were previously merchants, lawyers and engineers. Yakov gefen and Ramo work closely with me – they had already learnt their trade and are able to make frames and windows. Feingold has become an expert in lochsmithing and repairs roofs and other things in the ghetto. The women work sewing underwear and knitting, most of them faint from hunger and deprivation.

Kiblitsky is a good hearted and benevolent man, a dentist. He lives on the 3rd May St. and divides everything he has between the widows and orphans on Dluga St.

On Listowska St. in an old house there sits an old man – the Dayan (judge) Rabbi Simcha Zelig and his son in law, Rabbi Moshe Reuven. The house of Rabbi Zeev Soloveitchik is on the Aryan border – in it lives the rebbetzin and her children – the rabbi has gone to Vilna. Jewish policemen occupy part of the building. Before Pesach Rabbi Simcha Zelig and his son in law organized the secret baking of matzo and the distribution of the matzo for free to the needy. People arrive for the minyanim, the prayers services. The question "who will help us?" tears at the heart.

Dr. Gotbeiter (Reb David Dabirowski's daughter) helps runaway Jews from the district. Her husband was one of the first 5,000 Jews to be murdered. As well as the 5,000 Jews, 100s of Poles were employed in digging the graves and collecting the clothes and belongings from the murdered Jews. They were then also murdered so that there would not be any witnesses.

2nd June 1942.

There is a terrified panic amongst the Jews of the ghetto. In Rattner's yard on Dluga St., the Germans are digging pits. The commandant said that they were bringing a machine in to dig. People are anxious and afraid and say that this is for a mass grave. There was an order issued that all people over 50 years of age should report to the Gestapo, if not the whole ghetto would be liquidated. My mother hid herself in the attic. They arrested me and sent me to Kobryn to be shot. The Gestapo announced that if I revealed my mother's hiding place I would be released.

A new demand arose in Kobryn. The entire ghetto population was to present themselves in one hours time at the exit gate to the ghetto where the Gestapo would decide who would remain alive. My fate was to be selected to go to the right and remain alive. In that black hour 3,000 Jews perished, among them the Brest families: Borka Shatz, Kleinberg, Melamed, Mottel Mullier with his wife and son, Hayat with his family, Sarva's two daughters, Ginsberg and his family, Feivel Gluzman the baker, Meyer Tennenbaum the printer, his son in law Pack with his wife, Leibl Sini, Sheike Matzkevitch, Simcha Zbar, Esther Machlis –Sorkin, Avraham Shvartzman, Tuvia Lamazhevski, all with their families.

Leib Sini his wife and younger daughter were together with me in the Kobryn ghetto selection. When the daughter saw that she and her parents had been sent to the left, she began a frightened wailing: "I'm too young, I want to live". The supervisor of the labor committee wanted to transfer her to the right, but a moment later a bullet ended her young life.

We were returned to Brest. The issue arose of providing hot cooked food for the starving. Rabbi Simcha Zelig together with his son in law and Rabbi Eliezer Klepfisz made it be known to all that they would found a committee including amongst others: Yakov Rosenbaum, Nachum Savaniuk, the son in law of Butche Schochet, and Avraham David Feder. It was decided that every independent household would contribute some of their food to provide communal meals for the hungry.

2nd September 1942.

The rumors are that there are no more Jews left in Koval.These were the Brest families in the Koval ghetto: Shmuel Pomerantz, Leibl liberman, Michael Rapoport, Meyer Lederman, Zipporah pomerantz and her children, and Malchiel Pinchuk and his family. It was said that my uncle Leib Liberman, together with all the others, was locked up in a Koval school before being taken out and murdered. The Jews had cut themselves and dipped their fingers in their blood to write on the schoolhouse walls their names and where they came from. My uncle wrote on the wall that they were being led to their death, and he requested that the Brisker Rabbi, Zeev Soloveitchik, say Kaddish for them.

Everyone is preparing bunkers, attics, hiding places in cellars and under stairs and digging tunnels to the Aryan side. I am digging a pit under Gordon's house in Dluga St. The entry is through an opening next to the stove and this opening will be covered over with the floorboards and thick firewood.

Rosh Hashana 1942.

Small secret prayer meeting are held in secret on Dluga St. There were some Torah books that were rescued. They have a Torah in the small ghetto on Jagiellonska St. and they prayed in a small room at Motetski's. Gershon Rosenberg the son of Michael Rashes, led the prayers – from his throat came soft moans and wails: "God Almighty, vanquish our enemies." In my workers group we silently prayed for help. The prayers strengthened us and lifted our spirits.

Succoth and Simchat Torah 1942.

In the lanes between Siroka and Petrowska streets there are camouflaged Succahs topped with grass and straw. The Jews have a tiny amount of bread to eat – there are no Lulavs or Etrogs (palm branches and citrons). More deportees from the surroundings towns and villages arrive in Brest. The ghetto is a living hell. People walk around like the living dead and go crazy. They are unable to work and walk around crying piteously. The large square pit that we are digging is almost finished.

15th October 1942.

The courtyard of the Mizrachi building on Dluga St is full of people. There is great panic. They even buy poison to prepare for every eventuality. Whoever can do so, crosses over to the Aryan side. From mouth to ear it was silently whispered that tonight it would begin... those who returned from the Aryan side report that the police were massing and preparing to surround the ghetto.

The senses are dulled, one waits for death. From our hiding place we can hear the Jews being taken away like cattle in carriages to Bronnaya Gora.

Nine people lie in our hiding place, half dead. Outside - death. We are filthy, unshaven and half blind. It is already 2 months that we are lying there hungry and thirsty – tightly squashed together. We ran out of water – the murderers filled the well in the courtyard with stones and wood. We feel close to death.

From outside terrible screams reach us – somewhere the polce have discovered a hiding place. I can see how they lead a woman and small child – it's Hannah Nussenbaum's daughter with her daughter and other Jews. Ther cries are deafening. We silently say the prayers "Shema Israel" and "Viduyim". Several shots are heard, someone sings "Mi Yehiye (who will live)", and cries hysterically.

Mrs Dolinski left our hiding place and surrendered to her executioners, asking to be shot. Some complained that it was all in vain - that we should have died together with all the other Brest Jews.

Bialkin's wife had an attack of hysteria – the same occurred with others – on the outside the animals are celebrating in a drunken orgy. One of them said: " it's not true that there are no more Jews left in the ghetto. I received 5 kilos of sugar, sausage and lard for a caught Jew." From the bunker at Dr Josem's house the director of ORT and others emerged – they surrendered to the Germans and said loudly: " we are already 2 months without food and water, please give us some water and then shoot us. " The police laughed and brought them a full bucket of water – they undressed and were shot.

We possess only 4 more matches – we only cook in the middle of the night – we are preparing for death.

17th December 1942.

We are still in our bunker-hiding place. Mrs Bialkin, Simcha Bialkin, Tevele Bialkin, Mrs Geidan, Moshe Geidan, myself, my wife Beile and her mother, Rebbetzen Klepfish. Mrs Dolinski is not alive anymore.

3rd January 1943.

The murderers discover our hiding place. We beg and beseech. They said, "give us all your valuables". We gave them everything we had. They leave with their stolen 'treasure'. We begin to flee, running and tearing through the barbed wire. We are now on the outside on Dabrowska St. We hide ourselves and speak only in hushed Polish.

Mrs Geidan went to her Christian acquaintance, with whom she had left her furs and jewellery. The woman immediately called the Gestapo and she was shot. We sneak from one attic to another searching for a safe hiding place.

January 1943.

It is snowing. The icy cold cuts through our bodies, which are infested with lice and worms.... we are in the woods amongst the animals.... perhaps it is better to live with them.

10th January 1943.

We find ourselves in the small bathhouse on Listowska St. Vizer the owner told us that we could stay there for several weeks and that nothing would happen to us. We very much want to live, and what a great privilege it would be for us to survive. The bathhouse owner told us that between the 15th –18th October all the Jews were taken out from the ghetto through the gates on the corner of Dluga and Kosciusko streets. They caught Dr Kiblitzki; he covered his face when he was about to be shot. They murdered the members of the Judenrat behind Wartchen, a village close to Wysokie Litovsk.

Rabbi Simcha Zelig and his son in law, Rabbi Moshe Reuven and their families were taken to Bronnaya Gora and proudly went to their deaths in the name of God. My father was murdered together with the head of the Kamenetz Yeshiva. My father in law, Rabbi Avraham Klepfish, died before the liquidation of the ghetto.

November 1943.

They say that the Red Army is advancing. The desire for revenge seethes in me. We are lying in the roof of the bathhouse. In the suburb of Grayever Slobotka they caught and raped 15 and 16 year old girls. We hear the sounds and noise of the water as the murderers are bathing. As the Germans begin their retreat, it is said that there are gangs that attack Aryans – the Christians go to the villages at night for safety and return to the city in the morning. The Russian bombs rain overhead and make our hearts joyful and give us hope.

10th July 1944.

The uproar of machine guns and tanks – Pinsk is already liberated. I deliberately cut my face with the razor blade – I covered the wounds with iodine as if I had been wounded. I had a moustache like a real Pole. Leaning on a cane I barely dragged my legs along. My wife and my mother in law, both dressed like Polish women, helped me along and like this we crossed the bridge out of the city together. This is how we arrived at the village of Krinki.

The Germans are in retreat, their people fall like flies. There is shouting out:" Comrades, comrades, we are free!" We are surrounded and everyone embraces each other. There are several Jewish officers in the Russian army.

I walk through the streets of my hometown Brest with a broken heart. I reach the great synagogue and the prayer houses. I pick up pages from the torn and destroyed holy books which are scattered on the ground. I kiss them and wet them with my tears.

There is not even a minyan to say Kaddish. The streets are deserted, without Jews. The Great Synagogue proudly overlooks the city. Wherever one looks there are graves and destruction as if there never was any Jewish life there. There are mass graves in the courtyard of Rattner's building. There are 5000 martyrs buried between Kotelne and Zegielnia (the brickworks).

From my choked throat the words "Yiskadal ve Yiskadash" arise. Everything around me is full with sacred fallen victims.

Brest Holocaust survivors at a memorial gathering in Wasserborg, Germany 1947

[Page 601]

The Last Children of Brest

by Yitzhak Perlov

Translated by Dr. Samuel Chani and Jenni Buch

The days of Heshvan (October) are cooler, but dry and sunny with the beautiful sadness that comes with the Polish autumn. Berish is the only one to curse those sunshine days that shone on Hitler's luck – enabling him to march into the depths of Russia.

The evenings are thick and foggy; the nights are cutting cold with frost that glitters on the grass and moss, the tree trunks and fallen leaves. The frost particles remain into the crystal clear mornings, when the rays of the rising sun melt it into pearly droplets.

The smells of the forest are now more acute as if the trees had stretched and flexed their branches. Birds are scarce in this forest –their chirping is seldom heard. The wind howls like a shepherd with his flute complaining of the autumn.

Berish lies like a bear in the forest. A large fur covers his body and head. He is wildly unkempt – even his father did not have such a long beard; a monk does not feel such cold. His nails are long like those of a preying animal. Yes, he is a bear lying in the dug out grave of his bear's den. Here he lies with his bad temper like a bear before his hibernation. Woe to him who disturbs the bear's sleep.

But his rest was disturbed in the silvery frosty surroundings. His alert ears pricked up as he heard rustling leaves and twigs. He aimed his amchine gun and focused his gaze. He discerned a couple of dark spots quickly moving between the trees about 50 meters away from him. Germans? No. They were too small and low. Animals perhaps? No. They were people. Children? Yes they were children. What were children doing in the forest on such a frosty morning?

Children, how long had it been since he had seen a child? Perhaps they were spying gentile children sent into the forest by the German to find traces of partisans. Stop! He called out as he went towards them. They began to flee like frightened rabbits. Panicking, they ran in different directions. Stop or I'll shoot, he cried. The children stooped and tightly clung to the trees. Their eyes glittered with fear and their teeth chattered so much that they could not speak. They clung to the trees and it was some time before their words could come out. "Mercy sir, have mercy on us," and even lower "Shema Israel". Berish's heart was as if stabbed with a sharp knife. Alas, Jewish children. Thin emaciated bare legs, red from the cold, bare feet on the frosty moss. A boy of about 12 and an even younger girl. They were scratched and torn, their pale faces with runny noses and blue shivering lips. Dark black Jewish eyes full of fear and tears. Silver frost in their hair. Berish's tears flooded his cheeks. Alas, alas, Jewish children his voice trembled. Oy, oy, oy, a Jewish child. The children embraced each other; their eyes wide open in disbelief. The sudden shock had left them speechless. The girl still stammered in Polish for mercy.

Berish embraced them as if they were his own. He kissed their heads and pressed them to him. Now the children really began to cry as if in their father's arms. "Come and sit down," he threw his big fur at them and they sat on it. They clung together like lost sheep, he covered them with the fur and rubbed their feet for a long time with his hands and held them tight to warm their icy bodies. They shivered and their teeth chattered. "Hungry?" He asked. Certainly they were. He had some bread and sausage. He divided it between them with pleasurable heartache as he saw how they devoured the food like hungry wolf cubs. He also had brandy but how can one give alcohol to children to drink? Even to warm them up? No, he will not give them alcohol. Soon they will come to relieve him and he would take them to Vera's. Uncle Vanya would surely allow Vera to nurse them in her hospital until they recovered. They would bathe them and lay them on bedding, they would dress them and the children would become the children of the whole Otriad (partisan unit).

"What are your names?" he asked them. "I am Michael and she is Miriam", the boy who was bolder replied. "Is she your sister?" " No, she's a neighbour". " From where?" "From Brest ". As far away as Brest! " How far are we from Brest?" the boy asked. "I don't know but it's very far, have you been in the forest the whole time?" "Yes, in many forests, but we are too afraid to go to the villages – the peasants are hostile – they sool their dogs onto us and beat us like the Germans." "Did the Germans also beat you and how?" asked Berish.

"Myself, my little sister, my mother and father were all beaten before they were shot." "Shot? What do you mean? When and where?" "My parents, my sister, Miriam's parents with their other children, together with many other families with their children." "Where was this?" "Well, I told you it was in Brest in a large courtyard. They were all gathered together, beaten and shot. I was frightened and jumped into a rubbish bin to hide. I heard screaming, cries and constant shooting. My little sister cried louder than anyone else. Later on the shooting stooped and so did the crying. It got quiet. But I was too scared to leave the rubbish bin. I stayed there the whole night until I fell asleep. In the morning it was quiet – I peeped out and saw no Germans, so I crawled out of the bin and saw the entire yard was full of dead and bloodied Jews. I searched for my parents and sister but was too afraid to crawl over the mountains of dead bodies. Many had their eyes open and looked terrible. A dead person looks terrible so I ran home. The door was open – there was no one there. I wanted to leave but I heard a soft crying from the wardrobe.

I opened it but there was no one, but I still heard crying. I opened the drawer and there was Miriam. " What are you doing there?" I asked. "I want my mother," she said. I told her that her parents were dead, that I had seen them being shot in the courtyard together with her little brother, and that they shot all the Jews. I said let's run away because they are shooting all the Jews.She cried and said that dhe didn't want to go, that she would wait there for her mother. I pointed to the roof and said that her mother would not come and that she was lying dead in the courtyard. I took her by the arms and dragged her out of the house. We ran away to outside the city. On the road there were gentile children throwing stones at us. The adults encouraged their vicious dogs to attack us. The dogs bit us until our clothing was torn and bloody. "Enough, enough, I can't hear anymore!" The broad shouldered Berish cried like a child. A town with all it's Jews murdered? And here we are sitting in the forest? He got up and screamed like a wounded lion and began to run between the trees waving his machine gun as if randomly shooting out of frustration.

In the evening Uncle Maxim came to relieve Berish. He looked at the children and silently listened to their terrible ordeal with clenched teeth, he also had tears in his eyes. He gave the children his bread and sausage and whilst the children quickly devoured the food, Maxim advised Berish. He swore that he was a honest man and only had good intentions. "If the children can speak Polish, they should only speak Polish and have Polish names. Besides Uncle Vanya, and myself, no one should know what nationality they are." Berish was silent. Tears streamed down his cheeks. Maxim clapped him on his shoulders: "I understand you Boris, but if you want to save these children, do as I advise." "Alright Maxim, you are a dear friend, come on children." Berish went on his way and the children followed him stepping over branches and pinecones, scrambling in their bare feet like 2 wounded rabbits. " Do you speak Polish children?" "Yes we do, we went to a Polish primary school". "That's good; you must speak Polish to everyone as if you were gentiles. Do not say that your name is Michael – you will be Mikhaelic and you Miriam will be Maria. It must be this way, for your sakes, do you understand?" "Yes we do", the children answered like adults."When they ask where you are from say from a village. What the name of a village near Brest? Kotelne? Good. You are Mikhaelic and Maria from Kotelne and the Germans arrested your parents and you are going to Kowal to find your relatives." "We understand ", said the children. "All this is only if they ask ask you – speak as little as possible". Alright, we will be silent," Michael said. "But they will recognize us as Jews anyway", Miriam said. These were the first words she had spoken and they were said as if she was an adult already exhausted from fighting for her existence and resigned to whatever may happen.

A shudder went through Berish's body and he was unable to reply. Silently he walked with the children into the milky fog – the twigs under his feet groaned and snapped. Berish thought that the leaves fall from the trees but the trunks remain steady. Spring will come again and the trees will have new green shoots. But the Jewish forest with it's uprooted trees in the Brest courtyard where mothers and fathers lie like cut up logs, had only 2 remaining leaves blown by the storm into the forest.

Cursed will be the spring that comes to the world if the Jewish forest does not remain.

[Page 607]

Synagogues and Prayer Houses
that were destroyed in Brisk D'Lita

Translated by Dr. Samuel Chani and Jenni Buch

Throughout the generations Brest was famous in the Jewish world as a city of Torah and learning. People would travel from distant lands to its yeshivas. The city was full of prayer houses, not only to pray in but as centres of Torah and learning. In the evenings merchants and tradesmen would come to listen to a page of Gemarra, or a chapter from the Mishnah, Midrash or Ayin Yakov (the commentaries). In every street one would hear studying and praying. In the Mishmar prayer house there was a yeshiva where 100s of youth sat and studied. Businessmen would come to hear a lesson in the Shas study group. 100s of pupils studied in the Talmud Torahs and yeshivas that produced generations of great scholars and sages that were famous in the Jewish orthodox world. Some of these synagogues produced rabbis and sages in the bygone days when the community was still in the Altshtadt (before it was moved in 1837). These synagogues were named after their founders:

Saul Wahl, Israel Wolfs, and others that belonged to professional groups such as the Tailors synagogue, Butchers Synagogue, etc. The most famous was the Great Synagogue with its cantors and prayer leaders.

This is a list of 40 synagogues in Brest before the Holocaust and destruction:

1. The Great Synagogue on Listowska .
2. The Kadosh Synagogue on Bialystotska.
3. Rabbi Meir Padua.
4. Talmud Torah on Ksziwa St.
5. The Rabbi's (Soloveitchik) Synagogue on Dabrowska .
6. The New Synagogue on Szpitalna St. no.6
7. Mishmar Yeshiva Szpitalna no. 8
8. Chai Adam on Dluga St.
9. Chevra Levaya (The Funeral Society) on Dabrowska.
10. The Ox Traders Synagogue on Sadowa.
11. Tailors Synagogue on Dluga.
12. Butchers Synagogue on Pietrovska.
13. Chevra Chvekes on Pietrowska.
14. Zohar Synagogue.
15. Kobryner Synagogue on 3rd May St.
16. Green's Synagogue on Ksziwa.
17. Reb Feivel's Synagogue on Ksziwa.
18. Zyskind Synagogue on Topolowa.
19. Shamai Weint on Kosciusko.
20. Lisker Synagogue on Pietrowska.
21. Mordechai Itteles Synagogue on Bialystotska.
22. Reb Fishel's on Listowska.

23. Reb Yoel's on Dluga.
24. Israel Wolfs.
25. Reb Yitzchak Chavalisher on Jagiellonska.
26. Grayever Slobotka Synagogue (suburb).
27. Kiever (suburb).

Shteibls (prayer houses)

Slominer, Kobryner, Gerrer, Nieswiczer, Karlin – Stolin, Kotzker, Novo-Minsker, Domachever, Alexander, Harovechever and Chabad.

[Page 611]

BREST JEWS IN THE WORLD

The Landsmanschafts and the Story of the United Brisker Relief

by J. Finkelstein
Translated by Dr. Samuel Chani and Jenni Buch

Translators note: There is no exact English word for Landmans – Compatriot means people from the same country or place – however, compatriot or countryman/woman does not convey the deep bond the members of these organizations had. (JB).

The Landmanschafts were a great strength in the life of the Jews and played an important role for us in the U.S. For decades they carried with them the warmest emotions for their old hometowns. These organizations were built on the names of these towns. They participated fully in the community life of their new country but enthusiastically fulfilled their obligations to answer the requests from the old home.

A deep-rooted idealism motivated this voluntary work – time and money were given plus the highest sentiments of helping one's brother, from one country to another. Through their activities there developed a community life where people could involve themselves and hold important positions as activists and leaders of large national organizations in our country (U.S.A.)

There were two great waves of Jewish immigration to reach the shores of the U.S. The first was after the pogroms of 1882, the second after the great wave of anti-Semitism that followed the 1905 revolution in Russia, and the peasants rebellion in Romania with it's pogroms. These upheavals played a large part in the emigration of Jews – the other factor was the grinding poverty and miserable economic conditions – the pogroms were just the final straw to make them leave their homes.

The newly arrived migrant searched for a path in this new life. But he was attracted and drawn to people from his own home country and town - to those that spoke his language. This became his social home and nest, which to some degree eased his transition pains and gave him a glimpse of the atmosphere of his lost home. This served as a bridge from the past to the future. The spark of the old home gladdened the heart; the relatives and friends would always be in one's mind.

The Landmanschafts were the primary cells from which great national organizations have arisen. Fraternal societies that were concerned mainly in helping their own: Sickness benefits, insurance, medical assistance, and activities within the cultural sphere. The oldest Jewish society was established in 1843 and served as the Union of German Jews.

In later years whole rows of large national Jewish fraternal organizations of different backgrounds reached a membership of 100,000s.

The Brest Relief Committee was part of this network and was organized in 1915 in New York. An extraordinary meeting took place immediately after W.W.1. This emergency meeting was to establish life- saving relief for the destroyed cities and towns far away over land and sea. The Brest Relief Committee collected over 200,000 dollars for Brest itself in 1921.

W.W.1 had encompassed all of Europe in terror and flames that had destroyed our city. Terrible news came from the front – heartrending letters arrived for our townsman Hershel Freiluk, now Dr. Harry Freiluk. His letters were passed on to the committee and several Brest activists, members of the Brest National Workingman's Union and Brest Bundist Group. They got together with the aim of forming an assistance and relief organization for the city of Brest.

Out of love it was decided to establish a relief committee that would be dedicated to providing help for the people of Brest and the Brest Institutions.

At the first planning meeting which had taken place in 1914 at 179 E. Broadway at Sarzer's restaurant, a committee of three was elected: H. Frieluk, J. Finkelstein and Hersh (Yudel) Margolis.

The aim was to establish contacts with the following organizations: The Brest Branch (286) of the Workmans Circle, Brest Young Men, National Workers Union Branch, and Brest Bundists Organization. An explanatory assembly took place at Halperin's restaurant at 139 Henry St. in N.Y.

It was resolved to turn to the membership and the Brest organizations about the organizing of a large united conference.

The founders of the Brisker Relief 1914
R-L: Dr. H.R. Margolis, J. Finkelstein, and Dr. H. Freiluk.
(Absent Topolewski, Sarzer and Riger)

די ערשטע גרינדער פון דער בריסקער רעליעף קאמיטע

The Foundation Committee of the Brisker Relief

In January 1915 a great conference took place in a hall at 206 E. Broadway with the participation of all the N.Y. Brest organizations. All the delegates attended:

Branch no.286 of the Workman's Circle: H. Kleinberg, M. Mezrich, Y. Rosenberg.

The Brisk Bundists: J. Finkelstein, L. Raf, and H. Riger.

The Tiferet Israel Synagogue: R. Feldman, G. Sheinman, and L. Freidman.

Brisk Independent Young Men's Society: Hershel Yudel Margolis, S. Halperin, and R. Cherkies.

Lodge 337(AABS) A. Reis, B. Fisher, and M. Rubin.

Lodge 682 (IOBA): B. Stern, P. Rabinovitch.

Brisker-Semiatycher Society: L. Wilner, M. Dreyfus.

Rabbi Zylberstein's Lodge: S. Barmatz, Y. Grossbauer.

Brisk D' Lita Lodge: Wengerowski and Jacobson.

Brisk Support Society: Y. Rosenthal, Tesher.

Brisker Women's Organization: Mrs. Sarver, Mrs. Kushner, and Mrs. Wishnograd.

Brisker Self-Education Club: G. Sklar, W. Strummer, and D. Leibovitch.

This diverse gathering from every different faction, direction, and political affiliation came together and united with the sole aim of creating assistance and support for our brethren in Brest. This conference elected the following officials: Wilner – Chairman. M Dreyfus and Cherkas were the financial secretaries. H. Frieluk was executive secretary. H. Margolis, J. Finkelstein and B. Rubin - Publicity and correspondence secretaries. Dr. Bulkowstein – Treasurer.

The 1st meeting of the Brisker Relief took place January 1915, at Forsythe Hall, 206 Forsythe St. N.Y. The agenda of that evening declared that it's primary and greatest undertaking would be a large Charity Ball to be held in the New York Opera House. Immediately there was a conflict of opinions about organizing this first undertaking. Two differing opinions became obvious – the older Briskers with their approach to work, and the younger ones who had only recently arrived in the U.S. who sharply differed in their approach to practical work. The Charity Ball proposal did not succeed....

This first project ended in instant disappointment. The entire winter went on with only the usual meetings. No concrete fundraising eventuated. Upon the German expulsion of all the inhabitants of Brest, a group formed claiming that no help was needed: "because there were no Jews left in the city of Brest".

After an entire year spent squabbling, no practical results had been achieved. At a meeting of the Relief Fund, one of the members declared that: "since they were all expelled there is no one to help. Therefore, there was no necessity for the United Relief Fund". Upon hearing this, a portion of the older members left the hall. However Hyman Kleinberg made this statement at the same meeting: "We formed this Relief fund not to play games or to seek glory.

We are certain that the Briskers will return to their city and will need assistance". The following were elected to continue the work:

Philip Rabinovitch – Chairman. M. Mezrich – Financial Secretary. N. Sharon – Head secretary. H. Kleinberg – Treasurer. J. Finkelstein, B. Rubin and Dr. Margolis were the press committee.

As the war progressed our Brest people (compatriots) became more and more anxious and would come to the United Brisker Relief Committee asking for help in locating friends and relatives. After the Germans expelled the entire city, the Briskers wandered to various towns and villages in the district, as well as further away. The Relief began seeking ways of finding these scattered Briskers. The task was transferred to the press committee – J. Finkelstein, B. Rubin and Dr. Margolis.

The war had engulfed the whole of Europe and the delivery of mail had ceased, but the Brisker Relief did not rest until we had received from the Red Cross lists of Brest people that had been located in places like: Antopol, Pruzhany, Lukav, Mezrich, and Biale (Biala Podlaska). The U.B.R. called a mass meeting of all Briskers at the Aldrich St. Hall. Many found the relatives they were seeking in the lists. We received more names and places from the Red Cross and gave them to the Jewish press to print. Many people received news of their families in this way.

Brest Bundist Organization in N.Y. 1917

From R-L: Top Row: H. Sarzer, S. Riger, Leventhal.
2nd Row: Mrs.Shapiro, B. Rubin, D. Leibowitz, Sophia Katalanski
3rd Row, seated: H. Riger, S. Silver, P. Novick, Z. Zaldman, B. Katalanski,
Bottom Row: L.Raf, L. Kling, J. Finkelstein

The Brest Committee in Warsaw

In 1917 the newspaper "Morning Journal" printed a statement that Briskers had organized a committee in Warsaw to help the Brest homeless. It consisted of:

Raphael Shereshevski - Chairman. Moshe Perelstein - Secretary. Ber Finkelstein and Yitzhak Rodevski were Treasurers. Members: Michael Stock, Mordechai Baraks, L. Levine, Y, Badanski, N. Rosenberg, N. Finkelstein, Y. Ehrlich, N. Wein, A. Goldberg, S. Stock, Y, Licht, S. Lev, B. Yaffe, I. Tzemach, M, Halperin and A. Rodefski.

The Relief decided to send the committee in Warsaw $700 dollars - they confirmed receipt of this by telegram.

The Warsaw Committee for The Brest Homeless 1917
Standing R-L: P. Halperin, Avraham Goldberg, Isser Tzemach,
Eliezer Bloch, Dov Yaffe, Badanski, Rodevski and Chaim Halperin.
Seated: Y. Ehrlich, S. Stock, Raphael Shereshevski,
Yitzhak Rodevski and Moshe Feldstein

The situation deteriorated in 1917 when the U.S. entered the war and all contact with Europe was entirely cut off. The younger generation was called up to the U.S. Army. Many young Briskers joined a Jewish Brigade and served in the British Army. In that year the work of the U.B.R. abated.

Only at the end of the war in 1918 did the work resume. Vigorous efforts were made –several branches of the Brest Relief were organized in the city of New York and in the boroughs. We became aware that a great relief effort would be necessary when the Briskers returned to their hometown. The first branches were:

The Harlem Branch of the Brest Relief.

The founding members were Brest compatriots who carried love and nostalgia in their hearts for their old home. They were successful in raising large funds for the Brest Relief. We mention them, many have passed away since then but they earned our respect and pride: Shlomo Silver (Shlomo the tailor). Benzion Rubin, Lazar Raff, Max and Chaya Silver, Roshberg (now Mrs. Stock), Nathan Cohen, Wolinsky, Dora Yachsan, Miss Rubin, Kramer, Algaza, Melnik, Jenny Hoffman, Rabbi Margolis, Kunik, Steinberg, Yashke Israel and Meir Stock.

The Brownsville Branch of the Brest Relief

The activists who formed this branch were: Barnet Stern, Guske Sharon, and Schenker. They attracted members from the General Relief to the Brownsville Relief: H. Fein, Anna Strein, Gerin Wabnik, Tenenbaum, Patchilkey, Grossman, Weiner, Lederman, Goldman, Miss Liberman, Cohen, Brychman and Miller. They were very active in stirring the Briskers in their district and got very good results - collecting large sums of donation money that was transferred to the General Relief.

The Third Newark Branch

Newark is a neighboring city of New York, on the other side of the Hudson River where there are many Briskers involved in fundraising activities: The following are participants in this group: The Brisker Shul (Synagogue), and the Brisk Society.

The speakers from New York at the first meeting in the synagogue were - H. Kleinberg, Dr. Margolis, L. Komarovsky and J. Finkelstein. The first leaders of this branch were: Freidland, Weinstock, Watstein, Lederman, Blinder, Gevras, Belfuss, Shuchman and others. These leaders have shown great dedication. Until today there is a Newark chapter that does fundraising work. Thanks to Sam Gershonbaum, Kravetz, Freidland, Borodsky and others.

Briskers throughout the country heard of the United Brisker Relief in New York and it's fundraising work. The most important activities were always publicized in the Jewish press. It became apparent that Briskers wished to set up branches in other cities under the guidance of the New York committee. Three groups were established in Chicago, Cleveland, and Detroit. Cleveland especially distinguished itself – this was where the greatest number of Briskers became involved in helping their brethren and had great success... they were regarded as one of the most outstanding branches of the United Relief.

The Cleveland administration included: P. Hametz, Fredlis, Perlman, Fishman, Kaufman, Stein, Ross, Sandstein, Williams, Gerenstein, Sarzer, Dolinsky, Wolinetz, Rabinovitch, Goldstein, Pecker, and Max Gordon.

In Chicago there were less members involved in the fundraising work, but their leadership were very energetic and dedicated landsman – Weiss led the committee, which operated during the time that the Relief sent a delegation to Brest.

Detroit was the weakest branch; it was a large town with a lot of Briskers, but lacked leadership. Although the members showed great emotion and love for their hometown, they did not distinguish themselves with donations, but did achieve some material results and participated enthusiastically when the delegation went to Brest 1920-21.

With much effort and publicity in the press the Relief appealed to the other large cities such as Boston, Philadelphia, Cincinnati, and Atlanta – however the only ones to respond were the Briskers from Los Angeles.

The Los Angeles Branch

Their first chairman was an energetic and devoted Brisker – Sam Novick. Y. Ginsberg was the secretary. In a very short time they achieved great results and financial assistance for the Relief. In 1951 they sent food parcels and medicine to Briskers in the displaced persons camps in Germany, as well as money to the Brest survivors in Stettin Poland, and in Paris.

The most difficult times for the Relief in N.Y. and the rest of the country were the years 1919 -1921, after W.W.1. The inhabitants of Brest had been expelled from their homes for three years and had lived in exile in many surrounding towns and villages. They returned to their city to find it ruined and partially destroyed – hundreds of letters began arriving from the leaders of the Brest community and from private individuals to the Relief Fund and to friends and relatives. The call from everyone was "help, please help us". Sending money was very difficult – relatives sent money, by the time it arrived it had lost it's value due to the great inflation and devaluation of that time. There was a great demand from the people of Brest that the Relief should send a delegate to Brest. At a huge conference of all the branches it was decided to send a delegation to Brest – mass meetings were held in various parts of New York. At each of these it was unanimously decided to send a representative to Brest to personally bring aid and assistance for the city of Brest.

Within a short period the Briskers had collected 80,000 dollars to be sent to Brest for both the public institutions and pivate individuals. The first delegate elected to take the 80,000 dollars with him to Brest was Philip Rabinovitch. Although by that time (1921) the Polish government had established its authority - the Poznanchiks (anti–semitic hoodlums) were still agitating in Poland. They would cut Jew's beards, and throw them out of trains. In Brest they beat some Jews to death, including the elderly businessman Michael Weissman. The letters that arrived from Philip Rabinovitch were full of the fear that people experienced – they were frightened for their lives.

Our compatriot Pesach Novick was at that time in Vilna, he was a leading member of the Brest Relief Fund. In answer to our request he traveled to Brest and sent this report of his visit there in a letter:

"I immediately traveled to Brest upon receiving the letter from J. Finkelstein, 30th June 1919 asking me to go there. My friends, I can only write you of a mountain of woes, and this mountain of woes is our city. A committee of workers has been organized with 7 members, including participants from the Bund, the left Poale Zion and the communal kitchen, 1 from the primary school, 2 from the central headquarters of the professional unions, and myself

(P. Novick). I immediately came across the people's kitchen in Brest where they were feeding over 800 people daily, including widows and orphans as well as people that just recently were wealthy. Schools for the children are needed almost as urgently as food for the stomach.

The most important streets in the city have been severely damaged or destroyed completely. At present there are 20,000 inhabitants here now –75% need assistance. The once wealthy now beg for bread. The homeless roll around on benches, on the ground, in refuges and the synagogues. Assistance is needed urgently and as quickly as possible. Write if you can send parcels - I will immediately send you the addresses. The Brisker Relief and the Brest community cannot remain silent and must immediately respond to this cry for help."

After our delegate Philip Rabinovitch returned, we received many thank - you letters from individuals and institutions who wrote that thousands had been saved by our help and asking that another delegate should come to Brest. This request was relayed by our delegate Rabinovitch at a large assembly to which he described what the city looked like, the great poverty of the returned exiles, and their great hope that we would help them. This brought about the idea to send a second delegate.

At an executive meeting at the Relief office at 202 Broadway, we discussed this matter and decided to send two representatives – H. Kleinberg and J. Finkelstein. This decision was warmly endorsed by all the Brisker societies. The Brisker Relief committees of N.Y., Chicago, Cleveland, Detroit and Newark collected $109,000. The two delegates distributed this donation money in Brest assisting 3,500 individuals; in addition $15,000 was given directly to Brest institutions without discrimination or distinction to whatever political leaning or direction they came from.

This large sum of money that the delegates brought with them resuscitated and revitalized the city. Merchants began trading and workers found jobs. The institutions broadened their activities. The delegates felt the joy of the people in the rebirth of their city. Leaders and officials expressed their thanks directly to the Relief and the delegates for their work, and publicly in the press as well.

The Brisker Relief Delegates sent to Brest 1920-21
R-L: H. Kleinberg, P. Rabinovitch, J. Finkelstein

The Relief Delegates visit the Old Age Home in Brest

Moving and Emotional Moments that Occurred in Brest

The bridge to the railway station was full of holes from the heavy cannon fire, the further one went the heavier the heartache was to see all the destruction the war had caused to the beautiful city of Brest.

The people stood in the streets, on their front steps, on their verandas and looked through their windows awaiting the arrival of the Relief delegates.

At that time there was a rift between the American Relief delegates and the Brest community council (kehilla). The delegates tried to make peace but did not fully succeed in achieving unity. The delegates relayed greetings from their American brethren and appealed for unity for the sake of the city of Brest.

Rabbi Velvel Soloveitchik and Shmuel Pomerantz headed the American committee. Rabbi Avraham Bleiweiss and Begun headed the kehilla. The delegates pointed out the importance of being united for the sake of the city and for the sake of any future fundraising activities the Relief would conduct in the U.S.

They only managed to unite the workers and set up a United Workers Committee that had representatives from the Bund, right and left Poale Zion and also non-political members. The Relief left money for a United Workers Building, which brought great benefit to the schools, youth and professional clubs, and cultural organizations when it was built.

By this historic act of sending three representatives with large sums of money to help rehabilitate their city, the Relief demonstrated their brotherly aid in the time of great need of our compatriots on the other side of the ocean.

Many episodes were described by the delegates – the difficulties in transferring the monies from Warsaw to Brest. The risky business of transferring the money by freight train – there was no other means of transport in those days. The emotional scenes when the money was distributed. The invitation to the Slonimer Shteibl for the visit of the Slominer Rebbe when he visited his Chassidic followers in Brest. The conversation with the Bundist "Noah", and greetings from Vladimir Medes. The reception given by the community council, the photograph taken with Rabbi Velvel Soloveitchik, (he said that one should not be photographed however for the sake of the Relief he agreed but cast his eyes down).

The Progressive School for Children and the Talmud Torah School with 500 pupils. The communal kitchen, and meeting and talking with officials and ordinary folk.

Brest Officials with Relief delegates, 1921.
(Center Rabbi Velvel Soloveitchik)

Administration of the Relief committee in Brest 1921
(With Lubelsky, Rodevski, Shneider, Dr.Korman,
Greenberg, Finkelstein, etc.)

At a mass meeting the returned delegates Finkelstein and Kleinberg gave a detailed account of the situation in Brest. There were 21,000 inhabitants of the city – more than half suffered from hunger. Hundreds of children had no place to learn, and the soup kitchen daily provided meals for over 1,000 people. Of 1800 brick and timber houses only 832 remained. Only 8 synagogues remained. All the institutions were destitute, but had begun to rebuild by their own efforts and desperately needed support.

The large gathering at this meeting expressed their approval and thanks to the Brisker Relief for their vital work, which gave them the opportunity to help their relatives and brethren in Brest through the efforts of the Relief. The Relief sent Finkelstein to Chicago, Cleveland and Detroit to give his reports.

1924

Brest slowly rebuilt its life, which became more normal than the first years after the war. People who had relatives in Brest began sending money directly to them. Thanks to the publicity in the press the Relief had assisted the rebuilding of the city and its inhabitants. The call from individuals to their relatives became stronger and consequently the main work of fundraising for the Relief weakened.

In the years 1925-27 there were several meetings that took place at the Brisker Shul on Allen St .in N.Y. In 1927 the fundraising activity was weak, but those that remained found it difficult to leave the organization. The idea was raised to build a Brisker Center that would conduct cultural activities and provide a place for those newly arrived from Brest.

The Jewish Hospital in Brest

The Administration Board of the Brest Orphanage

The Orphanage in Brest

The Pogrom In Brest

We received the news that there had been a pogrom in Brest from the press. The secretary, J. Finkelstein immediately called the Relief officials and it was decided to call a mass meeting of all the Brest organizations. The Jewish press gave it a lot of coverage and wrote extensively about the pogrom that had occurred on the 13th May 1937. The conference was held with almost all the Brest organizations represented and also private individuals.

The Relief committee reorganized itself and the following were elected:

Chairman – J. Finkelstein.

Finance secretaries: Gewirtzman, A. Labris, Weiss and H. Frieluk.

Secretary – M. Bernstein. Treasurer – D. Zaidman.

Trustees - H. Fein, H. Letchinsky and Brodski.

Press committee – Y. Rosenberg, L.Kossofski, B. Rubin, Y. Leizerovitch, and J. Finkelstein.

The Relief called an assembly in the Brisker Shul "Tiferet Israel". On the 20th June 1937 a large protest meeting against the pogrom that was carried out by the Poles in Brest was held. The participants were representatives of all organizations and movements. The Jewish press, Jewish congress, Jewish People's Committee, the N.Y. City Hall employees, rabbis, Menachem Berisha, Pesach Novick, and others.

The following resolution was sent to President Roosevelt and the Congress, the Polish ambassador and the Polish government:

"The world was shaken to hear about this terrible pogrom that took place on the 13th May 1937 in Brest. The peaceful Jewish residents were attacked by Polish facist hooligans, who for twelve continuous hours in the presence of the Polish police, murderously beat Jews, and robbed and looted Jewish shops and homes. They destroyed property, both homes and work places. The murderers viciously attacked the townspeople of Brest – a city that has not fully recovered from the wounds of W.W.1. They damaged hundreds of houses and shops and over 5,000 people were affected.

These acts of pogroms against the Jewish communities of Poland is in full contradiction to what the Polish government and it's leadership guaranteed it's minorities at Versailles, when Poland gained independent government.

Instead of adhering to this agreement and defending it's citizens lives and possessions, the Jews of Brest have been attacked through pogroms and economic boycotts in order to exclude them from their existence in Brest.

The United Brest Relief, which represents 7 organizations in N.Y. with 1000s of members in the U.S., expresses the utmost and strongest protest against the destruction that the pogrom hooligans carried out on the peaceful community of Brest. The beating and maiming of 60 people – 3 of whom were murdered. We demand of the Polish government that they compensate the victims for the great economic damage suffered as a result. We also demand that they punish those responsible with the heaviest penalties and release those that took part in the self defence against the facist hooligans."

Signed: Chairman J. Finkelstein, Secretary H. Freiluk.

The United Brisker Relief, 20ᵗʰ June 1937.

The work of the Relief was drastically reorganized. In addition to New York, there were branches in Cleveland, Chicago, Detroit and Newark New Jersey. In order to awaken our Brest compatriots and to continue with the fundraising work our landsman R. Zaltzman gave a report of the operations of the institutions in Brest and their desperate financial situations. They needed assistance in order to continue their work. The whole country (Poland) was in economic crisis. At this meeting Yakov Pat also spoke of the general situation and stressed the terrible economic conditions that the reactionary Polish government had caused.

Two branches of the Brest societies cooperated in publishing a mutual journal called "Unser Wort" (our word). Writers who participated in this publication were: Menachem Berisha, Betzalel Freidman, P. Novick, Y. Laizerovitch, R. Saltzman, J. Finkelstein, Y. Rosenberg, B. Rubin, Y. Heftman, S. Asherovitch, L. Weiner, M. Rattner, M. Berenstein, B. Katalanski and others.

The Writer Menachem Berisha

In addition to it's welfare and assistance activites, the Brest Relief participated in the Jewish social and community life in the U.S.

1939 Conference of the Brest Organizations of New York and Newark

Brest in World War II

In 1939 Brest was assigned to the Soviet Union. It became obvious that no assistance could be requested from us or sent by us, as all the institutions were then under the control of the Soviet Government, and that there would be no further need for the Brest Relief. It was decided to hand over our funds ($1600) to the United Jewish Appeal and continue working with them. As soon as Hitler invaded Russia in 1941, the Relief renewed its efforts.

We joined the Council of Jewish Organizations and the Jewish Council for the Russian War Relief. We participated in various anti-Nazi activities and collected a fund for the people of Brest that would be necessary after the war. None of us dreamt that Hitler would create such carnage and murder all the Jews of Brest.

We read in the press that the Jews had all been concentrated into ghettos and death camps. That same fate befell Brest. The Relief did general work to help the war effort, sold war bonds, and took part in national conferences of the Jewish World Congress, the Joint, and demonstrations against Fascism and Nazism.

Many sons of Briskers fell in the battlefields of war. Amongst them was the only son of our long serving member and official Leon Kossovski.

On the 24th Jan 1943 there was a mourning and protest service at the Brisker Shul (Tiferet Israel), in memory of the thousands of sacred victims that had been murdered in Brest. The chairman of this meeting was Leon Kossovski, and the resolutions were sent to President Roosevelt, the Senate and Congress. A mass meeting was called at the Hotel Commodore to intensify the activity. A. Labris chaired this meeting and it was also attended by Rabbi Israel Chaim Kaplan, Rabbi Kalmanovitch, Rabbi Gorelik, Leon Kossovski, and J. Finkelstein.

American Jewish Soldiers originally from Brest who died in Europe during W.W.2
R-L: Sol Tenenbaum – Died 11th Oct 1944
Israel B. Margolis - Died 12th March 1945
Irving Marland – Died 13th March 1945

After World War II

Great celebrations were held at the Capitol Hotel 23rd August 1945 to celebrate the liberation of Brest from the Nazis. Representatives from all the different factions attended – speakers, writers, community leaders and officials. All spoke of the great Holocaust that the Nazis had committed against our people. J. Finkelstein was the chairman. The New York Brisker Relief decided to arouse the consciences of Briskers in the U.S. with a letter to the press. There was also a call to Chicago and Los Angeles where a new branch was being established. Committee members of the L.A. branch were:

S. Novick - Chairman. M. Goldfarb - Financial secretary. Savnik – secretary, Folget and Feldman were vice presidents, and Rosenblum was treasurer. They enlarged their committee and attracted many new members to the cause of helping the Brest Jews.

The first letters from Europe came from Stettin in Poland and were signed by secretary Shaina Lev, Y. Meyerovitch and M. Neumark. These letters arrived immediately after the end of the war and stated that Brest survivors were scattered in many small towns and villages and numbered over 200. The Relief sent support for these Brest survivors until 1949 – the amount came to over $6,000.

We received an appeal from Paris France – they had formed a Brest Committee to assist the Briskers who were now in Paris, these new immigrants needed assistance with their legal status, work, and accommodation. Over several years we sent the Paris committee over $6,000. According to their first letter to us, their leaders were: Shushkin, Gershon and Lerner, who were employed by the Paris committee.

Hundreds of letters arrived from various parts of the world asking for help. From the Displaced Persons camps in Germany, from Italy, Cyprus, Belgium, Sweden, Shanghai and Africa. Assistance was sent – parcels of food and help was organized in the German camps under the supervision of A. Lutenberg. The Relief was in contact with him and sent him many parcels for the Brest survivors and $500 was transferred from Paris.

At the same time, we were in contact with the committee in Israel that was led by L.Y.Winnikoff and Avraham Shtrickman. There were not so many Briskers in Israel at that time. The Relief sent the Israeli committee over $13,000 - with the establishment of the State of Israel in 1948 the entire work of the Relief was channeled to helping Israel.

Our compatriot and member Pesach Novick, the editor of "Morgen Freiheit", visited the Soviet Union in 1946. On this trip he stopped in Brest, his birthplace, and wrote several articles about life in post war Brest. The Brisker Relief organized a large meeting at the Hotel Diplomat on the 9th March 1947, at which Pesach Novick gave a detailed account of his visit to Brest. This was the first eyewitness account the hundreds of Briskers at the meeting had heard, and his account evoked many tears. Speaking about Hitler's atrocities and slaughter, he read out the accounts he had recorded from the few dozen Brest survivors he met whilst in the city. He related how he was taken by hundreds of surviving Jews from the surrounding towns and villages to the mass graves where the Nazis had murdered entire families, some buried whilst still alive.

This was the burial place for thousands of Brest Jews.

The city of Brest is still there, said Novick. It lives – but the Brest Jews, our dearest and most beloved who were brutally murdered by the Nazis – exist no more.

In 1947 Dr. Yitzchak Kagan and his family – his wife, daughter Minnie, and son in law Dr. Ferber arrived in the U.S. Dr. Kagan was a renowned figure of the Jewish community in Brest. He contributed significantly to the work of the Relief, but all the troubles and suffering that he and his family had endured during the war had weakened his heart, and after four years in the U.S., he died. During those four years he would sit and converse with us and never ran out of stories about his experiences until the last days of his life. Towards the end he had been appointed director and doctor at the Workman's Circle hospital. The Brisker Relief lost one of it's most sincere and dedicated members.

The young people of Israel were involved in a fierce struggle with their Arab enemies for their survival and independence. The Haganah (Israeli Army) called on world Jewry and all progressive forces in the world to help them in the struggle. The Relief decided to buy an ambulance equipped with X-ray machines for the Haganah. The response from our members was not enthusiastic - but our steadfast activists persisted until we attained this goal, and the ambulance bearing the name Brisk D'Lita and a medical car were sent. The military authorities in Tel Aviv acknowledged this gift and thanked the Brisker Relief in the U.S.

There was a celebration service in the Brisker Shul when the ambulance and car were sent to Israel on the 21st August 1948. The idea arose to build a cultural center in Tel Aviv in memory of the city of Brest. A group of Briskers: Rosinsky, Tepper, Fredlis, and Gonsher met and worked out a plan – they called for a conference with the aim of raising $50,000 to perpetuate the memory of the sacred 30,000 Brest victims of the Nazis. At a meeting at the Hotel Woodstock the speakers explained their plan of building a cultural center in Tel Aviv – the importance of commemorating the Brest name in Israel, and in helping build a new Israeli State.

The Relief decided to send a special delegation to visit the seven Brisker Relief branches in the States, but they were generally indifferent to the project and it was never achieved. The Relief turned to the secretary of the Brest committee in Tel Aviv, Shtrickman, and made it clear that American Briskers had not responded to this proposal. The raising of $50,000 was unattainable. We asked them what they intended to do, but never got a clear response. We continued to look for a way to commemorate the former community of Brisk D' Lita.

H. Leibner and Bader of Hashomer Hatzair proposed to commemorate the Brest community at Kibbutz Gal-On. The Relief sent the kibbutz $12,000 in machinery, and the kibbutz added the name Brisk Gal-On (in memory of the community of Brest). The kibbutz also explained that if any Briskers or orphans from Brest families wanted to apply for membership - they would have precedence in being accepted by the kibbutz. In honor of the first anniversary of the State of Israel the Relief sponsored a celebration for the Haganah that had fought for the new nation.

Kibbutz Gal – On (in memory of the community of Brest) in the Negev

In 1947 the idea was formed by the Brest committee in Israel to perpetuate the memory of the murdered 30,000 Jews of Brest by the publication of a Yizkor (memorial) book. P. Chinich wrote us that he was collecting material for a Brest Yizkor Book, and that the Brest committee in Israel would prepare it for publication.

J. Finkelstein replied that the decision of the Brest Relief was to publish a book by themselves. However, the problem arose of publishing the book with the cooperation of several countries: the U.S., Israel, France and Argentina. This plan was discussed at great length and with much correspondence between the various countries. In 1952, Chaim Barlas came to the U.S. as representative for the Encyclopedia of the Jewish Diaspora, which wanted to commemorate Jewish cities and communities, amongst them Brisk D'lita

N. Tenenbaum with the Commemorative Tablet at Kibbutz Gal-On

The Brest committee in Israel proposed to publish the book within this format, but at the same time established a book committee to prepare the book for publication. The members of this committee were: Gashner, Rosinsky, Tepper, Ravin, Hari and Wolski. The issue was much discussed and debated at great length at Relief meetings until a compromise was reached and it was decided to form a United Brest Yizkor Book committee that would collect and supply it's material for this book.

On the 12th March 1950 there was a meeting of over 400 Briskers from New York and surroundings. All the various factions were represented: Orthodox, Zionist, Socialist, Bundist, and non- affiliated. This was to demonstrate their unity for the great work that the Brisker Relief had carried out over the past 35 years, and to express their appreciation for the work of the executive secretary, J. Finkelstein. All of the 7 Brest societies in New York as well as the Brisker Synagogue were represented in large numbers. Greetings were sent from the L.A., Cleveland, Chicago and Newark chapters as well as from Israel, France, Poland and Argentina. Speakers from the United Jewish Appeal (UJA) expressed their appreciation and evaluation of the work carried out by the Brisker Relief during the last 35 years. All the speakers were unanimous in their opinions that the Brisker Relief was the only organization in the U.S. that had upheld and maintained the honor of the city of Brest. They had protected and helped their needy Brest brethren in both World Wars, wherever they were to be found.

There was a meeting farewelling the representatives of various Brest Relief organizations on the eve of their departure to Israel, especially member Tenenbaum. At this meeting it was suggested that the Brest Committee in Israel (Tel Aviv) find a suitable project for the Brest Relief to work towards that would perpetuate the memory of the community of Brest. In May 1952 the Relief heard Tenenbaum's report of his visit when he returned home. He reported about his visit to Kibbutz Gal On, and his meetings with the Tel Aviv Committee – he had chaired one of their meetings with A. Shtrickman acting as secretary. They had voted to improve and increase their work, passed a motion to establish a loans fund for their members, and emphasized the importance of the food parcels. The material assistance that this loans society gave became a significant factor in assisting Brest compatriots in Israel. The Relief also heard reports from members L.Fein, Dr. H. Freiluk, M. Harris and Malin who had also visited Israel.

Memorial Meeting in Tel Aviv in 1952 with N. Tenenbaum

In 1955 our member Rosinky visited Israel for a lengthy period and consolidated the work of the Brest committee in Israel. He chaired meetings of the Association of Briskers in Israel and visited Kibbutz Gal On.

The Brest Relief Committee 1953
Seated Left to Right: H. Aharonov, N. Tenenbaum,
Mrs Bender, J. Finkelstein, N. Shapiro.
Standing L to R: S. Lederman, B. Freidman, N. Liberman

The Landsmanschafts and the Story of the United Brisker Relief (cont.)
The Branches of the Brest Relief

The Brisker Shul "Tiferet Israel".

In 1873 Jews from Newtown and 176 Chaddam Square formed a society that was a vital spiritual center to it's people. On the 23rd of December 1873, a charter was granted to the following: Simon Halevitch, B. Barnet, Harry Berenstein, Max Halevitch, M. Rosenkranz, Hillel Berenstein, Leib Kaminsky, Josef Silberman and the Chazan (Cantor) Marcus.

Thus the Tiferet Israel Synagogue was founded. The office bearers were: President - Harry Berenstein, vice-president Simon Halevitch, - treasurer - Hillel Berenstein, and M. Halevitch - secretary. The cantor and preacher was Radi. The society purchased graves at Washington cemetery. Three years later they managed to lease a building on the Eldridge St Canal to be used as a synagogue. Later, they were forced to move from these premises because the people on the upper floors worked on the Sabbath. The society bought a place at 55 Hester St., corner of 26th St., for $72,000 dollars.

Those days were the beginning of the Torah, Work and Charity era. Many new members joined the "Ahavat Moshe Society", whose members were mainly from Pultusk. The president was Benjamin Davis, who managed to unite this society with "Achavat Achim Brisk D' Lita", and the new united society was called "Tiferet Israel", Brisker Shul.

The synagogue played a significant role in the Jewish life of those days. The president was Mr. Feldman who remained in this position for over 20 years. He was succeeded by Israel Avraham Gevirtzman who bought a property for the society in 1888, and was president for 16 years. City Hall decided to demolish this building and the society received a large sum of money as compensation. They built a new large synagogue at the corner of Climber St. and Bedford Avenue, Williamsburg, Brooklyn. Sam Gevirtzman succeeded his brother Israel Avraham after his death. The Brisker Shul actively participated in the work of the Brest Relief for the entire period of its existence. The following were active members: I.A. Gevirtzman, Sam Gevirtzman, S. Seidman, David Seidman, G. Shonblum, L. Freidman, Y. Leshinsky, S. Wengerovski, and Binenbaum.

The Brest Branch of the Workman's Circle no. 286

This organization was formed in April 1909. The first members were revolutionaries from Russia who had received their socialist education in the Bund in Brest. In 1904 they had established a group with the aim of collecting money for the Bundist organization in Brest. Later the group assumed the principles of the Workman's Circle in the U.S. and joined them in 1909 as the Brest Revolutionaries Branch no. 286 of the Workman's Circle. This group participated in all the workers struggles in the socialist movement in the U.S. They have produced activists that became leaders in the workers movement and in American society. This organization participated in various cultural and social activities. Their primary aim was to provide medical and fraternal help for their members. They have been amongst the builders and leaders of the Brest Relief, and the backbone in all that it has acheived. Until today, they remain our most committed members. One of the finest pages of their 47-year history is their role in the Brest Relief.

This branch also published a magazine on their anniversaries.

Leaders of the Brest Branch No. 286 of the Workman's Circle
Bottom row R-L: A. Weinstein, T. Kaplan, Y. Rosenberg, B. Freidman, S. Lederman
Middle row: Y. Black, M. Kravitz, A. Epstein, Sarah Freidental, R. Grossman, M. Berman
Top row: A. Weiner, P. Mattenberg, P. Grossman, Y. Bein

The Brest Young Men's Association

This organization was founded in 1908 by a group of Brest compatriots (landsmen). The founders and leaders were Zionist in their persuasion, although the membership was diverse. There were 150 members at the time of its inauguration. Nowadays their membership has fallen – they give brotherly assistance, have their own cemetery, and participate in community work, especially Zionist causes. They have been a significant force in the activity of the Relief and some of their leaders were amongst the founders of the Relief and active in it for years.

Brisker Young Men's Association
(With the attendence of L Kossovski, B. Hari, Halperin, Dr. Margolis and others)

The Brest Branch no. 15 of the Jewish People's Organization

People from the Brisker Center and the Independent Worker's circle decided in 1930 to join the Workers Movement as the Brest branch no. 35. Later this branch united with the Ciechanowitz under the name Brest - Ciechanowitz branch no.15. Within a short period of time this organization grew to 300 members. The Brest branch no. 15 was occupied with providing its members with medical and general insurance. It also conducted **compulsory** cultural activities and support for Yiddish authors. For a period of time it published a fortnightly newspaper for its members. They actively participated in all the work of the Brest Relief – its leaders were amongst the founders of the Relief.

After the pogrom of 1937, they took a very active financial role in the work of the Relief, and participated in the publishing of the journal "Unser Wort" the entire time.

The Brest Branch no.15 of the Jewish People's Organization

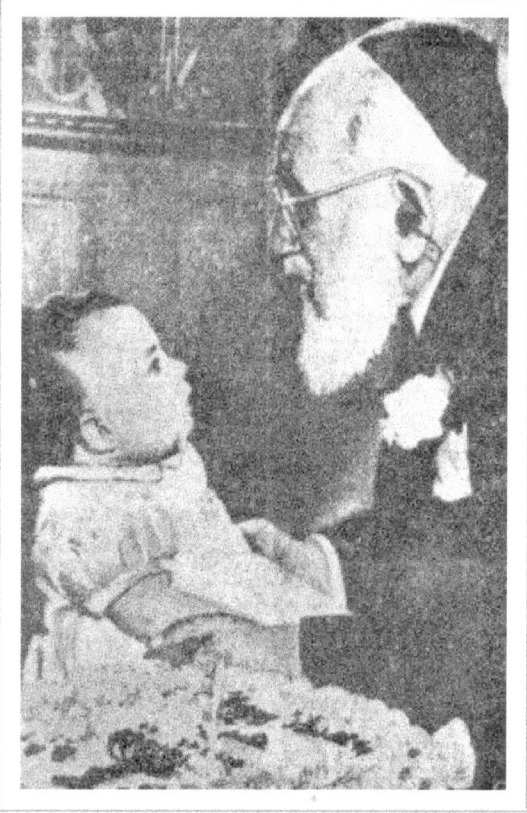

**One hundred year old Brisker gentleman,
Yitzchak Wolf Metchik in the U.S.
with his great- grandchild**

The Brest Benevolent Society

In 1890, after Passover, in the "Brisker Tea House" that was located on Eldridge St. N.Y.C., two Brisker gentlemen arrived and asked for a donation for a fellow Brisker. He had been evicted from his lodgings because he could not pay his rent. A collection of money was immediately organized so that he could return to his home. This event led to the foundation of the Brisker Benevolent Society.

The first meeting was at 150 Henry St. and the following officials were elected: President - L. Freidman. Vice President – Sam Watstein, Secretary – Abraham Weisfeld. The membership was about 100, and they paid a subscription of 10 cents a week. With their first income it was decided to buy cemetery plots. In 1900 the Society began to loan monies to its members. In 1905 they established a loan fund whereby their members could borrow $25. In 1906 they had over 300 members and a working capital of $5,000.

In 1911 a dispute arose – one side wanted to unite with the National Union of Benevolent Societies and the other side opposed this idea. This conflict went to court and the Society became on honorary organization only.

In 1917 the Brest Benevolent Society was re-established. It was the oldest of all the Brest branches in the U.S. – it had over 400 members who were mostly descendents of Briskers – it belonged to no political party or ideology and exclusively contributed to and participated in the work of the Brest Relief.

United Brest Society

In 1930 a group of 15 Brest compatriots united under the name "United Brest Society". The membership rapidly grew to hundreds in a short time. They purchased cemetery plots at the "Beth Olam" cemetery, and assisted their sick and needy members. This society met at Bables' "China Tea House" at 118 Orchard St. and their elected officials were: President – Sam Wengerowski, and Philip Rabinovitch was the secretary.

They participated in the Brest Relief through their dedicated members: S. Wengerowski, A. Rubin, A. Pomerantz, J. Reisman, who always gave their utmost to the Relief.

There were other Brest groups in N.Y. such as "Home Corner", but they did not participate in the work of the Relief nor in any of our fundraising appeals.

Brisk D'Lita Lodge

This Lodge was formed in 1907 by a group of Briskers. They united with the National Organization (identified as the Order of Abraham), and functioned as a branch of this organization. Within a short time they had grown to over 300 members. They provided fraternal assistance in matters of medical insurance, illness and burials. They participate in community work and support the U.J.A.

They are affiliated to the Brest Relief and make contributions from time to time. Their first officials were: President –A. Jacobson, Vice president - L. Farber, and J. Fisher – secretary. At present their secretary is Max Solomon.

Brest Leaders in the U.S.

Nathan Shapiro

Nathan Shapiro

He was the honorary president of the Brest Relief since its inception, and in its initial activities. He came to N.Y. from Brest aged 14, worked hard, and became an important figure in the clothing industry union. He published a book "The History of the Shapiro Family". He was active in orthodox circles and worked for yeshivas and the old- aged home. Loved and honored by all.

Jakob Finkelstein

Born in Brisk D' Lita to the poor but respected family of Reb 'Butche' Schochet. Jakob Finkelstein dedicated his life to the Brest community - he was one of the founders of the Brest Relief and its leader for 40 years. Arriving in N.Y. in 1910, he founded the Brest self-education fund in the Bund. He set up branches of the Brest Relief in Brownsville, Harlem, Newark, Chicago, Cleveland, and Detroit. In 1921 he was delegated to go to Brest with funds to assist the starving homeless returnees in the city after W.W.1.

He renewed his activity in the Brest Relief after the pogrom of 1937. His wife Clara had always stood at his side and helped him with all his community work. She passed away in 1944. He recently became a member of the U.J.A.

Clara Finkelstein

United Brest Relief Leaders – 1915 – 1953
From Top R- L: D. Kleinberg, Rosenthal, P. Rabinovitch, Y. Rosenberg,
N. Tenenbaum, A. Labris, j. Finkelstein, L. Kossovski, H. Riger, S. Silver,
B. Stern, N. Shapiro, A. Weiner, N. Liberman

Ruben Saltzman

Ruben Saltzman

He was a leader of the Bund in the U.S.A. He came from a poor family – he was apprenticed to a tailor. He was involved in conducting strikes during the Tsarist regime; as a result he was arrested and sent to Siberia. In 1911 he arrived in the U.S. He worked hard and became an active member of the Workman's Circle, and was one of the first to fight for a Yiddish primary school. In 1930 he founded the Progressive Help Organization. He was secretary of the International Workers Union that had over 50,000 Jewish members out of a total of 160,000. He was one of the founders of the Jewish Cultural Congress. In 1937, he was in Geneva and assisted the Brest Relief greatly - he also printed brochures about the Relief and its work in the U.S.

Yakov Greenberg

Yakov Greenberg

Originated from Brest. Arrived in the U.S. 63 years ago. His father Shepsel Greenberg was a learned man and scholar in Brest. He met the famous benefactor, Felix Warburg, who supported him and sent him to study in Paris – returning to the U.S., he immediately established a schools directorate. A longstanding member of the Jewish Education Council, he worked tirelessly to improve the standard of Jewish education in the U.S. he cared for both his students and teachers. He was always active in the Board of Education of N.Y. State, edited pedagogic journals, wrote textbooks and conducted research about teaching methods and education. Founded a course for teachers to teach Hebrew culture. He has close links with the education ministries of France, Israel and Greece.

David Dubinski

David Dubinski

One of the most popular and beloved members of the Workman's Circle, he became one of the leaders of American Jewry. David Dubinski was born in Brest in 1892, but his father, who was a poor baker, wandered away with his family to Lodz. David began work as a baker – at 15 he was the secretary of the baker's union and an active Bundist.

He organized a strike that led to his arrest. Freed on the condition that he leave Lodz, he arrived back at his relatives in Brest. But his political activities pulled him back to Lodz where he was immediately arrested and sent to Siberia. On this arduous long journey - he was forced to walk 10 hours a day and slept in prisons at night... he managed to escape and returned to Brest under an assumed name. He arrived in the U.S. in 1911 to join his brother. He learned a new profession as a cutter - and excelled at this work. With his organizational skills he quickly rose to important positions and in 1932 he was elected as President of the International Union of Clothing Industry Workers.

Within a short period, Dubinski had achieved wonders in this position – he organized 466 branches throughout the U.S. This union had an annual income of $7,000,000 from membership fees, and a turnover of tens of millions of dollars. It conducted compulsory educational activities as well. Today David Dubinski is one of the few Jewish labor activists who hold an important position in the forefront of the general labor movement. He visited Israel in 1955.

Secretaries and Treasurers of the Brest Relief since 1915

R-L top row: M. Dreyfus, B.Rubin, Mezrich, N. Sharon, M. Berenstein.
2nd row: P. Rabinovitch, J. Finkelstein, Mrs Bender, L. Kossovski, L. Raf
3rd row: Dr H. Freiluk, Silver, N. Liberman, H. Bernard, Dr. Margolis, and A. Epstein
(Inset): S. Lederman, B. Freidman, A. Labris
Bottom row: Treasurers – D. Seidman, H. Aronov, H. Kleinberg, N. Shapiro, D. Garin

Publications and Journals of the Brest Relief in N. Y.

The N.Y. Yizkor Book Committee 1957

Bottom row, seated L-R: J. Finkelstein, Y.Gunsher, A. Labris, N. Tenenbaum, N. Liberman, Z. Hari

Standing L-R: A. Epstein, Reizwin, B. Tepper, Dr. Freiluk, R. Rosensky, B. Wolsky, and Rabbi Golevetski

Absent: A. Pomerantz, Mrs. Heiden, M. Shwartzberg, Dr Eisen,

S. Gershenboim, S. Lederman, H. Aronov, Dr. Fein and N. Shapiro

[Page 657]

The Activities of the Joint in Brest

By A. Wertheim
Translated by Dr. Samuel Chani and Jenni Buch

The Joint organization was active in Poland from the end of W.W.1 until the outbreak of W.W.2 – 1918-1939. In it's early years it was exclusively involved in helping the victims of W.W.1 by distributing food, clothing and medical assistance. The department that oversaw the reconstruction and building work was not established in Poland until 1923. Brest was the only exception to this – due to the special circumstances that the city had experienced during the war – the construction work began almost immediately. During the war almost 70% of the city's housing had been destroyed. The exiled residents had fled in all directions. After W.W. 1, the Soviet Union and Poland conducted a war that ended in 1921. During this time the formers residents trickled back slowly – thousands of homeless Jews settled in the ruins of the destroyed and semi – destroyed houses. Many crowded into the synagogues and prayer houses for refuge. Dozens of men, women and children lived in the Great Synagogue - screening off their sleeping space with sheets. The noise and tumult was intolerable.

The ruined city

Refugees living in the Synagogue
(Image Before My Eyes)

Officials of the Joint in Brest
Standing R-L: Mordechai Yaffe, Lola Greenwald, Sara Pollack, Tzvi Lomazhevski
Seated R-L: Chana Spector, Moshe Machlis, Moshe Steinberg, Israel Tvirinovski

The Activities of the Joint in Brest (cont.)

Towards the end of 1921 the great writer Scholem Asch visited Brest and vividly described the densely crowded refuges in the packed synagogues and prayer houses.. The tragic scenes he saw moved him to tears. He later published several articles about the misery before the Holy Ark and the suffering of the returned exiles to Brest. His articles elicited a large response, not only from the Joint community in Poland, but also in the Joint circles in the U.S. They immediately set about rebuilding the city for the homeless returnees.

In 1922 I was sent by the Joint to Brest to oversee the Joint's many-sided relief, welfare, and assistance activities. We began with a budget of $100,000 that rapidly grew tenfold. Our activities concerned the following:

A. The erection of temporary housing of 2-3 rooms, which was allocated according to the size of the family.
B. Partially destroyed homes were leased for between 5 –15 years, the renovation costs being the rental. The rental payments were determined voluntarily.
C. We built a new suburb in a large street that was named after Felix Warburg, the then chairman of the Joint. The houses were two storeys and had an area for grass and garden. During 1922-23 we managed to build schools for the children of the poorer residents. Our activities in Brest were considered the crowning achievement of the Joint in Poland, all visiting dignitaries, officials and representatives went to see the beautiful houses in Brest – amongst them was James Marshall, the son of Louis Marshall.

The Felix Warburg Colony
(Pictures from Image Before our Eyes)

One of our most significant activities was the construction of Jewish schools in Brest. We established many schools of all the various factions - General Zionist, Tarbut, Talmud Torahs, yeshivas – all of which had been destroyed in the war. The Joint could not leave the city without schools – although we did not interfere in policy matters of education. Therefore, we paid great attention and effort in establishing the same schools that had existed in Brest previously. A huge and bitter political fight between the leaders of all these different factions resulted - with the Joint office trying to solve the educational issues. Every faction was afraid that they would lose their power and influence to their political opponents.

We established an orphanage hostel for the orphaned and abandoned children of Brest, which we divided between the various factions, according to the numbers in their schools. The Joint also established a large trades school that taught trades such as metalwork, lock smithing and carpentry; it was well equipped with instruments and machinery. In 1924 this school was handed over to the ORT organization and existed until the outbreak of W.W.2.

[Page 657]

The Brisker Landsmanschaft
in Australia

By Avraham Chani
Translated by Dr. Samuel Chani and Jenni Buch

Until 1938 there were almost no Briskers in Australia. In that year, as W.W. 2 neared 25 families arrived from Brest. The majority of these were artisans – it was very difficult at first to find employment for all of them, and only a small number managed to obtain employment. With the outbreak of war Australia experienced a shortage of manual labor and all the Brest migrants were able to find work. They organized themselves – 3 of the 25 families settled on farms away from Melbourne assisted by the Jewish Welfare Organization. The remainder remained in Melbourne, and lived in one neighbourhood. They all maintained close links with each other as one 'family'. They were also in constant contact with the relatives left behind in Brest.

When this contact was cut off we all went around in shock, and consequently we became even closer to each other – never did we miss a family event - celebration or tragedy, in the lives of our fellow Briskers. In 1942- 43 we received unsubstantiated and unbelievable news of the destruction that was occurring in Brest. We formed the idea to establish a Brisker Association in Melbourne with the aim of assisting our brethren in Brest at the first opportunity. In 1944 the news we received was clearer and more terrible. A meeting of all the Briskers was held on the 20th August 1944 at the home of A. Chani. An assistance fund was established to help any Briskers who would turn to us for help.

Our committee immediately sent letters to the Brisker Landmanschafts in NewYork, Buenos Aires and Tel Aviv. We informed them of our decisions and asked them for any news from Brest or about the Jews of Brest. Their replies contained no new information. We then sent letters to Moscow, to the offices of the "Unity" publication, and to the Council of Polish Jews. Alas, we never got a reply. But we did get a letter from a surviving Brest Jew, Asher Zisman, who described the destruction of Brest in detail, and how he and his wife had managed to save themselves. He also informed us about 14 other Brest Jews who had fled in various directions and survived. He himself was in Belgium. Letters began to arrive from other Brest survivors in Italy, Poland and Germany.

On the 30th July 1946, we received a collective letter from 12 Brest families who had returned from exile in Russia and were in a camp in Stettin Poland. They requested help and emigration permits for 7 families. From them we found out that dozens of Brest survivors were scattered in various towns throughout Poland. A committee was formed in Stettin, as this is where the largest group of Brest survivors was.

We immediately called an emergency meeting at the home of H. Rosenberg, and decided that the following Sunday every Brisker would bring food and clothing – the collection point was the factory of H.A. Woliniec. We packed and sent 24 parcels, each containing food, medicine and clothing. From then on this committee conducted a systematic and intensive assistance program. We received letters requesting help from survivors in various countries – not one request was unanswered.

Now that we knew the date of the massacre and liquidation of the town – 15th October 1942 – we began to hold an annual commemoration ceremony. At the first memorial ceremony we published a bulletin about the fate of the Jews of Brest that appeared as a Yiddish supplement in the Australian Jewish News. This bulletin included a historical article about the Jews of Brest by A. Chani, as well as the letter from the survivor Asher Zisman, followed by an article "20 years in Brest" by L. Greenberg, "Brest without Jews" by Y. Feldman, "Eternal Sorrow" by M. Wabnik, and the "Road to the Grave" by R. Mandelzweig.

We regularly hold meetings to organize effective assistance for all Briskers, as well as the annual Yizkor memorial services.

It is also noteworthy that the Brest Landsmanschaft belongs to the Australian Federation of Landsmanchafts, and we are represented by our President, Mrs Grace (Gruzhevski), who is the treasurer of this Federation. Our members also represent us at other Jewish community organizations in which they hold important positions.

Sending Parcels to Stettin Poland

Yizkor Memorial 1948

Yizkor Memorial 1949

[Page 665]

The Brisker Society in Paris
"Amicale Be Brest - Litowsk"

By B. Wolski (New York)
Translated by Dr. Samuel Chani and Jenni Buch

After the First World War, the Jewish youth of Brest found themselves in desperate circumstances without any future prospects for their existence. Therefore they sought any opportunity to emigrate. Not everyone could travel to the U.S.A. or Israel – some also immigrated to France. The majority of them settled in Paris, where they encountered great difficulties upon their arrival. Without family, friends or understanding of the language they had great difficulties in obtaining work permits. As foreigners they did not have the right to work and these permits were difficult to obtain. Overall their situation was grim.

On the "Pletzel" (the Jewish quarter of Paris) there was a shop owned by Leibl Prizant who sold underwear. This shop became the first gathering place at which the newly arrived Briskers would meet. The second place was the shoe repair shop owned by H. Gutmacher. Gutmacher was a young man from Brest, a genuine man of the people. Warm, friendly, big-hearted and always ready to help anyone – Gutmacher would lay down his tools and go with the newcomers to assist them –organizing their documents at the Police Prefecture to obtain their work permits.

The number of arrivals grew from day to day. Men of all different political persuasions and beliefs, who would never have mixed together in Brest, became friends in this foreign place. They would seek out opportunities to meet each other, to schmooze about their hometown, and to help each other. The two above mentioned businesses were not suitable for this purpose – a hall was needed for regular meetings and organized assistance for each other.

The writer of this article took upon himself the initiative to form a Brisker Society in Paris. He contacted several influential Parisians who had originated from Brest. One of them, Yitzhak Tilles, invited a group of Briskers to his home. Amongst them was Rabbi Chernaya, the son of Avremeleh the owner of the Paris Hall in Brest. Rabbi Chernaya was the rabbi of the Jewish community of Angen le Ben, a suburb of Paris. He was elected as Chairman of a temporary committee. Frequent meetings were held at Tilles' home, whilst they worked out the statutes of the new society, and collected addresses of Briskers who had settled in France.

At the beginning of 1924, a foundation meeting of the Brisker society in France was held. The following were elected: President: Rabbi Chernaya, Vice Presidents – the lawyers Frankel and Gorevitch, General Secretary – B. Wolski, Secretary – Sternberg, and Treasurer – A. Egdeshman.

Members were: Halbertal, Kranski, Leifer, Gerson, Gutmacher, L. Glozman, Kamenetski, Leibovitch, Morgenstern, Blackman, Itzkovitch, Shwartz, Hechtman, Eichenbaum and Leventhal.

The Society set itself the goal of giving moral support and material assistance to all the new arrivals from Brest, and to participate in their cultural and social lives. The society formed a loans fund, a reading room, and organized monthly cultural lectures about various topics like health, sociology, literature, history, etc.

When the influx of new arrivals decreased, the new immigrants were able to organize themselves and the Society evolved into a mutual – help organization, the purpose of which was to provide medical help for its' sick members, organizing graves and burials when they died, and covering their debts to the loans fund. They also provided support for widows and orphans. However, the society did not abandon its' cultural activities and also financially supported the ORT Trades school in Brest.

Committee of the Brisker Society in Paris
Seated R-L: Katzav, Engineer Shishkin, Gorevitch and Dr. Braverman
Standing R-L: Dr. Mintz, Kaplan, Gerson, Ginzberg, Glozman and Kamenetski

The new arrivals in France found adjusting to the French way of life difficult – during this period their children attended French schools and were quickly becoming assimilated. Due to this the initiative was raised to form a "Colony School" with the aim of providing supplemental Jewish schooling and summer activities and camps for Jewish children.

The "Colony School" achieved great success and was one of the most popular and liked Jewish organizations in Paris. It exists until this day and owns and runs 5 homes for orphans, a building that houses 150 residents at the seaside resort of Bourg Plage, and has a mobile clinic that provides free medical aid. It runs two Jewish supplementary schools, and many social activities for Jewish youth.

The fate of the author of this article was to become the Chairman of the Colony School and so I had to relinquish my position on the Brisker Society.

Brisker Landsleit (compatriots) in France

The first wave of immigrants from Brest to France occurred in 1906-08, after the Russo –Japanese War of 1905. The defeat of Russia caused a wave of anti Semitic riots and pogroms due to the economic upheavals and unrest. The following 20 years 1905-1925, saw a great increase of arrivals. A younger and dynamic element arrived that managed to quickly make contact with the older migrants who were able to assist them to find work, with their papers, legal status, and provide help for the urgent needy cases. The foundation meeting of the new Landsmanschaft of the Brisker Society was held on the 14th Febuary 1925. On the 7th December 1926, a Loans fund that provided interest free loans was established. This was an autonomous organization that gave long-term interest free loans to small businessmen, tradesmen, and students.

The Brisker Society provided medical treatment and medicines, financial support in case of serious illness, burial costs, and support for the widows and orphans of the deceased. There was also an active cultural program; lectures were regularly held, as well as group tours of places of historical interest in and outside of Paris, museums etc. They also held an annual Ball that was the traditional get- together of all the Briskers in France. Thanks to the initiative of the Brisker Society, the 'Colony School' that provided supplemental Jewish education for the children of the Brest migrants was established. In the same year (1926) an appeal for the hungry children of Poland and the orphans of Brest was held. In 1930 an appeal for the Jewish schools of Brest was held. At the outbreak of war in 1939, the Brisker Society organized itself to morally and materially support their members who were fighting on the battlefront and their family members at home.

Many Briskers fought in the French underground during Hitler's occupation. Amongst the first 48 French resistance members to be shot was our Brest brother, Hersh Leib Meirovitch.

Immediately after the liberation of France, a general meeting of all Brest survivors was called in September 1945, at which a plan of material and moral support was worked out. The Society played a vital role in the lives of the young Jewish children and orphans of W.W.2. They held summer colonies for the elderly; the Society supported all the Jewish organizations that provided financial and moral assistance to the French Jewish community, and their anti-defamation, anti-semitism and anti-racism work. It took an active role in the movement against German rearmament, and support for the activities of the Haganah in the early days of the State of Israel. (They raised 500,000 francs). In 1956, the Brisker Society celebrated its 30th anniversary in France. They received congratulations from all over the world – from the U.S.A, Argentina, Israel, Warsaw and Stettin Poland, and Australia. All expressed the hope that we would never forget the tragic destruction of our 1000-year-old community, and that we would remain in close contact with all the Briskers from all the corners of the world.

The committee of the Brisker Society consisted of the following members:

Honorary president: Evel Gorevitch. President: David Lerner. Vice presidents: Lazar Glozman, Albert Gutmacher, and Bernard Gerson. Secretary: Moshe Shishkin. Treasurers: Ovsei Tashkin, and Mordechai Kamenetski.

Members: Aaron Mintz, Yosef Farwein, Yekutiel Kaplan, Dr. Shmuel Danovski, Kalman Ginzberg, Yosef Glozman, Alexander Sochowolski,Jacques Glozman, Boris Mular and Yitzhak Levenberg.

Amongst the members who had distinguished themselves with their dedication and work were: Leiber Rimland, Moshe Sternberg, Felix Morgenstern, Mrs M. Katz, Henri Ramo, Mottel Berman, Moshe Katzaf, and Armand Leventhal.

The French Memorial in Honor of the Brest Martyrs

[Page 671]

The Brisker Landsmanschaft in Argentina

Translated by Dr. Samuel Chani and Jenni Buch

The stream of immigration out of Poland after the First World War did not miss Argentina. The Jews who fled anti Semitic Poland arrived here without any means, and without any knowledge of the local language and conditions. Therefore, they required a great deal of material and moral support.

Amongst these immigrants were some Jews from Brest. The Brest Jews that had arrived in Argentina previously, were the ones that provided the necessary assistance and help for their newly arrived brethren. Early in 1923 the Society of Brisker People was formed. The founders were: Tabachnik, Bacharach and Munk. The Society's goals were the assistance of new arrivals from Brest, helping them obtain accommodation and employment, as well as establishing links with Brest and providing support for the social and cultural institutions of their hometown. They had already organized a book collection for the Trade Unions Library in Brest in 1925. In 1929 a Brest Bank was established which existed until 1935.

With the outbreak of W.W.2 all contact with Brest was severed. This weakened the activity of the Society, which began to disintegrate, if not for the foresight of several members who foresaw that the Society would encounter far more urgent challenges. When the first news of the destruction and Holocaust in Brest arrived, the Society strengthened and began intensifying it's activities of aid and assistance for Holocaust survivors, with priority for those from Brest.

In 1949 a split occurred within the Society. A group of Briskers who did not agree with the "Progressive Faction" and who had strong ties to the State of Israel, established their own group under the name Union of Brisk D'Lita and District. At the head of this Union were: Y. Zajonc, P. Glazer, M Youngerman, A. Kandel, Weinstein and others. During the time of its' existence this Union managed to organize and send food parcels to Israel, and collect money for the Keren Kayemet Leisrael to perpetuate the memory of the sacred victims of Brest with a memorial forest. It also published a newsletter for the group called "The New Word" (Dem Neie Wort). This Union has very close links to the Brisker Association in Israel.

Committee of Briskers in Buenos Aires, Argentina

[Page 673]

Surviving Brest Jews In Poland

By Mordechai Neumark
Translated by Dr. Samuel Chani and Jenni Buch

Group of Brest Survivors in Siberia 1946

Discussing the Brest survivors in Poland, I cannot omit relating to Brest specifically as I saw it myself whilst travelling through on our return journey by train from Russia to Poland.

This was on the 19th- 20th May 1946. A group of Brest families including Aaron Rosenberg, Mordechai Neumark, Pesach Kempel, Shlomo Shapiro, Rochel Fernig, and Genia Storch were returning from Russia to Poland after the war. We arrived in transit at the Brest railway station, where we were told to transfer to a Polish train that went to Warsaw and Lodz. In the interval the passengers, both Poles and Jews, could wander around the city to have a look, and say our goodbyes before crossing the border into Poland.

I felt duty bound to visit Dr. David Gotlib on Listowska St. Walking through the streets; I did not come across one familiar face. Only one, Mrs. Bertha Kandelsbrat, a noted music teacher, who embraced me warmly and gave me a hearty welcome from the remaining Jews of Brest. 1 was warmly received at Dr. Gotlib's by his wife Rachel. I also found Dr. Mendel Kummel there from whom I heard that there was barely a minyan of Jews (10) left in the city. I said my farewells and returned to the station. On my way back I saw the deserted Great Synagogue, without any people praying, without its shammes, Reb David.

The next day Piotr Grigoriev, Moshe Katzav, Genia Shedrovitzka, Raizel Razel, and others who had heard from Dr. Gotlieb that we were there, arrived at the station to see us. Piotr Grigoriev, a Christian, was a great friend of the Jews, and the treasurer of the Brest City Council until 1939. He asked me to take his greetings to all the Brest Jews and not to forget him. This man would come to the synagogue every year to hear Kol Nidre for over 27 years.

On the journey to Stettin Yosef Meirovitch, Israel Furmanovitch and Eliezer Ratnovski joined us. The journey to Stettin took a week, and Shamai Hazan met us on our arrival.

On the 5th June 1946, we established a "local committee of Briskers" in Stettin with the participation of Yakov Koppelman, Mordechai Neumark, Aaron Rosenberg, Shaina Lev and Yosef Meirovitch. The committee immediately established contact with the Brisker organizations in the U.S., Israel, Argentina and Australia.

At the same time we formed contacts with the Briskers in Lodz, Poland, who had also formed a committee that included Moshe Lev, Eliezer Hatz, Chaya Israel, Max Rottenberg, etc

After the pogrom in Kielce, many Jews left Poland. From our committee in Stettin Koppelman and Rosenberg emigrated.

It was difficult to obtain the exact numbers of Briskers remaining in Poland. The committee established a figure of 200 Briskers who were concentrated in the towns of Stettin, Lodz, Wroclaw, Warsaw, Dzergeniev, Bialalewa, Walbrzych, Krakow, Bytom, Ziembice and Klutski.

Many of these Briskers had changed their names to Polish names but it was very seldom that they had left their Jewish religious heritage. They worked in government and communal positions, in factories and cooperatives. Amongst them were Moscinska, who worked in the Government Communications department, Zelig Rosenzweig, Josef Goldman who worked in the Ministry of Trade, Leizer Gruzhevski, Adam Savaniuk, Leizer Petchanik who worked at the "Solidarnosc" co-op., Genia Silecks, who worked for the Jewish Historical Institute, Shaina Lev the director of the Yiddish primary school in Stettin named after I.L. Peretz, Miriam Weingarten who was the director of the Jewish kindergarten in Stettin and then worked for the Israeli Consulate. Eliezer Hatz worked for Keren Kayemet Leisrael, Max Rottenberg worked for the TOZ central organization, Mordechai Neumark worked for the Jewish community in Stettin, Mania Shachnievska – Graevska worked for the Jewish committee in Ziembice, Shimon Kritzin – Jewish committee in Bialaleva, Shabtai Bishkowitz – teacher in Walbzrych, Josef Meirovitch – Yiddish library Stettin, Sarah Shapiro – nurse in Klutski.

The majority of Briskers have left Poland and are now to be found in Israel, France,Belgium, Australia, etc. A very small number remained in Poland.

**Memorial Service For the Brest Holocaust Victims
held in Stettin Poland ,1947**

[Page 675]

Organization of Brest Descendants in Israel (Irgun Yotzei Brisk)

By A. Shtrickman
Translated by Dr. Samuel Chani and Jenni Buch

For us, the Briskers in Israel, the idea of a Landsmanschaft was a foreign concept. We did not represent any activity or identify with the social structure of the "Old Country". It was our intention to put down roots in Israel and to contribute to the creation and character of this new Israeli nation.

Until the Great Holocaust occurred. In 1944 a group of Briskers decided to call a meeting with the aim of establishing an organization that would gather any news of our town. A committee was elected which consisted of: Winnikoff, Ludski, Kastrinski, Dlugin, Zweiboim, Shtickman and Kachel. At that first meeting we decided to publish the "Book of Brest".

The first activity of the board was to collect and gather any information about the fate of the Jews of Brest, with the assistance of the Jewish Agency and any other means, also to provide food parcels for the needy.

In May 1945, we received the first letter from a surviving Brest Jew, Asher Zisman, who described in detail the destruction of the Jews of Brest. On the 17th June 1945, we held our first commemoration service, and it was decided to establish the 6th Cheshvan (15th October) as our memorial date. Then the first of the Brest survivors arrived in Israel and we tried to assist them with settling in Israel. Contacts were established with Brisker Landsmanschafts in other countries, with the Brest Relief in New York, Australia, Argentina and France. The closest links were with the Brest Relief in New York, which until today is the most active of all these organizations. The organizations of the other countries concentrated on helping Brest survivor refugees where they were located in Poland, Germany, and France. Therefore our requests did not find a receptive response.

In the great wave of post- war immigration, we helped the new migrants to find housing and work. We did not receive any assistance from abroad until 1948, when the first help came from the Brest Relief in New York specifically for the refugees from the British camps on Cyprus.

Over the course of time we met with many Briskers from abroad that were visiting Israel. From Argentina - Chaim Finkelstein, P. Gingold from Chicago, H. Kossovski from New York, H. Neuman from Chicago, Dr H. Freiluk and Pomerantz from New York, members of the Brest Society from Paris - H. Shushkin, Minc, and Lerner. N. Tenenbaum the chairman of the Brest Relief in New York, H. Yungerman from Argentina, Diana Yanov and Freidlis from New York. Thanks to those meetings an ongoing and lively contact was established with the Brest organizations abroad. At the Brest Relief conference in New York, our member H. Trubovitch represented us.

The Israeli committee took on the task of perpetuating the memory of our city and made great efforts towards the publishing of the Brisk D' Lita Yizkor book. We were in constant contact with the Brest organizations of various countries. A committee was established especially to collect material for this book – this committee consisted of: Dlugin, Chinich, Kastrinski and A. Levinson.

In New York, Jonah Ganzer headed their book committee. When Chaim Barlas visited the U.S. the matter of publishing the book in two languages was agreed on - Hebrew and Yiddish. We must note the great voluntary effort and dedication of Nachum Chinich. This member of the book committee painstakingly collected and prepared the material before it was sent for publication by the Encyclopedia of the Diaspora.

With the visit of H. Tenenbaum, Chairman of the Brest Relief in New York, a Loan Fund was established which helped many Briskers in Israel.

These are the members of the Brest Committee in Israel:

Honorary Chairman - Rabbi I. Y Unterman, the Chief Rabbi of Tel Aviv and Jaffa. Committee members from 1944-1950: Y.L. Winnikoff, Chairman. Aaron Ludski, Avraham Shtrickman – Secretary. B. Kastrinski, Shlomo Dlugin, Eliezer Fein, Fania Artzi – Pomerantz and Bat-Sheva Segal.

In 1957 the committee members were: D. Zisman, A. Shtrickman, M. Neumark, M. Zamichovski, B. Kastrinski, and S. Shwartz. The editorial committee for the Yizkor book: Dr. S. Orchov, S. Golubovitch, Engineer P. Barkai and M. Breinhendler.

The Briskers and their descendants are spread throughout the cities, settlements, and kibbutzim of Israel. According to our estimates they number about 1,000 families.

Organization of Brest Descendants in Israel 1950
Seated R-L Y.L. Winnikoff, Rabbi A.Y. Unterman
Standing R-L: A. Lutenberg, A. Pomeranitz, A. Dolgin, N. Chinich,
M. Neumark,A, Ludski, A.Shtrickman, B. Kastrinski

Organization of Brest Descendants in Israel (Irgun Yotzei Brisk)

Members of the Haifa Committee
R-L: M. Breinhendler, S. Rubin, H. Kachel and S. Zmichovski

[Page 681]

Briskers Who Fell in the War of Independence

Translated by Dr. Samuel Chani and Jenni Buch

Let us remember our children that originated in Brest and gave their lives in the great struggle for liberation and the establishment of the State of Israel.

Joseph Guss. Son of Rachel and Shmaryahu Guss

Born in Brest in 1929, fell at Gush Etzion 21st Nissan 1948. He immigrated with his parents to Israel in 1934. After finishing primary school, he studied at evening high school classes, and worked at a clerical job during the day to help his parents.

Joseph was active in the Haganah, after the United Nation's partitioning of the country; he was amongst the first to volunteer to accompany the convoys trying to break through the blockade and reach Jerusalem. He was transferred by air to the besieged Gush Etzion when the situation deteriorated there. When his parents asked where he was going he said proudly "who but the young can protect our lives? Or should we go like sheep to the slaughter like our beloved ones did in Brest?"

He was proud of his voluntary contribution to the struggle for the establishment of the new nation. Despite the great difficulties that he knew existed in Gush Etzion, he reassured his parents that they should not worry and that the nation would be established in spite of their Arab enemies.

On the 5th May 1948, the Arab Legion under the guidance of the British Army attacked Gush Etzion with tanks and heavy artillery. The defenders of Gush Etzion withstood the attack but suffered heavy losses. Twelve heroes fell on that day, amongst them Joseph who was not quite 19.

Yakov Getzel

Born In Brest 1915, fell in the fields of Benyamina 1947.

The Getzel family was exiled from Brest to Siberia during W.W.1 – the family returned to Brest in 1925. Yakov studied at the Tachkamoni Hebrew primary school in Brest, and then at the Ort tradeschool where he learnt metal trades and locksmithing. He was known as strong and fearless, and always ready to defend the weak. He was never wounded in the fights between the Polish and Jewish youths, and was a graduate of Betar.

He arrived in Israel in 1935 and worked at Hadera. He was also a guard at Tulkarem and Kalkiliya. The members of the local farming settlements (moshavs) liked him because of his fearlessness. Yakov was arrested by the British at Hadera as the result of taking part in retaliatory action by the underground. He sat in Acre prison for several months.

After being freed from prison he was sent by the Haganah to Hanita where he was given the task of training himself to assemble and handle weapons in the armory of the British Army. He became a specialist in this field.

In 1947 he was sent to obtain weapons from the Arabs and never returned. He fell at his guard post in the fields of Benyamina.

David Gratzer, son of Chaya and Yakov Gratzer

Born 28th Tevet 1921 in Ramat Gan and fell 3rd Iyar 1948 at a radar station. David was raised in Kfar Yehoshua and was liked by his friends and teachers. David was quiet gentle and serious, he loved nature and prepared for a career in agriculture. His ambition was to have a rural life working the land.

When he was mobilized in March 1948 he was sent to the besieged Jerusalem, for weeks his family awaited his return, but he never did – he fell on road to Jerusalem.

Gershon Dubinboim, son of Mala and Tanchum

Born 26th April 1927 in Brest. Fell on the 21st Tishrei 1948 on the Negev Front.

The Dubinboim family made Aliyah from Brest to Israel in 1935. Gershon finished his primary school in Rechovot. Due to the difficult financial situation of his family he interrupted his studies and began to work at 15. He was accepted into Kibbutz Degania – and was sent to an instructor's course by the Haganah. Returning to Degania he gave all his free time to working for the Haganah.

When W.W.2 ended Gershon and his family became aware that all of their nearest and dearest in Brest had been murdered by the Nazis. Gershon decided to enlist in the Palmach where he took part in the most dangerous missions. He distinguished himself and studied to further increase his military expertise.

In December 1947 he was sent with his battalion to the Negev. He became battalion leader and took on the defence of the Yad Mordechai and Gvar Am district to ensure to communication lines there. This area quickly became the most difficult and bloodiest of battles of the whole Negev campaign. When the decisive battle broke out in Yad Mordechai, although his battalion headquarters was stationed further away, Gershon personally participated in its defence. Thanks to him the evacuation of the children was carried out successfully in the last moments before the Egyptian surrounded them and the decisive battle began.

With typical skill and courage he also fought with his battalion in the siege of Beer Sheba and was involved with the Stern group in bringing reinforcements to Hebron and destroying the bridge at Dahariya. He was hit by anti tank shrapnel there and died the following day, the 21st Tishrei 1948.

Gershon was beloved by the men of his battalion – he always demanded more of himself than of others. He was wholehearted in his dedication. The city of Rechovot honored his memory by naming a new street in Rechovot after him – Rechov Gershon.

Tzvi Drori, son of Ida and Gershon Drori

Born in Tammuz 1928 in Tel Aviv. Fell 10th Tammuz 1948. Tzvi Drori came from a deeply rooted Zionist family. His grandfather was Reb Shmuel Halperin, from the family of Rabbi Chaim Volozhyn, who was a great scholar and a dedicated Zionist. After W.W.1 he founded the Mizrachi organization in Brest and the Tachkmoni Hebrew School. He brought up all his children in the spirit of Torah and Zionism and was granted that all his children made aliyah to Israel and survived the Holocaust.

His son Gershon was Tzvi's father and an impassioned Zionist from his youth. He went to Israel together with his pioneer group aged 18. He worked on a railway gang and built the railroad between Sarafen and Lod. He endured all sorts of backbreaking work and in 1932 was one of the founders of a settlement at Yarkona.

From his mother's family he received the influence of Jewish culture and Zionism. His maternal grandfather was Kadish Tennewitzki, a committed Zionist official and worker all his life. He had made aliyah with all his family to Israel in 1938, but had returned to Brest to liquidate his business interests and perished in the Brest ghetto.

Tzvi was 3 years old when his family settled in Yarkona, and was still at school when his father died, forcing him to assume the role of provider for his family. He worked during the day and at night he studied with the Gadna (military cadets), training hard. At 14 years of age he became a member of the Haganah. When the terrible news about the 35 martrys of Gush Etzion arrived, he hastened to help the besieged at Gush Etzion. He went to his mother and said:" I'm going to replace them". He excelled in his leadership abilities and took part in battles at Jaffa, the Sharon district, and the sieges at Latrun, Migdal Tzedek, and Rosh Ayin.

In the battle over Kola where his company found themselves in a difficult situation, he ordered his men to withdraw and left himself to cover their retreat. The company escaped unharmed but their leader Tzvi fell. It was his 20th birthday.

Tzvi's heroic deed

He shot at the approaching enemy tanks with his machine gun, even when they were only 200 meters away. At this critical moment, his machine gun jammed – Tzvi did not lose control and calmed and encouraged his men – he ordered a group of his soldiers to shoot at the tanks whilst he repaired his gun and began shooting again so that his men could retreat safely.

From the official report on Kola – the ambush of the village and the defence against it. 1948.

David Tash (Tour Shalom), son of Tziporah and Eliezer Tash By E. Tash

Born on the 28th Iyar 1928 in Brest. Fell on the 8th Shevet 1948 on the road to Gush Etzion.

David was born in Brest, on his mother's side he was a descendant of both Rabbi Nachum of Chernobyl and Rabbi Pinchas Koritzer. He inherited his love of Israel from his home, and his schooling at Tarbut further deepened this love. As a three-year-old child he loved the story of David and Goliath. Winnikoff's daughter would jokingly call the three year old to the phone and say: " David, how did David kill Goliath?" he would reply: " with five small stones." Ironically his fate was that he, together with his group of 35 comrades, heroically fought in the same area that David killed Goliath with stones from the river.

It is possible that in their last tragic moments, they realized that they had no more bullets, and only had stones as ammunition. (The Arabs said that one of the 35 was found with a stone in his clenched hand).

In Israel he was brought up in the idealistic spirit of love for Israel and was active in the labor movement. He joined the Gadna (military cadets) where he was active; he studied sociology, philosophy and law at university. At the same time he was a youth instructor, cultural officer and guard in the Gadna. He lectured in factories, and was also involved in the theatre group.

Notwithstanding that he was exempt from active combat duties, according to one of his commanding officers: " he willingly chose to be on the front line and volunteered to take part in the desperate attempt to break the blockade at the beseiged Gush Etzion. There together with his entire group he fell after a long and hard battle".

The editor of the newspaper "Am Oved" (working nation) published a book of David's writings titled: "David Tash, one of the 35".

Benjamin Yarchi (Pitcharski). Son of Nathan

Bejamin Yarchi was born in Tel Aviv in 1927. He graduated from the Geula High school. He was amongst those who led the drive and penetration into the Negev, even before the establishment of the State of Israel. He fell on the road to Falugia.

An only son, his parents could not survive this great tragedy and both died shortly after him.

David Neumark

Born into a distinguished old Brest family. His father Baruch Neumark (Noy) was the mayor of Acre. His grandfather was Ben Zion Neumark, a famous Zionist activist in Brest. When he was a child his family migrated to New Zealand. Although he adjusted successfully there the youth never stopped yearning to go to Eretz Israel.

In 1945 the entire Neumark family made Aliyah to Israel, and it was then that I met David for the first time, a quiet shy youth. Underneath he had an unforgettable lust for life. He was friendly, loyal and popular. The day when he entrusted his secret to me is etched into my memory – he told me that he had been accepted for Gadna training and how his face lit up with joy.

On the 29th Dec 1947, a month after the U.N. resolution to establish a Jewish State, one of the underground divisions attacked the Arab suburb of Romema, which held a nest of Arab bandits.

The British arrived to assist the 'innocent' Arabs. They shot at the neighboring Jewish settlements from their armored cars. The 16-year-old David who was incidentally passing along the street at this time was shot and killed by one of their murderous bullets.

(A friend).

Ben Zion Fogel. Son of Nechama and Yitzchak

Born 11th Elul 1930 in Rechovot, fell 3rd Tammuz 1948.

Ben Zion's father Yitzchak was educated at the ORT Trades School and hostel in Brest, where he was brought up in the Zionist spirit. He came to Israel with the first group of Zionist pioneers from the hostel in 1926 and worked as a laborer in Rechovot. His mother Nechama arrived in Israel in 1926 and immediately went to on a kibbutz.

His parents went to work the land together and were part of the founding group that established the first worker's moshav of 'Kfar Bilu'. Their son Ben Zion was educated at first in this village, then at high school in Rechovot, and later graduated from the Max Fein Trades School as a machinist. He excelled himself with his diligence and good nature, and was very much like by his friends and teachers. He was devoted to the Haganah where he trained from his early youth. In the battles for liberation he was amongst the best at creating diversions and an excellent organizer. He took part in dozens of actions including escorting convoys to Jerusalem, Kfar Uriah., Nachshon, Latrun, Tel Arish and the "Maccabee" action. He was finally transferred to the 52nd battalion in the Nitzanim area where he participated in some bloody battles. On a Saturday night the 4th Tammuz he was sent to collect the dead and wounded, where he was wounded himself. He said to the medics that he was only lightly wounded and could carry on helping others. However, he died shortly afterwards. He was not yet 18 years old.

Yitzchak Shuster. Son of Chaya and Eliezer

Born on the 1st Iyar 1924. Fell on the 17th Tishrei 1948.

Yitzchak finished primary school in Brest. He then endured and survived all the horrors of W.W.2 in Europe. After the war he was a member of the kibbutz Ichud group in Germany and came to Israel in the "Haportzim" refugee ship which arrived at Nahariya January 1948. He worked as a barber in Hadera. He was mobilized into the Israeli army and served as a medic in the 'Givati' battalion. He participated in the battles for the Negev and was wounded at Negba. After recovering he returned to the battlefront and was killed on the 19th October 1948, during the attempt to break the siege of Moav Akiva, whilst fulfilling his duties as a medic. He was laid to rest at Kfar Warberg.

[Page 691]

SMALL NOTES

Customs and Folklore in Brest

by Benjamin Gruzhevski
Translated by Dr. Samuel Chani and Jenni Buch

The Keren Kayemet Tax

Brisk D'Lita was greatly under the influence of its rabbi – Rabbi Chaim Soloveitchik. It had a great many yeshivas and synagogues, both Chassidic and Orthodox (Mitnagdim). Rich businessmen and merchants supported these institutions, large and small, and even such "Mitzvas" such as Hoshannas.

The Zionists were a majority in the city. They included most of the intelligentsia led by Colonel Dr. Shteinberg, who had full authorization from the Odessa Committee (The Zionist Headquarters in Russia). Leaders were C. Padua, M. Rabinovitch, Ben Zion Neumark, Leon Horoditche, and A. Pochachevski (from the first Chovevei Zion) – they had participated in the first Zionist Congress.

After our successful annual collection of donations for settlements in Eretz Israel on the Eve of Yom Yippur in the synagogues, we decided to levy a special Keren Kayemet tax on all the Jews of Brest. Because of our opponents, we decided to keep this decision secret. After Yom Kippur we formed a special committee that would collect the Hoshannas. Three days before Hoshanna Raba we sent out people who stood in pairs the entire day and night on all the corners of the city, on the roads that led to the villages that supplied all the branches for the Hoshannas.

We tried to buy all their stock, but many of the village peasants refused to sell us their branches at our offered price – they thought that they would get a better price in the city. This was a risk that would damage our whole plan; therefore our members, after arguing with the villagers, tore the leaves off the branches. The stripped branches were therefore rendered worthless. The peasants did not understand and stood all day in the city awaiting their fortune. Hundreds of Jews passed by and saw the damaged branches and would not touch them. A day before Hoshanna Raba there was disquiet in the city due to the lack of the Hoshanna branches – at this stage the Zionists posted notice in all the central spots announcing that 'Kosher hoshannas' would be sold at certain locations. Every Jew that wanted to carry out the mitzvah of Hoshanna ran quickly to purchase them. Many became enraged when they discovered that it was a Zionist scheme, but they had no choice other than to purchase from us. The price was higher – we earned a kopeck from each sale. All the money went to the Keren Kayemet.

There were some individuals who refused to buy from the Zionists. The Zionists decided to delay the prayers and sent special messengers to the villages to buy branches for them. The rabbi had to buy from us and willingly paid the tax. That particular Simcha Torah was characterized by especially joyous dancing.

The Keren Kayemet Congress In Brest 1913
Including: Zisman, Kvianovski, Lubelski, Koloditzki,
B.Z. Neumark, Markran, Henich, and Kviatkovski

Letterheads and Stamps of Various Brest Institution

Folk Stories

by Meyer Ashkenazi
Translated by Dr. Samuel Chani and Jenni Buch

The people's doctor, Dr. Shteinberg, used to say: I have the recipe for long life, to live until 120. He would explain thus on every eve of Yom Kippur, Passover, and Simchat Torah: One's home should always be as clean as on the eve of Passover, one should always eat until full as on the eve of Yom Kippur, and one should always rejoice as if it were Simchat Torah.

* * *

When he would visit a sick patient he would accept payment for his services, even on the Sabbath. When the rabbi, Chaim Soloveitchik, raised this matter with him, he replied: "Rabbi, if the women know that I won't accept payment on the Sabbath, they'll all get sick on the Sabbath! It is written that the Sabbath is a day of rest – what sort of rest would I get every Sabbath? Rabbi Chaim replied: " you bow to the golden calf the entire week, at least on the Sabbath free your soul from the weekly work. You are a physician of the sick and a liberator of the oppressed. Are you then not duty bound?

* * *

He would charge ten kopecks a visit. Upon departing, he once heard a woman say: "the doctor, came, took a tenner and departed! Hopefully he took the illness with him..." She thought that he was a Gentile, but he immediately replied to her in Yiddish: "yes I took the tenner, but the illness is still with the patient, and it will be a miracle from heaven if he survives!"

* * *

When there was an outbreak of cholera in the fortress, 28 Gentile and 8 Jewish soldiers were stricken, Dr. Shteinberg ordered that a huge pot of stew be cooked and given to the sick soldiers. All the Gentile soldiers recovered and the Jews died. When asked why he replied: " from this we learn that Jews can't tolerate pork!"

* * *

Brest was renowned as a bastion of the Mitnagdim. One of them, an educated young man married into a Chassidic family. His new father in law wanted him to become a Chassid and said: " I don't care whether you go to the Gerrer or Kotzker Rebbe, as long as you are a Chassid, I don't mind...." The young man replied: " I don't believe in either the Gerrer or Kotzker rebbes, I only believe in what one says about the other!"

* * *

Reb Shmuel Landau, a learned Jew, came to Rabbi Chaim Soloveitchik on Purim and said: "I wanted to send the rabbi the best wine as a Purim gift, but I could not find a suitably expensive container for such a good wine. I decided that the most expensive container is myself, so I drank the wine and then I came to you!"

* * *

My grandfather Reb Meyer Ashkenazi was born in the old Brest (before they shifted the city) and died in the new Brest when he was aged 101. When he was ninety years of age, my grandfather fasted on Tisha B'Av. My grandmother, seeing that he was weakened, asked him to eat something - he took her by the hand and led her outside to the street. He showed her how the entire sky was lit by fire, and said: "see how the synagogue is burning and you tell me to eat!

My grandmother died aged 100.

* * *

My father Reb Gershon Moshe, blessed be his name, died aged 98. He was never sick, never wore glasses and led the prayers at the lectern at the 'Hakodesh' synagogue on the High Holydays. When he turned 98, he was confined to his bed for 2 days and passed away peacefully without any suffering.

My mother, Bashe was born in Bialystok and died in Brest aged 96. She did a great deal for the poor and saw to it that no one would go hungry on the Sabbath.

Brest Jews in Military Service of Various Countries
From R-L top to bottom: Pesach Barkai (Burkowstein) Served in the Israeli Army
M.Bikov – Polish Army
L. Raf – British Army W.W.1
S. Ramo – Soviet Union Military
C. Finkelstein – U.S. Army W.W.1
D. Tennenbaum - U.S. Army W.W.2
Silver – Jewish Legion (British) W.W.1
Josef Butkovski – Tsarist Russian

[Page 699]

Brest In World Events

Translated by Dr. Samuel Chani and Jenni Buch

Events of great historical and political importance took place in Brest on the 20th Century. The peace treaty between the Russian Bolsheviks and the Imperial Germany was signed there, and 22 years later in 1939 the Communist Soviet Union met there for talks with the German Nazi regime. The first shots fired when the Germans invaded The Soviet Union in 1941 were crossing the Bug River into Brest.

Brest is entered in the annals of world history with various other historical events. It is impossible to mention all of these occurrences - but we publish here the recollections of Count Atkater Tchernin 1872-1932. Tchernin was an Austrian diplomat and foreign minister of Austria 1916-1918. He played an active role in drafting the peace treaty signed in Brest Litovsk in 1918. An excerpt from Trotski's "My Life" (Trotski was the famous Soviet representative). An excerpt from Winston Churchill's book "The Second World War".

"No War No Peace", Brest the 20th December 1917

We arrived at Brest station at 5 a.m. We were met by the Chief of Staff General Hoffman, acoompanied by his retinue of about 10 people including special envoys Von Rosenberg and Murray. After a short discussion about the latest events, I went back into the train carriage and sat and thought about what we needed to establish at the negotiating table. At 6 a.m. I traveled to General Hoffman's. He spoke about the tension and boasted that no one could equal him in the number of his successful military battles. About 100 people attended the breakfast banquet, which was presided over by the Count of Bavaria. Next to him sat the leader of the Russian delegation, the Jew Yaffe, who had only recently been released from a Siberian prison. Next to Yaffe sat generals and ambassadors. Besides Yaffe, Kaminiev also distinguished himself with his excellent conversational skills – he had also been recently freed from prison.

Later on I had a long conversation with Yaffe. He was of the opinion that first all the peoples of the world should be liberated - only then would we accheive true brotherhood. When I remarked that this could lead to conflict, unrest, and civil war in the whole world – he did not deny this and stressed that such a war would fulfill human ideals and therefore be justified.

Brest 4th January 1918

During the night there was a terrible snowstorm. The heating in the carriages froze. When I awoke the train on the tracks opposite ours consisted of the Bulgarian and Turkish carriages. Kulamin told me that they were angry in Berlin, he had proposed to Ludendorf that he himself should come to Brest to take part in the peace negotiations, but it became clear to Kulamin that Ludendorf did himself not know what he wanted, and that his journey would be superfluous. He would only spoil matters. It was clear that if the Russians wanted to cease the negotiations, the situation would only become more difficult. In the evening a telegram arrived from St. Petersburg announcing that the foreign minister Leon Trotski was leading a delegation that was departing for Brest.

The Brest Fortress January 10th 1918

Trotski gave a beautiful speech in which he conceded all of the 5 major points – he accepted the German Austro –Hungarian ultimatum. He was staying in Brest, he said, just not to give us the pleasure of blaming the Russians for further extending the war.

Brest 11th Febuary 1918

Trotski said whilst signing the peace treaty: "no peace, no war". This slogan was written on the wall of the Brest Fortress, and covered by a protective glass. This short sentence that caused so much upheaval in the world.

From the memoirs of Count Tchernin about the peace negotiations after the W.W.1. Archives of the Russian Revolution. 1921.

To Peace by Leon Trotsky

At the request of Lenin, I traveled to Brest. Not counting the old buildings outside the old city where the German Command was housed, the city of Brest actually did not exist anymore... The Kaiser's Imperial Army had violently ransacked, burnt and destroyed the city. Food and furniture was extremely basic. Through the city ran a broad strategic road – on my morning walks I came across a sign written on a wall – "every Russian that is caught would be shot".

From "My Life" by L. Trotsky

1939 - When the Storm Erupted

On the 17th September 19139, the Russian military crossed the Polish border which was almost undefended at the time. The Russians created a wide western front. By the 18th they had reached Vilna and they met with their allies the Germans in Brest Litovsk. The Bolsheviks and the Germans had signed a separate peace treaty there towards the end of W.W.1, demonstrating the difficult situation of those days. This time it was the German Nazis and the Russian communists who shook hands and smiled.

Winston Churchill " The Second World War"

1941 – The German Military Invasion of Russia

This occurred at 3.30 a.m. on the 22nd June 1941. With the changing of the border guards on the bridge over the Bug river between the two territories. The Germans shot their Russian comrades instead of saluting them. Thus began the invasion of the Soviet Union.

Willian Exner "This is the Enemy" London 1943

**The City Of Tel Aviv decided to perpetuate the memory of the
Jewish Community of Brest by naming a street - Rehov Kehillat Brisk D' Lita**

[Page 703]

Brest 1954

by M. Almoni
Translated by Dr. Samuel Chani and Jenni Buch

Do not wonder that I write these few words. An extraordinary event happened to me two days ago when I visited Brest Litovsk en route on my trip to Russia, - and I wish to share my experiences with you.

I had to exchange trains in Brest and had a five-hour wait there. I took a taxi to the city center and walked through the streets of the city, strolling through the main and side streets, looking at the faces of the passers-by, searching for a Jew but could not find one.

The city had not changed a great deal, (the ruins had almost disappeared). There were many new buildings and nice gardens that had been planted in the city squares. On the corner of Dabrowska and The 3rd of May Sts. (the main intersection of the city) where I thought there had once been a cinema, there now was a small park with a statue of Stalin in the middle.

The Great Synagogue was still standing but had been changed into a cinema. I peered inside – nothing had changed except for the rows of seats in a semi – circle, where the Holy Ark once was – now stood the large picture screen.

The city was tinged with greenery. I saw many men in military uniforms – a typical provincial city. The streets have new names: Topolowska = Karl Marx St., Dabrowska = Soviet Army St. There are bus services running to Kobryn, Pruzhany and Pinsk.

I chatted to a bus driver who told me about the liquidation of the Jews of Brest. Some of them were sent to Kobryn and were murdered there. Now there are a few Jews, almost all of them had not lived in Brest before the war. The majority of residents seemed to be Poles that had remained there from before the war. Those that had come froms the towns of Biala and Janow, for example, and had occupied Jewish homes and their contents until today.

It is very difficult for me to describe my emotions duriing those hours – to walk around the streets of Brest, devoid of any Jews. When I spotted a face which looked Jewish, I stopped the person and asked him – he denied it and avoided me...

It was also strange to travel through the neighboring towns and villages such as Mezrich, Biala, Terespol, Zhabinka and Bereza etc, etc, and not find a Jew there either. I did not go to Kobryn although I was only 15 kilometers from there.

With comradely greetings and regards, M. Almoni (Anonymous in Hebrew).

The Memorial on the site of a Massacre of Jews at 124 Dluga St.
Photo taken by Dr. Sam Chani in 1965
Translator's note: This monument was vandalized and destroyed in the 1970s

[Page 705]

The History of This Book

by N. Chinich
Translated by Dr. Samuel Chani and Jenni Buch

At a general assembly of the Organization of Brest Immigrants in Israel that took place in Tel Aviv in 1944, it was decided to publish a memorial book about this famous and historic community. I undertook to manage this difficult task and issued a plea for support in the press, both in Israel and abroad. I requested that all the Briskers in the world send in their memoirs, recollections, photos, memorabilia, political and institutional records. This request was printed in the U.S., Australia, South Africa, Argentina, Europe, Mexico and Brazil. I also sent more than 300 personal letters, both in Israel and overseas.

Over the following eight years we collected enough material for a book - I also visited with elderly Briskers in Israel and recorded their recollections. When I visited the grey haired Beinish Koloditzky in Petach Tikvah he was very moved by the idea of a memorial book. With tears in his eyes, he related his memoirs to me for hours. With his faint and tired voice: "I'm already 84 years old, but I want to tell you about our city. I want to live to see the publication of this book about Brest and it's people. " He drew from his memories great figures and personalities such as Shereshevski, Shteinberg, Rabbi Butche, and Rabbi Simcha Zelig. He said he had been an official for the Keren Kayemet for over 30 years, and had the privilege of living in his own country, and could not want anything more. He thought for a bit and then said he wanted to tell me about the co-operative movement in Brest in the old days, and that the Briskers were the first to establish this practice. He said he would tell me more about this subject later. He never did as he died a few weeks later.

I also travelled to Ramat Yitzhak to interview the elderly Doba Yaffa. The old lady told me about the Great Synagogue, about her family, about the fortress, about the community leaders, the old cemetery, and her memories of bygone years, but I did not see her again as the old lady passed away. I spent long hours recording what the elderly Levi Yitzhak Winnikoff related to me about Brest officials and personalities, who no longer were alive and had not been granted the privilege of coming to Eretz Israel.

I had the nerve to approach the great professor Albert Einstein who had worked closely with Yakov Gromer as his teacher and co-worker. The great scientist sent me a personal reply and said that he regretted that he had no photo of Gromer. Yitzhak Greenbaum sent me his biographies of Avraham Goldberg and N.Finkelstein from his cell in the British prison at Latrun. The elderly Michael Pochachevsky sent me his interesting memoirs but refused to sent his photo, saying "who am I to have my photo in a book about Brest?" Friends loaned us articles from the Yiddish press – editorials from the Polessie

Shtimme, I searched all the references to Brest in the Hebrew press archives: Hamelitz, Hamagid, Ha Yom, Ha Dor, Ha Zman, Ha Tzophe, and Ha Tzphira. We also collected over 200 photographs.

A huge amount of material was collected; everything remained as a collection of works as we were unable to edit the work for publication. Our comrades also lost hope that it would ever appear in book form but then we found a saviour in Chaim Barlas. A native of Brest, Chaim Barlas was the editor of the Encyclopedia of the Diaspora and he made our goal a reality. Praise should be given to the book committee of the Organization of Brest Immigrants in Israel: B. Kastrinski, A. Shtrickman, S. Orchov, M. Neumark who gave their hearts and souls to this project, also A. Zamir, blessed be his memory, who helped a great deal with the collection of material. The many people who helped collect and edit the information – M. Zinovitch who gave us valuable information about the rabbis of Brisk D'Lita.

Special thanks should be given to the Brest Relief in New York and the members of its book committee: H.H. Gonsher, Y. Finkelstein, B. Wolsky, Frieluk and others who assisted greatly to make this matter a reality and get this book published.

The Memorial book for our great and famous hometown of Brest, its people, their sufferings and torments, and the tragic demise of the ancient city of Brisk D' Lita.

[Page 707]

The Three Periods of Brisk D' Lita

by Avraham Levinson
Translated by Dr. Samuel Chani and Jenni Buch

The first mention of Jews in Brest was in the 14th century, when the first Jews settled on Lithuanian soil. Throughout the generations the city of Brest acquired a special economic, political, and social significance, which it maintained during all of these three periods of the existence of the Jewish community. These periods were defined by the name changes to the city.

The first period was the establishment of the Jewish settlement, whose existence was due to the privileges granted by the king and princes, despite the opposition of the church and the aristocracy. Their persecutions and accusations of ritual blood libel did not stop the commercial and cultural development of the city and it grew and stood at the head of all the Jewish communities of Lithuania. The city produced famous personalities, rabbis and sages. They built yeshivas and synagogues that attracted scholars from many lands.

In the period of the Council of Four Lands, the economic and political importance of Brest rose greatly. This was a bloody period of pogroms in

Lithuania and the Ukraine. Over a period of ten terrible years almost the entire population of Brest was murdered – only a small number of Jews in the west of the city remained.

Gradually Brest recovered from this great massacre and destruction. The hatred from the Polish townsmen, the harassment, the charges of blood libel from the Catholic and Russian orthodox churches did not cease. The Jews were forced again to seek protection and privileges from the king who obliged willingly in order not to lose his revenue from the taxes and charges that his Jews paid him.

When Jewish autonomy was established in Brest, the city did not lose it's elevated position – the stronger the political opposition and economic need, the higher the spiritual walls of the city were strengthened. The rabbis and sages of Brest had great influence over the Jews of the entire nation. In 1796, after the second Polish partition, the city passed into Russian hands and its name was changed to Brest Litovsk.

A new flood of misfortune and troubles was unleashed. Every day brought new persecutions. One of the greatest plagues that befell the city were the fires. No other cities endured and suffered as much from fires as Brest. In a hundred years, there were four large fires –(1802, 1825, 1895 and 1901), that caused great destruction and suffering.

Despite all this, the city arose from its ashes and rebuilt its youth. Its strategic position as a junction between Moscow, Kiev, and Warsaw, the two rivers Bug and Mukhavets, on which it was positioned, the reinforced fortress, all combined to create an economic revival and an increase in the number of inhabitants of the city. The Jews were occupied in developing commerce and trade, manufacturing, communications, and supplying the needs of the large military presence in Brest.

In Brest the beginnings of a new culture were felt. Under a banner of conspiratorial secrecy sprouted the first rays of radical thought. The first of the Zionists were the Chovevei Zion (Lovers of Zion), who found a responsive audience in Brest. In 1892 Rabbi Shmuel Maliever passed through on his way to Warsaw and met with Rabbi Joseph Ber Soloveitchik and Rabbi Eliahu Chaim Maizel.

The fame of Brest far transcended its borders – many Briskers wandered off to other cities and countries. They participated in the building of Hebrew and Jewish culture. Notable amongst them were: A.L. Feinstein, author of "Ir Tehillah", which has not lost its scientific and research value to this day. It is still the greatest single writing about Brest, not counting the two small monographs from the military rabbi of the German prison camp (for prisoners of war) that was written by A Tanzer and A. Kaplan about the destruction of the city during W.W.1. The brothers Moshe and Samuel Minc who belonged to the founding pioneer group BILU that originated in Kharkov and made aliyah to Eretz Israel. The author Dr. Benjamin Shereshevski, a pioneer of the Jewish settlement in Israel, known by his pseudonym "Powers of Nature" (of which he was the author) and "Six Degrees of Science". Senator Dr. Marcus Brodie who was the rabbi in Lodz Poland, an official of the National High School education board, and a founder of the Judaica Institute in Warsaw. Beinish Michalevitch-Itzbitski, a leader of the Bund in Poland. Professor Y.N. Halevi – Epstein, historical researcher and lecturer in Hebrew Literature at the Hebrew University of Jerusalem. The famous Yiddish novelist Menachem Berisha, who settled in the U.S.A, the writer Benjamin Chaim Reis, author of "The Siberian Stories' and "Memories of a Wanderer", the actor Mischa Apelboim and many others....

This is how Brisk D' Lita was in the Russian period – a city whose people suffered oppressions, troubles, endured fires and wars - survived, but still did not stop radiating life and light. After the First World War, the city entered its third historical period – it became the Polish "Brzesc nad Bugiem".

The old Jewish residents returned together with newcomers from the surrounding towns. It was the beginning of a superhuman task to rebuild the city from its ruins. The central responsible authority and source of financial assistance was the Joint Organization that built the Warburg Colony (the new model suburb), the orphanage, schools, health organizations, and the Artisans Union building. Gradually a new Jewish community re emerged with a new Jewish identity and pride.

It turned out that the New Poland had learnt nothing from its former history of enslavement. The Polish republic was actually a continuation of the Old Polish Monarchy. In this Poland there was no room for privileges granted to Jews, for further spreading the oral traditions, the legends about Esterke, and Saul Wahl, who was king for one day. The political and economic reality was depressing; the conditions were miserable and insulting. After a short period of liberalism there was a rising militarism from an aggressive and chauvinistic Polish government. In Brest just as in the other towns of the Cressy (former Russian held territories) the authorities began to wipe off any traces of the former Russian rule, eradicating any traces of the Old Russian Regime. This was followed by the Polonization of the soul, the culture, and the economy - the provincial Mayors, Governors, chiefs of police and military leaders executed the chauvinistic policies with a heavy hand.

Their presence in the streets and schools was meant to strengthen the Polish element and weaken the Jewish community. They imposed heavy taxation, distanced the Jews for obtaining government employment, and blocked Jews from getting government projects. The blocking of funds to the Jewish high schools and the erection of modern Polish suburbs isolating the Jewish community further weakened the Jewish community.

Apart from a few, Brest with all its merchants and shopkeepers, tradesmen, artisans, office workers and labourers, was a city of poor people who struggled for their daily existence. The Jewish representatives in the city council were well aware of their opportunity to defend their rights and resist the injustices. The entire Polish administration was riddled with anti Semitism.

Despite all that Brest remained Brest Litovsk - the Jewish Brest with all it's political parties: Zionist, Mizrachi, both branches of Poale Zion, the Unity party and also the Bund. They understood the importance of preserving the purity of their idealistic struggle. The Zionist organization with all its factions was the center of all our social life – it did not rule by the power of numbers but by its moral influence on the Brest institutions. It also had economic power in its hands – its influence with the Jewish banks, and its moral authority found direction in the Jewish education and schools. The Hebrew High School was officially accredited for university entrance examinations. There was also a trade school run by Ort, a children's orphanage and hostel, and a Jewish hospital and library.

In the last years we saw the gathering clouds over our heads. The horizon darkened but no one could have foreseen the horrible end. However, we were never without the feeling that we were going from one disaster to another – spinning downwards. The bloody events of 1937 showed the brutality in frightening detail - the helplessness of the Polish Jews. The day of the terrible destruction arrived – the final conflagration in which the entire Jewish population was destroyed in a sacrifice to inhumanity. The executioner's final blow to the beautiful Jewry of Poland, severing 1000 years of Jewish culture.

There is no consolation in revenge.

Table of Figures and Photographs

INDEX

Orchov, 82, 136, 269, 270, 275, 298, 442, 460

Orenstein, 17, 27, 42, 103, 261, 307

P

Padkorene, 351

Padua, 11, 12, 17, 27, 39, 70, 82, 84, 148, 189, 243, 252, 261, 284, 290, 349, 350, 352, 389, 449

Padva, 341

Padwa, 323

Papeh, 190

Paskievitch, 72

Pat, 405

Patchilkey, 396

Patzalnik, 31

Paznitzki, 230

Pearlman, 87

Pechta, 134

Pecker, 396

Perelstein, 395

Peretz, 31, 55, 82, 133, 134, 158, 160, 179, 182, 200, 233, 236, 253, 280, 303, 328, 440, 465

Perlis, 269, 270, 286, 375

Perlman, 269, 396

Perlmutter, 98

Perlov, 202, 281, 285, 386

Persitz, 231

Pesach, 31

Petchanik, 439

Petrovski, 360

Petrushka, 293

Piasetzki, 286

Piatkowski, 286

Pilsudski, 51, 183, 294, 328, 338

Pinchuk, 382

Pinchus, 26

Pinczuk, 376

Pinsky, 201

Pitcharski, 447

Pitlik, 255

Pochachevski, 1, 107, 116, 185, 186, 187, 216, 244, 269, 284, 375, 449, 464

Podva, 87, 100

Polani, 246, 465

Polefski, 246

Poliachik, 148

Poliak, 207

Politshanski, 282

Politzik, 275

Pollack, 427

Pollak, 72, 246, 269, 465

Pollig, 71

Pomeraniec, 376

Pomeranitz, 293, 442

Pomerantz, 2, 56, 70, 217, 269, 286, 307, 345, 350, 381, 382, 400, 418, 425, 441, 442, 464

Poniatowski, 16

Popievska, 362

Porat, 319

Posniak, 201

Pozezhinski, 244, 269

Pozezinski, 324

Pozhinski, 269

Poznanski, 98

Pragel, 245

Pregel, 300, 301, 347, 349

Preger, 322, 466

Priludski, 339

Prizant, 433

Propes, 280

Prostig, 324

R

Rabinovitch, 125, 202, 251, 269, 276, 292, 293, 299, 306, 307, 324, 325, 393, 394, 396, 397, 398, 399, 418, 421, 424, 449, 465, 466

Rachkes, 163

Rachowski, 33

Rade, 355, 356

Radevski, 227

Radevsky, 130

Radi, 413

Radzivill, 30

Raf, 393, 394, 424, 454

Raff, 396

Ragazhik, 244

Raheling, 133, 134

Rakov, 284

Ramah, 289

Ramo, 10, 12, 250, 307, 350, 351, 381, 436, 454

Rapoport, 382

Rascovitch, 7

Rashal, 9

Rashes, 23, 126, 128, 382

Rashkes, 72

Rassin, 221

www.ingramcontent.com/pod-product-compliance
Lightning Source LLC
Chambersburg PA
CBHW082006150426

42814CB00005BA/247